The Adventures of Arthur O'Leary

Charles Lever

BIBLIOLIFE

THE ADVENTURES

OF

ARTHUR O'LEARY

BY

CHARLES LEVER

AUTHOR OF "CHARLES O'MALLEY"

WITH ILLUSTRATIONS

LONDON

GEORGE ROUTLEDGE AND SONS

THE BROADWAY, LUDGATE

NEW YORK: 416, BROOME STREET

LONDON:
WOODFALL AND KINDER, PRINTERS,
MILFORD LANE, STRAND, W.C.

CONTENTS.

THE ADVENTURES

OF

ARTHUR O'LEARY.

CHAPTER I.

THE " ATTWOOD."

OLD Woodcock says, that if Providence had not made him a Justice of the Peace, he'd have been a vagabond himself. No such kind interference prevailed in my case. I was a vagabond from my cradle I never could be sent to school, alone, like other children—they always had to see me there safe, and fetch me back again. The rambling bump monopolized my whole head. I'm sure my godfather must have been the Wandering Jew, or a king's messenger Here I am again, *en route*, and sorely puzzled to know whither? There's the fellow for my trunk.

" What packet, sir ?"

" Eh ? What packet? The vessel at the Tower stairs ?"

"Yes, sir; there are two with the steam up—the Rotterdam and the Hamburgh."

" Which goes first ? "

" Why, I think the ' Attwood,' sir."

" Well, then, shove aboard the ' Attwood.' Where is she for ? "

B

"She's for Rotterdam.——He's a queer cove, too," said
the fellow under his teeth, as he moved out of the room;
" and don't seem to care where he goes."

A capital lesson in life may be learned from the few
moments preceding departure from an inn. The surly
waiter that always said "coming" when he was leaving
the room, and never came, now grown smiling and smirking; the landlord expressing a hope to see you again, while
he watches your upthrown eyebrows at the exorbitancy
of his bill; the Boots attentively looking from your feet to
your face, and back again; the housemaid passing and
repassing a dozen times on her way nowhere, with a look
half saucy, half shy; the landlord's son, an abortion of
two feet high, a kind of family chief-remembrancer, that
sits on a high stool in the bar, and always detects something you have had that was not "put down in the bill'
—two shillings for a cab, or a "brandy and water;" a
curse upon them all; this poll-tax upon travellers is utter
ruin; your bill, compared to its dependencies, is but
Falstaff's "pennyworth of bread" to all the score for sack.

Well, here I am at last "Take care, I say! you'll
upset us. Shove off, Bill, ship your oar," splash, splash.
"Bear a hand. What a noise they make!" bang! crash!
buzz! what a crowd of men in pilot coats and caps;
women in plaid shawls and big reticules, band-boxes, bags,
and babies, and what higgling for sixpences with the
wherrymen!

All the places round the companion are taken by pale
ladies in black silk, with a thin man in spectacles beside
them; the deck is littered with luggage, and little groups
seated thereon; some very strange young gentlemen, with
many-coloured waistcoats, are going to Greenwich, and
one as far as Margate, a widow and daughters, rather
prettyish girls, for Herne Bay; a thin, bilious-looking man
of about fifty, with four outside coats, and a bear-skin
round his legs, reading beside the wheel, occasionally
taking a sly look at the new arrivals—I've seen him
before; he is the Secretary of Embassy at Constantinople;
and here's a jolly-looking, rosy-cheeked fellow, with a fat
florid face, and two dashing-looking girls in black velvet.
Eh! who's this?—Sir Peter, the steward calls him; a

London alderman going up the Rhine for two months—
he's got his courier, and a strong carriage, with the
springs well corded for the *pavé ;*—but they come too fast
for counting ; so now I'll have a look after my berth.

Alas ! the cabin has been crowded all the while by some
fifty others, wrangling, scolding, laughing, joking, complaining, and threatening, and not a berth to be had.

"You've put me next the tiller," said one ; " I'm over
the boiler," screamed another.

" I have the pleasure of speaking to Sir Willoughby
Steward," said the captain, to a tall, grey-headed, soldier-
like figure, with a closely-buttoned blue frock. " Sir
Willoughby, your berth is No 8."

" Eh ! that's the way they come it," whispers a Cockney
to his friend. " That 'ere chap gets a berth before us
all."

" I beg your pardon, sir," says the baronet, mildly, " I
took mine three days ago."

" Oh ! I didn't mean anything, " stammers out the
other, and sneaks off.

" Laura-Mariar—where's Laurar ? " calls out a shrill
voice from the aft-cabin.

" Here, ma," replies a pretty girl, who is arranging
her ringlets at a glass, much to the satisfaction of a
young fellow in a braided frock, that stands gazing at
her in the mirror with something very like a smile on his
lip.

There's no mistaking that pair of dark-eyed fellows
with aquiline noses and black ill-shaven beards—Hamburgh or Dutch Jews, dealers in smuggled lace, cigars,
and Geneva watches, and occasionally small money-
lenders. How they scan the company, as if calculating
the profit they might turn them to ! The very smile they
wear seems to say, " *Comme c'est doux de tromper les
Chrétiens.*" * But, halloa ! there was a splash ! we *are*
moving, and the river is now more amusing than the
passengers.

I should like to see the man that ever saw London
from the Thames ; or any part of it, save the big dome of

* How sweet it is to take the Christians in.

B 2

St. Paul's, the top of the Monument, or the gable of the great black wharf inscribed with "Hodgson's Pale Ale." What a devil of a row they do make! I thought we were into that fellow. See, here's a wherry actually under our bow; where is she now? are they all lost already? No ' there they go, bobbing up and down, and looking after us, as if asking why we didn't sail over them. Ay! there comes an Indiaman, and that little black slug that's towing her up against the stream, is one of the Tug Company's craft; and see how all the others at anchor keep tossing and pitching about as we pass by, like an awkward room-full of company, rising at each new arrival.

There's Greenwich! a fine thing Greenwich. I like the old fellows that the First Lord always makes stand in front, without legs or arms; a cheery sight : and there's a hulk, or an hospital ship, or something of that kind.

"That's the 'Hexcellent,'" said a shrill voice behind me.

"Ah! I know her, she's a revenue cruiser."

Lord! what liars the Cockneys are ! The plot thickens every moment; here come little bright green and gold things, shooting past like dragon-flies skimming the water, steaming down to Gravesend. What a mob of parasols cover the deck, and what kissing of hands and waving of handkerchiefs to anonymous acquaintances nowhere. More steamers—here's the "Boulogne boat," followed by the Ostender, and there, rounding the reach, comes the Ramsgate ; and a white funnel, they say, is the Cork packet; and yonder, with her steam escaping, is the Edinburgh, her deck crowded with soldiers.

"Port—port it is—steady there—steady."

"Do you dine, sir?" quoth the steward to the pale gentleman. A faint "Yes." "And the ladies too ?" A more audible "No."

"I say, steward," cries Sir Peter, "what's the hour for dinner ?"

"Four o'clock, sir, after we pass Gravesend."

'Bring me some brandy and water and a biscuit, then."

"Lud, pa! "

" To be sure, dear, we shall be sick in the pool. They say there's a head wind."

How crowded they are on the fore-part of the vessel ! six carriages and eight horses; the latter belong to a Dutch dealer, who, by the bye, seems a shrewd fellow, and well knowing the extreme sympathy between horses and asses, leaves the care of his to some Cockneys, who come down every half-hour to look after the tarpaulins, inspect the coverings, see the knee-caps safe, and ask if they want " 'ay ; " and all this, that to some others on board they may appear as sporting characters, well versed in turf affairs, and quite up to stable management.

When the life and animation of the crowded river is passed, how vexatious it is to hear for the thousandth time the dissertations on English habits, customs, and constitution, delivered by some ill-informed, under-bred fellow or other to some eager German—a Frenchman, happily, is too self-sufficient ever to listen—who greedily swallows the farrago of absurdity, which, according to the politics of his informant, represents the nation in a plethora of prosperity, or the last stage of inevitable ruin. I scarcely know which I detest the more ; the insane toryism of the one is about as sickening as the rabid radicalism of the other. The absurd misapprehensions foreigners entertain about us, are, in nine cases out of ten, communicated by our own people ; and in this way, I have always remarked a far greater degree of ignorance about England and the English to prevail among those who have passed some weeks in the country, than among such as had never visited our shores. With the former, the Thames Tunnel is our national boast ; raw beef and boxing our national predilections , the public sale of our wives a national practice.

" But what's this ? our paddles are backed. Anything wrong, steward ? "

" No, sir, only another passenger coming aboard "

" How they pull, and there's a stiff sea running, too. A queer figure that is in the stern sheets ; what a beard he has ! "

I had just time for the observation, when a tall, athletic man, wrapped in a wide blue cloak, sprang on the deck—

his eyes were shaded by large green spectacles and the
broad brim of a very projecting hat; a black beard a
rabbi might have envied, descended from his chin, and
hung down upon his bosom; he chucked a crown-piece
to the boatman as he leaned over the bulwark, and then
turning to the steward, called out—

"Eh, Jem! all right?"

"Yes, sir, all right," said the man, touching his hat
respectfully.

The tall figure immediately disappeared down the companion ladder, leaving me in the most puzzling state of
doubt as to what manner of man he could possibly be.
Had the problem been more easy of solution I should
scarcely have resolved it when he again emerged—but
how changed! The broad beaver had given place to a
blue cloth foraging cap with a gold band around it; the
beard had disappeared totally, and left no successor save
a well-rounded chin; the spectacles also had vanished,
and a pair of sharp, intelligent grey eyes, with a most
uncommon degree of knowingness in their expression,
shone forth; and a thin and most accurately curled
moustache graced his upper lip, and gave a character of
Vandykism to his features, which were really handsome.
In person he was some six feet two, gracefully but strongly
built; his costume, without anything approaching conceit, was the perfection of fashionable attire—even to his
gloves there was nothing which d'Orsay could have criticized, while his walk was the very type of that mode of
progression which is only learned thoroughly by a daily
stroll down St James's-street, and the frequent practice
of passing to and from Crockford's, at all hours of the
day and night.

The expression of his features was something so striking,
I could not help noting it. There was a jauntiness, an
ease, no smirking, half-bred, self-satisfied look, such as a
London linendraper might wear on his trip to Margate;
but a consummate sense of his own personal attractions
and great natural advantages had given a character to his
features which seemed to say—it's quite clear there's no
coming up to *me*, don't try it—*nascitur non fit*. His very
voice implied it. The veriest commonplace fell from him

with a look, a smile, a gesture, a something or other that made it tell ; and men repeated his sayings without knowing that his was a liquor that was lost in decanting. The way in which he scanned the passengers—and it was done in a second—was the practised observance of one who reads character at a glance. Over the Cockneys, and they were numerous, his eyes merely passed without bestowing any portion of attention ; while to the lady part of the company his look was one of triumphant satisfaction, such as Louis XIV. might have bestowed when he gazed at the thousands in the garden of Versailles, and exclaimed, " *Oui ! ce sont mes sujets*."* Such was the Honourable Jack Smallbranes, younger son of a peer, ex-captain in the Life Guards, winner of the Derby, but now the cleared-out man of fashion flying to the Continent to escape from the Fleet, and cautiously coming aboard in disguise below Gravesend, to escape the bore of a bailiff, and what he called the horror of bills " detested."

We read a great deal about Cincinnatus cultivating his cabbages, and we hear of Washington's retirement when the active period of his career had passed over ; and a hundred similar instances are quoted for our admiration of men who could throw themselves at once from all the whirlwind excitement of great events, and seek in the humblest and least obtrusive position, an occupation and an enjoyment. But I doubt very much if your ex-man of fashion, your *ci-devant* winner of the Derby—the adored of Almack's—the *enfant chéri* of Crockford's and the Clarendon, whose equipage was a model, whose plate was perfection, for whom life seemed too short for all the fascinations wealth spread around him, and each day brought the one embarrassment how to enjoy enough—I repeat it, I doubt much if he, when the hour of his abdication arrives—and that it will arrive sooner or later not even himself entertains a doubt—when Holditch protests, and Bevan proceeds ; when steeds are sold at Tattersall's and pictures at Christie's ; when the hounds pass over to the next new victim, and the favourite for the St. Leger, backed with mighty odds, is now entered under another name ; when in lieu of the bright eyes and honied words

* Yes ! these are my subjects.

that make life a fairy tale, his genii are black-whiskered
bailiffs and auctioneers' appraisers—if he, when the tide
of fortune sets in so strong against him, can not only
sustain himself for a while against it, and when too
powerful at last, can lie upon the current and float as gaily
down, as ever he did joyously up, the stream—then, say I,
all your ancient and modern instances are far below him.
All your warriors and statesmen are but poor pretenders
compared to him, they have retired like rich shop-keepers,
to live on the interest of their fortune, which is fame;
while he, deprived of all the accessories which gave him
rank, place, and power, must seek within his own resources
for all the future springs of his pleasure, and be satisfied to
stand spectator of the game in which he was once the
principal player.   A most admirable specimen of this
philosophy was presented by our new passenger, who, as
he lounged against the binnacle, and took a deliberate
survey of his fellow-travellers, formed the very ideal of
unbroken ease and undisturbed enjoyment.   He knew he
was ruined; he knew he had neither house in town or
country; neither a steed, nor a yacht, nor a preserve; he
was fully aware that Storr and Mortimer, who but yesterday would have given him a mountain of silver, would not
trust him with a mustard-pot to-day, that even the "legs"
would laugh at him if he offered the odds on the Derby;
and yet if you were bound on oath to select the happiest
fellow on board, by the testimony of your eyes, the choice
would not have taken you five minutes.   His attitude was
ease itself; his legs slightly crossed, perhaps the better to
exhibit a very well-rounded instep, which shone forth in
all the splendour of French varnish; his travelling cap
jauntily thrown on one side so as to display to better
advantage his perfumed locks, that floated in a graceful
manner somewhat lengthily on his neck; the shawl around
his neck had so much of negligence as to show that the
splendid enamel pin that fastened it was a thing of little
moment to the wearer.   All were in keeping with the
nonchalant ease and self-satisfaction of his look, as with
half-drooping lids he surveyed the deck, caressing with his
jewelled fingers the silky line of his moustache, and
evidently enjoying in his inmost soul the triumphant scene

of conquest his very appearance excited. Indeed, a less practised observer than himself could not fail to remark the unequivocal evidences the lady portion of the community bore to his success · the old ones looked boldly at him with that fearless intrepidity that characterizes conscious security, their property was insured, and they cared not how near the fire came to them; the very young participated in the sentiment from an opposite reason — theirs was the unconsciousness of danger; but there was a middle term, what Balzac calls " *la femme de trente ans,*" and she either looked over the bulwarks, or at the funnel, or on her book, anywhere in short but at our friend, who appeared to watch this studied denial on her part with the same kind of enjoyment the captain of a frigate would contemplate the destruction his broadsides were making on his enemy's rigging; and perhaps the latter never deemed his conquest more assured by the hauling down of the enemy's colours than did the " Honourable Jack." when a let-down veil convinced him that the lady could bear no more

I should like to have watched the proceedings on deck, where, although no acquaintance had yet been formed, the indications of such were clearly visible. The alderman's daughters evincing a decided preference for walking on that side where Jack was standing, he studiously performing some small act of courtesy from time to time as they passed, removing a seat, kicking any small fragment of rope, &c ; but the motion of the packet warned me that note-taking was at an end, and the best thing I could do would be to " compose " myself.

" What's the number, sir ? " said the steward, as I staggered down the companion.

" I have got no berth," said I, mournfully.

" A dark horse, not placed," said the Honourable Jack, smiling pleasantly as he looked after me, while I threw myself on a sofa, and cursed the sea.

CHAPTER II.

THE PASSPORT—A PERILOUS ADVENTURE—MINE HOST OF THE BOAR'S
HEAD.

IF the noise and bustle which attend a wedding, like trumpets in a battle, are intended as provisions against reflection, so firmly do I feel the tortures of sea-sickness are meant as antagonists to all the terrors of drowning, and all the horrors of shipwreck.

Let him who has felt the agonies of that internal earthquake which the "pitch and toss" motion of a ship communicates—who knows what it is to have his diaphragm vibrating between his ribs and the back of his throat, confess how little to him was all the confusion which he listened to over head! how poor the interest he took in the welfare of the craft wherein he was "only a lodger," and how narrowed were all his sympathies within the small circle of bottled porter, and brandy and water, the steward's infallibles in suffering.

I lay in my narrow crib, moodily pondering over these things, now wondering within myself what charms of travel could recompense such agonies as these; now muttering a curse, "not loud, but deep," on the heavy gentleman whose ponderous tread on the quarter-deck seemed to promenade up and down the surface of my own pericranium. The greasy steward, the jolly captain, the brown-faced, black-whiskered king's messenger, who snored away on the sofa, all came in for a share of my maledictions, and I took out my cares in curses upon the whole party. Meanwhile I could distinguish, amid the other sounds, the elastic tread of certain light feet that pattered upon the quarter-deck; and I could not mistake the assured footstep which accompanied them, nor did I need the happy roar of laughter that mixed with the noise to satisfy myself that the "Honourable Jack" was then cultivating the alderman's daughters, discoursing most

eloquently upon the fascinations of those exclusive circles
wherein he was wont to move, and explaining, on the
clearest principles, what a frightful chasm his absence
must create in the London world—how deplorably flat
the season would go off, where he was no actor—and
wondering who, among the aspirants of high ambition,
would venture to assume his line of character, and supply
his place, either on the turf or at the table.

But at length the stage of semi-stupor came over me ;
the noises became commixed in my head, and I lost all
consciousness so completely, that, whether from brandy
or sickness, I fancied I saw the steward flirting with the
ladies, and the "Honourable Jack" skipping about with
a white apron, uncorking porter bottles, and changing
sixpences.

  *   *   *   *   *   *
  *   *   *   *   *   *

The same effect which the announcement of dinner
produces on the stiff party in the drawing-room, is caused
by the information of being alongside the quay, to the
passengers of a packet. It is true the procession is not
so formal in the latter as in the former case. The tur-
baned dowagers that take the lead in one, would more
than probably be last in the other ; but what is lost in
decorum, is more than made up in hilarity What
hunting for carpet-bags ! what opening and shutting of
lockers ! what researches into portmanteaus, to extricate
certain seizable commodities, and stow them away upon
the person of the owner, till at last he becomes an imper-
sonation of smuggling, with lace in his boots, silk stockings in his hat, brandy under his waistcoat, and jewelry
in the folds of his cravat. There is not an item in the
tariff that might not be demonstrated in his anatomy.
From his shoes to his night-cap, he is a living sarcasm
upon the revenue. And, after all, what is the searching
scrutiny of your Quarterly Reviewer, to the all-penetrating
eye of an excise officer? He seems to look into the whole
contents of your wardrobe before you have unlocked the
trunk "warranted solid leather," and with a glance
appears to distinguish the true man from the knave,

knowing, as if by intuition, the precise number of cambric handkerchiefs that befit your condition in life, and whether you have transgressed the bounds of your station by a single bottle of " *Eau-de-Cologne.*"

What admirable training for a novelist would a year or two spent in such duties afford; what singular views of life; what strange people must he see; how much of narrative would even the narrow limits of a hat-box present to him; and how naturally would a story spring from the rosy-cheeked old gentleman, paying his duty upon a "*pâté de foie gras*" to his pretty daughter, endeavouring, by a smile, to diminish the tariff on her French bonnet, and actually captivate a custom-house officer by the charms of her "*robe à la Victorine.*"

The French "*douaniers*" are droll fellows, and are the only ones I have ever met who descend from the important gravity of their profession, and venture upon a joke. I shall never forget entering Valenciennes late one night, with a large "Diligence" party, among which was a corpulent countryman of my own, making his first continental tour. It was in those days when a passport presented a written portrait of the bearer: when the shape of your nose, the colour of your hair, the cut of your beard, and the angle of incidence of your eyebrow, were all noted down and commented on, and a general summing-up of the expression of your features, collectively, appended to the whole; and you went forth to the world with an air "mild," or "military;" "feeble," "fascinating," or "ferocious," exactly as the Foreign Office chose. It was in those days, I say, when, on entering the fortress of Valenciennes, the door of the "Diligence" was rudely thrown open, and, by the dim flicker of a lamp, we beheld a moustached, stern-looking fellow, who rudely demanded our passports. My fat companion, suddenly awakened from his sleep, searched his various pockets with all the trepidation of a new traveller, and at length produced his credentials, which he handed, with a polite bow, to the official. Whatever the nature of the description might have been I cannot say, but it certainly produced the most striking effect on the passport officers, who laughed loud and long as they read it over.

" *Descendez, Monsieur*," said the chief of the party, in a tone of stern command.

" What does he say ? " said the traveller, in a very decided western accent.

" You must get out, sir," said I.

" Tare-and-ages," said Mr. Moriarty, " what's wrong ? "

After considerable squeezing, for he weighed about twenty stone, he disengaged himself from the body of the " Diligence," and stood erect upon the ground. A second lantern was now produced, and while one of the officers stood on either side of him, with a light beside his face, a third read out the clauses of the passport, and compared the description with the original. Happily Mr Moriarty's ignorance of French saved him from the penalty of listening to the comments which were passed upon his " *nez retroussé*," " *bouche ouverte*," &c. ; but what was his surprise when, producing some yards of tape, they proceeded to measure him round the body, comparing the number of inches his circumference made, with the passport.

" *Quatre-vingt-dix pouces*,"* said the measurer, looking at the document. " *Il en a plus*,"† added he, rudely.

" What is he saying, sir, if I might be so bowld ? " said Mr. Moriarty to me, imploringly.

" You measure more than is set down in your passport," said I, endeavouring to suppress my laughter.

" Oh, murther ! that dish of boiled beef and beet-root will be the ruin of me. Tell them, sir, I was like a greyhound before supper."

As he said this, he held in his breath, and endeavoured with all his might to diminish his size ; while the Frenchmen, as if anxious to strain a point in his favour, tightened the cord round him, till he almost became black in the face.

" *C'est ça*," said one of the officers, smiling blandly as he took off his hat , " *Monsieur peut continuer sa route*."‡

" All right," said I ; " you may come in, Mr. Moriarty."

" 'Tis civil people I always heard they wor," said he ; " but it's a sthrange country where it's against the laws to grow fatter."

---

* Ninety-eight inches.   † He measures more.
‡ The gentleman may proceed on his journey.

I like Holland ;—it is the antipodes of France. No one is ever in a hurry here. Life moves on in a slow majestic stream, a little muddy and stagnant, perhaps, like one of their own canals, but you see no waves, no breakers—not an eddy, nor even a froth-bubble breaks the surface. Even a Dutch child, as he steals along to school, smoking his short pipe, has a mock air of thought about him. The great fat horses, that wag along, trailing behind them some petty, insignificant truck, loaded with a little cask, not bigger than a life-guardsman's helmet, look as .though Erasmus was performing duty as a quadruped, and walking about his own native city in harness. It must be a glorious country to be born in. No one is ever in a passion ; and as to honesty, who has energy enough to turn robber ? The eloquence which in other lands might wind a man from his allegiance, would be tried in vain here. Ten minutes' talking would set any audience asleep, from Zetland to Antwerp. Smoking, beer-drinking, stupefying, and domino-playing, go on in summer, before, in winter, within, the *cafés ;* and every broad flat face you look upon, with its watery eyes and muddy complexion, seems like a coloured chart of the country that gave it birth.

How all the industry, that has enriched them, is ever performed—how all the cleanliness, for which their houses are conspicuous, is ever effected, no one can tell. Who ever saw a Dutchman labour ? Everything in Holland seems typified by one of their own drawbridges, which rises as a boat approaches, by invisible agency, and then remains patiently aloft, till a sufficiency of passengers arrives to restore it to its place ; and Dutch gravity seems the grand centre of all prosperity.

When, therefore, my fellow-passengers stormed and swore because they were not permitted to land their luggage ; when they heard that until nine o'clock the following morning, no one would be astir to examine it ; and that the Rhine steamer sailed at eight, and would not sail again for three days more. and cursed the louder thereat , I chuckled to myself that I was going nowhere, that I cared not how long I waited, nor where, and began to believe that something of very exalted philosophy must have been infused into my nature, without my ever being aware of it.

For twenty minutes and more, Sir Peter abused the Dutch; he called them hard names in English, and some very strong epithets in bad French. Meanwhile, his courier busied himself in preparations for departure, and the "Honourable Jack" undertook to shawl the young ladies, a performance which, whether from the darkness of the night, or the intricacy of the muffling, took a most unmerciful time to accomplish.

"We shall never find the hotel at this hour," said Sir Peter, angrily.

"The house will certainly be closed," chimed in the young ladies.

"Take your five to two on the double event," replied Jack, slapping the alderman on the shoulder, and preparing to book the wager.

I did not wait to see it accepted, but stepped over the side, and trudged along the "Boomjes," that long quay, with its tall elm trees, under whose shade many a burgomaster has strolled at eve, musing over the profits which his last venture from Batavia was to realize; and then, having crossed the narrow bridge at the end, I traversed the Erasmus Platz, and rang boldly, as an old acquaintance has a right to do, at the closed door of the "Schwein Kopf." My summons was not long unanswered, and following the many-petticoated handmaiden along the well-sanded passage, I asked, "Is the Holbein chamber unoccupied?" while I drew forth a florin from my purse.

"Ah, Mynheer knows it, then," said she, smiling. "It is at your service. We have had no travellers for some days past, and you are aware that, unless we are greatly crowded, we never open it."

This I knew well; and having assured her that I was an *habitué* of the "Schwein Kopf," in times long past, I persuaded her to fetch some dry wood and make me a cheerful fire, which, with a "krug of schiedam" and some "canastre," made me happy as a king.

The "Holbeiner Kammer." owes its name, and any repute that it enjoys, to a strange, quaint portrait, of that master, seated at a fire, with a fair-headed, handsome child, sitting cross-legged on the hearth before him. A certain half resemblance seems to run through both faces, although the age and colouring are so different   But the same contemplative expression, the deep-set eye, the massive forehead and pointed chin, are to be seen in the child as in the man.

Tnis was Holbein and his nephew, Franz von Holbein, who in after years served with distinction in the army of Louis Quatorze. The background of the picture represents a room exactly like the chamber—a few highly-carved oak chairs, the Utrecht-velvet backs glowing with their scarlet brilliancy, an old-fashioned Flemish bed, with groups of angels, Neptunes, bacchanals, and dolphins, all mixed up confusedly in quaint carving ; and a massive frame to a very small looking-glass, which hung in a leaning attitude over the fireplace, and made me think, as I gazed at it, that the plane of the room was on an angle of sixty-five, and that the least shove would send me clean into the stove.

"Mynheer wants nothing ? " said the *Vrow* with a curtsey.

" Nothing," said I, with my most polite bow.

" Good night, then," said she ; "*schlaf wohl*, and don't mind the ghost."

"Ah, I know him of old," replied I, striking the table three times with my cane. The woman, whose voice the moment before was in a tone of jest, suddenly grew pale, and, as she crossed herself devoutly muttered—" *Nein !* *nein !* don't do that," and, shutting the door, hurried downstairs with all the speed she could muster

I was in no hurry to go to bed, however. The " krug " was racy, the " canastre " excellent · so, placing the light where its rays might fall with good effect on the Holbein, I stretched out my legs to the blaze ; and, as I looked upon the canvas, began to muse over the story with which it was associated, and which I may as well jot down here for the reader's sake.

Frank Holbein, having more ambition and less industry than the rest of the family, resolved to seek his fortune ; and early in the September of the year 1681, he found himself wandering in the streets of Paris, without a *liard* in his pocket, or any prospects of earning one. He was a fine-looking, handsome youth, of some eighteen or twenty years, with that Spanish cast of face for which so many Dutch families are remarkable. He sat down, weary and hungry, on one of the benches of the Pont de la Cité, and looked about him wistfully, to see what piece of fortune might come to his succour. A loud shout, and the noise of people hastening in every direction, attracted him. He jumped up and saw persons running hither and thither to escape from a calèche, which a pair of runaway horses were tearing along at a frightful rate. Frank blessed himself, threw off his cloak, pressed his cap firmly upon his brow and dashed forward. The affrighted animals slackened their speed as he stood before them, and endeavoured to pass by; but he sprang to their heads, and, with one vigorous plunge, grasped the bridle. Though he held on manfully, they continued their way; and, notwithstanding his every effort, their mad speed scarcely felt his weight, as he was dragged along beside them. With one tremendous effort, however, he wrested the near horse's head from the pole, and thus compelling him to cross his forelegs, the animal tripped, and came headlong to the ground with a smash that sent poor Frank spinning some twenty yards before them. Frank soon got up again; and though his forehead was bleeding, and his hand severely cut, his greatest grief was his torn doublet, which, threadbare before, now hung around him in ribbons.

"It was you who stopped them?—are you hurt?" said a tall, handsome man, plainly but well dressed, and in whose face the trace of agitation was clearly marked.

"Yes, sir," said Frank, bowing respectfully. "I did it; and see how my poor doublet has suffered!"

"Nothing worse than that?" said the other, smiling blandly. "Well, well, that is not of so much moment. Take this," said he, handing him his purse; "buy yourself a new doublet, and wait on me to-morrow by eleven."

With these words the stranger disappeared in a calèche, which seemed to arrive at the moment, leaving Frank in a state of wonderment at the whole adventure.

"How droll he should never have told me where he

C

lives !" said he, aloud, as the bystanders crowded about him, and showered questions upon him.

"It is Monsieur le Ministre, man—M. de Louvois himself—whose life you've saved. Your fortune is made for ever."

The speech was a true one. Before three months from that eventful day, M. de Louvois, who had observed and noted down certain traits of acuteness in Frank's character, sent for him to his *bureau*.

"Holbein," said he, "I have seldom been deceived in my opinion of men—You can be secret, I think ?"

Frank placed his hand upon his breast, and bowed in silence.

"Take the dress you will find on that chair; a carriage is now ready, waiting in the courtyard; get into it, and set out for Bâle. On your arrival there, which will be—mark me well—about eight o'clock on the morning of Thursday, you'll leave the carriage, and send it into the town, while you must station yourself on the bridge over the Rhine, and take an exact note of everything that occurs, and every one that passes, till the cathedral clock strikes three Then, the calèche will be in readiness for your return: and lose not a moment in repairing to Paris."

It was an hour beyond midnight, in the early part of the following week, that a calèche, travel-stained and dirty, drove into the court of the minister's hotel, and five minutes after, Frank, wearied and exhausted, was ushered into M. de Louvois' presence.

"Well, Monsieur," said he, impatiently, "what have you seen ?"

"This, may it please your Excellency," said Frank, trembling, "is a note of it: but I am ashamed that so trivial an account——"

"Let us see—let us see," said the minister.

"In good truth, I dare scarcely venture to read such a puerile detail."

"Read it at once, Monsieur," was the stern command.

Frank's face became deep-red with shame, as he began thus ·

"Nine o'clock.—I see an ass coming along, with a child

leading him. The ass is blind of one eye.—A fat German sits on the balcony, and is spitting into the Rhine——"

" Ten.—A livery servant from Bâle rides by, with a basket. An old peasant in a yellow doublet——"

" Ah, what of him ?"

" Nothing remarkable, save that he leans over the rails and strikes three blows with his stick upon them."

" Enough, enough," said M. de Louvois, gaily. " I must awake the king at once."

The minister disappeared, leaving Frank in a state of bewilderment. In less than a quarter of an hour he entered the chamber, his face covered with smiles.

" Monsieur," said he, " you have rendered his majesty good service. Here is your brevet of colonel. The king has this instant signed it."

In eight days after was the news known in Paris that Strasburg, then invested by the French army, had capitulated, and been reunited to the kingdom. The three strokes of the cane being the signal which announced the success of the secret negotiation between the ministers of Louis XIV. and the magistrates of Strasburg.

This was the Franz Holbein of the picture, and if the three *coups de bâton* are not attributable to his ghost, I can only say I am totally at a loss to say where they should be charged; for my own part, I ought to add, I never heard them, conduct which I take it was the more ungracious on the ghost's part, as I finished the schiedam, and passed my night on the hearth-rug, leaving the feather bed with its down coverlet quite at Master Frank's disposal.

Although the " Schwein Kopf" stands in one of the most prominent squares of Rotterdam, and nearly opposite the statue of Erasmus, it is comparatively little known to English travellers. The fashionable hotels which are near the quay of landing, anticipate the claims of this more primitive house; and yet, to any one desirous of observing the ordinary routine of a Dutch family, it is well worth a visit. The buxom Vrows who trudge about with short but voluminous petticoats, their heads ornamented by those gold or silver circlets which no Dutch peasant seems ever to want, are exactly the very types

c 2

of what you see in an Ostade or a Teniers. The very host himself, old Hoogendorp, is a study; scarcely five feet in height, he might measure nearly nine in circumference, and in case of emergency could be used as a sluice-gate should anything happen to the dykes. He was never to be seen before one o'clock in the day, but exactly as the clock tolled that hour, the massive souptureen, announcing the commencement of the *table d'hôte*, was borne in state before him, while with "solemn step and slow," ladle in hand, and napkin round his neck, he followed after. His conduct at table was a fine specimen of Dutch independence of character; he never thought of bestowing those petty attentions which might cultivate the good-will of his guests; he spoke little, he smiled never; a short nod of recognition bestowed upon a townsman was about the extent of royal favour he was ever known to confer, or occasionally, when any remark made near him seemed to excite his approbation, a significant grunt of approval ratified the wisdom of the speech, and made a Solon of the speaker. His ladle descended into the soup, and emerged therefrom with the ponderous regularity of a crane into the hold of a ship. Every function of the table was performed with an unbroken monotony, and never, in the course of his forty years' sovereignty, was he known to distribute an undue quantity of fat, or an unseemly proportion of beet-root sauce, to any one guest in preference to another.

The *table d'hôte*, which began at one, concluded a little before three, during which time our host, when not helping others, was busily occupied in helping himself, and it was truly amazing to witness the steady perseverance with which he waded through every dish, making himself master in all its details of every portion of the dinner, from the greasy soup to that *acmè* of Dutch epicurism—Utrecht cheese. About a quarter before three, the long dinner drew to its conclusion. Many of the guests, indeed, had disappeared long before that time, and were deep in all their wonted occupations of timber, tobacco, and train-oil. A few, however, lingered on to the last   A burly major of infantry, who, unbuttoning his undress rock towards the close of the feast would sit smoking and sipping his coffee as if unwilling to desert the field; a grave, long-haired professor; and perhaps an officer of the excise, waiting for the re-opening of the custom-house, would form the company. But even these dropped off at last, and, with a deep bow to mine host, passed away to their homes or their haunts. Meanwhile the waiters hurried hither and thither, the cloth was removed, in its place a fresh one was spread, and all the preliminaries for a new dinner was set about with the same activity as before. The napkins enclosed in their little horn cases, the decanters of beer, the small dishes of preserved fruit, without which no Dutchman dines, were all set forth, and the host, without stirring from his seat, sat watching the preparations with calm complacency. Were you to note him narrowly, you could perceive that his eyes alternately opened and shut, as if relieving guard, save which, he gave no other sign of life, nor even at last, when the mighty stroke of three rang out from the cathedral, and the hurrying sound of many feet proclaimed the arrival of the guests of the second table, did he ever exhibit the slightest show or mark of attention, but sat calm, and still, and motionless.

For the next two hours it was merely a repetition of the performance which preceded it, in which the host's part was played with untiring energy, and all the items of soup, fish, *bouilli*, fowl, pork, and vegetables, had not to complain of any inattention to their merits, or any undue preference for their predecessors of an hour before If the traveller was astonished at his appetite during the first table, what would he say to his feats at the second As for myself, I honestly confess I thought that some harlequin-trick was concerned, and that mine host of the " Schwein Kopf" was not a real man, but some mechanical contrivance by which, with a trap-door below him, a certain portion of the dinner was conveyed to the apartments beneath. I lived, however, to discover my error; and after four visits to Rotterdam, was at length so far distinguished as actually to receive an invitation to pass an evening with "Mynheer" in his own private den, which, I need scarcely say, I gladly accepted.

I have a note of that evening somewhere—ay, here it is—

"Mynheer is waiting supper," said a waiter to me, as I
sat smoking my cigar, one calm evening in autumn, in the
porch of the " Schwein Kopf." I followed the man through
a long passage, which, leading to the kitchen, emerged on
the opposite side, and conducted us through a little garden
to a small summer-house. The building, which was of
wood, was painted in gaudy stripes of red, blue, and yellow,
and made in some sort to resemble those Chinese pagodas
we see upon a saucer. Its situation was conceived in the
most perfect Dutch taste—one side, flanked by the little
garden of which I have spoken, displayed a rich bed of
tulips and ranunculuses, in all the gorgeous luxuriance of
perfect culture—it was a mass of blended beauty and perfume superior to anything I have ever witnessed On the
other flank lay the sluggish, green-coated surface of a
Dutch canal, from which rose the noxious vapours of a
hot evening, and the harsh croakings of ten thousand
frogs, "fat, gorbellied knaves," the very burgomasters of
their race, who squatted along the banks, and who, except
for the want of pipes, might have been mistaken for small
Dutchmen enjoying an evening's promenade. This building was denominated " Lust und Rust," which, in letters
of gold, was displayed on something resembling a sign-
board, above the door, and intimated to the traveller that the
temple was dedicated to pleasure and contentment. To a
Dutchman, however, the sight of the portly figure who sat
smoking at the open window, was a far more intelligible
illustration of the objects of the building, than any let-
tered inscription. Mynheer Hoogendorp, with his long
Dutch pipe, and tall flagon, with its shining brass lid,
looked the concentrated essence of a Hollander, and might
have been hung out, as a sign of the country, from the
steeple of Haarlem.

The interior was in perfect keeping with the designation of the building. Every appliance that could suggest
ease, if not sleep, was there : the chairs were deep, plethoric-
looking Dutch chairs, that seemed as if they had led a
sedentary life, and throve upon it; the table was a short,
thick-legged one, of dark oak, whose polished surface reflected the tall brass cups, and the ample features of Mynheer, and seemed to hob-nob with him when he lifted the

capacious vessel to his lips; the walls were decorated with
quaint pipes, whose large porcelain bowls bespoke them of
home origin; and here and there a sea-fight, with a Dutch
three-decker hurling destruction on the enemy. But the
genius of the place was its owner, who, in a low fur cap and
slippers, whose shape and size might have drawn tears of
envy from the Ballast Board, sat gazing upon the canal in
a state of Dutch rapture, very like apoplexy. He motioned
me to a chair without speaking—he directed me to a pipe,
by a long whiff of smoke from his own—he grunted out a
welcome, and then, as if overcome by such unaccustomed
exertion, he lay back in his chair, and sighed deeply.

We smoked till the sun went down, and a thicker haze,
rising from the stagnant ditch, joined with the tobacco
vapour, made an atmosphere like mud reduced to gas.
Through the mist, I saw a vision of soup tureens, hot meat,
and smoking vegetables. I beheld as though Mynheer
moved among the condiments, and I have a faint dreamy
recollection of his performing some feat before me; but
whether it was carving, or the sword exercise, I won't be
positive.

Now, though the schiedam was strong, a spell was upon
me, and I could not speak; the great green eyes that
glared on me through the haze, seemed to chill my very
soul; and I drank, out of desperation, the deeper.

As the evening wore on, I waxed bolder; I had looked
upon the Dutchman so long, that my awe of him began to
subside, and I at last grew bold enough to address him.

I remember well, it was pretty much with that kind of
energy, that semi-desperation, with which a man nerves
himself to accost a spectre, that I ventured on addressing
him. How or in what terms I did it, Heaven knows!
Some trite every-day observation about his great knowledge of life—his wonderful experience of the world, was
all I could muster; and when I had made it, the sound of
my own voice terrified me so much, that I finished the
can at a draught, to reanimate my courage.

"Ja! Ja!" said Van Hoogendorp, in a cadence as
solemn as the bell of the cathedral; "I have seen many
strange things; I remember what few men living can
remember. I mind well the time when the ' Hollandische

Vrow' made her first voyage from Batavia, and brought back a paroquet for the burgomaster's wife; the great trees upon the Boomjes were but saplings when I was a boy; they were not thicker than my waist;" here he looked down upon himself with as much complacency as though he were a sylph. "Ach Gott! they were brave times, schiedam cost only half a guilder the krug"

I waited in hopes he would continue, but the glorious retrospect he had evoked, seemed to occupy all his thoughts, and he smoked away without ceasing

"You remember the Austrians, then?" said I, by way of drawing him on.

"They were dogs," said he, spitting out.

"Ah!" said I, "the French were better then?"

"Wolves!" ejaculated he, after glowring on me fearfully.

There was a long pause after this; I perceived that I had taken a wrong path to lead him into conversation, and he was too deeply overcome with indignation to speak. During this time, however, his anger took a thirsty form, and he swigged away at the schiedam most manfully.

The effect of his libations became at last evident, his great green stagnant eyes flashed and flared, his wide nostrils swelled and contracted, and his breathing became short and thick, like the convulsive sobs of a steam-engine when they open and shut the valves alternately. I watched these indications for some time, wondering what they might portend, when at length he withdrew his pipe from his mouth, and with such a tone of voice as he might have used if confessing a bloody and atrocious murder, he said—

"I will tell you a story."

Had the great stone figure of Erasmus beckoned to me across the market-place, and asked me the news "on Change," I could not have been more amazed; and not venturing on the slightest interruption, I refilled my pipe, and nodded sententiously across the table, while he thus began.

CHAPTER III.

MINE HOST'S TALE.

" It was in the winter of the year 1806, the first week of December, the frost was setting in, and I resolved to pay a visit to my brother, whom I hadn't seen for forty years ; he was burgomaster of Antwerp. It is a long voyage and a perilous one, but with the protection of Providence, our provisions held out, and on the fourth night after we sailed, a violent shock shook the vessel from stem to stern, and we found ourselves against the quay of Antwerp.

" When I reached my brother's house I found him in bed, sick ; the doctors said it was a dropsy ; I don't know how that might be, for he drank more gin than any man in Holland, and hated water all his life. We were twins, but no one would have thought so, I looked so thin and meagre beside him.

" Well, as I was there, I resolved to see the sights of the town ; and the next morning, after breakfast, I set out by myself, and wandered about till evening. Now there were many things to see—very strange things too ; the noise, and the din, and the bustle, addled and confused me ; the people were running here and there, shouting as if they were mad, and there were great flags hanging out of the windows, and drums beating, and, stranger than all, I saw little soldiers with red breeches and red shoulder-knots, running about like monkeys.

" ' What is all this ? ' said I, to a man near me.

" ' Methinks,' said he, ' the burgomaster himself might well know what it is.'

" ' I am not the burgomaster,' quoth I, ' I am his brother, and only came from Rotterdam yesterday.'

" ' Ah ! then,' said another, with a strange grin, ' you didn't know these preparations were meant to welcome your arrival.'

" ' No,' said I ; 'but they are very fine, and if there were not so much noise, I would like them well.'

" And so I sauntered on till I came to the great Platz, opposite the cathedral—that was a fine place—and there was a large man carved in cheese over one door, very wonderful to see ; and there was a big fish, all gilt, where they sold herrings ; but in the town-hall there seemed something more than usual going on, for great crowds were there, and dragoons were galloping in and galloping out, and all was confusion.

" ' What's this ? ' said I. 'Are the dykes open ? '

" But not one would mind me ; and then suddenly I heard some one call out my name.

" ' Where is Van Hoogendorp ? ' said one ; and then another cried, ' Where is Van Hoogendorp ? '

" ' Here I am,' said I ; and at the same moment two officers, covered with gold lace, came through the crowd, and took me by the arms.

" ' Come along with us, Monsieur de Hoogendorp,' said they, in French ; ' there is not a moment to lose ; we have been looking for you everywhere.'

" Now, though I understand that tongue, I cannot speak it myself, so I only said ' Ja, Ja,' and followed them.

" They led me up an oak stair, and through three or four large rooms, crowded with officers in fine uniforms, who all bowed as I passed, and some one went before us, calling out in a loud voice, ' Monsieur de Hoogendorp ! '

" ' This is too much honour,' said I, ' far too much ;' but as I spoke in Dutch, no one minded me. Suddenly, however, the wide folding-doors were flung open, and we were ushered into a large hall, where, although above a hundred people were assembled, you might have heard a pin drop ; the few who spoke at all did so only in whispers.

" ' Monsieur de Hoogendorp ! ' shouted the man again.

" ' For shame,' said I ; ' don't disturb the company ;' and I thought some of them laughed, but he only bawled the louder, ' Monsieur de Hoogendorp ! '

" ' Let him approach,' said a quick, sharp voice, from the fireplace.

" ' Ah ! ' thought I, ' they are going to read me an address. I trust it may be in Dutch.'

" They led me along in silence to the fire, before which, with his back turned towards it, stood a short man, with a sallow, stern countenance, and a great, broad forehead, his hair combed straight over it. He wore a green coat with white facings, and over that a grey surtout trimmed with fur. I am particular about all this, because this little man was a person of consequence.

" ' You are late, Monsieur de Hoogendorp,' said he, in French; ' it is half-past four;' and so saying, he pulled out his watch, and held it up before me.

" ' Ja !' said I, taking out my own, ' we are just the same time.'

' At this he stamped upon the ground, and said something I thought was a curse.

" ' Where are the *Echevins,* monsieur ? ' said he.

" ' God knows,' said I, ' most probably at dinner.'

" ' *Ventre bleu!*——'

" ' Don't swear,' said I. ' If I had you in Rotterdam, I'd fine you two guilders.'

" ' What does he say ? ' while his eyes flashed fire. ' Tell *La grande morue* to speak French.'

" ' Tell him I am not a cod-fish,' said I.

" ' Who speaks Dutch here ? ' said he. ' General de Ritter, ask him where are the *Echevins,* or, is the man a fool ? '

" ' I have heard,' said the General, bowing obsequiously —' I have heard, your Majesty, that he is little better.'

" ' *Tonnerre de Dieu !*' said he; ' and this is their chief magistrate ! Marat, you must look to this to-morrow; and as it grows late now, let us see the citadel at once, he can show us the way thither, I suppose;' and with this he moved forward, followed by the rest, among whom I found myself hurried along, no one any longer paying me the slightest respect or attention.

" ' To the citadel,' said one.

" ' To the citadel,' cried another.

" ' Come, Hoogendorp, lead the way,' cried several together; and so they pushed me to the front, and, notwithstanding all I said, that I did not know the citadel from the Dome Church, they would listen to nothing, but only called the louder, ' Step out, old " *Grande culotte,*" ' and hurried me down the street, at the pace of a boar-hunt.

"'Lead on,' cried one. 'To the front,' said another. 'Step out,' roared three or four together; and I found myself at the head of the procession, without the power to explain or confess my ignorance

"'As sure as my name is Peter van Hoogendorp, I'll give you all a devil's dance,' said I to myself; and with that I grasped my staff, and set out as fast as I was able. Down one narrow street we went, and up another; sometimes we got into a *cul de sac*, where there was no exit, and had to turn back again; another time we would ascend a huge flight of steps, and come plump into a tanner's yard, or a place where they were curing fish, and so we blundered on till there wasn't a blind alley nor crooked lane of Antwerp that we didn't wade through, and I was becoming foot-sore and tired, myself, with the exertion.

"All this time the Emperor—for it was Napoleon—took no note of where we were going; he was too busy conversing with old General de Ritter to mind anything else. At last, after traversing a long narrow street, we came down upon an arm of the Scheldt, and so overcome was I then that I resolved I would go no further without a smoke, and I sat myself down on a butter firkin, and took out my pipe, and proceeded to strike a light with my flint. A titter of laughter from the officers now attracted the Emperor's attention, and he stopped short and stared at me as if I had been some wonderful beast.

"'What is this?' said he. 'Why don't you move forward.'

"'It's impossible,' replied I; 'I never walked so far since I was born.'

"'Where is the citadel?' cried he in a passion.

"'In the devil's keeping,' said I, 'or we should have seen it long ago.'

"'That must be it yonder,' said an aide-de-camp, pointing to a green, grassy eminence, at the other side of the Scheldt.

"The Emperor took the telescope from his hand, and looked through it steadily for a couple of minutes.

" ' Yes,' said he, ' that's it: but why have we come all
this round ? the road lay yonder.'

" ' Ja ! ' said I, ' so it did.'

" ' *Ventre bleu !* ' roared he, while he stamped his foot
upon the ground, ' *Le gaillard se moque de nous.*' *

" ' Ja ! ' said I again, without well knowing why.

" ' The citadel is there ! It is yonder ! ' cried he, pointing with his finger.

" ' Ja ! ' said I, once more.

" ' *En avant !* then,' shouted he, as he motioned me
to descend the flight of steps which led down to the
Scheldt ; ' if this be the road you take, *par Saint Denis !*
you shall go first.'

" Now the frost, as I have said, had only set in a few
days before, and the ice on the Scheldt would scarcely
have borne the weight of a drummer-boy ; so I remon-
strated at once, at first in Dutch, and then in French, as
well as I was able, but nobody minded me. I then endeavoured to show the danger his Majesty himself would
incur ; but they only laughed at this, and cried—

" ' *En avant, en avant toujours,*' and before I had time
for another word, there was a corporal's guard behind me
with fixed bayonets ; the word ' march ' was given and
out I stepped.

" I tried to say a prayer, but I could think of nothing
but curses upon the fiends, whose shouts of laughter
behind put all my piety to flight. When I came to the
bottom step, I turned round, and, putting my hand to my
sides, endeavoured by signs to move their pity ; but they
only screamed the louder at this, and at a signal from
an officer, a fellow touched me with a bayonet.

" ' That was an awful moment,' said old Hoogendorp,
stopping short in his narrative, and seizing the can, which
for half an hour he had not tasted. I think I see the
river before me still, with its flakes of ice, some thick and
some thin, riding on each other ; some whirling along in
the rapid current of the stream ; some lying like islands
where the water was sluggish. I turned round, and
I clenched my fist, and I shook it in the Emperor's face,

---

* The fellow is laughing at us.

and I swore by the bones of the Stadtholder, that if I had
but one grasp of his hand, I'd not perform that dance
without a partner. Here I stood,' quoth he, 'and the
Scheldt might be, as it were, there. I lifted my foot thus,
and came down upon a large piece of floating ice, which,
the moment I touched it, slipped away, and shot out into
the stream.' "

At this moment Mynheer, who had been dramatizing
this portion of his adventure, came down upon the waxed
floor with a plump that shook the pagoda to its centre,
while I, who had during the narrative been working
double tides at the schiedam, was so interested at the
catastrophe that I thought he was really in the Scheldt,
in the situation he was describing. The instincts of
humanity were, I am proud to say, stronger in me than
those of reason. I kicked off my shoes, threw away
my coat, and plunged boldly after him. I remember well
catching him by the throat, and I remember, too, feeling
what a dreadful thing was the grip of a drowning man,
for both his hands were on my neck, and he squeezed me
fearfully. Of what happened after, the waiters or the
Humane Society may know something. I only can tell
that I kept my bed for four days, and when I next
descended to the *table d'hôte*, I saw a large patch of black
sticking-plaster across the bridge of old Hoogendorp's nose,
and I never was a guest in ' Lust und Rust ' afterwards.

*　　　*　　　*　　　*　　　*
*　　　*　　　*　　　*　　　*

The loud clanking of the *table d'hôte* bell aroused me,
as I lay dreaming of Frank Holbein and the yellow
doublet. I dressed hastily and descended to the *saal;*
everything was exactly as I left it ten years before; even
to the cherrywood pipe-stick that projected from Mynheer's breeches-pocket, nothing was changed. The clatter
of post-horses and the heavy rattle of wheels drew me
to the window, in time to see the Alderman's carriage,
with four posters, roll past; a kiss of the hand was thrown
me from the rumble. It was the " Honourable Jack" himself, who, somehow, had won their favour, and was already
installed their travelling companion.

"It is odd enough," thought I, as I arranged my napkin across my knee, "what success lies in a well-curled whisker—particularly if the wearer be a fool."

CHAPTER IV.

STRANGE CHARACTERS.

It was through no veneration for the memory of Van Hoogendorp's adventure, that I found myself one morning at Antwerp. I like the old town   I like its quaint, irregular streets—its glorious cathedral—the old "Place," with its alleys of trees; I like the Flemish women, and their long-eared caps; and I like the *table d'hôte* at the "St. Antoine"—among other reasons, because, being at one o'clock, it affords a capital argument for a hot supper at nine.

I do not know how other people may feel, but to me, I must confess, much of the pleasure the Continent affords me, is destroyed by the jargon of the "*Commissionaires*," and the cant of guide-books. Why is not a man permitted to sit down before that great picture, "The Descent from the Cross," and "gaze his fill" on it? Why may he not look till the whole scene is, as it were, acted before him, and all those faces of grief, of care, of horror, and despair, are graven in his memory, never to be erased again? Why, I say, may he not study this in tranquillity and peace, without some coarse, tobacco-reeking fellow at his elbow, in a dirty blouse and wooden shoes, explaining, in *patois* French, the merits of a work which he is as well fitted to paint as to appreciate?

But I must not myself commit the very error I am reprobating. I will not attempt any description of a

picture which, to those who have seen it, could realize not
one of the impressions the work itself afforded, and to
those who have not, would convey nothing at all. I will
not bore my reader with the tiresome cant of " effect,"
" expression," " force," " depth," and " relief," but, instead
of all this, will tell him a short story about the painting,
which, if it has no other merit, has at least that of
authenticity.

Rubens—who, among his other tastes, was a great florist
—was very desirous to enlarge his garden, by adding to
it a patch of ground adjoining   It chanced, unfortunately,
that this piece of land did not belong to an individual
who could be tempted by a large price, but to a society or
club called the " Arquebussiers," one of those old Flemish
guilds which date their origin several centuries back.
Insensible to every temptation of money, they resisted
all the painter's offers, and at length only consented to
relinquish the land on condition that he would paint a
picture for them, representing their patron saint, St.
Christopher. To this, Rubens readily acceded, his only
difficulty being to find out some incident in the good
saint's life which might serve as a subject. What St.
Christopher had to do with cross-bows or sharpshooters,
no one could tell him ; and for many a long day he puzzled
his mind, without ever being able to hit upon a solution
of the difficulty. At last, in despair, the etymology of
the word suggested a plan ; and " Christopheros," or
cross-bearer, afforded the hint on which he began his great
picture of " The Descent." For months long, he worked
industriously at the painting, taking an interest in its
details, such as he confesses never to have felt in any of
his previous works. He knew it to be his *chef-d'œuvre*,
and looked forward, with a natural eagerness, to the
moment when he should display it before its future
possessors, and receive their congratulations on his
success

The day came , the " Arquebuss " men assembled, and
repaired in a body to Rubens' house ; the large folding
shutters which concealed the painting were opened, and
the triumph of the painter's genius was displayed before
them : but not a word was spoken ; no exclamation of

admiration or wonder broke from the assembled throng; not a murmur of pleasure, or even surprise, was there. On the contrary, the artist beheld nothing but faces expressive of disappointment and dissatisfaction; and at length, after a considerable pause, one question burst from every lip—" Where is St. Christopher ? "

It was to no purpose that he explained the object of his work. In vain he assured them that the picture was the greatest he had ever painted, and far superior to what he had contracted to give them. They stood obdurate and motionless. It was St. Christopher they wished for; it was for him they bargained, and him they would have.

The altercation continued long and earnest Some of them, more moderate, hoping to conciliate both parties, suggested that, as there was a small space unemployed in the left of the painting, St. Christopher could be introduced there, by making him somewhat diminutive. Rubens rejected the proposal with disgust his great work was not to be destroyed by such an anomaly as this· and so, breaking off the negotiation at once, he dismissed the " Arquebuss " men, and relinquished all pretension to the "promised land."

Matters remained for some months thus, when the burgomaster, who was an ardent admirer of Rubens' genius. happened to hear of the entire transaction, and, waiting on the painter, suggested an expedient by which every difficulty might be avoided, and both parties rest content. " Why not," said he, " make a St Christopher on the outside of the shutter? You have surely space enough there, and can make him of any size you like." The artist caught at the proposal, seized his chalk, and in a few minutes sketched out a gigantic saint, which the burgomaster at once pronounced suited to the occasion.

The " Arquebuss" men were again introduced, and, immediately on beholding their patron, professed themselves perfectly satisfied. The bargain was concluded, the land ceded, and the picture hung up in the great cathedral of Antwerp, where, with the exception of the short period that French spoliation carried it to the Louvre, it has remained ever since, a monument of the artist's genius, the greatest and most finished of all his works. And now that I have done my story, I'll try and find out that little quaint hotel they call the "Fischer's Haus."

Fifteen years ago, I remember losing my way one night in the streets of Antwerp. I couldn't speak a word of Flemish : the few people I met couldn't understand a word of French. I wandered about for full two hours, and heard the old cathedral clock play a psalm tune, and the St. Joseph tried its hand on another. A watchman cried the hour through a cow's horn, and set all the dogs a-barking; and then all was still again, and I plodded along, without the faintest idea of the points of the compass.

In this moody frame of mind I was, when the heavy clank of a pair of sabots, behind, apprised me that some one was following. I turned sharply about, and accosted him in French.

"English?" said he, in a thick, guttural tone.

"Yes, thank Heaven," said I, "do you speak English?"

"Ja, Mynheer," answered he.

Though this reply didn't promise very favourably, I immediately asked him to guide me to my hotel, upon which he shook his head gravely, and said nothing.

"Don't you speak English?" said I.

"Ja!" said he once more.

"I've lost my way," cried I; "I am a stranger."

He looked at me doggedly for a minute or two, and then, with a stern gravity of manner and a phlegm I cannot attempt to convey, he said—

"D——n *my* eyes!"

"What," said I, "do you mean?"

"Ja!" was the only reply

"If you know English, why won't you speak it?"

"D——n *his* eyes!" said he with a deep solemn tone.

"Is that all you know of the language?" cried I, stamping with impatience. "Can you say no more than that?"

"D——n *your* eyes!" ejaculated he, with as much composure as though he were maintaining an earnest conversation.

When I had sufficiently recovered from the hearty fit of laughter this colloquy occasioned me, I began by signs, such as melo-dramatic people make to express sleep, placing my head in the hollow of my hand, snoring and yawning, to represent that I stood in need of a bed.

" Ja !" cried my companion with more energy than before, and led the way down one narrow street, and up another, traversing lanes where two men could scarcely go abreast, until at length we reached a branch of the Scheldt, along which we continued for about twenty minutes. Suddenly the sound of voices shouting a species of Dutch tune—for so its unspeakable words, and wooden turns, bespoke it—apprised me that we were near a house where the people were yet astir.

" Ha !" said I, " this is a hotel then."

Another " Ja !"

" What do they call it ? "

A shake of the head.

' That will do ; good night," said I, as I saw the bright lights gleaming from the small diamond panes of an old Flemish window ; " I am much obliged to you "

" D——n *your* eyes !" said my friend, taking off his hat politely, and making me a low bow, while he added something in Flemish, which I sincerely trust was of a more polite and complimentary import than his parting benediction in English.

As I turned from the Fleming, I entered a narrow hall, which led by a low-arched door into a large room, along which a number of tables were placed, each crowded by its own party, who clinked their cans and vociferated a chorus which, from constant repetition, rings still in my memory—

> " Wenn die wein ist in die mann,
> Der weisdheid den ist in die kan ;"

or in the vernacular—

> " When the wine is in the man,
> Then is the wisdom in the can ;"

a sentiment which a very brief observation of their faces induced me perfectly to concur in. Over the chimney-piece an inscription was painted in letters of about a foot

long, "Hier verkoopt man Bier," implying, what a very
cursory observation might have conveyed to any one,
even on the evidence of his nose, that beer was a very
attainable fluid in the establishment. The floor was
sanded, and the walls whitewashed, save where some
pictorial illustrations of Flemish habits were displayed in
black chalk, or the smoke of a candle.

As I stood uncertain whether to advance or retreat, a
large portly Fleming, with a great waistcoat, made of the
skin of some beast, eyed me steadfastly from head to foot,
and then, as if divining my embarrassment, beckoned me
to approach, and pointed to a seat on the bench beside him.
I was not long in availing myself of his politeness, and
before half an hour elapsed, found myself with a brass can
of beer, about eighteen inches in height, before me ; while
I was smoking away as though I had been born within
the "dykes," and never knew the luxury of dry land

Around the table sat some seven or eight others, whose
phlegmatic look and sententious aspect convinced me they
were Flemings. At the far end, however, was one whose
dark eyes, flashing beneath heavy shaggy eyebrows, huge
whiskers, and bronzed complexion, distinguished him
sufficiently from the rest. He appeared, too, to have
something of respect paid him, inasmuch as the others
invariably nodded to him whenever they lifted their cans
to their mouths. He wore a low fur cap on his head, and
his dark blue frock was trimmed also with fur, and slashed
with a species of braiding, like an undress uniform.

Unlike the rest, he spoke a great deal, not only to his
own party, but maintaining a conversation with various
others through the room—sometimes speaking French,
then Dutch, and occasionally changing to German or
Italian, with all which tongues he appeared so familiar,
that I was fairly puzzled to what country to assign him.

I could mark at times that he stole a sly glance over
towards where I was sitting, and, more than once, I
thought I observed him watching what effect his voluble
powers as a linguist was producing upon me. At last our
eyes met, he smiled politely, and taking up the can before
him, he bowed, saying, "*A votre santé, monsieur.*"

I acknowledged the compliment at once, and seizing the

opportunity, begged to know of what land so accomplished a linguist was a native. His face brightened up at once, a certain smile of self-satisfied triumph passed over his features, he smacked his lips, and then poured out a torrent of strange sounds, which, from their accent, I guessed to be Russian.

"Do you speak Slavonic ? " said he in French ; and as I nodded a negative, he added—" Spanish,—Portuguese ? "

" Neither," said I.

" Where do you come from, then ? " asked he, retorting my question.

"Ireland, if you may have heard of such a place."

" Hurroo ! " cried he, with a yell that made the room start with amazement. " By the powers ! I thought so ; come up, my hearty, and give me a shake of your hand."

If I were astonished before, need I say how I felt now ?

"And you are really a countryman of mine ? " said I, as I took my seat beside him.

" Faith, I believe so. Con O'Kelly does not sound very like Italian, and that's my name, anyhow ; but wait a bit, they're calling on me for a Dutch song, and when I've done we'll have a chat together."

A very uproarious clattering of brass and pewter cans on the tables announced that the company was becoming impatient for Mynheer O'Kelly's performance, which he immediately began ; but of either the words or air, I can render no possible account ; I only know there was a kind of *refrain* or chorus, in which all, round each table, took hands, and danced a "grand round," making the most diabolical clatter with wooden shoes I ever listened to. After which, the song seemed to subside into a low droning sound, implying sleep. The singer nodded his head, the company followed the example, and a long heavy note, like snoring, was heard through the room, when suddenly, with a hiccup, he awoke, the others did the same, and then the song broke out once more, in all its vigour, to end as before, in another dance, an exercise in which I certainly fared worse than my neighbours, who tramped on my corns without mercy, leaving it a very questionable fact how far his " pious, glorious, and immortal memory " was

to be respected, who had despoiled my country of "wooden
shoes," when walking off with its brass money.

The melody over, Mr. O'Kelly proceeded to question
me somewhat minutely, as to how I had chanced upon
this house, which was not known to many, even of the
residents of Antwerp

I briefly explained to him the circumstances which led
me to my present asylum, at which he laughed heartily

" You don't know, then, where you are ? " said he, looking at me, with a droll half-suspicious smile.

" No ; it's a Schenck Haus, I suppose," replied I.

" Yes, to be sure, it is a Schenck Haus; but it's the
resort only of smugglers, and those connected with their
traffic.   Every man about you, and there are, as you see,
some seventy or eighty, are all either sea-faring folks, or
landsmen associated with them, in contraband trade."

" But how is this done so openly ? the house is surely
known to the police "

" Of course, and they are well paid for taking no notice
of it."

" And you ? "

" Me!   Well, *I* do a little that way too, though it's
only a branch of my business.   I'm only Dirk Hatteraick,
when I come down to the coast · then you know a man
doesn't like to be idle ; so that when I'm here, or on the
Bretagny shore, I generally mount the red cap, and buckle
on the cutlass, just to keep moving , as, when I go inland,
I take an occasional turn with the gipsy folk in Bohemia,
or their brethren in the Basque provinces.   There's nothing
like being up to everything—that's *my* way."

I confess I was a good deal surprised at my companion's
account of himself, and not over impressed with the rigour
of his principles ; but my curiosity to know more of him
became so much the stronger.

" Well," said I, " you seem to have a jolly life of it ;
and, certainly a healthful one."

" Ay, that it is," replied he quickly.   " I've more than
once thought of going back to Kerry, and living quietly
for the rest of my days, for I could afford it well enough ;
but, somehow, the thought of staying in one place, talking
always to the same set of people, seeing every day the

same sights, and hearing the same eternal little gossip about little things, and little folk, was too much for me, and so I stuck to the old trade, which I suppose I'll not give up now as long as I live."

"And what may that be?" asked I, curious to know how he filled up moments snatched from the agreeable pursuits he had already mentioned.

He eyed me with a shrewd, suspicious look, for above a minute, and then, laying down his hand on my arm, said—

"Where do you put up at, here in Antwerp?"

"The 'St. Antoine.'"

"Well, I'll come over for you to-morrow evening about nine o'clock; you're not engaged, are you?"

"No, I've no acquaintance here."

"At nine, then, be ready, and you'll come and take a bit of supper with me; and in exchange for your news of the old country, I'll tell you something of my career."

I readily assented to a proposal which promised to make me better acquainted with one evidently a character; and after half an hour's chatting, I arose.

"You're not going away, are you?" said he. "Well, I can't leave this yet; so I'll just send a boy to show you the way to the 'St. Antony.'"

With that he beckoned to a lad at one of the tables, and addressing a few words in Flemish to him, he shook me warmly by the hand. The whole room rose respectfully as I took my leave, and I could see that "Mr. O'Kelly's friend" stood in no small estimation with the company.

The day was just breaking when I reached my hotel; but I knew I could poach on the daylight for what the dark had robbed me; and besides, my new acquaintance promised to repay the loss of a night's sleep, should it even come to that.

Punctual to his appointment, my newly-made friend knocked at my door exactly as the cathedral was chiming for nine o'clock. His dress was considerably smarter than on the preceding evening, and his whole air and bearing bespoke a degree of quiet decorum and reserve, very different from his free-and-easy carriage in the "Fischer's Haus." As I accompanied him through the

porte-cochère, we passed the landlord, who saluted us with
much politeness, shaking my companion by the hand like
an old friend.

" You are acquainted here, I see," said I.

" There are few landlords from Lubeck to Leghorn I
don't know by this time," was the reply, and he smiled as
he spoke

A calèche with one horse was waiting for us without,
and into this we stepped. The driver had got his directions, and plying his whip briskly, we rattled over the
paved streets, and passing through a considerable part of
the town, arrived at last at one of the gates. Slowly
crossing the draw-bridge at a walk, we set out again at a
trot, and soon I could perceive, through the half light,
that we had traversed the suburbs and were entering the
open country.

" We've not far to go now," said my companion, who
seemed to suspect that I was meditating over the length
of the way ; " where you see the lights yonder—that's our
ground."

The noise of the wheels over the stones soon after
ceased, and I found we were passing across a grassy lawn
in front of a large house, which, even by the twilight, I
could detect was built in the old Flemish taste. A square
tower flanked one extremity, and from the upper part of
this the light gleamed to which my companion pointed

We descended from the carriage at the foot of a long
terrace, which, though dilapidated and neglected, bore
still some token of its ancient splendour. A stray statue
here and there remained, to mark its former beauty, while,
close by, the hissing splash of water told that a *jet d'eau*
was playing away, unconscious that its river gods, dolphins,
and tritons had long since departed.

" A fine old place once," said my new friend ; " the old
chateau of Overghem—one of the richest seignories of
Flanders in its day—sadly changed now ; but come,
follow me."

So saying, he led the way into the hall, where detaching
a rude lantern that was hung against the wall, he ascended
the broad oak stairs.

I could trace, by the fitful gleam of the light, that the

walls had been painted in fresco, the architraves of the
windows and doors being richly carved in all the grotesque
extravagance of old Flemish art; a gallery which traversed the building, was hung with old pictures, apparently family portraits, but they were all either destroyed
by damp or rotting with neglect. At the extremity of
this, a narrow stair conducted us by a winding ascent to
the upper story of the tower, where, for the first time, my
companion had recourse to a key; with this he opened a
low pointed door, and ushered me into an apartment, at
which I could scarcely help expressing my surprise aloud
as I entered.

The room was of small dimensions, but seemed actually
the boudoir of a palace. Rich cabinets in buhl graced the
walls, brilliant in all the splendid costliness of tortoise-
shell and silver inlaying—bronzes of the rarest kind, pictures, vases, curtains of gorgeous damask covered the
windows, and a chimney-piece of carved black oak, representing a pilgrimage, presented a depth of perspective,
and a beauty of design, beyond anything I had ever witnessed. The floor was covered with an old tapestry of
Oudenarde, spread over a heavy Persian rug, into which
the feet sank at every step, while a silver lamp, of antique
mould, threw a soft, mellow light around, revolving on an
axis, whose machinery played a slow but soothing melody
delightfully in harmony with all about.

"You like this kind of thing," said my companion, who
watched with evident satisfaction the astonishment and
admiration with which I regarded every object around
me. "That's a pretty bit of carving there; that was done
by Van Zoost, from a design of Schneider's; see how the
lobsters are crawling over the tangled sea-weed there, and
look how the leaves seem to fall heavy and flaccid, as if
wet with spray. This is good, too; it was painted by
Gherard Dow. It is a portrait of himself; he is making
a study of that little boy who stands there on the table;
see how he has disposed the light so as to fall on the little
fellow's side, tipping him from the yellow curls of his
round bullet head to the angle of his white sabot.

"Yes, you're right, that is by Van Dyk, only a sketch,
to be sure, but has all his manner. I like the Velasquez

yonder better, but they both possess the same excellence.
They could represent *birth* Just see that dark fellow
there; he's no beauty, you'll say; but regard him closely,
and tell me if he's one to take a liberty with ; look at his
thin, clenched lip, and that long, thin, pointed chin, with
its straight, stiff beard—can there be a doubt he was a
gentleman ? Take care; gently, your elbow grazed it.
That is a specimen of the old Japan china—a lost art
now—they cannot produce the blue colour you see there,
running into green. See, the flowers are laid on after
the cup is baked, and the birds are a separate thing after
all. But come, this is, perhaps, tiresome work to you ;
follow me."

Notwithstanding my earnest entreaty to remain, he took
me by the arm, and opening a small door, covered by a
mirror, led me into another room, the walls and ceiling
of which were in dark oak wainscot ; a single picture
occupied the space above the chimney, to which, however,
I gave little attention, my eyes being fixed upon a most
appetizing supper, which figured on a small table in the
middle of the room Not even the savoury odour of the
good dishes, or my host's entreaty to begin, could turn
me from the contemplation of the antique silver covers,
carved in the richest fashion. The handles of the knives
were fashioned into representations of saints and angels,
the costly ruby glasses, of Venetian origin, were surrounded
with cases of gold filagree, of most delicate and beautiful
character.

" We must be our own attendants," said the host.
" What have you there ? Here are some Ostend oysters,
' *en matelot ;* ' that is a small capon *truffé;* and here are
some cutlets ' *aux points d asperge.*' But let us begin, and
explore as we proceed A glass of Chablis with your
oysters; what a pity these Burgundy wines are inaccessible to you in England Chablis scarcely bears the sea ;
of half a dozen bottles, one is drinkable, the same of the
red wines; and what is there so generous ? Not that
we are to despise our old friend, Champagne ; and now
that you've helped yourself to a *paté,* let us have a bumper. By the bye, have they abandoned that absurd notion
they used to have in England about Champagne ? When

I was there, they never served it during the first course. Now Champagne should come immediately after your soup—your glass of Sherry or Madeira is a holocaust offered up to bad cookery; for if the soup were safe, Chablis or Sauterne is your fluid. How is the capon?—good? I'm glad of it. These countries excel in their *poulardes*."

In this fashion my companion ran on, accompanying each plate with some commentary on its history or concoction, a kind of dissertation, I must confess, I have no manner of objection to, especially when delivered by a host who illustrates his theorem, not by "plates" but "dishes."

Supper over, we wheeled the table to the wall, and drawing forward another, on which the wine and dessert were already laid out, prepared to pass a pleasant and happy evening in all form.

" Worse countries than Holland, Mr. O'Leary," said my companion, as he sipped his Burgundy, and looked with ecstasy at the rich colour of the wine through the candle

" When seen thus," said I, " I don't know its equal "

" Why, perhaps this is rather a favourable specimen of a smuggler's cave, " replied he, laughing. " Better than old Dirk's, eh? By the bye, do you know Scott?"

" No; I am sorry to say that I am not acquainted with him."

" What the devil could have led him into such a blunder as to make Hatteraick, a regular Dutchman, sing a German song? Why, 'Ich Bin liederlich' is good Hoch-Deutsch and Saxon to boot. A Hollander might just as well have chanted modern Greek, or Coptic. I'll wager you that Rubens there, over the chimney, against a crown-piece, you'll not find a Dutchman, from Dort to Nimwegen, could repeat the lines that he has made a regular national song of; and again, in Quentin Durward, he has made all the Liège folk speak German. That was even a worse mistake. Some of them speak French; but the nation, the people, are Walloons, and have as much idea of German as a Hottentot has of the queen of hearts. Never mind, he s a glorious fellow for all that, and here's his health. When will Ireland have his equal to chronicle her feats of field and flood, and make her land as classic as Scott has done his own!"

While we rambled on, chatting of all that came uppermost, the wine passed freely across the narrow table, and the evening wore on. My curiosity to know more of one who, on whatever he talked, seemed thoroughly informed, grew gradually more and more; and at last I ventured to remind him that he had half promised me the previous evening to let me hear something of his own history.

"No, no," said he," laughing; "story-telling is poor work for the teller and the listener too, and when a man's tale has not even brought a moral to himself, it's scarcely likely to be more generous towards his neighbour."

" Of, course," said I; " I have no claim as a stranger—"

" Oh, as to that," interrupted he, "somehow I feel as though we were longer acquainted. I've seen much of the world, and know by this time that some men begin to know each other from the starting-post—others never do, though they travel a life long together; so that, on that score, no modesty. If you care for my story, fill your glass, and let's open another flask; and here it's for you, though I warn you beforehand the narrative is somewhat of the longest."

CHAPTER V.

'I can tell you but little about my family," said my host,
stretching out his legs to the fire, and crossing his arms
easily before him. "My grandfather was in the Austrian
service, and killed in some old battle with the Turks.
My father, Peter O'Kelly, was shot in a duel by an
attorney from Youghal. Something about nailing his ear
to the pump, I've heard tell was the cause of the row; for
he came down to my father's with a writ, or a process, or
something of the kind. No matter—the thief had pluck
in him; and when Peter—my father that was—told him
he'd make a gentleman of him, and fight him, if he'd give
up the bill of costs, why, the temptation was too strong to
resist, he pitched the papers into the fire, went out the
same morning, and faith he put in his bullet as fair as if
he was used to the performance. I was only a child then,
ten or eleven years old, and so I remember nothing of the
particulars; but I was packed off the next day to an old
aunt's, a sister of my father's, who resided in the town
of Tralee.

"Well, to be sure, it was a great change for me, young
as I was, from Castle O'Kelly to Aunt Judy's. At home
there was a stable full of horses, a big house, generally
full of company, and the company as full of fun; we had
a pack of harriers went out twice or thrice a week, had
plenty of snipe-shooting, and a beautiful race-course was
made round the lawn. And though I wasn't quite of an
age to join in these pleasures myself, I had a lively taste
for them all, and relished the free-and-easy style of my
father's house, without any unhappy forebodings that the
amusements there practised would end in leaving me a
beggar.

"Now, my Aunt Judy lived in what might be called a

state of painfully-elegant poverty. Her habitation was somewhat more capacious than a house in a toy-shop; but then it had all the usual attributes of a house. There was a hall door, and two windows, and a chimney, and a brass knocker, and, I believe, a scraper; and within there were three little rooms, about the dimensions of a mail-coach, each. I think I see the little parlour before me, now this minute: there was a miniature of my father in a red coat over the chimney, and two screens painted by my aunt—landscapes, I am told they were once; but time and damp had made them look something like the moon seen through a bit of smoked glass; and there were fire-irons as bright as day, for they never performed any other duty than standing on guard beside the grate—a kind of royal beef-eaters, kept for show; and there was a little table covered with shells and minerals, bits of coral, conchs, and cheap curiosities of that nature, and over them, again, was a stuffed macaw. Oh, dear! I see it all before me, and the little tea service, that if the beverage had been vitriol, a cupful couldn't have harmed you. There were four chairs;—human ingenuity couldn't smuggle in a fifth. There was one for Father Donnellan, another for Mrs. Brown, the post-mistress, another for the barrack-master, Captain Dwyer, the fourth for my aunt herself; but then no more were wanted. Nothing but real gentility, the 'ould Irish blood,' would be received by Miss Judy; and if the post-mistress wasn't fourteenth cousin to somebody, who was aunt to Phelim O'Brien, who was hanged for some humane practice towards the English in former times, the devil a cup of bohea she'd have tasted there! The priest was *ex officio*, but Captain Dwyer was a gentleman born and bred. His great-grandfather had an estate; the last three generations had lived on the very reputation of its once being in the family ' *they* weren't upstarts, no, sorrow bit of it;' ' when they had it they spent it,' and so on, were the current expressions concerning them. Faith, I will say, that in my time in Ireland—I don't know how it may be now—the aroma of a good property stood to the descendants long after the substance had left them, and if they only stuck fast to the place where the family had once been great, it took at least a couple of generations before they need think of looking out for a livelihood.

"Aunt Judy's revenue was something like eighty pounds a year; but in Tralee she was not measured by the rule of the 'income tax.' 'Wasn't she own sister to Peter O'Kelly of the Castle; didn't Brien O'Kelly call at the house when he was canvassing for the member, and leave his card; and wasn't the card displayed on the little mahogany table every evening, and wiped and put by every morning, for fifteen years ; and sure the O'Kellys had their own burial-ground, the 'O'Kellys' pound,' as it was called, being a square spot inclosed within a wall, and employed for all 'trespassers' of the family within death's domain. Here was gentility enough, in all conscience, even had the reputation of her evening parties not been the talk of the town. These were certainly exclusive enough, and consisted as I have told you.

"Aunt Judy loved her rubber, and so did her friends; and eight o'clock every evening saw the little party assembled at a game of 'longs,' for penny points. It was no small compliment to the eyesight of the players, that they could distinguish the cards ; for with long use they had become dimmed and indistinct. The queens had contracted a very tatterdemalion look, and the knaves had got a most vagabond expression for want of their noses, not to speak of other difficulties in dealing, which certainly required an expert hand, all the corners having long disappeared, leaving the operation something like playing at quoits.

"The discipline of such an establishment, I need scarcely say, was very distasteful to me. I was seldom suffered to go beyond the door, more rarely still, alone. My whole amusement consisted in hearing about the ancient grandeur of the O'Kellys, and listening to a very prosy history of certain martyrs, not one of whom I didn't envy in my heart; while in the evening I slept beneath the whist table, being too much afraid of ghosts to venture upstairs to bed. It was on one of those evenings, when the party were assembled as usual ; some freak of mine—I fear I was a rebellious subject—was being discussed between the deals, it chanced that by some accident I was awake, and heard the colloquy.

" ' 'Tis truth I'm telling you, ma'am,' quoth my aunt; 'you'd think he was mild as milk, and there isn't a name for the wickedness in him.'

" ' When I was in the Buffs there was a fellow of the name of Clancy——'

" ' Play a spade, captain,' said the priest, who had no common horror of the story he had heard every evening for twenty years.

" 'And did he really put the kitten into the oven?' inquired Mrs. Brown.

" ' Worse than that—he brought in Healy's buck goat yesterday, and set him opposite the looking-glass, and the beast, thinking he saw another opposite him, bolted straightforward, and, my dear, he stuck his horns through the middle of it. There isn't a piece as big as the ace of diamonds.'

" ' When I was in the Buffs——'

" ' 'Tis at say he ought to be—don't you think so, captain?' said the priest —'them's trumps.'

" ' I beg your pardon, Father Donnellan ; let me look at the trick. Well I'm sure I pity you, Miss O'Kelly.'

" 'And why wouldn't you ! his mother had a bad drop in her, 'tis easy seen. Sure, Peter that's gone, rest his soul in peace, he never harmed man nor beast ; but that child there has notions of wickedness that would surprise you. My elegant cornelian necklace he's taken the stones out of, till it nearly chokes me to put it on.'

" ' When I was in the Buffs, Miss O'Kelly, there was——'

" ' Pay fourpence,' said the priest, pettishly, 'and cut the cards As I was saying, I'd send him to " say," and if the stories be thrue I hear, he's not ill-fitted for it ; he does be the most of his time up there at the caves of Ballybunnion, with the smugglers.'

" My aunt crimsoned a little at this, as I could see from my place on the hearth-rug, for it was only the day before I had brought in a package of green tea, obtained from the quarter alluded to.

" ' I'd send him to Banagher to-morrow,' said he, resolutely ; ' I'd send him to school.'

" 'There was one Clancy, I was saying, a great devil he was——'

" ' And faix ould Martin will flog his tricks out of him, if birch will do it,' said the priest.

" ' 'Tis only a fortnight since he put hot cinders in the letter-box, and burned half the Dublin bag,' said Mrs. Brown. 'The town will be well rid of him.'

" This was exactly the notion I was coming to myself, though differing widely as to the destination by which I was to manage my exchange out of it. The kind wishes of the party towards me, too, had another effect—it nerved me with a courage I never felt before—and when I took the first opportunity of a squabble at the whist-table to make my escape from the room, I had so little fear of ghosts and goblins, that I opened the street-door, and, although the way led under the wall of the churchyard, set out on my travels, in a direction which was to influence all my after life.

" I had not proceeded far when I overtook some cars on their way to Tarbert, on one of which I succeeded in obtaining a seat; and, by daybreak, arrived at the Shannon, the object of my desires, and the goal of all my wishes.

" The worthy priest had not calumniated me in saying that my associates were smugglers. Indeed, for weeks past, I never missed any opportunity of my aunt leaving the house, without setting out to meet a party who frequented a small public-house, about three miles from Tralee, and with whom I made more than one excursion to the caves of Ballybunnion. It was owing to an accidental piece of information I afforded them—that the revenue force was on their track—that I first learned to know these fellows; and from that moment I was a sworn friend of every man among them. To be sure, they were a motley crew. The craft belonged to Flushing, and the skipper himself was a Fleming; the others were Kinsale fishermen, Ostenders, men from the coast of Bretagne, a Norwegian pilot, and a negro who acted as cook. Their jovial style of life, the apparent good humour and good fellowship that subsisted among them, a dash of reckless devil-may-care spirit, resembling a schoolboy's love of fun

E

—all captivated me ; and when I found myself on board
the ' Dart,' as she lay at anchor under the shadow of the
tall cliffs, and saw the crew burnishing up pistols and
cutlasses, and making ready for a cruise, I had a proud
heart when they told me I might join and be one among
them. I suppose every boy has something in his nature
that inclines him to adventure. It was strong enough in
me, certainly.

" The hardy, weather-beaten faces of my companions—
their strong muscular frames—their coarse uniform of
striped Jersey wear, with black belts crossing on the chest
—all attracted my admiration : and from the red bunting
that floated at our gaff, to the brass swivels that peeped
from our bows, the whole craft delighted me. I was not
long in acquiring the rough habits and manners of my
associates, and speedily became a favourite with every one
on board. All the eccentricities of my venerable aunt, all
the peculiarities of Father Donnellan, were dished up by me
for their amusement, and they never got tired laughing at
the description of the whist-table. Besides, I was able to
afford them much valuable information about the neigh-
bouring gentry. all of whom I knew, either personally or
by name. I was at once, therefore, employed as a kind of
diplomatic envoy to ascertain if Mr. Blennerhassett
wouldn't like a hogshead of brandy, or the Knight of
Glynn a pipe of claret, in addition to many minor embassies among the shebeen houses of the country, concerning
nigger-heads of tobacco, packages of tea, smuggled lace,
and silk handkerchiefs.

" Thus was my education begun ; and an apter scholar,
in all the art and mystery of smuggling, could scarcely
have been found. I had a taste for picking up languages ;
and, before my first cruise was over, had got a very toler-
able smattering of French, Dutch, and Norwegian, and
some intimacy with the fashionable dialect used on the
banks of the Niger. Other accomplishments followed
these. I was a capital pistol shot—no bad hand with
the small-sword—could reef and steer, and had not my
equal on board in detecting a revenue officer, no matter
how artfully disguised. Such were my professional—my
social qualifications far exceeded these. I could play a

little on the violin and the guitar, and was able to throw
into rude verse any striking incident of our wild career,
and adapt an air to it, for the amusement of my companions. These I usually noted down in a book, accompanying them with pen illustrations and notes ; and I assure
you, however little literary reputation this volume might
have acquired, ' O'Kelly's Log,' as it was called, formed
the great delight of ' Saturday night at sea.' These
things were all too local and personal in their interest to
amuse any one who didn't know the parties ; but mayhap
one day or other I'll give you a sight of the ' log,' and let
you hear some of our songs.

"I won't stop to detail any of the adventures of my
seafaring life; strange and wild enough they were in all
conscience : one night staggering under close-reefed canvas
under a lee-shore ; another, carousing with a jolly set in a
'Schenck Haus' at Rotterdam or Ostend ; now hiding in
the dark caves of Ballybunnion while the craft stood out to
sea ; now disguised, taking a run up to Paris, and dining
in the ' Café de l'Empire,' in all the voluptuous extravagance of the day. Adventure fast succeeding on adventure, escape upon escape, had given my life a character of
wild excitement, which made me feel a single day's repose
a period of *ennui* and monotony.

" Smuggling, too, became only a part of my occupation.
My knowledge of French, and my power of disguising my
appearance, enabled me to mix in Parisian society of a
certain class without any fear of detection In this way I
obtained, from time to time, information of the greatest
consequence to our government ; and once brought some
documents from the war department of Napoleon, which
obtained for me the honour of an interview with Mr. Pitt
himself. This part of my career, however, would take me
too far away from my story, were I to detail any of the
many striking adventures which marked it ; so I'll pass on
at once to one of those eventful epochs of my life, two or
three of which have changed for the time the current of
my destiny.

" I was about eighteen : the war with France had just
broken out, and the assembled camp at Boulogne threatened the invasion of England. The morning we left the
E 2

French coast, the preparations for the embarkation of the
troops were in great forwardness, and certain particulars
had reached us which convinced me that Napoleon really
intended an attempt, which many were disposed to believe
was merely a menace.   In fact, an officer of the staff had
given me such information as explained the mode of the
descent, and the entire plan of the expedition.   Before I
could avail myself of this, however, we had to land our
cargo, an unusually rich one, on the west coast of Ireland,
for my companions knew nothing all this time of the
system of 'espionage' I had established, and little suspected that one of their crew was in relation with the
Prime Minister of England.

"I have said I was about eighteen.   My wild life, if it
had made me feel older than my years, had given a hardi-
hood and enterprise to my character which heightened for
me the enjoyment of every bold adventure, and made me
feel a kind of ecstasy in every emergency where danger
and difficulty were present.   I longed to be the skipper of
my own craft, sweeping the seas at my own will; a bold
buccaneer, caring less for gain than glory, until my name
should win for itself its own meed of fame, and my feats
be spoken of with awe and astonishment.

" Old Van Brock, our captain, was a hardy Fleming,
but all his energy of character, all his daring, were
directed to the one object—gain.   For this there was
nothing he wouldn't attempt, nothing he wouldn't risk.
Now, our present voyage was one in which he had embarked all his capital; the outbreak of a war warned him
that his trade must speedily be abandoned—he could no
longer hope to escape the cruisers of every country that
already filled the channel.   This one voyage, however, if
successful, would give him an ample competence for life,
and he determined to hazard everything upon it.

"It was a dark and stormy night in November when
we made the first light on the west coast of Ireland.   Part
of our cargo was destined for Ballybunnion; the remainder, and most valuable portion, was to be landed in the
Bay of Galway.   It blew a gale from the south'ard and
westward, and the sea ran mountains high, not the short
jobble of a land-locked channel, but the heavy roll of the

great Atlantic—dark and frowning, swelling to an enormous height, and thundering away on the iron-bound coast to leeward with a crash that made our hearts quiver. The 'Dart' was a good sea-boat, but the waves swept her from stem to stern, and though nothing but a close-reefed topsail was bent, we went spinning through the water at the rate of twelve knots the hour. The hatchways were battened down, and every preparation made for a rough night, for as the darkness increased, so did the gale.

"The smuggler's fate is a dark and gloomy one. Let the breeze fall, let the blue sky and fleecy clouds lie mirrored on the glassy deep, and straight a boat is seen sweeping along with sixteen oars, springing with every jerk of the strong arms to his capture. And when the white waves rise like mountains, and the lowering storm descends, sending tons of water across his decks, and wetting his highest rigging with the fleecy drift, he dares not cry for help; the signal that would speak of his distress would be the knell to toll his ruin. We knew this well. We felt that, come what would, from others there was nothing to be hoped. It was then with agonizing suspense we watched the little craft as she worked in the stormy sea ; we saw that with every tack we were losing. The strong land current that set in towards the shore told upon us at every reach; and when we went about, the dark and beetling cliffs seemed actually toppling over us, and the wild cries of the sea-fowl rang like a dirge in our ears. The small storm-jib we were obliged to set sunk us by the head, and at every pitch the little vessel seemed threatening to go down, bow foremost.

" Our great endeavour was to round the headland which forms the southern shore of the Shannon's mouth There is a small sound there, between this point and the rocks they call the ' Blasquets,' and for this we were making with all our might. Thus passed our night, and, when day broke, a cheer of joy burst from our little crew, as we beheld the Blasquets on our weather bow, and saw that the sound lay straight before us. Scarce had the shout died away, when a man in the rigging cried out—

" ' A sail to windward ;' and the instant after added, ' a man-o'-war brig.'

"The skipper sprang on the bulwark, and setting his glass in the shrouds, examined the object, which to the naked eye was barely a haze in the horizon.

"She carries eighteen guns,' said he, slowly, 'and is steering our course. I say, O'Kelly, there's no use in running in shore to be pinioned—what's to be done ?'

"The thought of the information I was in possession of flashed across me. Life was never so dear before, but I could not speak. I knew the old man's all was on the venture; I knew, too, if we were attacked, his resolve was to fight her to the last spar that floated.

"' Come,' said he, again, ' there's a point more south'ard in the wind ; we might haul her close and make for Galway Bay. Two hours would land the cargo—at least enough of it ; and if the craft must go——'

"A heavy squall struck us as he spoke ; the vessel reeled over, till she laid her crosstrees in the sea. A snap like the report of a shot was heard, and the topmast came tumbling down upon the deck, the topsail falling to leeward and hanging by the bolt-ropes over our gunwale. The little craft immediately fell off from the wind, and plunged deeper than ever in the boiling surf; at the same instant a booming sound swept across the water, and a shot striking the sea near, ricochetted over the bowsprit, and passed on, dipping and bounding towards the shore.

"She's one of their newly-built ones,' said the second mate, an Irishman, who chewed his quid of tobacco as he gazed at her, as coolly as if he was in a dockyard. 'I know the ring of her brass guns.'

"A second and a third flash, followed by two reports, came almost together; but this time they fell short of us, and passed away in our wake.

"We cut away the fallen rigging, and seeing nothing for it now but to look to our own safety, we resolved to run the vessel up the bay, and try if we could not manage to conceal some portions of the cargo before the man-o'-war could overtake us. The caves along the shore were all well known to us ; every one of them had served either as a store or a place of concealment. The wind, however, freshened every minute; the storm-jib was all we could carry, and this, instead of aiding, dipped us heavily by the head, while the large ship gained momentarily on us, and now her tall masts and white sails lowered close in our wake.

" ' Shall we stave these puncheons? ' said the mate in a whisper to the skipper; ' she'll be aboard of us in no time.'

" The old man made no reply, but his eyes turned from the man-o'-war to shore, and back again, and his mouth quivered slightly.

" ' They'd better get the hatches open, and heave over that tobacco,' said the mate, endeavouring to obtain an answer.

" ' She's hauled down her signal for us to lie-to,' observed the skipper, ' and see there, her bow ports are open —here it comes.'

" A bright flash burst out as he spoke, and one blended report was heard, as the shots skimmed the sea beside us.

" ' Run that long gun aft,' cried the old fellow, as his eyes flashed and his colour mounted. ' I'll rake their after-deck for them, or I'm mistaken.'

" For the first time the command was not obeyed at once. The men looked at each other in hesitation, and as if not determined what part to take.

" ' What do you stare at there ? ' cried he, in a voice of passion. ' O'Kelly, up with the old bunting, and let them see who they've got to deal with.'

" A brown flag, with a Dutch lion in the centre, was run up the signal-halliards, and the next minute floated out bravely from our gaff.

" A cheer burst from the man-o'-war's crew, as they beheld the signal of defiance. Its answer was a smashing discharge from our long swivel that tore along their decks, cutting the standing rigging, and wounding several as it went. The triumph was short-lived for us. Shot after shot poured in from the brig, which, already to windward, swept our entire decks ; while an incessant roll of small-arms showed that our challenge was accepted to the death.

" ' Down helm,' said the old man in a whisper to the sailor at the wheel—' down helm ; ' while already the spitting waves that danced half a mile ahead, betokened a reef of rocks, over which at low water a row-boat could not float.

" ' I know it, I know it well,' was the skipper's reply to the muttered answer of the helmsman.

" By this time the brig was slackening sail, and still his fire was maintained as hotly as ever. The distance between us increased at each moment, and, had we sea-room, it was possible for us yet to escape.

" Our long gun was worked without ceasing, and we could see from time to time that a bustle on the deck denoted the destruction it was dealing; when suddenly a wild shout burst from one of our men—'the man-o'-war's aground,—her topsails are aback.' A mad cheer—the frantic cry of rage and desperation—broke from us; when, at the instant, a reeling shock shook us from stem to stern. The little vessel trembled like a living thing, and then, with a crash like thunder, the hatchways sprang from their fastenings, and the white sea leaped up and swept along the deck One drowning cry, one last mad yell burst forth.

" 'Three cheers, my boys ! ' cried the skipper, raising his cap above his head.

" Already she was settling in the sea—the death-notes rang out high over the storm ; a wave swept me over-board at the minute, and I saw the old skipper clinging to the bowsprit, while his long grey hair was floating wildly behind: but the swooping sea rolled over and over me. A kind of despairing energy nerved me, and after being above an hour in the water, I was taken up, still swim-ming, by one of the shore-boats, which, as the storm abated, had ventured out to the assistance of the sloop; and thus was I shipwrecked within a few hundred yards of the spot where first I had ventured on the sea, being the only one saved of all the crew. Of the ' Dart,' not a spar reached shore ; the breaking sea tore her to atoms.

" The ' Hornet ' scarcely fared better. She landed eight of her crew, badly wounded; one man was killed, and she herself was floated only after months of labour, and never, I believe, went to sea afterwards.

" The sympathy which in Ireland is never refused to misfortune, no matter how incurred, stood me in stead now; for although every effort was made by the authorities to discover if any of the smuggler's crew had reached shore alive, and large rewards were offered, no one would betray me; and I lay as safely concealed beneath the thatch of an humble cabin, as though the proud walls of a baronial castle afforded me their protection.

" From day to day I used to hear of the hot and eager inquiry going forward to trace out, by any means, something of the wrecked vessel; and, at last, news reached me that a celebrated thief-taker from Dublin had arrived in the neighbourhood to assist in the search.

" There was no time to be lost now. Discovery would not only have perilled my own life, but also have involved those of my kind protectors. How to leave the village was, however, the difficulty. Revenue and man-of-war boats abounded on the Shannon since the day of the wreck; the Ennis road was beset by police, who scrutinized every traveller that passed on the west coast. The alarm was sounded, and no chance of escape presented itself in that quarter. In this dilemma, fortune, which so often stood my friend, did not desert me. It chanced that a strolling company of actors, who had been performing for some weeks past in Kilrush, were about to set off to Ennistymon, where they were to give several representations. Nothing could be easier than to avoid detection in such company; and I soon managed to be included in the corps, by accepting an engagement as a ' walking gentleman,' at a low salary, and on the next morning found myself seated on the ' van,' among a very motley crew of associates, in whose ways and habits I very soon contrived to familiarize myself, becoming, before we had gone many miles, somewhat of a favourite in the party.

" I will not weary you with any account of my strolling life. Every one knows something of the difficulties which beset the humble drama; and ours was of the humblest. Joe Hume himself could not have questioned one solitary item in our budget; and I defy the veriest quibbler on a grand jury to ' traverse ' a spangle on a pair of our theatrical smallclothes.

" Our scenes were two in number: one represented a cottage interior—pots, kettles, a dresser, and a large fire being depicted in smoke-coloured traits thereon—this,

with two chairs and a table, was convertible into a parlour
in a private house; and again, by a red-covered arm-chair,
and an old banner, became a baronial hall, or the saloon in
a palace : the second represented two houses on the flat,
with an open country between them, a mill, a mountain, a
stream, and a rustic bridge inclusive.   This, then, was
either a street in a town, a wood, a garden, or any other
out-of-door place of resort for light comedy people, lovers,
passionate fathers, waiting-maids, robbers, or chorus
singers.

   " The chiefs of our corps were Mr and Mrs. M'Elwain,
who, as their names bespoke, came from the north of Ireland, somewhere near Coleraine I fancy, but cannot pretend to accuracy ; but I know it was on the borders of
' Darry.'

   " Who, or what, had ever induced a pair of as commonplace, matter-of-fact folk as ever lived, to take to the
Thespian art Heaven can tell.   Had Mr. Mac been a bailiff,
and madam a greengroceress, Nature would seem to have
dealt fairly with them ; he being a stout, red-faced, black-
bearded tyke, with a thatch of straight black hair, cut in
semicircles over his ears, so as to permit character wigs
without inconvenience, heavy in step, and plodding in gait.
She, a tall, raw-boned woman, of some five-and-forty, with
piercing grey eyes, and a shrill, harsh voice, that would
have shamed the veriest whistle that ever piped through a
keyhole.   Such were the Macbeth and the Lady Macbeth
—the Romeo and Juliet—the Hamlet and Ophelia of the
company ; but their appearance was a trifle to the manner
and deportment of their style.   Imagine Juliet with a
tattered Leghorn bonnet, a Scotch shawl, and a pair of
brown boots, declaiming somewhat in this guise—

> " ' Come, *gantle* night, come loving black-browed night,
> *Gie* me my *Romo !* and when he shall *dee,*
> *Tak'* him, and cut him into *lectle* stars,
> And he will *mak'* the face of heaven *sae* fine,
> That *a'* the *warld* will be in *lo'e* with him.'

   "With these people I was not destined long to continue.   The splendid delusion of success was soon dispelled ; and the golden harvest I was to reap settled

down into something like four shillings a week, out of
which came stoppages of so many kinds and shapes, that
my salary might have been refused at any moment, under
the plea that there was no coin of the realm in which to
pay it.

"One by one every article of my wardrobe went to
supply the wants of my stomach; and I remember well
my greatcoat, preserved with the tenacity with which a
shipwrecked mariner hoards up his last biscuit, was converted into mutton to regale Messrs. Iago, Mercutio, and
Cassius, with Mesdames Ophelia, Jessica, Desdemona, and
Co. It would make the fortune of an artist could he
only have witnessed the preparations for our entertainment.

"The festival was in honour of, what the manager was
pleased by a singular figure of speech to call, my ' benefit;'
the only profit accruing to me from the aforesaid benefit
being any satisfaction I might feel in seeing my name in
capitals, and the pleasure of waiting on the enlightened
inhabitants of Kilrush, to solicit their patronage.

"There was something to me of indescribable melancholy in that morning's perambulation, for, independent
of the fact that I was threatened by one with the stocks
as a vagabond, another set a policeman to dog me as a
suspicious character, and a third mistook me for a ratcatcher; the butcher, with whom I negotiated for the
quarter of mutton, came gravely up, and examined the
texture of my raiment, calling in a jury of his friends to
decide if he wasn't making a bad bargain.

"Night came, and I saw myself dressed for Petruchio,
the character in which I was to bring down thunders of
applause, and fill the treasury to overflowing. What a
conflict of feelings was mine—now rating Katharina in
good round phrase before the audience—now slipping behind the flats to witness the progress of the ' cuisine ' for
which I longed with the appetite of starvation,—how the
potatoes split their jackets with laughing, as they bubbled
up and down in the helmet of Coriolanus, for such I
grieve to say was the vessel used on the occasion; the
roasting mutton was presided over by ' a gentleman of
Padua,' and Christopher Sly was employed in concocting

some punch, which, true to his name, he tasted so frequently it was impossible to awake him towards the last
act

" It was in the first scene of the fourth act, in which,
with the feelings of a famished wolf, I was obliged to
assist at a mock supper on the stage, with wooden beef,
parchment fowls, wax pomegranates, and gilt goblets, in
which only the air prevented a vacuum. Just as I came
to the passage—

> 'Come, Kate, sit down—I know you have a stomach ;
> Will you give thanks, sweet Kate, or else shall I ?
> What is this – mutton ?'

" At that very moment, as I flung the ' pine saddle'
from one end of the stage to the other, a savoury odour
reached my nose ; the clatter of knives, the crash of plates,
the sounds of laughter and merriment, fell upon my ears—
the wretches were at supper! Even the ' first servant,'
who should have responded to my wrath, bolted from the
stage like a shot, leaving his place without a moment's
warning , and ' Katharina, the sweetest Kate in Christendom, my dainty Kate,' assured me, with her mouth full,
' the meat was well, if I were so contented.' Determined
to satisfy myself on the point—regardless of everything
but my hunger, I rushed off the stage, and descended like a
vulture in the midst of the supper party. Threats, denunciations, entreaties, were of no use, I wouldn't go back;
and let the house storm and rage, I had helped myself to
a slice of the joint, and cared for nobody. It was in vain
they told me that the revenue officer and his family were
outrageous with passion ; and as to the apothecary in the
stage box, he had paid for six tickets in ' senna mixture;'
but Heaven knows I wasn't a case for such a regimen.

" All persuasions failing, Mr. M'Elwain, armed all in
proof, rushed at me with a tin scimitar, while Madame,
more violent still, capsized the helmet and its scalding
contents over my person, and nearly flayed me alive
With frantic energy I seized the joint, and, fighting my
way through the whole company, rushed from the spot.

> "' Romans,' ' countrymen,' and 'lovers,'

' dukes,' ' duennas,' ' demigods,' and ' dancers,' with a loud
yell, joined in the pursuit Across the stage we went,
amid an uproar that would have done credit to Pande-
monium.   I was ' nimblest of foot,' however, and having
forced my way through an ' impracticable ' door, I jumped
clean through the wood, and having tripped up an ' angel'
that was close on my heels, I seized a candle, ' thirty-six to
the pound,' and applying it to the edge of the kitchen
aforementioned, bounded madly on, leaving the whole
concern wrapped in flames.   Down the street I went as if
bloodhounds were behind me, and never stopped my wild
career until I reached a little eminence at the end of the
town ; then I drew my breath, and turned one last look
upon the ' Theatre Royal.'   It was a glorious spectacle to
a revengeful spirit.   Amid the volume of flame and smoke
that rose to heaven (for the entire building was now en-
veloped) might be seen the discordant mass of actors and
audience mixed up madly together,—Turks, tailors, tum-
blers and tide-waiters, grandees and grocers, imps and
innkeepers,—there they were, all screaming in concert,
while the light material of the ' property-room ' was
ascending in myriads of sparks.   Castles and forests,
baronial halls and robbers' caves, were mounting to mid-
heaven amid the flash of blue-lights and the report of
stage combustibles.

" You may be sure, that however gratifying to my feelings this last scene of the drama was, I did not permit
myself much leisure to contemplate it, a very palpable
conviction staring me full in the face that such a spectacle
might not exactly redound to my ' benefit.'   I, therefore,
addressed myself to the road, moralizing as I went somewhat in this fashion · I have lost a respectable, but homely
suit of apparel, and instead, I have acquired a green
doublet, leathern hose, jack boots, a slouched hat and a
feather.   Had I played out my part, by this time I should
have been strewing the stage with a mock supper.   Now
I was consoling my feelings with real mutton, which, however wanting its ordinary accompaniments, was a delicacy
of no common order to me.   I had not, it is true, the
vociferous applause of a delighted audience to aid my
digestion as Petruchio.   But the pleasant whisper of a

good conscience was a more flattering reward to Con O'Kelly. This balanced the account in my favour, and I stepped out with that light heart which is so unequivocal an evidence of an innocent and happy disposition.

" Towards daybreak I had advanced some miles on the road to Killaloe, when before me I perceived a drove of horses, coupled together with all manner of strange tackle, halters, and hay-ropes. Two or three country lads were mounted among them, endeavouring, as well as they were able, to keep them quiet, while a thick, short, red-faced fellow, in dirty ' tops' and a faded green frock, led the way, and seemed to preside over the procession. As I drew near, my appearance caused no common commotion; the drivers, fixing their eyes on me, could mind nothing else ; the cattle, participating in the sentiments, started, capered, plunged, and neighed fearfully ; while the leader of the corps, furious at the disorder he witnessed, swore like a trooper, as with a tremendous cutting whip he dashed here and there through the crowd, slashing men and horses with a most praiseworthy impartiality. At last his eyes fell upon me, and for a moment I was full sure my fate was sealed, as he gripped his saddle closer, tightened his curb rein, and grasped his powerful whip with redoubled energy.

" The instincts of an art are very powerful; for, seeing the attitude of the man, and beholding the savage expression of his features, I threw myself into a stage position, slapped down my beaver with one hand, and, drawing my sword with the other, called out in a rich melodramatic howl—' Come on, Macduff!' My look, my gesture, my costume, and above all my voice, convinced my antagonist that I was insane, and as quickly the hard unfeeling character of his face relaxed, and an expression of rude pity passed across it.

" ''Tis Billy Muldoon, sir, I'm sure,' cried one of the boys, as with difficulty he sat the plunging beast under him.

" ' No, sir,' shouted another, ' he's bigger nor Billy, but he has a look of Hogan about the eyes.'

" ' Hould your prate,' cried the master. ' Sure Hogan was hanged at the summer assizes.'

" ' I know he was, sir,' was the answer, given as coolly as though no contradiction arose on that score.

" ' Who are you ? ' cried the leader; ' where do you come from ? '

" ' From Ephesus, my lord,' said I, bowing with stage solemnity, and replacing my sword within my scabbard.

" ' Where ? ' shouted he, with his hand to his ear.

" ' From Kilrush, most potent,' replied I, approaching near enough to converse without being overheard by the others: while in a few words I explained, that my costume and appearance were only professional symbols, which a hasty departure from my friends prevented my changing.

" ' And where are you going now ? ' was the next query.

" ' May I ask you the same ? ' said I.

" ' Me ? Why, I'm for Killaloe—for the fair to-morrow.'

" ' That's exactly my destination,' said I.

" ' And how do you mean to go ? ' retorted he. ' It's forty miles from here.'

" ' I have a notion,' replied I, ' that the dark chestnut there, with the white fetlock, will have the honour of conveying me.'

" A very peculiar grin, which I did not half admire, was the reply to this speech.

" ' There's many a one I wouldn't take under five shillings from, for the day,' said I; 'but the times are bad, and somehow I like the look of you. Is it a bargain ? '

" ' Faix, I'm half inclined to let you try the same horse,' said he. ' It would be teaching you something, any how. Did ye ever hear of the Playboy ? '

" ' To be sure I did. Is that he ? '

" He nodded.

" ' And you're Dan Moone ? ' said I.

" ' The same,' cried he, in astonishment.

" ' Come, Dan, turn about's fair play. I'll ride the horse for you to-morrow—where you like, and over what you like—and in reward, you'll let me mount one of the others

as far as Killaloe : we'll dine together at the cross roads.'—
Here I slipped the mutton from under the tail of my coat.
' Do you say done ? '

" 'Get upon the grey pony,' was the short rejoinder ;
and the next moment I was seated on the back of as
likely a cob as I ever bestrode.

" My first care was to make myself master of my companion's character, which I did in a very short time, while
affecting to disclose my own, watching, with sharp eye,
how each portion of my history told upon him. I saw
that he appreciated, with a true horse-dealer's ' onction,'
anything that smacked of trick or stratagem ; in fact, he
looked upon all mankind as so many ' screws,' he being the
cleverest fellow who could detect their imperfections and
unveil their unsoundness. In proportion as I recounted
to him the pranks and rogueries of my boyish life, his
esteem for me rose higher and higher ; and, before the day
was over, I had won so much of his confidence, that he
told me the peculiar vice and iniquity of every horse he
had, describing with great satisfaction the class of pur-
chasers he had determined to meet with

" ' There is little Paul there,' said he, ' that brown cob,
with the cropped ears, there isn't such a trotter in Ireland,
but somehow, though you can see his knees from the
saddle when he's moving, he'll come slap down with you,
as if he was shot, the moment you touch his flank with
the spur, and then there's no getting him up again till you
brush his ear with the whip—the least thing does it—he's
on his legs in a minute, and not a bit the worse of his
performance.

" Among all the narratives he told, this made the
deepest impression on me. That the animal had been
taught the accomplishment, there could be no doubt ; and
I began to puzzle my brain in what way it might best be
turned to advantage. It was of great consequence to me
to impress my friend at once with a high notion of my
powers; and here was an admirable occasion for their
exercise, if I could only hit on a plan.

" The conversation turned on various subjects, and at
last, as we neared Killaloe, my companion began to
ponder over the most probable mode in which I could be

of service to him on the following day. It was at last
agreed upon, that, on reaching town, I should exchange
my Petruchio costume for that of a 'squireen,' or half-
gentleman ; and repair to the ordinary at the ' Green
Man,' where nearly all the buyers put up, and all the talk
on sporting matters went forward This suited me perfectly ; I was delighted to perform a new part, particularly
when the filling-up was left to my own discretion Before
an hour elapsed after our arrival, I saw myself attired
in a very imposing suit—blue coat, cords and tops,
that would have fitted me for a very high range of
character in my late profession. O'Kelly was a name, as
Pistol says, ' of good report,' and there was no need to
change it ; so I took my place at the supper-table, among
some forty others, comprising a very fair average of the
raffs and raps of the county. The mysteries of horse-
flesh were, of course, the only subject of conversation ;
and before the punch made its appearance, I astonished
the company by the extent of my information and the
acuteness of my remarks. I improvised steeple-chases
over impossible countries, invented pedigrees for horses
yet unfoaled, and threw out such a fund of anecdote about
the ' turf ' and the 'chase,' that I silenced the old-estab-
lished authorities of the place, and a general buzz went
round the table of, ' Who can he be at all—where did he
come from ? '

  " As the evening wore apace, my eloquence grew warm—
I described my stud and my kennel, told some very curious
instances of my hunting experience, and when at last a
member of the party, piqued at my monopoly of the conversation, endeavoured to turn my flank by an allusion
to grouse-shooting, I stopped him at once, by asserting
with vehemence, that no man deserved the name of sportsman who shot over dogs—a sudden silence pervaded the
company, while the last speaker turned towards me with
a malicious grin, begged to know how I bagged my game,
for that, in *his* county, they were ignorant enough to
follow the old method.

  " ' With a pony, of course,' said I, finishing my glass.

  " ' A pony ! ' cried one after the other—' how do you
mean ? '

F

" 'Why,' resumed I, ' that I have a pony sets every species of game, as true as the best pointer that ever " stopped." '

" A hearty roar of laughing followed this declaration, and a less courageous spirit than mine would have feared that all his acquired popularity was in danger.

" 'You have him with you, I suppose,' said a sly old fellow from the end of the table.

" 'Yes,' said I carelessly—'I brought him over here to take a couple of days' shooting, if there is any to be had.'

" 'You would have no objection,' said another, insinu- atingly, ' to let us look at the beast?'

" ' Not the least,' said I.

" ' Maybe you'd take a bet on it,' said a third.

" 'I fear I couldn't,' said I ; 'the thing is too sure—the wager would be an unfair one.'

" ' Oh, as to that,' cried three or four together, ' we'll take our chance, for even if we were to lose, it's well worth paying for.'

" The more I expressed my dislike to bet, the more warmly they pressed me ; and I could perceive that a general impression was spreading that my pony was about as apocryphal as many of my previous stories.

" ' Ten pounds with you, he doesn't do it,' said an old hard-featured squire.

" ' The same from me,' cried another.

" ' Two to one in fifties,' shouted a third, until every man at table had proffered his wager, and I gravely called for pen, ink, and paper, and booked them, with all due form.

" 'Now, when is it to come off ?' was the question of some half-dozen.

" 'Now, if you like it—the night seems fine.'

" ' No, no,' said they, laughing, ' there's no such hurry as that; to-morrow we are going to draw Westenra's cover; what do you say if you meet us there by eight o'clock, and we'll decide the bet.'

" ' Agreed,' said I ; and shaking hands with the whole party, I folded up my paper, placed it in my pocket, and wished them good night.

" Sleep was, however, the last thing in my thoughts. Repairing to the little public-house where I left my friend Dan, I asked him if he knew any one well acquainted with the country, and who could tell at a moment where a hare or a covey was to be found.

" ' To be sure,' said he at once; ' there's a boy below knows every puss and every bird in the country. Tim Daly would bring you, dark as the night is, to the very spot where you'd find one '

" In a few minutes I had made Mr. Tim's acquaintance, and arranged with him to meet me at the cover on the following morning, a code of signals being established between us, by which he was to convey to me the information of where a hare was lying, or a covey to be sprung

" A little before eight I was standing beside ' Paul ' on the appointed spot, the centre of an admiring circle, who, whatever their misgivings as to his boasted skill, had only one opinion about his shapes and qualities.

" ' Splendid forehand '—' what legs '—' look at his quarters '—' and so deep in the heart '—were the exclamations heard on every side—till a rosy-cheeked fat little fellow, growing impatient at the delay, cried out—

" ' Come, Mr. O'Kelly, mount, if you please, and come along.'

" I tightened my girth, sprang into the saddle—my only care being to keep my toes in as straight a line as I could with my feet. Before we proceeded half a mile, I saw Tim seated on a stile, scratching his head in a very knowing manner; upon which I rode out from the party, and looking intently at the furze cover in front, called out—

" ' Keep back the dogs there –call them off—hush, not a word.'

" The hounds were called in, the party reined back their horses, and all sat silent spectators of my movements.

" When suddenly I touched ' Paul ' in both flanks, down he dropped, like a parish clerk, stiff and motionless as a statue.

" ' What's that? ' cried two or three behind.

" ' He's setting,' said I, in a whisper.

F 2

" 'What is it, though?' said one.

" 'A hare!' said I, and at the same instant I shouted to lay on the dogs, and tipping Paul's ears, forward I went. Out bolted puss, and away we started across the country, I leading, and taking all before me.

" We killed in half an hour, and found ourselves not far from the first cover; my friend Tim, being as before in advance, making the same signal as at first. The same performance was now repeated. 'Paul' went through his part to perfection; and notwithstanding the losses, a general cheer saluted us as we sprung to our legs, and dashed after the dogs.

" Of course I didn't spare him. Everything now depended on my sustaining our united fame; and there was nothing too high or too wide for me that morning.

" 'What will you take for him, Mr. O'Kelly?' was the question of each man, as he came up to the last field.

" 'Would you like any other proof?' said I. 'Is any gentleman dissatisfied?'

" A general 'No' was the answer; and again the offers were received from every quarter, while they produced the bank-notes, and settled their bets. It was no part of my game, however, to sell him; the trick might be discovered before I left the country, and if so, there wouldn't be a whole bone remaining in my skin

" My refusal evidently heightened both *my* value and *his*, and I sincerely believe there was no story I could tell, on our ride back to town, which would not have met credence that morning; and, indeed, to do myself justice, I tried my popularity to its utmost.

" By way of a short cut back, as the fair was to begin at noon, we took a different route, which led across some grass fields and a small river. In traversing this I unfortunately was in the middle of some miraculous anecdote, and entirely forgot my pony and his requirements; and as he stopped to drink, without thinking of what I was doing, with the common instinct of a rider, I touched him with the spur. Scarcely had the rowel reached his side, when down he fell, sending me head foremost over his neck into the water. For a second or two the strength of the current carried me along, and it was only after a devil of a scramble I gained my legs, and reached the bank wet through, and heartily ashamed of myself.

" ' Eh, O'Kelly, what the deuce was that?' cried one of the party, as a roar of laughter broke from amongst them.

" ' Ah! ' said I, mournfully, ' I wasn't quick enough.'

" ' Quick enough!' cried they. ' Egad, I never saw anything like it. Why, man, you were shot off like an arrow.'

" ' Leaped off, if you please,' said I, with an air of offended dignity—' leaped off—didn't you see it?'

" ' See what?'

" ' The salmon, to be sure. A twelve-pounder, as sure as my name's O'Kelly. He " set " it.'

" ' Set a salmon!' shouted twenty voices in a breath. ' The thing's impossible.'

" ' Would you like a bet on it?' asked I, drily.

" ' No, no—damn it; no more bets; but surely——'

" ' Too provoking, after all,' muttered I, ' to have lost so fine a fish, and get such a ducking ,' and with that I mounted my barb, and, waving my hand, wished them a good-bye, and galloped into Killaloe.

" This story I have only related because, insignificant as it was, it became in a manner the pivot of my then fate in life. The jockey at once made me an offer of partnership in his traffic, displaying before me the numerous advantages of such a proposal. I was a disengaged man—my prospects not peculiarly brilliant—the state of my exchequer by no means encouraging the favourite nostrum of a return to cash payments, and so I acceded, and entered at once upon my new profession with all the enthusiasm I was always able to command, no matter what line of life solicited my adoption.

" But it's near one o'clock, and so now, Mr. O'Leary, if you've no objection, we'll have a grill and a glass of Madeira, and then, if you can keep awake an hour or so longer, I'll try and finish my adventures."

CHAPTER VI.

THE SMUGGLER'S STORY—(*continued*).

" I LEFT off at that flattering portion of my history where
I became a horse-dealer. In this capacity I travelled over
a considerable portion of Ireland, now larking it in the
West, jollifying in the South, and occasionally suffering a
penance for both enjoyments by a stray trip to Ulster.
In these rambles I contrived to make acquaintance with
most of the resident gentry, who, by the special free-
masonry that attends my calling, scrupled not to treat me
on terms of half equality, and even invite me to their
houses, a piece of condescension on their part, which they
well knew was paid for in more solid advantages.

" In a word, Mr. O'Leary, I became a kind of moral
amphibia, with powers to sustain life in two distinct and
opposite elements ; now brushing my way among frieze-
coated farmers, trainers, dealers, sharpers, and stablemen ;
now floating on the surface of a politer world, where the
topics of conversation took a different range, and were
couched in a very different vocabulary.

" My knowledge of French, and my acquaintance with
Parisian life, at least as seen in that class in which I used
to mix, added to a kind of natural tact, made me, as far
as manners and ' usage ' were concerned, the equal of those
with whom I associated, and I managed matters so well,
that the circumstance of my being seen in the morning
with cords and tops of jockey cut, showing off a ' screw,'
or extolling the symmetry of a spavined hackney, never
interfered with the pretensions I put forward at night,
when, dressed in a suit of accurate black, I turned over
the last new opera, or delivered a very scientific criticism
on the new ' ballet ' in London, or the latest fashion imported from the Continent.

" Were I to trace this part of my career, I might perhaps amuse you more by the incidents it contained than

by any other portion of my life. Nothing indeed is so
suggestive of adventure as that anomaly which the French
denominate so significantly—' a false position.' The man
who—come, come, don't be afraid, though that sounds
very like Joseph Surface, I'm not going to moralize—the
man, I say, who endeavours to sustain two distinct lines
in life is very likely to fail in both, and so I felt it; for
while my advantages all inclined to one side, my taste
and predilections leaned to the other; I could never adopt
knavery as a profession—as an amateur I gloried in it.
Roguery, without risk, was a poor pettifogging policy that
I spurned; but a practical joke that involved life or limb,
a hearty laugh, or a heavy reckoning, was a temptation
I never could resist. The more I mixed in society, the
greater my intimacy with persons of education and refine-
ment, the stronger became my repugnance to my actual
condition, and the line of life I had adopted. While my
position in society was apparently more fixed, I became
in reality more nervously anxious for its stability The
fascinations which in the better walks of life are thrown
around the man of humble condition, but high aspirings,
are strong and sore temptations, while he measures and
finds himself not inferior to others to whom the race is
open and the course is free, and yet feels in his own heart
that there is a bar upon his escutcheon which excludes
him from the lists. I began now to experience this in all
· its poignancy. Among the acquaintances I had formed,
one of my most intimate was a young baronet, who had
just succeeded to a large estate in the county of Kilkenny.
Sir Harvey Blundell was an Anglo-Irishman in more
than one sense. From his English father he had inherited
certain staid and quiet notions of propriety, certain conventional ideas regarding the observance of etiquette, which
are less valued in Ireland; while from his mother, he
succeeded to an appreciation of native fun and drollery, of
all the whims and oddities of Irish life, which, strange
enough, are as well understood by the Anglo-Irishman as
by one ' to the manner born.'

" I met Sir Harvey at a supper party in College. Some
song I had sung of my own composing, or some story of
my inventing, I forget which, tickled his fancy. He

begged to be introduced to me, drew his chair over to my side of the table, and ended by giving me an invitation to his house for the partridge-shooting, which was to begin in a few days. I readily assented; it was a season in which I had nothing to do, my friend Dan had gone over to the Highlands to make a purchase of some ponies; I was rather flush of cash, and consequently in good spirits. It was arranged that I should drive him down in my drag, a turn-out with four spanking greys, of whose match and colour, shape and action, I was not a little vain.

"We posted to Carlow, to which place I had sent on my horses, and arrived the same evening at Sir Harvey's house in time for dinner. This was the first acquaintance I had made, independent of my profession. Sir Harvey knew me as Mr. O'Kelly, whom he met at an old friend's chambers in College; and he introduced me thus to his company, adding to his intimates in a whisper I could overhear—'devilish fast fellow, up to everything—knows life at home and abroad, and has such a team!' Here were requisites enough, in all conscience, to win favour among any set of young country gentlemen, and I soon found myself surrounded by a circle who listened to my opinions on every subject, and recorded my judgments with the most implicit faith in their wisdom, no matter on what subject I talked,—women, wine, the drama, play, sporting, debts, duns, or duels,—my word was law.

"Two circumstances considerably aided me in my present supremacy. First, Sir Harvey's friends were all young men from Oxford, who knew little of the world, and less of that part of it called Ireland; and secondly, they were all strangers to me, and consequently my liberty of speech was untrammelled by any unpleasant reminiscences of dealing in fairs or auctions.

"The establishment was presided over by Sir Harvey's sister, at least nominally so, her presence being a reason for having ladies at his parties; and although she was only nineteen, she gave a tone and character to the habits of the house which without her it never could have possessed. Miss Blundell was a very charming person, combining in herself two qualities which, added to beauty, made a very irresistible *ensemble*. She had the greatest

flow of spirits, with a retiring and almost timidly bashful
disposition; courage for anything, and a delicacy that
shrunk abashed from all that bordered on display, or bore
the slightest semblance of effrontery. I shall say no more,
than that before I was a week in the house I was over
head and ears in love with her; my whole thoughts centred in her; my chief endeavour was to show myself in
such a light as might win her favour.

"Every accomplishment I possessed—every art and
power of amusing, I exerted in her service; and at last
perceived that she was not indifferent to me. Then, and
then for the first time, came the thought—who was I,
that dared to do this—what had I of station, rank, or
wealth to entitle me to sue—perhaps to gain, the affections of one like her? The duplicity of my conduct started
up before me, and I saw for the first time how the mere
ardour of pursuit that led me on and on—how the daring
to surmount a difficulty had stirred my heart, at first to
win, and then to worship her. The bitterness of my self-
reproach at that moment became a punishment, which,
even now, I remember with a shudder. It is too true! The
great misfortunes of life form more endurable subjects for
memory in old age, than the instances, however trivial,
where we have acted amiss, and where conscience rebukes
us. I have had my share of calamity, one way or other—
my life has been more than once in peril—and in such
peril as might well shake the nerve of the boldest: 1 can
think on all these, and do think on them often, without
fear or heart-failing; but never can I face the hours, when
my own immediate self-love and vanity brought their own
penalty on me, without a sense of self-abasement as vivid
as the moment I first experienced it. But I must hasten
over this. I had been now about six weeks in Sir
Harvey's house, day after day determining on my departure, and invariably yielding, when the time came, to
some new request to stay for something or other—now,
a day's fishing on the Nore—now, another morning at the
partridge—then, there was a boat-race, or a music party,
or a picnic—in fact, each day led on to another, and I
found myself lingering on, unable to tear myself from
where, 1 felt, my remaining was ruin.

"At last I made up my mind, and determined, come what would, to take my leave, never to return. I mentioned to Sir Harvey in the morning that some matter of importance required my presence in town, and by a half-promise to spend my Christmas with him, obtained his consent to my departure.

"We were returning from an evening walk — Miss Blundell was leaning on my arm—we were the last of the party, the others having, by some chance or other, gone forward, leaving us to follow alone. For some time neither of us spoke. What were her thoughts I cannot guess; mine were, I acknowledge, entirely fixed upon the hour I was to see her for the last time, while I balanced whether I should speak of my approaching departure, or leave her without even a ' good-bye.'

" I did not know at the time so well as I now do, how much of the interest I had excited in her heart depended on the mystery of my life. The stray hints I now and then dropped—the stories into which I was occasionally led—the wild scenes, and wilder adventures, in which I bore my part—had done more than stimulate her curiosity concerning me. This, I repeat, I knew not at the time, and the secret of my career weighed like a crime upon my conscience. I hesitated long whether I should not disclose every circumstance of my life, and, by the avowal of my utter unworthiness, repair, as far as might be, the injury I had done her. Then came that fatal '*amour propre,*' that involved me originally in the pursuit, and I was silent. We had not been many minutes thus, when a servant came from the house, to inform Miss Blundell that her cousin, Captain Douglas, had arrived. As she nodded her head in reply, I perceived the colour mounted to her cheek, an expression of agitation passed over her features.

" ' Who is Captain Douglas ? ' said I, without, however, venturing to look more fully at her.

" ' Oh ! a cousin—a second or third cousin, I believe ; but a great friend of Harvey's.'

" ' And of his sister's, too, if I might presume so far ? '

" 'Quite wrong for once,' said she, with an effort to seem at ease : 'he's not the least a favourite of mine, although——'

" '*You* are of his!' I added, quickly. ' Well, well, I really beg pardon for this boldness of mine.' How I was about to continue, I know not, when her brother's voice, calling her aloud, broke off all further conversation.

" ' Come, Fanny,' said he, ' here's Harry Douglas, just come with all the London gossip—he's been to Windsor, too, and has been dining with the Prince. O'Kelly, you must know Douglas, you are just the men to suit each other.—He's got a heavy book on the Derby, and will be delighted to have a chat with you about the turf.'

" As I followed Miss Blundell into the drawing-room, my heart was heavy and depressed.

" Few of the misfortunes in life come on us without foreboding. The clouds that usher in the storm, cast their shadows on the earth before they break; and so it is with our fate. A gloomy sense of coming evil presages the blow about to fall, and he who would not be stunned by the stroke, must not neglect the warning.

" The room was full of people—the ordinary buzz and chit-chat of an evening party was going forward, among which I heard my name bandied about on every side

" ' O'Kelly will arrange this,' cried one—' leave it all to O'Kelly—he must decide it;' and so on, when suddenly Blundell called out—

" ' O'Kelly, come up here,' and then, taking me by the arm, he led me to the end of the room, where, with his back turned towards us, a tall, fashionable-looking man was talking to his sister.

" 'Harry,' cried the host, as he touched his elbow, 'let me introduce a very particular friend of mine—Mr. O'Kelly.'

" Captain Douglas wheeled sharply round, and fixing on me a pair of dark eyes, overshadowed with heavy beetling brows, looked at me sternly without speaking. A cold thrill ran through me from head to foot as I met his gaze ; the last time we had seen each other was in a square of the Royal Barracks, where *he* was purchasing a remount for his troop, and *I* was the horse-dealer.

" ' *Your* friend, Mr. O'Kelly !' said he, as he fixed his glass in his eye, and a most insulting curl, half smile, half sneer, played about his mouth.

" How very absurd you are, Harry,' said Miss Blundell, endeavouring, by an allusion to something they were speaking of, to relieve the excessive awkwardness of the moment.

" ' Yes, to be sure, *my* friend,' chimed in Sir Harvey, ' and a devilish good fellow too, and the best judge of horse-flesh.'

" ' I haven't a doubt of it,' was the dry remark of the Captain ; ' but how did he get here ? '

" ' Sir,' said I, in a voice scarce audible with passion, ' whatever, or whoever I am, by birth at least I am fully your equal.'

" ' D——n your pedigree,' said he, coolly.

" ' Why, Harry ? ' interrupted Blundell ; ' what are you thinking of ? Mr. O'Kelly is——'

" ' A jockey—a horse-dealer, if you will, and the best hand at passing off a screw I've met for some time. I say, sir,' continued he, in a louder tone, ' that roan charger hasn't answered his warranty—he stands at Dycer's for you.'

" Had a thunderbolt fallen in the midst of us, the consternation could not have been greater ; as for me, everything around bore a look of mockery and scorn. Derision and contempt sat on every feature, and a wild uncertainty of purpose, like coming insanity, flitted through my brain. What I said, or how I quitted the spot, I am unable to say ; my last remembrance of that accursed moment was the burst of horrid laughter that filled my ears as I rushed out. I almost think that I hear it still, like the yell of the furies ; its very cadence was torture. I ran from the house—I crossed the fields without a thought of whither I was going—escape, concealment, my only object. I sought to hide myself for ever from the eyes of those who had looked upon me with such withering contempt, and I should have been thankful to him who would have given me refuge beneath the dank grass of the churchyard.

" Never did a guilty man fly from the scene of his crime with more precipitate haste than I did from the spot which had witnessed my shame and degradation. At every step I thought of the cruel speeches, the harsh railings, and the bitter irony of all before whom, but one hour ago, I stood chief and pre-eminent; and although I vowed to myself never to meet any of them again, I could not pluck from my heart the innate sense of my despicable condition, and how low I must now stand in the estimation of the very lowest I had so late looked down upon. And here let me passingly remark, that while we often hold lightly the praise of those upon whose powers of judgment and reach of information we place little value, by some strange contrariety we feel most bitterly the censure of these very people whenever any trivial circumstance, any small or petty observance with which they are acquainted, gives them, for the time, the power of an opinion. The mere fact of our contempt for them adds a poignancy to their condemnation, and I question much if we do not bear up better against the censure of the wise than the scoff of the ignorant.

"On I went, and on, never even turning my head; for though I had left all the little wealth I possessed in the world, I would gladly have given it, ten times told, to have blotted out even a particle of the shame that rested on my character. Scarcely had I reached the high road, when I heard the quick tramp of horses and the rattle of wheels behind me; and, so strong were the instincts of my fear, that I scarcely dared to look back: at length I did so, and beheld the mail-coach coming towards me at a rapid pace. As it neared, I hailed the coachman, and without an inquiry as to where it was going, I sprang up to a place on the roof, thankful that ere long I should leave miles between me and my torturers.

"The same evening we arrived in Cork. During the journey I made acquaintance with a sergeant of a light dragoon regiment, who was proceeding in charge of three recruits to the depôt at Cove. With the quick eye of his calling, the fellow saw something in my dispirited state that promised success to his wishes; and he immediately began the thousand-times-told tale of the happiness of a soldier's life. I stopped him short at once, for my mind was already made up, and before the day broke I had enlisted in his Majesty's 12th Light Dragoons, at that time serving in America.

"If I have spared you the recital of many painful passages in my life, I shall also pass over this portion of my career, which, though not marked by any distinct feature of calamity, was, perhaps, the most painful I ever knew. He who thinks that in joining the ranks of an army, his only trials will be the severity of an unaccustomed discipline, and the common hardships of a soldier's life, takes but a very shallow view of what is before him. Coarse and vulgar associates—depraved tastes and brutal habits —the ribald jest of the barrack-room—the comrade spirit of a class, the very lowest and meanest—these are the trials, the almost insupportable trials, of him who has known better days.

"As hour by hour he finds himself yielding to the gradual pressure of his fate, and feels his mind assuming, one by one, the prejudices of those about him, his self-esteem falls with his condition, and he sees that the time is not distant when all inequality between him and his fellows shall cease, and every trait of his former self be washed away for ever.

"After four months of such endurance as I dare not even now suffer myself to dwell upon, orders arrived at Cove for the recruits of the different regiments at once to proceed to Chatham, whence they were to be forwarded to their respective corps. I believe, in my heart, had this order not come I should have deserted, so unendurable had my life become. The thought of active service, the prospect of advancement, however remote, cheered my spirits, and, for the first time since I joined, my heart was light on the morning when the old 'Northumberland' transport anchored in the harbour, and the signal for embarking the troops floated from the mast-head. A motley crew we were—frieze-coated, red-coated, and no-coated; some, ruddy-cheeked farmers' boys, sturdy good-humoured fellows, with the bloom of country life upon their faces; some, the pale, sickly inhabitants of towns, whose sharpened features and quick penetrating eyes betokened how much their wits had contributed to their maintenance. A few there were, like myself, drawn from a better class, but already scarce distinguishable amid the herd. We were nearly five hundred in number, one feature of equality pervading all—none of us had any arms. Some

instances of revolt and mutiny that had occurred, a short
time previous, on ·board troop-ships, had induced the
Horse Guards to adopt this resolution, and a general order
was issued that the recruits should not receive arms before
their arrival at Chatham. At last we weighed anchor, and
with a light easy wind stood out to sea. It was the first
time I had been afloat for many a long day, and as I
leaned over the bulwark, and heard the light rustle of the
waves as they broke on the cut-water, and watched the
white foam as it rippled past, I thought on the old days of
my smuggling life, when I trod the plank of my little
craft, with a step as light and a heart as free as ever did
the proudest admiral on the poop-deck of his three-decker ;
and as I remembered what I then had been, and thought
of what I now was, a growing melancholy settled upon
me, and I sat apart and spoke to none.

"On the third night after we sailed, the breeze, which
had set in at sunset, increased considerably, and a heavy
sea rolled in from the westward. Now, although the
weather was not such as to endanger the safety of a good
ship with an able crew, yet was it by no means a matter
of indifference in an old rotten craft like the 'Northumberland,' condemned half a dozen years before, and barely
able to make her voyage in light winds and fine weather.
Our skipper knew this well, and I could see by the agitation of his features, and the altered tones of his voice, how
little he liked the freshening gale, and the low moaning
sound that swept along the sea, and threatened a storm.
The pumps had been at work for some hours, and it was
clear that the most we could do was to keep the water
from gaining on us. A chance observation of mine had
attracted the skipper's attention, and after a few minutes'
conversation he saw that I was a seaman not only better
informed, but more habituated to danger than himself; he
was, therefore, glad to take counsel from me, and at my
suggestion a spare sail was bent, and passed under the
ship's bottom, which soon arrested the progress of the
leak, and, at the same time, assisted the vessel's sailing.
Meanwhile the storm was increasing, and it now blew
what the sailors call 'great guns.'

"We were staggering along under light canvas, when

the look-out-ahead announced a light on the weather-
bow ; it was evidently coming towards us, and scarce half
a mile distant, we had no more than time to hang out
a lantern in the tops and put up the helm, when a large
ship, whose sides rose several feet above our own, swept
by us, and so close, that her yard-arms actually touched
our rigging as she yawed over in the sea. A muttered
thanksgiving for our escape, for such it was, broke from
every lip ; and hardly was it uttered, when again a voice
cried out, ' Here she comes to leeward,' and sure enough
the dark shadow of the large mass moving at a speed
far greater than ours passed under our lee, while a harsh
summons was shouted out to know who we were, and
whither bound. ' The " Northumberland," with troops,'
was the answer ; and before the words were well out, a
banging noise was heard—the ports of the stranger ship
were flung open—a bright flash, like a line of flame, ran
her entire length, and a raking broadside was poured into
us. The old transport reeled over and trembled like a
thing of life,—her shattered sides and torn bulwarks let
in the water as she heeled to the shock, and for an instant,
as she bent beneath the storm, I thought she was settling,
to go down by the head. I had little time, however, for
thought ; one wild cheer broke from the attacking ship—
its answer was the faint, sad cry, of the wounded and
dying on our deck. The next moment the grapples were
thrown into us, and the vessel was boarded from stem
to stern. The noise of the cannonade, and the voices
on deck, brought all our men from below, who came tumbling up the hatches, believing we had struck.

" Then began a scene, such as all I have ever witnessed
of carnage and slaughter cannot equal. The Frenchmen,
for such they were, rushed down upon us as we stood
defenceless, and unarmed : a deadly roll of musketry
swept our thick and trembling masses. The cutlass and
the boarding-pike made fearful havoc among us, and an
unresisted slaughter tore along our deck, till the heaps
of dead and dying made the only barrier for the few
remaining.

" A chance word in French, and a sign of masonry,
rescued me from the fate of my comrades, and my only

injury was a slight sabre-wound in the fore-arm, which I received in warding off a cut intended for my head. The carnage lasted scarce fifteen minutes; but in that time, of all the crew that manned our craft—what between those who leaped overboard in wild despair, and those who fell beneath fire and steel—scarce fifty remained, appalled and trembling, the only ones rescued from this horrible slaughter.

"A sudden cry of 'She's sinking!' burst from the strange ship, and in a moment the Frenchmen clambered up their bulwarks, the grapples were cast off, the dark mass darted onwards on her course, and we drifted away to leeward—a moving sepulchre!

"As the clouds flew past, the moon shone out and threw a pale, sickly light on the scene of slaughter, where the dead and dying lay in indiscriminate heaps together— so frightful a spectacle never did eye rest upon! The few who, like myself, survived, stood trembling, half stunned by the shock, not daring to assist the wretched men as they writhed in agony before us. I was the first to recover from this stupor, and turning to the others, I made signs to clear the decks of the dead bodies—speak I could not. It was some time before they could be made to understand me: unhappily, not a single sailor had escaped the carnage; some raw recruits were the only survivors of that dreadful night.

"After a little they rallied so far as to obey me, and I, taking the wheel, assumed the command of the vessel, and endeavoured to steer a course for any port on the west coast of England.

"Day broke at length, but a wide waste of waters lay around us. The wind had abated considerably, but still the sea ran high; and although our foresail and trysail remained bent, as before the attack, we laboured heavily, and made little way through the water. Our decks were quite covered with the dying, whose heart-rending cries, mingled with the wilder shouts of madness, were too horrible to bear. But I cannot dwell on such a picture. Of the few who survived, scarcely three were serviceable. Some sat cold and speechless from terror, and seemed insensible to every threat or entreaty; some sternly refused

to obey my orders, and prowled about between decks in
search of spirits, and one, maddened by the horrors he
beheld, sprang with a scream into the sea, and never was
seen more.

"Towards evening we heard a hail, and on looking out
saw a pilot-boat making for us, and in a short time we
were boarded by a pilot, who, with some of his crew, took
charge of the vessel, and before sunset we anchored in
Milford.

"Immediately on landing, I was sent up to London
under a strong escort, to give an account of the whole
affair to the Admiralty. For eight days my examination
was continued during several hours every day, and at last
I was dismissed, with promotion to the rank of sergeant
for my conduct in saving the ship, and appointed to the
40th Foot, then under orders for Quebec.

"Once more at sea and in good spirits, I sailed for
Quebec on a fine morning in April, on board the "Aber-
crombie" Nothing could be more delightful than the
voyage. The weather was clear, with a fair fresh breeze
and a smooth sea; and at the third week we dropped our
lead on the green bank of Newfoundland, and brought
up again a cod-fish every time we heaved it. We now
entered the Gulf of St. Lawrence, and began anxiously
to look for land.

"On the third morning after we made the 'Gulf,' a
heavy snow-storm came on, which prevented our seeing a
cable's length ahead of us. It was so cold, too, that few
remained on deck; for although the first of May, it was
about as severe a day as I remember. Anxious to see
something of the country, I remained with the look-out-
ahead, straining my eyes to catch a glimpse of the land
through the dense snow-drift. All I could distinguish,
however, was the dim outline of distant mountains, apparently covered with snow; but, as the day wore on, we
came in sight of the long low island of Anticosti, which,
though considerably more than a hundred miles in length,
is not in any part more than fifteen feet above the level of
the water.

"Towards evening the land became much clearer to
view; and now I could perceive tall, peaked mountains

some thousand feet in height, their bases clad with stunted pine-trees—their white summits stretching away into the clouds. As I looked, my astonishment was great to find that the vast gulf, which at daybreak was some sixty miles in width, seemed now diminished to about eight or ten, and continued to narrow rapidly as we proceeded on our course.

"The skipper, who had only made the voyage once before, seemed himself confused, and endeavoured to explain our apparent vicinity to the land as some mere optical delusion—now, attributing it to something in the refraction of the light; now, the snow. Although he spoke with all the assurance of knowledge, it was evident to me that he was by no means satisfied in his own mind of the facts he presented to ours.

"As the snow-storm abated, we could see that the mountains which lay on either side of us met each other in front, forming a vast amphitheatre without any exit.

"'This surely is not the Gulf of St. Lawrence?' said I to an old sailor who sat leisurely chewing tobacco with his back to the capstern.

"'No, that it ain't,' said he, coolly; 'it's Gaspé Bay, and I shouldn't wish to be in a worse place.'

"'What could have brought us here, then?—the skipper surely doesn't know where we are?'

"'I'll tell you what has brought us here. There's a current from the Gulf Stream sets in to this bay at seven or eight knots the hour, and brings in all the floating ice along with it——There, am I right? do you hear that?'

"As he spoke, a tremendous crash, almost as loud as thunder, was heard at our bow; and as I rushed to the bulwark and looked over, I beheld vast fragments of ice more than a foot thick, encrusted with frozen snow, flying past us in circling eddies; while, farther on, the large flakes were mounting, one above the other, clattering and crashing as the waves broke among them. Heaven knows how much farther our mulish Cumberland skipper would have pursued his voyage of discovery, had not the soundings proclaimed but five fathom water. Our sails were now backed; but as the current continued to bear us along, a boat was got out, and an anchor put in readiness to warp us astern; but, by an unhappy accident, the anchor slipped in lowering over the side, stove in the boat, and of the four poor fellows who were under it, one was carried under the ice, and never seen again. This was a bad beginning, and matters now appeared each moment more threatening. As we still continued to drift with the current, a bower-anchor was dropped where we were, and the vessel afterwards swung round head to wind, while the ice came crashing upon the cut-water, and on the sides, with a noise that made all else inaudible. It was found by this time that the water was shoaling, and this gave new cause for fear, for if the ship were to touch the ground, it was clear all chance of saving her was at an end.

"After a number of different opinions given and canvassed, it was determined that four men should be sent ashore in the yawl, to find out some one who knew the pilotage of the bay; for we could descry several log-huts along the shore, at short distances from each other. With my officer's permission, I obtained leave to make one of this party, and I soon found myself tugging away at the bow-oar through a heavy surf. After rowing about an hour, the twilight began to fall, and we could but faintly perceive the outline of the ship, while the log-huts on shore seemed scarcely nearer than at the moment when we quitted the vessel. By this time large fields of ice were about us on every side; rowing was no longer possible, and we groped along with our boat-hooks, finding a channel where we could avoid the floating masses.

"The peril of this proceeding grew with every moment: sometimes our frail boat would be struck with such force as threatened to stave in every plank; sometimes she was driven high upon a piece of ice, which took all our efforts to extricate her from, while, as we advanced, no passage presented itself before us, but flake upon flake of frozen matter, among which were fragments of wrecks and branches of trees, mixed up together. The sailors, who had undertaken the enterprise against their will, now resolved they would venture no farther, but make their way back to the ship while it was yet possible. I alone opposed this plan: to return, without at least having reached the shore, I told them, would be a disgrace—the safety of all on board was in a manner committed to our efforts; and I endeavoured by every argument to induce them to proceed. To no purpose did I tell them this; of no use was it that I pointed out the lights on shore, which we could now see moving from place to place, as though we had been perceived, and that some preparations were making for our rescue. I was outvoted, however; back they would go; and one of them, as he pushed the boat's head round, jeeringly said to me—

" ' Why, with such jolly good foot-way, don't you go yourself? you'll have all the honour, you know.'

" The taunt stung me to the quick, the more as it called forth a laugh from the rest. I made no answer, but seizing a boat-hook, sprang over the side upon a large mass of ice. The action drove the boat from me. I heard them call to me to come back; but, come what would, my mind was made up. I never turned my head, but, with my eyes fixed on the shore-lights, I dashed on, glad to find that with every stroke of the sea the ice was borne onwards towards the land. At length the sound of the breakers ahead made me fearful of venturing farther, for, as the darkness fell, I had to trust entirely to my hearing as my guide. I stood then rooted to the spot, and, as the wind whistled past, and the snow-drift was borne in eddying currents by me, I drove my boat-hook into the ice, and held on firmly by it. Suddenly, through the gloom a bright flash flared out, and then I could see it flitting along, and at last I thought I could mark it directing its course towards the ship. I strained my eyes to their utmost, and in an ecstasy of joy I shouted aloud, as I beheld a canoe manned by Indians, with a pine torch blazing in the prow. The red light of the burning wood lit up their wild figures as they came along, now carrying their light bark over the fields of ice, now launching it into the boiling surf; and thus, alternately walking and sailing, they came at a speed almost inconceivable. They soon heard my shouts, and directed their course to where I stood, but the excitement of my danger, the dreadful alternations of hope and fear thus suddenly ceasing, so stunned me that I could not speak, as they took me in

their arms and placed me in the bottom of the canoe. Of
our course back to shore I remember little. The intense
cold, added to the stupefaction of my mind, brought on a
state resembling sleep, and even when they lifted me on
land, the drowsy lethargy clung to me; and only when
I found myself beside the blaze of a wood-fire, did my
faculties begin to revive, and, like a seal under the rays of
the sun, did I warm into life once more. The first thing I
did when morning broke, was to spring from my resting-
place beside the fire, and rush out to look for the ship.
The sun was shining brilliantly; the bay lay calm as a
mirror before me, reflecting the tall mountains and the
taper pines : but the ship was gone, not a sail appeared in
sight; and now I learned that when the tide began to
make, and she was enabled to float, a land-breeze sprang
up which carried her gently out to sea, and that she was
in all likelihood by that time some thirty miles in her
course up the St. Lawrence. For a moment, my joy at
the deliverance of my companions was unchecked by any
thought of my own desolate condition; the next minute I
remembered myself, and sat down upon a stone, and gazed
out upon the wide waters with a sad and sinking heart."

CHAPTER VII.

THE SMUGGLER'S STORY—(*concluded*).

"LIFE had presented too many vicissitudes before me to make much difference in my temperament, whatever came uppermost. Like the gambler, who, if he lose to-day, goes off consoling himself that he may be a winner to-morrow, I had learned never to feel very acutely any misfortune, provided only that I could see some prospect of its not being permanent; and how many are there who go through the world in this fashion, getting the credit all the while of being such true philosophers, so much elevated above the chances and changes of fortune, and who, after all, only apply to the game of life the same rule of action they practise at the '*rouge et noir*' table!

"The worthy folks among whom my lot was now cast, were a tribe of red men, called the Gaspé Indians, who, among other pastimes peculiar to themselves, followed the respectable and ancient trade of wreckers, in which occupation the months of October and November usually supplied them with as much as they could do: after that, the ice closed in on the bay, and no vessel could pass up or down the St. Lawrence before the following spring.

"It was for some time to me a puzzle how people so completely barbarous as they were, possessed such comfortable and well-appointed dwellings; for not only had they log-huts well jointed and carefully put together, but many of the comforts of civilized life were to be seen in the internal decorations. The reason I at length learned from the chief, in whose house I dwelt, and with whom I had already succeeded in establishing a sworn friendship. About fifteen years previous, this bay was selected by a party of emigrants as the *locale* of a settlement. They had been wrecked on the island of Anticosti themselves, and made their escape to Gaspé with such remnants of their effects as they could rescue from the wreck. There they built houses for themselves, made clearings in the forest, and established a little colony, with rules and regulations for its government.   Happily for them, they possessed within their number almost every description of artificer requisite for such an undertaking, their original intention being to found a settlement in Canada; and thus carpenters, shoemakers, weavers, tailors, millwrights, being all ready to contribute their aid and assistance to each other, the colony made rapid progress, and soon assumed the appearance of a thriving and prosperous place.   The forest abounded in wild deer and bears, the bay was not less rich in fish, while the ground, which they sowed with potatoes and Indian corn, yielded most successful crops; and as the creek was never visited by sickness, nothing could surpass the success of their labours.

"Thus they lived, till in the fall of the year a detachment of the Gaspé Indians, who came down every autumn for the herring-fishery, discovered that their territory was occupied, and that an invading force were in possession of their hunting grounds.   The result could not be doubted: the red men returned home to their friends with the news, and speedily came back again with reinforcements of the whole tribe, and made an attack upon the settlement. The colonists, though not prepared, soon assembled, and being better armed, for their firearms and cutlasses had all been saved, repelled their assailants, and having killed and wounded several of them, drove them back into the forest. The victory, however complete, was the first day of their misfortunes · from that hour they were never safe; sometimes a marauding party of red men would dash into the village at nightfall, and carry away some of the children before their cries could warn their parents.   Instead of venturing, as before, into the 'bush' whenever they pleased, and in small numbers, they were now obliged to go with the greatest circumspection and caution, stationing scouts here and there, and, above all, leaving a strong garrison to protect the settlement against attack in their absence.   Fear and distrust prevailed everywhere, and instead of the peace and prosperity that attended the first year of their labours, the land now remained but half tilled, the hunting yielded scarcely any benefit, and all their efforts were directed to their safety, and their time consumed in erecting outworks and forts to protect the village.

" While matters were in this state, a large timber-ship, bound for England, struck on a reef of rocks at the entrance of the bay. The sea ran high, and a storm of wind from the north-west soon rent her in fragments. The colonists, who knew every portion of the bay well, put out the first moment they could venture to the wreck, not, however, to save the lives and rescue the poor fellows who yet clung to the rigging, but to pillage the ship ere she went to pieces. The expedition succeeded far beyond their most ardent hopes, and a rich harvest of plunder resulted from this venture ; casks of powder, flour, pork, and rum were landed by every tide at their doors, and once more the sounds of merriment and rejoicing were heard in the village. But how different from before was it ! Then they were happy and contented settlers, living like one united family in brotherly affection and kind good-will; now, it was but the bond of crime that bound, and the wild madness of intoxication that excited them. Their hunting-grounds were no longer cared for ; the fields, with so much labour rescued from the forest, were neglected ; the fishing was abandoned ; and a life given up to the most intemperate abandonment, succeeded to days of peaceful labour and content. Not satisfied with mere defence, they now carried the war into the Indian settlements, and cruelties the most frightful ensued in their savage reprisals.

" In this dangerous coast a winter never passed without several wrecks occurring, and as they now practised every device, by false signals and fires, to lure vessels to their ruin, their infamous traffic succeeded perfectly, and wrecking became a mode of subsistence far more remunerative than their former habits of quiet industry.

" One long reef of rocks that ran from the most southerly point of the bay, and called by the Indians ' the Teeth,' was the most fatal spot of the whole coast; for while these rocks stretched for above a mile to sea, and were only covered at high water, a strong land current drew vessels towards them, which, with the wind on shore, it was impossible to resist.

" To this fatal spot each eye was turned at daybreak, to see if some ill-starred vessel had not struck during the night. This was the last point each look was bent on as the darkness was falling; and when the wind howled, and the sea ran mountains high, and dashed its white foam over their little huts, then was every one astir in the village. Many an anxious gaze pierced through the mist, hoping some white sail might gleam through the storm, or some bending spar show where a perishing crew yet cried for help. The little shore would then present a busy scene; boats were got out, coils of rope and oars strewed on every side, lanterns flitted rapidly from place to place. With what energy and earnestness they moved! how their eyes gleamed with excitement, and how their voices rung out, in accents of hoarse command! Oh! how horrible to think that the same features of a manly nature—the bold and daring courage that fears not the rushing wave nor the sweeping storm, the heroic daring that can breast the wild breakers as they splash on the dark rocks, can arise from impulses so opposite; and that humanity the fairest, and crime the blackest, have but the same machinery to work with!

" It was on a dark November night—the heavy sough of a coming storm sent large and sullen waves on shore, where they broke with that low, hollow cadence, that seamen recognize as boding ill. A dense, thick fog obscured all objects seaward; and though many scouts were out upon the hills, they could detect nothing: still, as the night grew more and more threatening, the wreckers felt assured a gale was coming, and already their preparation was made for the approaching time. Hour after hour passed by; but though the gale increased, and blew with violence on the shore, nothing could be seen. Towards midnight, however, a scout came in to say that he thought he could detect at intervals, through the dense mist and spray, a gleaming light in the direction of 'the Teeth.' The drift was too great to make it clearly perceptible, but still he persisted he had seen something.

" A party was soon assembled on the beach, their eyes turned towards the fatal rocks, which at low water rose some twelve or fifteen feet above the surface. They gazed long and anxiously, but nothing could they make out, till, as they were turning away, one cried out, 'Ay, see there—there it is now!' and as he spoke, a red forked flame shot up through the drifting spray, and threw a lurid flash upon the dark sea. It died away almost as quickly, and though seen at intervals again, it seemed ever to wax fainter and fainter. 'She's on fire!' cried one. 'No, no; it's a distress signal,' said another. 'One thing is certain,' cried a third, 'the craft that's on "the Teeth" on such a night as this won't get off very readily; and so, lads, be alive and run out the boats.'

"The little colony was soon astir. It was a race of avarice, too; for, latterly, the settlement had been broken up by feuds and jealousies into different factions, and each strove to overreach the other. In less than half an hour, eight boats were out, and, breasting the white breakers, headed out to sea. All, save the old and decrepit, the women and children, were away, and even they stood watching on the shore, following with their eyes the boats in which they felt most interested.

"At last they disappeared in the gloom—not a trace could be seen of them, nor did the wind carry back their voices, over which the raging storm was now howling. A few still remained, straining their eye-balls towards the spot where the light was seen—the others had returned towards the village—when all of a sudden a frightful yell, a long-sustained and terrible cry arose from the huts, and the same instant a blaze burst forth, and rose into a red column towards the sky. The Indians were upon them. The war-shout—that dreadful sound they knew too well—resounded on every side. Then began a massacre which nothing in description can convey. The dreadful rage of the vengeful savage—long pent up, long provoked—had now its time for vengeance. The tomahawk and the scalping-knife ran red with blood, as women and infants rushed madly hither and thither in flight. Old men lay weltering in their gore beside their daughters and grand-children; while the wild red men, unsated with slaughter, tore the mangled corpses as they lay, and bathed them-selves in blood. But not there did it end. The flame that gleamed from 'the Teeth' rocks was but an Indian

device to draw the wreckers out to sea. A pine-wood fire
had been lighted on the tallest cliff at low water, to attract their attention, by some savages in canoes, and left
to burn away slowly during the night.

" Deceived and baffled, the wreckers made towards
shore, to which already their eyes were turned in terror,
for the red blaze of the burning huts was seen, miles off,
in the bay. Scarcely had the first boat neared the shore,
when a volley of fire-arms poured in upon her, while the
war-cry that rose above it told them their hour was come.
The Indians were several hundreds in number, armed to
the teeth ; the others few, and without a single weapon.
Contest, it was none. The slaughter scarce lasted many
minutes, for ere the flame from the distant rock subsided,
the last white man lay a corpse on the bloody strand.
Such was the terrible retribution that followed on crime,
and, at the very moment, too, when their cruel hearts
were bent on its perpetration.

" This tale, which was told me in a broken jargon, between Canadian-French and English, concluded with
words which were not to me, at the time, the least shock-
ing part of the story, as the narrator, with glistening
eyes, and in a voice whose guttural tones seemed almost
too thick for utterance, said, ' It was I that planned it ! '

" You will ask me, by what chance did I escape with
life among such a tribe. An accident—the merest accident
—saved me. When a smuggler, as I have already told
you I was, I once, when becalmed in the Bay of Biscay,
got one of the sailors to tatoo my arm with gunpowder, a
very common practice at sea. The operator had been
in the North American trade, and had passed ten years as
a prisoner among the Indians, and brought away with him
innumerable recollections of their habits and customs.
Among others, their strange idols had made a great impression on his mind , and, as I gave him a discretionary
power as to the frescoes he was to adorn me with, he
painted a most American-looking savage with two faces
on his head, his body all stuck over with arrows and spear-
points, while he, apparently unmoved by such visitors,
was skipping about, in something that might be a war-
dance.

"This, with all its appropriate colours—for, as the heraldry folk say, 'It was proper'—was a very conspicuous object on my arm, and no sooner seen by the chief, than he immediately knelt down beside me, dressed my wounds, and tended me; while the rest of the tribe, recognizing me as one whose existence was charmed, showed me every manner of respect, and even devotion.

"Indeed I soon felt my popularity to be my greatest difficulty; for whatever great event was going forward among the tribe, it became the etiquette to consult me on it, as a species of soothsayer, and never was a prophet more sorely tested. Sometimes it was a question of the whale-fishery—whether 'bottle-noses,' or 'sulphur-bottoms,' were coming up the bay, and whether, in the then season, it was safe, or not, to strike the 'calf whales' first. Now it was a disputed point as to the condition of bears; or, worse than either, a little marauding party would be undertaken into a neighbour's premises, where I was expected to perform a very leading part, which, not having the same strong convictions of my invulnerable nature as my worthy associates, I undertook with as few feelings of satisfaction as you may imagine. But these were not all; offers of marriage from many noble families pressed me on every side; and though polygamy to any extent was permissible, I never could persuade myself to make my fortune in this manner. The ladies, too, I am bound to say, were not so seductive as to endanger my principles. Flattened heads, bent-down noses, and lip-stones, are very strong antidotes to the tender passion. And I was obliged to declare, that I was compelled by a vow not to marry for three moons. I dared not venture on a longer period of amnesty, lest I should excite suspicion of any insult to them on a point where their vengeance never forgives; and I hoped, ere that time elapsed, that I should be able to make my escape—though how, or when, or where to, were points I could not possibly guess at.

"Before the half of my probation had expired, we were visited by an old Indian of a distant tribe—a strange old fellow he was, clothed in goats' skins, and wearing strong leather boots and rackets (snow shoes), a felt hat, and a kind of leather sack strapped on his back, and secured by a lock. This singular-looking fellow was 'the post.' He travelled once a year from a small settlement near Miri-michi, to Quebec, and back, carrying the letters to and from these places, a distance of something like seven hundred miles, which he accomplished entirely on foot, great part of it through dense forests and over wild uninhabited prairies, passing through the hunting-grounds of several hostile tribes, fording rivers and climbing mountains, and all for the moderate payment of ten pounds a year, half of which he spent in rum before he left Quebec, and while waiting for the return mail; and, strangest of all, though for forty years he had continued to perform this journey, not only no accident had ever occurred to the letters, but he himself was never known to be behind his appointed time at his destination.

"'Tahata,' for such was his name, was, however, a character of great interest, even to the barbarous tribes through whose territories he passed. He was a species of savage newspaper, recounting various details respecting the hunting and fishing seasons—the price of skins at Quebec or Montreal—what was the peltry most in request, and how it would bring its best price. Cautiously abstain-ing from the local politics of these small states, his infor-mation only bore on such topics as are generally useful and interesting, and never for a moment partook of any partisan character; besides, he had ever some petty com-mission or other from the squaws to discharge at Quebec. There was an amber bead, or a tin ornament, a bit of red ribbon, or a glass button, or some such valuable, every-where he went; and his coming was an event as much longed and looked for as any other that marked their monotonous existence.

" He rested for a few days at our village, when I learned these few particulars of his life, and at once resolved, come what might, to make my escape with him, and, if possible, reach Quebec. An opportunity, fortunately, soon offered for my doing so with facility. The day of the courier's departure was fixed for a great fishing excursion, on which the tribe were to be absent for several days. Affecting illness, I remained on shore, and never stirred from the wigwam till the last canoe had disappeared from

sight; then I slowly sauntered out, and telling the squaws
that I would stroll about, for an hour or so, to breathe the
air, I followed the track which was pointed out to me by
the courier who had departed early on the same morning.
Before sunset I came up with my friend, and with a heart
overflowing with delight, sat down to partake of the little
supper he had provided for our first day's journey; after
that, each day was to take care of itself.

"Then began a series of adventures, to which all I have
hitherto told you are as nothing. It was the wild life of the
prairies in companionship with one who felt as much at
home in the recesses of a pine forest as ever I did in the
snug corner of mine inn. Now, it was a night spent
under the starry sky, beside some clear river's bank, where
the fish lay motionless beneath the red glare of our watch-
fire; now, we bivouacked in a gloomy forest, planting
stockades around to keep off the wild beasts; then, we
would chance upon some small Indian settlement, where
we were regaled with hospitality, and spent half the night
listening to the low chant of a red man's song, as he
deplored the downfall of his nation, and the loss of their
hunting-grounds. Through all, my guide preserved the
steady equability of one who was travelling a well-worn
path—some notched tree, some small stone heap, some
fissured rock, being his guide through wastes, where, it
seemed to me, no human foot had ever trod. He lightened
the road with many a song and many a story, the latter
always displaying some curious trait of his people, whose
high sense of truth and unswerving fidelity to their word,
once pledged, appeared to be an invariable feature in every
narrative; and though he could well account for the feeling
that makes a man more attached to his own nation, he
more than once half expressed his surprise, how, having
lived among the simple-minded children of the forest, I
could ever return to the haunts of the plotting and design-
ing white men.

"This story of mine," continued Mr. O'Kelly, "has
somehow spun itself out far more than I intended. My
desire was, to show you briefly in what strange and dissimilar situations I have been thrown in life—how I have
lived among every rank and class, at home and abroad, in

comparative affluence—in narrow poverty; how I have
looked on at the world, in all its gala dress of wealth, and
rank, and beauty—of power, of station, and command of
intellect; and how I have seen it poor, and mean, and
naked—the companion of gloomy solitudes, and the denizen
of pathless forests; and yet found the same human passions, the same love and hate, the same jealousy and fear,
courage and daring—the same desire for power, and the
same wish to govern in the red Indian of the prairie, as in
the star-bedecked noble of Europe The proudest rank
of civilized life has no higher boast than in the practice of
such virtues as I have seen rife among the wild dwellers
in the dark forest. Long habit of moving thus among my
fellow-men has worn off much of that conventional reverence for class which forms the standing point of all our
education at home. The tarred and weather-beaten sailor,
if he be but a pleasant fellow, and has seen life, is to me
as agreeable a companion as the greatest admiral that
ever trod a quarter-deck. My delight has been thus, for
many a year back, to ramble through the world, and look
on its game, like one who sits before the curtain, and has
no concern with the actors, save in so far as they amuse
him.

"There is no cynicism in this. No one enjoys life
more than I do. Music is a passion with me—in painting, I take the greatest delight, and beauty has still her
charm for me. Society never was a greater pleasure.
Scenery can give me a sense of happiness which none
but solitary men ever feel—yet, it is less as one identified
with these, than as a mere spectator. All this is selfish
and egotistical, you will say—and so it is. But then,
think what chance has one like me of any other pleasure!
To how many annoyances should I expose myself, if I
adopted a different career. Think of the thousand in-
quiries, of—who is he? what is his family? where did he
come from? what are his means? and all such queries,
which would beset me, were I the respectable denizen of
one of your cities. Without some position, some rank,
ome settled place in society, you give a man nothing—he
can neither have friend nor home. Now, I am a wanderer
—my choice of life happily took an humble turn. I have

placed myself in a good situation for seeing the game—
and I am not too fastidious if I get somewhat crushed by
the company about me: but now, to finish this long story,
for I see the day is breaking, and I must leave Antwerp
by ten o'clock.

"At last, then, we reached Quebec, It was on a bright,
clear, frosty day, in December, when all the world was
astir—sledges flying here and there—men slipping along
in rackets—women wrapped up in furs, sitting snugly in
chairs, and pushed along the ice some ten or twelve miles
the hour—all gay, all lively, and all merry-looking—while
I and my Indian friend bustled our way through the crowd
towards the post-office. He was a well-known character,
and many a friendly nod and knowing shake of the head
welcomed him as he passed along. I, however, was an
object of no common astonishment, even in a town where
every variety of costume, from full dress to almost
nakedness, was to be met with daily. Still, something
remained as a novelty, and it would seem I had hit on it.
Imagine, then, an old and ill-used foraging cap, drawn
down over a red night cap, from beneath which my hair
descended straight, somewhere about a foot in length—
beard and moustaches to match—a red uniform coat,
patched with brown seal-skin, and surmounted by a kind
of blanket of buffalo hide—a pair of wampum shorts,
decorated with tin and copper, after the manner of a
marqueterie table—gray stockings, gartered with fish skin
—and mocassins made after the fashion of high-lows, an
invention of my own, which I trust are still known as
'O'Kellys' among my friends the red men

"That I was not an Indian, was sufficiently apparent—
if by nothing else, the gingerly delicacy with which I trod
the pavement after a promenade of seven hundred miles,
would have shown it; and yet there was an evident re-
luctance on all sides to acknowledge me as one of themselves. The crowd that followed our steps had by this
time attracted the attention of some officers, who stopped
to see what was going forward, when I recognized the
major of my own regiment among the number. I saw,
however, that he did not remember me, and hesitated
with myself whether I should return to my old servitude.

The thought that no mode of subsistence was open to me —that I was not exactly prepossessing enough to make my way in the world by artificial advantages—decided the question, and I accosted him at once.

" I will not stop to paint the astonishment of the officer, nor shall I dwell on the few events which followed the recognition—suffice it to say, that, the same evening I received my appointment, not as a sergeant, but as regimental interpreter between our people and the Indians, with whom we were then in alliance against the Yankees. The regiment soon left Quebec for Trois Rivières, where my ambassadorial functions were immediately called into play —not, I am bound to confess, under such weighty and onerous responsibilities as I had been led to suspect would ensue between two powerful nations—but on matters of less moment, and fully as much difficulty, viz. the barter of old regimental coats and caps for bows and arrows ; the exchange of rum and gunpowder for mocassins and wampum ornaments—in a word, the regulation of an Anglo-Indian tariff, which accurately defined the value of everything, from a black fox-skin to a pair of old gaiters—from an Indian tomahawk to a tooth-pick.

" In addition to these fiscal regulations, I drew up a criminal code—which, in simplicity at least, might vie with any known system of legislation—by which it was clearly laid down, that any unknown quantity of Indians were only equal to the slightest inconvenience incurred or discomfort endured by an English officer: that the condescension of any intercourse with them was a circumstance of the greatest possible value—and its withdrawal the highest punishment. A few other axioms of the like nature greatly facilitated all bargains, and promoted universal good feeling. Occasionally, a knotty point would arise, which somewhat puzzled me to determine. Now and then, some Indian prejudice, some superstition of the tribe, would oppose a barrier to the summary process of my cheap justice ; but then, a little adroitness and dexterity could soon reconcile matters—and as I had no fear that my decisions were to be assumed as precedents, and still less dread of their being rescinded by a higher court, I cut boldly, and generally severed the difficulty at a blow.

"My life was now a pleasant one enough—for our officers treated me on terms of familiarity, which gradually grew into intimacy, as our quarters were in remote stations, and as they perceived that I possessed a certain amount of education—which, it is no flattery to say, exceeded their own. My old qualities of convivialism, also, gave me considerable aid; and as I had neither forgotten to compose a song, nor sing it afterwards, I was rather a piece of good fortune in this solitary and monotonous state of life. Etiquette prevented my being asked to the mess, but, most generously, nothing interfered with their coming over to my wigwam almost every evening, and taking share of a bowl of sangaree and a pipe—kindnesses I did my uttermost to repay, by putting in requisition all the amusing talents I possessed: and certainly, never did a man endeavour more for great success in life, nor give himself greater toil, than did I, to make time pass over pleasantly to some half-dozen silly subalterns, a bloated captain or two, and a plethoric old snuff-taking major, that dreamed of nothing but rappee, punch, and promotion. Still, like all men in an ambiguous, or a false position, I felt flattered by the companionship of people whom, in my heart, I thoroughly despised and looked down upon; and felt myself honoured by the society of the most thick-headed set of noodles ever a man sat down with—Ay! and laughed at their flat witticisms, and their old stale jokes—and often threw out hints for *bon mots*, which, if they caught, I immediately applauded, and went about, saying, did you hear ' Jones's last?'—' do you know what the major said this morning?' bless my heart! what a time it was. Truth will out—the old tuft-hunting leaven was strong in me, even yet—hardship and roughing had not effaced it from my disposition—one more lesson was wanting, and I got it.

"Among my visitors was an old captain of the rough school of military habit, with all the dry jokes of the recruiting service, and all the coarseness which a life spent most part in remote stations and small detachments, is sure to impart. This old fellow, Mat Hubbart, a wellknown name in the Glengarries, had the greatest partiality for practical jokes, and could calculate to a nicety the precise amount of a liberty which any man's rank in the service permitted, without the risk of being called to account; and the same scale of equivalents by which he established the momenclature for female rank in the army, was regarded by him as the test for those licenses he permitted himself to take with any man beneath him ; and as he spoke of the colonel's 'lady,' the major's ' wife,' the captain's ' woman,' the lieutenant's 'thing,' so did he graduate his conduct to the husbands, never transgressing for a moment on the grade by any undue familiarity or any unwonted freedom. With me, of course, his powers were discretionary, or rather, had no discretion whatever. I was a kind of military outlaw that any man might shoot at, and certainly he spared not his powder in my behalf.

"Among the few reliques of my Indian life, was a bear-skin cap and hood, which I prized highly. It was a present from my old guide—his parting gift—when I put into his hands the last few pieces of silver I possessed in the world. This was then to me a thing which, as I had met with not many kindnesses in the world, I valued at something far beyond its mere price, and would rather have parted with any, or everything I possessed, than lose it. Well, one day on my return from a fishing excursion, as I was passing the door of the mess-room, what should I see but a poor idiot that frequented the barrack, dressed in my bear-skin.

"'Halloa ! Rokey,' said I, 'where did you get that?' scarce able to restrain my temper.

"'The captain gave it me,' said the fellow, touching his cap, with a grateful look towards the mess-room window, where I saw Captain Hubbart standing, convulsed with laughter.

"'Impossible !' said I, yet half fearing the truth of his assertion. 'The captain couldn't give away what's mine, and not his.'

"'Yes, but he did though,' said the fool, 'and told me, too, he'd make me the "talk man" with the Indians, if you didn't behave better in future.'

"I felt my blood boil up as I heard these words. I saw at once that the joke was intended to insult and offend

me ; and probably meant as a lesson for my presumption
a few evenings before, since I had the folly, in a moment of
open-hearted gaiety, to speak of my family, and perhaps
to boast of my having been a gentleman. I hung my
head in shame, and all my presence of mind was too little
to allow me to feign a look of carelessness as I walked by
the window, from whence the coarse laughter of the captain was now heard peal after peal. I shall not tell you
how I suffered when I reached my hut, and what I felt at
every portion of this transaction. One thing forcibly impressed itself upon my mind, that the part I was playing
must be an unworthy one, or I had never incurred such a
penalty ; that if these men associated with me, it was on
terms which permitted all from them—nothing in return ;
and for a while I deemed no vengeance enough to satisfy
my wounded pride. Happily for me my thoughts took
another turn, and I saw that the position in which I had
placed myself invited the insolence it met with ; and
that if any man stoop to be kicked in this world, he'll
always find some kind friend ready to oblige him with the
compliment. Had an equal so treated me, my course
had presented no difficulty whatever. Now, what could
I do ?

"While I pondered over these things a corporal came
up to say that a party of the officers were about to pay me
a visit after evening parade, and hoped I'd have something
for supper for them. Such was the general tone of their
invitations, and I had received in my time above a hundred similar messages, without any other feeling than
one of pride at my being in a position to have so many
distinguished guests. Now, on the contrary, the announcement was a downright insult. My long-sleeping
pride suddenly awakened, I felt all the contumely of my
condition ; and my spirit, sunk for many a day in the
slavish observance of a miserable vanity, rebelled against
further outrage. I muttered a hasty 'all right' to the
soldier, and turned away to meditate on some scheme of
vengeance.

"Having given directions to my Indian follower, a half-
breed fellow of the most cunning description, to have all
ready in the wigwam, I wandered into the woods. To

no use was it that I thought over my grievance, nothing presented itself in any shape as a vindication of my wounded feelings, nor could I see how anything short of ridicule could ensue from all mention of the transaction. The clanking sound of an Indian drum broke on my musings, and told me that the party were assembled, and on my entering the wigwam I found them all waiting for me. There were full a dozen ; many who had never done me the honour of a visit previously, came on this occasion to enjoy the laugh at my expense the captain's joke was sure to excite. Husbanding their resources, they talked only about indifferent matters—the gossip and chit-chat of the day—but still with such a secret air of something to come, that even an ignorant observer could notice that there was in reserve somewhat that must abide its time for development. By mere accident I overheard the captain whisper, in reply to a question of one of the subalterns, 'No! no!—not now—wait till we have the punch up.' I guessed at once that such was the period they proposed to discuss the joke played off at my cost, and I was right; for no sooner had the large wooden bowl of sangaree made its appearance, than Hubbart, filling his glass, proposed a bumper to our new ally, Rokey ; a cheer drowned half his speech, which ended in a roar of laughter, as the individual so complimented stood at the door of the wigwam, dressed out in full costume with my bear-skin.

"I had just time to whisper a command to my Indian imp, concluding with an order for another bowl of sangaree, before the burst of merriment had subsided—a hail-storm of jokes, many poor enough, but still cause for laughter, now pelted me on every side. My generosity was lauded, my good taste extolled, and as many impertinences as could well be offered up to a man at his own table went the round of the party. No allusion was spared either to my humble position as interpreter to the force, or my former life among the Indians, to furnish food for joke. Even my family—of whom, as I have mentioned, I foolishly spoke to them lately—they introduced into their tirade of attack and ridicule, which nothing but a sense of coming vengeance could have enabled me to endure.

" ' Come, come,' said one, ' the bowl is empty. I say,
O'Kelly, if you wish us to be agreeable, as I'm certain
you find us, will you order a fresh supply ? '

" ' Most willingly,' said I, ' but there is just enough left
in the old bowl to drink the health of Captain Hubbart,
to whom we are certainly indebted for most of the amusement of the evening. Now, therefore, if you please, with
all the honours, gentlemen ; for let me say, in no one
quality has he his superior in the regiment. His wit we
can all appreciate ; his ingenuity I can speak to ; his
generosity—you have lauded *mine*, but think of *his*.' As
I spoke I pointed to the door, where my ferocious-looking
Indian stood in all his war-paint, wearing on his head the
full-dress cocked-hat of the captain, while over his shoulders was thrown his large blue military cloak, over which
he had skilfully contrived to make a hasty decoration of
brass ornaments and wild-bird's feathers.

" ' Look there ! ' said I, exultingly, as the fellow nodded
his plumed hat and turned majestically round to be fully
admired.

" ' Have you dared, sir ? ' roared Hubbart, frothing with
passion and clenching his fist towards me—but a perfect
cheer of laughter overpowered his words. Many rolled
off their seats, and lay panting and puffing on the ground ;
some turned away half-suffocated with their struggles,
while a few, more timid than the rest, endeavoured to
conceal their feelings, and seemed half alarmed at the
consequences of my impertinence. When the mirth had
a little subsided, it was remarked that Hubbart was gone
—no one had seen how or when, but he was no longer
among us.

" ' Come, gentlemen,' said I, ' the new bowl is ready for
you, and your toast is not yet drunk. All going so early ?
Why, it's not eleven yet.'

" But so it was. The impulse of merriment over, the
esprit de corps came back in all its force, and the man
whose feelings they had not scrupled to outrage and insult,
they turned on the very moment he had the courage to
assert his honour. One by one passed out, some with
a cool nod ; others a mere look ; many never even noticed
me at all : and one, the last, I believe, dropping a little

behind, whispered as he went, 'Sorry for you, faith, but
all your own doing, though.'

"'My own doing,' said I, in bitterness, as I sat me
down at the door of the wigwam. 'My own doing!' and
the words ate into my very heart's core. Heaven knows,
had any one of them who left me but turned his head and
looked at me then as I sat—my head buried in my hands,
my frame trembling with strong passion—he had formed
a most false estimate of my feelings. In all likelihood,
he would have regarded me as a man sorrowing over a
lost position in society; grieved at the mistaken vanity
that made him presume upon those who associated with
him by grace especial, and never on terms of equality.
Nothing in the world was then farther from my heart.
No, my humiliation had another source—my sorrowing
penetrated into a deeper soil. I awoke to the conviction
that my position was such that even the temporary countenance they gave me by their society was to be deemed
my greatest honour, as its withdrawal should be my
deepest disgrace—that these poor heartless, brainless fools
for whom I taxed my time, my intellect, and my means,
were in the light of patrons to me. Let any man who
has felt what it is to live among those on whose capacity
he has looked down, while he has been obliged to pay
homage to their rank—whose society he has frequented,
not for pleasure nor enjoyment—not for the charm of
social intercourse, or the interchange of friendly feeling,
but for the mere vulgar object that he might seem to
others to be in a position to which he had no claim—to
be intimate when he was only endured—to be on terms of
ease when he was barely admitted; let him sympathize
with me. Now I awoke to the full knowledge of my
state, and saw myself at last in a true light. 'My own
doing!' repeated I to myself. 'Would it had been so
many a day since, ere I lost self-respect, ere I had felt the
humiliation I now feel.'

"'You are under arrest, sir,' said the sergeant, as, with
a party of soldiers, he stood prepared to accompany me to
the quarters.

"'Under arrest! By whose orders?'

"'The colonel's orders,' said the man, briefly, and in a

voice that showed I was to expect little compassion from one of a class who had long regarded me as an upstart giving himself airs unbecoming his condition.

"My imprisonment, of which I dared not ask the reason, gave me time to meditate on my fortunes, and think over the vicissitudes of my life; to reflect on the errors which had rendered abortive every chance of success in whatever career 1 adopted; but, more than all, to consider how poor were all my hopes of happiness in the road I had chosen, while I dedicated to the amusement of others the qualities which, if cultivated for myself, might be made sources of contentment and pleasure. If I seem prolix in all this—if I dwell on these memories, it is, first, because few men may not reap a lesson from considering them ; and again, because on them hinged my future life.

" There, do you see that little drawing yonder ? it is a sketch, a mere sketch I made from recollection of the room I was confined in. That's the St. Lawrence flowing beneath the window, and there, far in the distance, you see the tall cedars of the opposite bank. On that little table I laid my head the whole night long ; I slept, too, and soundly , and when I awoke the next day I was a changed man.

" ' You are relieved from arrest,' said the same sergeant who conducted me to prison, ' and the colonel desires to see you on parade.'

"As I entered the square, the regiment was formed in line, and the officers, as usual, stood in a group, chatting together in the centre. A half smile, quickly subdued as I came near, ran along the party.

" ' O'Kelly,' said the colonel, ' I have sent for you to hear a reprimand which it is fitting you should receive at the head of the regiment, and which, from my knowledge of you, I have supposed would be the most effectual punishment I could inflict for your late disrespectful conduct to Captain Hubbart.'

" ' May I ask, colonel, have you heard of the provocation which induced my offence ? '

" ' I hope, sir,' replied he, with a look of stern dignity, ' you are aware of the difference of your relative rank and

station, and that, in condescending to associate with you,
Captain Hubbart conferred an honour which doubly com-
pensated for any liberty he was pleased to take.   Read
the general order, Lieutenant Wood.'

"A confused murmur of something, from which I could
collect nothing, reached me ; a vague feeling of weight
seemed to press my head, and a giddiness that made me
reel, was on me ; and I only knew the ceremony was over
as I heard the order to march given, and saw the troops
begin to move off the ground.

" 'A moment, colonel,' said I, in a voice that made him
start, and drew on me the look of all the others.   ' I have
too much respect for you, and I hope also for myself,
to attempt any explanation of a mere jest, where the
consequences have taken a serious turn ; besides, I feel
conscious of one fault, far too grave a one to venture on
an excuse for any other I have been guilty of.   I wish
to resign my post.   I here leave the badge of the only
servitude I ever did, or ever intend to submit to ; and
now, as a free man once more, and a gentleman, too, if
you'll permit me, I beg to wish you adieu ; and as for
you, captain, I have only to add, that whenever you feel
disposed for a practical joke, or any other interchange of
politeness, Con O'Kelly will be always delighted to meet
your views—the more so as he feels, though you may not
believe it, something still in your debt.'

" With that I turned on my heel, and left the barrack-
yard, not a word being spoken by any of the others, nor
any evidence of their being so much amused as they
seemed to expect from my exposure.

" Did it never strike you as a strange thing, that while
none but the very poorest and humblest people can bear
to confess to present poverty, very few men decline to
speak of the narrow circumstances they have struggled
through—nay, rather take a kind of pleasure in relating
what difficulties once beset their path—what obstacles
were opposed to their success?   The reason perhaps is,
there is a reflective merit in thus surmounting opposition.
The acknowledgment implies a sense of triumph.   It
seems to say—Here am I, such as you see me now, and
yet time was, when I was houseless and friendless—when

the clouds darkened around my path, and I saw not even
the faintest glimmer of hope to light up the future; yet,
with a stout heart and strong courage, with the will came
the way; and I conquered. I do confess I could dwell,
and with great pleasure too, on those portions of my life
when I was poorest and most forsaken, in preference to the
days of my prosperity, and the hours of my greatest wealth.
Like the traveller who, after a long journey through some
dark winter's day, finds himself at the approach of night,
seated by the corner of a cheery fire in his inn; every
rushing gust of wind that shakes the building, every
plash of the beating rain against the glass, but adds to
this sense of comfort, and makes him hug himself with
satisfaction to think how he is no longer exposed to such a
storm—that his journey is accomplished — his goal is
reached—and as he draws his chair closer to the blaze, it
is the remembrance of the past gives all the enjoyment to
the present. In the same way, the pleasantest memories
of old age are of those periods in youth when we have
been successful over difficulty, and have won our way
through every opposing obstacle. 'Joy's memory is indeed
no longer joy.' Few can look back on happy hours without thinking of those with whom they spent them, and
then comes the sad question, Where are they now? What
man reaches even the middle term of life with a tithe of
the friends he started with in youth; and as they drop off,
one by one, around him, comes the sad reflection that the
period is past when such ties can be formed anew—The
book of the heart once closed, opens no more. But why
these reflections? I must close them, and with them my
story at once.

"The few pounds I possessed in the world enabled me
to reach Quebec, and take my passage in a timber vessel
bound for Cork. Why I returned to Ireland, and with
what intentions, I should be sorely puzzled to explain.
Some vague, indistinct feeling of home connected with my
birthplace, had, perhaps, its influence over me. So it was
—I did so.

" After a good voyage of some five weeks, we anchored
in Cove, where I landed, and proceeded on foot to Tralee.
It was night when I arrived. A few faint glimmering

lights could be seen here and there, from an upper window, but all the rest was in darkness. Instinctively I wandered on, till I came to the little street where my aunt had lived. I knew every stone in it. There was not a house I passed but I was familiar with all its history. There was Mark Cassidy's provision store, as he proudly called a long dark room, the ceiling thickly studed with hams and bacon, coils of rope, candles, flakes of glue, and loaves of sugar; while a narrow pathway was eked out below between a sugar-hogshead, some sacks of flour and potatoes, hemp-seed, tar, and treacle, interspersed with scythe-blades, reaping-hooks, and sweeping-brushes — a great coffee-roaster adorning the wall, and forming a conspicuous object for the wonderment of the country people, who never could satisfy themselves whether it was a new-fashioned clock, or a weather-glass, or a little threshing-machine, or a money-box. Next door was Maurice Fitzgerald's, the apothecary, a cosy little cell of eight feet by six, where there was just space left for a long-practised individual to grind with a pestle, without putting his right elbow through a blue glass bottle that figured in the front window, or his left into active intercourse with a regiment of tinctures that stood up, brown, and muddy, and fœtid, on a shelf hard by. Then came Joe M'Evoys, 'licensed for spirits and enthertainment,' where I had often stood as a boy to listen to the pleasant sounds of Larry Branaghan's pipes, or to the agreeable ditties of 'Adieu, ye shinin' daisies, I loved you well and long,' as sung by him, with an accompaniment. Then there was Mister Moriarty's, the attorney, a great man in the petty sessions, a bitter pill for all the country gentlemen. He was always raking up knotty cases of their decisions, and reporting them to the *Limerick Vindicator* under the cognomen of ' Brutus' or ' Coriolanus.' I could just see by the faint light that his house had been raised a story higher, and little iron balconies, like railings, stuck to the drawing-room windows. Next came my aunt's. There it was—my foot was on the door where I stood as a child, my little heart wavering between fears of the unknown world without, and hopes of doing something—heaven knows what— which would make me a name hereafter; and there I was

now, after years of toil and peril of every kind, enough to
have won me distinction, success enough to have made me
rich, had either been but well directed; and yet I was
poor and humble, as the very hour I quitted that home   I
sat down on the steps, my heart heavy and sad, my limbs
tired, and before many minutes fell fast asleep, and never
awoke till the bright sun was shining gaily on one side
of the little street, and already the preparations for the
coming day were going on about me.   I started up, afraid
and ashamed of being seen, and turned into the little ale-
house close by, to get my breakfast.   Joe himself was not
forthcoming; but a fat, pleasant-looking, yellow-haired
fellow, his very image, only some dozen years younger,
was there, bustling about among some pewter quarts and
tin measures, arranging tobacco-pipes, and making up
little pennyworths of tobacco.

" ' Is your name M'Evoy ? ' said I.

" ' The same, at your service,' said he, scarce raising his
eyes from his occupation.

" ' Not Joe M'Evoy ? '

" ' No, sir, Ned M'Evoy; the old man's name was Joe.'

" ' He's dead, then, I suppose ? '

" ' Ay, sir; these eight years come micklemass; is it a
pint or a naggin of sperits ? '

" ' Neither; it's some breakfast, a rasher and a few
potatoes, I want most.   I'll take it here, or in the little
room.'

" ' Faix, ye seem to know the ways of the place,' said he,
smiling, as he saw me deliberately push open a small door,
and enter a little parlour once reserved for favourite
visitors.

" ' It's many years since I was here before,' said I to
the host, as he stood opposite to me, watching the progress
I was making with my breakfast; ' so many that I can
scarce remember more than the names of the people I knew
very well.   Is there a Miss O'Kelly living in the town ?
It was somewhere near this, her house.'

" ' Yes, above Mr. Moriarty's, that's where she lived;
but sure, she's dead and gone, many a day ago.   I mind
Father Donellan, the priest that was here before Mr. Nolan,
saying masses for her sowl, when I was a slip of a boy.'

" 'Dead and gone,' repeated I to myself sadly—for though I scarcely expected to meet my poor old relative again, I cherished a kind of half hope that she might still be living. 'And the priest, Father Donellan, is he dead too?'

" 'Yes, sir; he died of the fever, that was so bad four years ago.'

" 'And Mrs Brown that kept the post-office?'

" 'She went away to Ennis when her daughter was married there; I never heard tell of her since.'

" 'So that, in fact, there are none of the old inhabitants of the town remaining. All have died off?'

" 'Every one, except the ould captain; he's the only one left.'

" 'Who is he?'

" 'Captain Dwyer; maybe you knew him?'

" 'Yes, I knew him well; and he's alive?—he must be very old by this time?'

" 'He's something about eighty-six or seven; but he doesn't let on to more nor sixty, I believe; but sure, talk of ——, God preserve us, here he is.'

"As he spoke, a thin withered-looking old man, bent double with age, and walking with great difficulty, came to the door, and in a cracked voice called out,—

" 'Ned M'Evoy, here's the paper for you, plenty of news in it too about Mister O'Connell and the meetings in Dublin. If Cavanagh takes any fish, buy a sole or a whiting for me, and send me the paper back.'

" 'There's a gentleman, inside here, was just asking for you, sir,' said the host.

" 'Who is he? Is it Mr. Creagh? At your service, sir,' said the old man, sitting down on a chair near me, and looking at me from under the shadow of his hand spread over his brow. 'You're Mr. Studdart, I'm thinking?'

" 'No, sir; I do not suspect you know me; and, indeed, I merely mentioned your name as one I had heard of many years ago when I was here, but not as being personally known to you.'

" 'Oh! troth and so you might, for I'm well known in these parts—eh, Ned?' said he, with a chuckling cackle, that sounded very like hopeless dotage. 'I was in the army—in the "Buffs;" maybe you knew one Clancy who was in them?'

"'No, sir; I have not many military acquaintances. I came here this morning on my way to Dublin, and thought I would just ask a few questions about some people I knew a little about—Miss O'Kelly——'

"'Ah, dear! Poor Miss Judy—she's gone these two or three years.'

"'Ay, these fifteen,' interposed Ned.

"'No, it isn't though,' said the captain, crossly, 'it isn't more than three at most—cut off in her prime too; she was the last of an old stock—I knew them all well There was Dick—blazing Dick O'Kelly, as they called him, that threw the sheriff into the mill-race at Kilmacud, and had to go to France afterwards; and there was Peter—Peter got the property, but he was shot in a duel. Peter had a son—a nice devil he was too—he was drowned at sea; and except the little girl that has the school up there, Sally O'Kelly—she is one of them—there's none to the fore.'

"'And who was she, sir?'

"'Sally was—what's this? Ay, Sally is daughter to a son Dick left in France; he died in the war in Germany, and left this creature, and Miss Judy heard of her, and got her over here, just the week she departed herself. She's the last of them now—the best family in Kerry—and keeping a child's school! Ay, ay, so it is, and there's property too coming to her, if they could only prove that chap's death, Con O'Kelly; but sure no one knows anything where it happened. Sam Fitzsimon advertised him in all the papers, but to no use.'

"I did not wait for more of the old captain's reminiscences, but snatching up my hat, I hurried down the street, and in less than an hour was closeted with Mr Samuel Fitzsimon, attorney-at-law, and gravely discussing the steps necessary to be taken for the assumption of my right to a small property, the remains of my Aunt Judy's; a few hundred pounds, renewal fines of lands, that had dropped since my father's death. My next visit was to the little school, which was held in the parlour, where poor Aunt Judy used to have her little card parties The old stuffed macaw—now from dirt and smoke he might have

passed for a raven, was still over the fireplace, and there
was the old miniature of my father, and on the other side,
was one which I had not seen before, of Father Donellan,
in full robes.   All the little old conchologies were there too,
and except the black plethoric-looking cat, that sat staring
fixedly at the fire, as if she was grieving over the price of
coals, I missed nothing.   Miss Sally was a nice modest-
looking woman, with an air of better class about her, than
her humble occupation would seem to imply.   I made
known my relationship in a few words, and having told
her that I had made all arrangements for settling whatever property I possessed upon her, and informed her that
Mr. Fitzsimon would act as her guardian, I wished her
good-bye and departed   I saw that my life must be passed
in occupation of one kind or other—idleness would never
do, and with the only "fifty" I reserved to myself of my
little fortune, I started for Paris.   What I was to do, I
had no idea whatever; but I well knew, you have only
to lay the bridle on Fortune's neck, and you'll seldom be
disappointed in adventures.

"For some weeks I strolled about Paris, enjoying myself as thoughtlessly as though I had no need of any effort
to replenish my failing exchequer.   The mere human tide
that flowed along the Boulevards, and through the gay
gardens of the Tuileries, would have been amusement
enough for me.   Then there were theatres, and *cafés* and
restaurants, of every class, from the costly style of the
'Rocher,' down to the dinner beside the fountain 'Des
Innocents,' where you feast for four sous, and where the
lowest and poorest class of the capital resorted.   Well—
well, I might tell you some strange scenes of those days,
but I must hurry on.

"In my rambles through Paris, visiting strange and
out-of-the-way places, dining here, and supping there,
watching life under every aspect I could behold it, I
strolled one evening across the Pont Neuf into the 'Ile
St Louis,' that quaint old quarter, with its narrow strag-
gling streets, and its tall gloomy houses, barricadoed like
fortresses.   The old *porte-cochère* studded with nails, and
barred with iron, and having each a small window to peer
through at the stranger without, spoke of days when out-

rage and attack were rife, and it behoved every man to
fortify his stronghold as best he could. There, were now
to be found the most abandoned and desperate of the
whole Parisian world—the assassin, the murderer, the
housebreaker, the coiner, found a refuge in this confused
wilderness of gloomy alleys and dark dismal passages.
When night falls, no lantern throws a friendly gleam
along the streets—all is left in perfect darkness, save
when the red light of some cabaret lamp streams across
the pavement. In one of these dismal streets I found myself when night set in, and although I walked on, and on,
somehow, I never could extricate myself, but continually
kept moving in some narrow circle, so I guessed at least,
for I never wandered far from the deep-toned bell of
'Notre Dame,' that went on chanting its melancholy peal
through the stillness of the night air. I often stopped to
listen—now it seemed before, now behind me, the rich
solemn sound floating through those cavernous streets, had
something awfully impressive. The voice that called to
prayer, heard in that gloomy haunt of crime, was indeed
a strange and appalling thing. At last it ceased, and all
was still. For some time I was uncertain how to act; I
feared to knock at a door and ask my way; the very confession of my loneliness would have been an invitation to
outrage, if not murder. No one passed me; the streets
seemed actually deserted.

"Fatigued with walking, I sat down on a door-sill and
began to consider what was best to be done, when I heard
the sound of heavy feet moving along towards me, the
clattering of sabots on the rough pavement, and shortly
after, a man came up, who, I could just distinguish,
seemed to be a labourer. I suffered him to pass me a few
paces, and then called out—

"'Halloa, friend, can you tell me the shortest way to
the "Pont Neuf?"'"

"He replied by some words in a *patois* so strange I
could make nothing of it. I repeated my question, and
endeavoured by signs to express my wish. By this time
he was standing close beside me, and I could mark, was
evidently paying full attention to all I said. He looked
about him once or twice, as if in search of some

I

one, and then turning to me, said in a thick guttural voice—

"'*Halte la*, I'll come:' and with that he moved down in the direction he originally came from, and I could hear the clatter of his heavy shoes, till the sounds were lost in the winding alleys.

"A sudden thought struck me that I had done wrong. The fellow had evidently some dark intention by his going back, and I repented bitterly having allowed him to leave me; but then, what were easier for him than to lead me where he pleased, had I retained him; and so I reflected, when the noise of many voices speaking in a half-subdued accent came up the street. I heard the sound, too, of a great many feet; my heart sickened as the idea of murder, so associated with the place, flashed across me; and I had just time to squeeze myself within the shelter of the doorway, when the party came up.

"'Somewhere hereabouts, you said, wasn't it?' said one in a good accent, and a deep clear voice.

"'*Oui da !*' said the man I had spoken to, while he felt with his hands upon the walls and doorway of the opposite house. 'Halloa there,' he shouted.

"'Be still, you fool; don't you think that he suspects something by this time? Did the others go down the Rue des Loups?'

"'Yes, yes,' said a voice close to where I stood.

"'Then all's safe; he can't escape that way. Strike a light, Pierre.'

"A tall figure, wrapped up in a cloak, produced a tinder-box, and began to clink deliberately with a steel and flint. Every flash showed me some savage-looking face, where crime and famine struggled for mastery, while I could mark that many had large clubs of wood, and one or two were armed with swords. I drew my breath with short efforts, and was preparing myself for the struggle, in which, though I saw death before me, I resolved to sell life dearly, when a hand was passed across the pillar of the door, and rested on my leg. For a second it never stirred; then slowly moved up to my knee, where it stopped again. My heart seemed to cease its beating; I felt like one around whose body some snake is coiling, fold after fold, his slimy grasp.   The hand was gently withdrawn, and before I could recover from my surprise, I was seized by the throat and hurled out into the street. A savage laugh rang through the crowd, and a lantern, just lighted, was held up to my face, while he who spoke first called out—

" ' You didn't dream of escaping us, *bête*, did you ? ' at the same moment hands were thrust into my various pockets ; the few silver pieces I possessed were taken ; my watch torn off; my hat examined, and the lining of my coat ripped open, and all so speedily, that 1 saw at once I had fallen into experienced hands.

" ' Where do you live in Paris ? ' said the first speaker, still holding the light to my face, and staring fixedly at me, while I answered.

" ' I am a stranger and alone,' said I, for the thought struck me, that in such a circumstance, frankness was as good policy as any other.   ' I came here to-night to see the cathedral, and lost my way in returning '

" ' But where do you live ? in what quarter of Paris ? '

" ' The Rue d'Alger ; number 12 ; the second story.'

" ' What effects have you there in money ? '

" ' One English bank-note for five pounds ; nothing more.'

" ' Any jewels, or valuables of any kind ? '

" ' None ; I am as poor as any man in Paris.'

" ' Does the porter know your name, in the house ? '

" ' No; I am only known as the Englishman of number 12.'

" ' What are your hours ? irregular, are they not ? '

" ' Yes, I often come home very late '

" ' That's all right.   You speak French well.   Can you write it ? '

" ' Yes ; sufficiently so for any common purpose.'

" ' Here, then,' said he, opening a large pocket-book, ' write an order which I'll tell you, to the *concierge* of the house.   Take this pen.'

" With a trembling hand I took the pen, and waited for his direction.

" ' Is it a woman keeps the door of your hotel ? '

" ' Yes,' said I.

" 'Well, then, begin—Madame La Concierge, let the bearer of this note have the key of my apartment——'

" As I followed with my hand the words, I could mark that one of the party was whispering in the ear of the speaker, and then moved slowly round to my back.

" 'Hush! what's that?' cried the chief speaker. 'Be still there;' and as we listened, the chorus of a number of voices singing in parts, was heard at some little distance off.

" 'That infernal nest of fellows must be rooted out of this, one day or other,' said the chief; 'and if I end my days on the Place de Grève, I'll try and do it. Hush there—be still—they're passing on.' True enough, the sound began to wax fainter, and my heart sank heavily, as I thought the last hope was leaving me · suddenly a thought dashed through my mind—death in one shape is as bad as another. I'll do it—I stooped down as if to continue my writing, and then collecting my strength for the effort, and taking a deep breath, I struck the man in front a blow, with all my might, that felled him to the ground, and clearing him with a spring, bounded down the street. My old Indian teaching had done me good service here; few white men could have caught me in an open plain, with space and sight to guide me—and I gained at every stride; but, alas, I dared not stop to listen whence the sounds proceeded, and could only dash straight forward, not knowing where it might lead me; down a steep rugged street, that grew narrower as I went, I plunged—when, horror of horrors, I heard the Seine plashing at the end; the rapid current of the river surged against the heavy timbers that defended the banks, with a sound like a death-wail.

"A solitary, trembling light, lay afar off in the river, from some barge that was at anchor there; I fixed my eye upon it, and was preparing for a plunge, when, with a half-suppressed cry, my pursuers sprang up from a low wharf I had not seen, below the quay, and stood in front of me. In an instant they were upon me; a shower of blows fell upon my head and shoulders—and one, armed with desperate resolution, struck me on the forehead, and felled me on the spot.

"'Be quick now, be quick,' said a voice I well knew—'into the river with him—the "filets de St. Cloud" will catch him by daybreak—into the river with him.' They tore off my coat and shoes, and dragged me along towards the wharf—my senses were clear, though the blow had deprived me of all power to resist—and I could calculate the little chance still left me, when once I had reached the river—when a loud yell, and a whistle was heard afar off—another, louder, followed—the fellows around me sprang to their legs, and with a muttered curse, and a cry of terror, darted off in different directions. I could hear now several pistol-shots following quickly on each other, and the noise of a scuffle with swords ; in an instant it was over, and a cheer burst forth like a cry of triumph. ' Any one wounded there ? ' shouted a deep manly voice, from the end of the street : I endeavoured to call out, but my voice failed me. ' Halloa, there, any one wounded ? ' said the voice again, when a window was opened over my head, and a man held a candle out, and looked into the street. ' This way, this way,' said he, as he caught sight of my shadow where I lay. ' Ay, I guessed they went down here,' said the same voice I heard first, as he came along, followed by several others. ' Well, friend, are you much hurt, any blood lost ? '

"'No, only stunned,' said I, ' and almost well already.'

"'Have you any friends here—were you quite alone ? '

"'Yes; quite alone.'

"'Of course you were—why should I ask? That murderous gang never dared to face two men yet. Come, are you able to walk? Oh, you're a stout fellow, I see—come along with us. Come, Ludwig, put a hand under him, and we'll soon bring him up.'

"When they lifted me up, the sudden motion caused a weakness so complete, that I fainted, and knew little more of their proceedings, till I found myself lying on a sofa in a large room, where some forty persons were seated at a long table, most of them smoking from huge pipes of regular German proportions.

"'Where am I ? ' was my question, as I looked about, and perceived that the party wore a kind of blue uniform,

with fur on the collar and cuffs—and a greyhound worked
in gold on the arm.

" ' Why, you're safe, my good friend,' said a friendly
voice beside me—' that's quite enough to know at present, isn't it ? '

" ' I begin to agree with you,' said I, coolly—and so,
turning round on my side, I closed my eyes, and fell into
as pleasant a sleep as ever I remember in my life.

" They were, indeed, a very singular class of restoratives which my kind friends thought proper to administer
to me; nor am I quite sure that a *bavaroise* of chocolate,
dashed with rum, and friction over the face, with hot Eau
de Cologne, are sufficiently appreciated by the ' faculty ;'
but this I do know, that I felt very much revived by the
application without, and within, and with a face somewhat
the colour of a copper preserving-pan, and far too hot
to put anything on, I sat up, and looked about me.   A
merrier set of gentlemen, not even my experience had
ever beheld. They were mostly middle-aged, grizzly-looking
fellows, with very profuse beards and moustachios; their
conversation was partly French, partly German, here and
there a stray Italian diminutive crept in; and, to season
the whole, like cayenne in a *ragoût*, there was an odd
curse in English.

" Their strange dress, their free and easy manner, their
intimacy with each other, and above all, the *locale* they
had chosen for their festivities, made me, I own, a little
suspicious about their spotless morality, and I began conjecturing to what possible calling they might belong.
Now, guessing them smugglers—now, police of some kind
or other—now, highwaymen outright, but without ever
being able to come to any conclusion that even approached
satisfaction.   The more I listened, the more did my puzzle
grow on me ; that they were either the most distinguished and exalted individuals, or the most confounded
story-tellers, was certain.   Here, was a fat greasy little
fellow, with a beard like an Armenian, who was talking
of a trip he made to Greece with the Duke of Saxe
Weimar ; apparently they were on the best of terms together, and had a most jolly time of it.   There was a large
handsome man, with a short black moustache, describing

a night attack by wolves, made on the caravan he was in, during a journey to Siberia. I listened with intense interest to his narrative; the scenery, the danger, the preparation for defence, had all those little traits that bespeak truth, when, confound him! he destroyed the whole in a moment as he said, 'At that moment the Archduke Nicholas said to *me*'—the Archduke Nicholas, indeed— very good that—he's just as great a liar as the other.

" ' Come,' thought I, ' there's a respectable-looking old fellow with a bald head; let us hear him; there's no boasting of the great people he ever met with from that one, I'm sure.'

" We were now coming near to Vienna,' continued he, ' the night was dark as pitch, when a *vidette* came up to say, that a party of brigands, well known thereabouts, were seen hovering about the post station the entire evening. We were well armed, but still by no means numerous, and it became a grave question what we were to do? I got down immediately, and examined the loading and priming of the carbines; they were all right, nothing had been stirred. "What's the matter?" said the duke.'

" ' Oh,' said I, ' then there's a duke here also '

" ' What's the matter? ' said the Duke of Wellington.

" ' Oh, by Jove! that beats all,' cried I, jumping up on the sofa, and opening both my hands with astonishment. ' I'd have wagered a trifle on that little fellow, and hang me, if he isn't the worst of the whole set.'

" ' What's the matter?—what's happened? ' said they all, turning round in amazement at my sudden exclamation. ' Is the man mad? '

" ' It's hard to say,' replied I; ' but if I'm not, you must be; unless I have the honour, which is perfectly possible, to be at this moment in company with the Holy Alliance; for, so help me, since I've sat here and listened to you, there is not a crowned head in Europe, not a queen, not an archduke, ambassador, and general-in-chief, some of you have not been intimate with; and the small man with a red beard has just let slip something about the Shah of Persia.'

" The torrent of laughter that shook the table never

ceased for a full quarter of an hour. Old and young, smooth and grizzly, they laughed, till their faces were seamed with rivulets, like a mountain in winter; and when they would endeavour to address me, they'd burst out again, as fresh as ever.

" Come over and join us, worthy friend,' said he who sat at the head of the board, ' you seem well equal to it; and perhaps our character as men of truth may improve on acquaintance.'

" ' What, in Heaven's name, are you ? ' said I.

" Another burst of merriment was the only reply they made me. I never found much difficulty in making my way in certain classes of society, where the tone was a familiar one: where a *bon môt* was good currency, and a joke passed well, there I was at home, and to assume the features of the party was with me a kind of instinct which I could not avoid. It cost me neither effort nor strain—I caught up the spirit as a child catches up an accent, and went the pace as pleasantly as though I had been bred among them. I was therefore but a short time at table, when, by way of matriculation, I deemed it necessary to relate a story; and certainly, if they had astounded me by the circumstances of their high and mighty acquaintances, I did not spare them in my narrative, in which the Emperor of Japan figured as a very commonplace individual, and the King of Candia came in, just incidentally, as a rather dubious acquaintance might do.

" For a time they listened, like people who are well accustomed to give and take these kind of miracles; but when I mentioned something about a game of leap-frog on the wall of China with the Celestial himself, a perfect shout of incredulous laughter interrupted me.

" ' Well,' said I, ' don't believe me, if you don't like; but here have I been the whole evening listening to you, and if I've not bolted as much as that, my name's not Con O'Kelly.'

" But it is not necessary to tell you how, step by step, they led me to credit all they were saying, but actually to tell my own real story to them, which I did from beginning to end, down to the very moment I sat there, with a large glass of hot claret before me, as happy as might be.

" ' And you really are so low in purse?' said one.

" ' And have no prospect of any occupation, nor any idea of a livelihood?' cried another.

" ' Just as much as I expect promotion from my friend the Emperor of China,' said I.

" ' You speak French and German well enough though?'

" ' And a smattering of Italian,' said I.

" ' Come, you'll do admirably; be one of us.'

" 'Might I make bold enough to ask what trade that is?'"

" ' You don't know; you can't guess even?'

" ' Not even guess,' said I, ' except you report for " the papers," and come here to make up the news.'

" ' Something better than that, I hope,' said the man at the head of the table. ' What think you of a life that leads a man about the world from Norway to Jerusalem— that shows him every land the sun shines on, and every nation of the globe, travelling with every luxury that can make a journey easy, and a road pleasant; enables him to visit whatever is remarkable in every city of the universe; to hear Pasta at St. Petersburgh in the winter, and before the year's end to see an Indian war-dance among the red men of the Rocky Mountains; to sit beneath the shadow of the Pyramids, as it were to-day, and, ere two months be over, to stand in the spray of Trolhattan, and join a wolf-chase through the pine forests of the north; and not only this, but to have opportunities of seeing life, on terms the most intimate; that society should be unveiled to an extent that few men of any station can pretend to; to converse with the greatest, and the wisest, the most distinguished in rank, ay! and better than all, the most beautiful women of every land in Europe, who depend on your word, rely on your information, and permit a degree of intimacy, which in their own rank is unattainable; to improve your mind by knowledge of languages, acquaintance with works of art, scenery, and more still, by habits of intelligence which travelling bestows.'

" ' And to do this,' said I, burning with impatience at a picture that realized all I wished for, ' to do this——'

" ' Be a Courier,' said thirty voices in a cheer.   ' Vive la
Grande Route ! ' and with the word each man drained his
glass to the bottom.

" ' Vive la Grande Route ! ' exclaimed I, louder than the
rest ; ' and here I join you.'   From that hour I entered on
a career, that each day I follow is becoming dearer to me.
It is true, I sit in the rumble of the carriage, while ' *mon-
seigneur*,' or my lord, reclines within ; but would I exchange his ennui and depression for my own light-hearted-
ness and jollity ? would I give up the happy independence
of all the intrigue and plotting of the world I enjoy, for
all his rank and station ?   Does not Mont Blanc look as
grand in his hoary panoply to *me* as to *him* ? are not the
Danube and the Rhine as fair ?   If I wander through the
gallery of Dresden, have I not the sweet smile of the great
Raphael's Madonna bent on *me*, as blandly as it is on him ?
Is not mine host, with less of ceremony, far more cordial
to *me* than to *him* ?   Is not mine a rank known, and
acknowledged, in every town, in every village ?   Have I
not a greeting wherever I pass ?   Should sickness overtake
me, where have I not a home ?   Where am I among
strangers ?   Then, what care I for the bill—mine is a royal
route where I never pay ?   As, lastly, how often is the
soubrette of the rumble as agreeable a companion as the
pale and careworn lady within ?

" Such is my life.   Many would scoff and call it menial.
Let them, if they will.   I never *felt* it so : and once more
I say, ' Vive la Grande Route ! '

"But your friends of the Fischer's Haus ? "

"A jolly set of smugglers, with whom, for a month or
two in summer, I take a cruise, less for profit than pleasure.   The blue water is a necessary of life, to the man
that has been some years at sea.   My little collection has
been made in my wanderings ; and if ever you come to
Naples, you must visit a cottage I have at Castella Mare,
where you'll see something better worth your looking at.
And now, it does not seem very hospitable, but I must
say, adieu."   With these words Mr. O'Kelly opened a
drawer, and drew forth a blue jacket, lined with rich dark
fur, and slashed with black braiding ; a greyhound was
embroidered in gold twist on the arm, and a similar decora-

tion ornamented the front of his blue cloth cap. "I start for Genoa in half an hour—we'll meet again, and often, I hope."

"Good-bye," said I, "and a hundred thanks for a pleasant evening, and one of the strangest stories I ever heard. I half wish I were a younger man, and I think I'd mount the blue jacket too."

"It would show you some strange scenes," said Mr. O'Kelly, while he continued to equip himself for the road. "All I have told is little compared to what I might, were I only to give a few leaves of my life '*en Courier*,' but, as I said before, we'll live to meet again. Do you know who my party is this morning?"

"I can't guess."

"My old flame, Miss Blundell; she's married now, and has a daughter, so like what I remember herself once. Well, well, it's a strange world. Good-bye."

With that we shook hands for the last time, and parted; and I wandered back to Antwerp when the sun was rising, to get into a bed and sleep for the next eight hours.

CHAPTER VIII.

TABLE-TRAITS.

MORGAN O'DOGHERTY was wrong—and, sooth to say, he was not often so—when he pronounced a "Mess" to be "the perfection of dinner society" In the first place, there can be no perfection anywhere, or in anything, it is evident, where ladies are not. Secondly, a number of persons so purely professional, and therefore so very much alike in their habits, tone of thinking, and expression, can scarcely be expected to make up that complex amalgam so indispensable to pleasant society. Lastly, the very fact of meeting the same people each day, looking the very same way too, is a sad damper to that flow of spirits, which, for their free current, demand all the chances and vicissitudes of a fresh audience. In a word, in the one case, a man becomes like a Dutch canal, standing stagnant and slow between its trim banks; in the other, he is a bounding rivulet, careering pleasantly through grassy meadows and smiling fields, now, basking in the gay sunshine, now, lingering in the cool shade; at one moment, hurrying along between rocks and moss-grown pebbles, brawling, breaking, and foaming; at the next, expanding into some little lake, calm, and deep, and mirror-like.

It is the very chances and changes of conversation, its ups and downs, its lights and shadows—so like those of life itself—that make its great charm; and for this generally, a mixed party gives the only security. Now, a Mess has very little indeed of this requisite; on the contrary, its great stronghold is the fact, that it offers an easy tableland for all capacities. It has its little, dry, stale jokes, as flat and as dull as the orderly book; the regular quiz about "Jones's" whiskers, or "Tobin's horse;" the hackneyed stories about Simpson of "Ours." or Nokes of "Yours," of which the major is never tired, and the newly-joined sub. is enraptured. Bless their honest hearts, very little fun goes far in the army! like the regimental allowance of wine, it will never intoxicate, and no man is expected to call for a fresh supply.

I have dined at more messes than any red-coat of them all, at home and abroad, cavalry, artillery, and infantry —"horse, foot, and dragoons," as Grattan has it; in gala parties, with a general and his staff for guests; after sweltering field-days, where all the claret could not clear your throat of pipe-clay and contract powder; in the colonies, where flannel jackets were substituted for regulation coats; and land-crabs and pepper-pot for saddles and sirloins; in Connemara, Calcutta, or Corfu, it was all the same,—*cœlum non animum*——&c.

Not but that they had all their little peculiarities among themselves; so much so, indeed, that I offer a fifty, if you set me down blindfolded at any Mess in the service, to tell you what "corps" they belong to, before the cheese appears; before the bottle goes half round, I'll engage to distinguish the hussars from the heavies, and the fusileers from the light-bobs; and when the president is ringing for more claret, it will go hard with me, if I don't make a shrewd guess at the number of the regiment

The great charm of the Mess is to those young, ardent spirits, fresh from Sandhurst or Eton, sick of mathematics and bored with false quantities. To them the change is indeed a glorious one, and I'd ask nothing better than to be sixteen, and enjoy it all; but for the old stagers, it is slow work indeed. A man curls his whiskers at forty, with far less satisfaction than he surveys their growth and development at eighteen; he tightens his waist too, at that period, with a very different sense of enjoyment. His first trip to Jamaica is little more than a "lark;" his fourth or fifth, with a wife and four brats, is scarcely a party of pleasure; and all these things react on the Mess. Besides, it is against human nature itself to like the people who rival us; and who could enjoy the jokes of a man that stands between him and a majority? Yet, taking them all in all, the military cut up better than any other professionals. The doctors might be agreeable; they know a vast deal of life, and in a way too, that other people never see it; but meet them *en masse*, they are little better than body-snatchers; there is not a malady too dreadful, nor an operation too bloody, to tell you over your soup; every slice of the turkey suggests an amputation, and they sever a wing with the anatomical precision they would extirpate a thigh bone. Life to them has no interest except where it verges on death; and from habit and hardening, they forget that human suffering has any other phase than a source of wealth to the medical profession.

The lawyers are even worse. To listen to them, you would suppose that the highest order of intellect was a skill in chicanery; that trick and stratagem were the foremost walks of talent; that to browbeat a poor man, and to confound a simple one, were great triumphs of genius; and that the fairest gift of the human mind was that which enabled a man to feign every emotion of charity, benevolence, pity, anger, grief, and joy, for the sum of twenty pounds sterling, wrung from abject poverty, and briefed by an "honest attorney."

As to the parsons, I must acquit them honestly of any portion of this charge. It has been my fortune to "assist" at more than one visitation dinner, and I can safely aver, that never by any accident did the conversation become professional, nor did I hear a word of piety during the entertainment.

Country gentlemen are scarcely professional, however the similarity of their tastes and occupations might seem to warrant the classification—fox-hunting, grouse-shooting, game-preserving, road-jobbing, rent-extracting, land-tilling, being propensities in common. They are the slowest of all: and the odds are long, against any one keeping awake after the conversation has taken its steady turn, into "shorthorns," Swedish turnips, subsoiling, and southdowns.

Artists are occasionally well enough, if only for their vanity and self-conceit.

Authors are better still, for ditto and ditto.

Actors are most amusing from the innocent delusion they labour under, that all that goes on in life is unreal, except what takes place in Covent Garden or Drury Lane; in a word, professional cliques are usually detestable, the individuals who compose them being frequently admirable ingredients, but intolerable when unmixed, and society, like a "Macedoine," is never so good as when its details are a little incongruous.

For my own part, I know few things better than a *table d'hôte*—that pleasant reunion of all nations, from Stockholm to Stamboul; of every rank, from the grand-duke to the bag-man—men and women—or, if you like the phrase better, ladies and gentlemen; some, travelling for pleasure, some, for profit; some, on wedding tours; some, in the grief of widowhood; some, rattling along the road of life, in all the freshness of youth, health, and well-stored purses; others, creeping by the way-side, cautiously and quietly: sedate and sententious English, lively Italians, plodding Germans, witty Frenchmen, wily Russians, and stupid Belgians—all pell-mell, seated side by side, and actually shuffled into momentary intimacy by soup, fish, fowl, and *entremets*. The very fact that you are *en route*, gives a frankness and a freedom to all you say. Your passport is signed, your carriage packed; to-morrow you will be a hundred miles away. What matter, then, if the old baron with the white moustache has smiled at your German, or if the thin-faced lady in the Dunstable bonnet has frowned at your morality; you'll never, in all likelihood, meet either again. You do your best to be agreeable—it is the only distinction recognized, here are no places of honour—no favoured guests—each starts fair in the race, and a pleasant course I have always deemed it.

Now, let no one, while condemning the vulgarity of this taste of mine, for such I anticipate as the ready objection—though the dissentient should be a tailor from Bond-street, or a schoolmistress from Brighton—for a moment suppose, that I mean to include all *table d'hôtes* in this sweeping laudation—far, very far from it. I, Arthur O'Leary, have travelled some hundreds of thousands of miles in every quarter and region of the globe, and yet would have considerable difficulty in enumerating even six such as fairly to warrant the praise I have pronounced.

In the first place, the "*table d'hôte*," to possess all the requisites I desire, should not have its *locale* in any first-rate city, like Paris, London, or St. Petersburgh; no, it should rather be in Brussels, Dresden, Munich, Berne, or Florence. Again, it should not be in the great overgrown mammoth-hotel of the town, with three hundred daily devourers, and a steam-engine to slice the "bouilli." It should, and will usually, be found in some retired and quiet spot; frequently within a small court, with orange-trees round the walls, and a tiny modest *jet d'eau* in the middle, a glass-door entering from a flight of low steps into a neat antechamber, where an attentive, but unobtrusive waiter is ready to take your hat and cane, and, instinctively divining your dinner intentions, ushers you respectfully into the *salon*, and leans down your chair beside the place you select.

The few guests already arrived have the air of "habitués;" they are chatting together when you enter, but they conceive it necessary to do the honours of the place to the stranger, and at once include you in the conversation; a word or two suffices, and you see that they are not chance folk, whom hunger has overtaken at the door, but daily visitors, who know the house, and appreciate it. The table itself is far from large—at most sixteen persons could sit down at it; the usual number is about twelve or fourteen. There is, if it be summer, a delicious bouquet in the midst; and the snowy whiteness of the cloth, and the clear lustre of the water, strike you instantly. The covers are as bright as when they left the hands of the silversmith, and the temperature of the room at once shows that nothing has been neglected that can contribute to the comfort of the guests. The very plash of the fountain is a grateful sound, and the long necks of the hock-bottles, reposing in the little basin, have an air of luxury far from unpleasing; while the champagne indulges its more southern character in the ice-pails in the shade, a sweet, faint odour of pine-apples and nectarines is diffused about; nor am I disposed to quarrel with the chance view I catch between the orange-trees, of a window, where asparagus, game, oranges, and melons, are grouped confusedly together, yet with a harmony of colour and effect Schneider would have gloried in.

There is a noiseless activity about—a certain air of preparation—not such as by bustle can interfere with the placid enjoyment you feel, but something which denotes care and skill; you feel, in fact, that impatience on your part would only militate against your own interest, and that, when the moment arrives for serving, the "potage" has then received the last finishing touch of the artist. By this time, the company are assembled; the majority are men, but there are four or five ladies. They are *en chapeau* too; but it is a toilet that shows taste and elegance, and the freshness—that delightful characteristic of foreign dress—the freshness, of their light muslin dresses —is in keeping with all about. Then follows that little pleasant bustle of meeting; the interchange of a number of small courtesies, which cost little, but are very delightful; the news of the theatre for the night; some *soirée*, well known, or some promenade, form the whole— and we are at table.

The destiny that made me a traveller, has blessed me with either the contentment of the most simple, or the perfect enjoyment of the most cultivated "cuisine;" and if I have eaten *tripe de rocher* with Parry at the Pole, I have never lost thereby the acme of my relish for truffles at the "Frères;" therefore, trust me that in my mention of a *table d'hôte*, I have not forgotten the most essential of its features—for this, the smallness, and consequent selectness of the party, is always a guarantee. Thus, then, you are at table; your napkin is spread, but you see no soup; the reason is at once evident, and you accept with gratefulness the little plate of Ostend oysters, each somewhat smaller than a five-franc piece, that are before you. Who would seek for pearls without when such treasures are to be found within the shell—cool, and juicy, and succulent; suggestive of delights to come, and so suited to the limpid glass of Chablis. What preparatives for the "potage," which already I perceive to be a "printanière." But why dwell on all this? These memoranda of mine were intended rather to form an humble companion to some of John Murray's inestimable treatises on the road; some stray recollection of what in my rambles had struck me as worth mention, something that might

K

serve to lighten a half hour here or an evening there; some
hint for the wanderer, of a hotel, or a church, or a view, or
an actor, or a poet, a picture, or a *paté*, for which his halting-place is remarkable, but of whose existence he knew
not—and to come back once more, such a picture as I have
presented is but a weak and imperfect sketch of the " Hotel
de France " in Brussels, at least, of what I once remember
it   Poor Biennais, he was an artiste!   He commenced
his career under Chicaud, and rose to the dignity of
" rotisseur " under Napoleon.   With what enthusiasm he
used to speak of his successes during the empire, when
Bonaparte gave him *carte blanche* to compose a dinner for
a " party of kings."   Napoleon himself was but an inferior gastronome: with him, the great requisite was, to
serve anywhere, and at any moment; and though the bill
of fare was a modest one, it was sometimes a matter of
difficulty to prepare it in the depths of the Black Forest,
or on the sandy plains of Prussia, amid the mud-covered
fields of Poland, or the snows of Muscovy—a poulet, a
cutlet, and a cup of coffee was the whole affair; but it
should be ready as if by magic

Among his followers were several distinguished *gour-
mets*.   Cambacérès was well known; Murat also, and
Decrés, the minister of marine, kept admirable tables.   Of
these, Biennais spoke with ecstasy: he remembered their
various tastes, and would ever remark, when placing some
masterpiece of skill before you, how the King of Naples
loved, or the arch-chancellor praised it.   To him, the over-
throw of the empire was but the downfall of the " cuisine;"
and he saw nothing more affecting in the last days of
Fontainebleau, than that the Emperor had left untouched
a " fondue " he had always eaten of with delight.   " After
that," said Biennais, " I saw the game was up."   With
the Hundred Days, he was " restored," like his master,
but, alas, the empire of casserolles was departed; the
thunder of the cannon foundries, and the roar of the shot
furnaces, were more congenial sounds than the simmering
of sauces and the gentle murmur of a stew-pan   No
wonder, thought he, there should come a Waterloo, when
the spirit of the nation had thus degenerated.

Napoleon spent his last days in exile; Biennais took his

departure for Belgium ; the park was his Longwood; and, indeed, he himself saw invariable points of resemblance in the two destinies. Happily for those who frequented the Hotel de France, he did not occupy his remaining years in dictating his memoirs to some Las Casas of the kitchen, but persevered to the last in the practice of his great art, and died, so to speak, ladle in hand.

To me, the Hotel de France has many charms. I re-member it—I shall not say how many years; its cool, delightful *salon*, looking out upon that beautiful little park whose shady alleys are such a resource in the evenings of summer ; to sit beneath the lime trees and sip your coffee, as you watch the groups that pass and repass before you, weaving stories to yourself which become thicker and thicker as the shade deepens, and the flitting shapes are barely seen as they glide along the silent alleys ; a distant sound of music—some air of the Fatherland—is all that breaks the stillness, and you forget in the dreamy silence, that you are in the midst of a great city.

The " Hotel de France " has other memories than these, too ; I'm not sure that I shall not make a confession, yet somehow I half shrink from it. You might call it a love adventure, and I should not like that ; besides, there is scarcely a moral in it—though who knows ?

CHAPTER IX.

A DILEMMA.

IT was in the month of May—I won't confess to the year—that I found myself, after trying various hotels in the Place Royale, at last deposited at the door of the Hotel de France. It seemed to me, in my then ignorance, like a *pis aller*, when the postilion said, "Let us try 'The France,'" and little prepared me for the handsome, but somewhat small, hotel before me. It was nearly five o'clock when I arrived, and I had only time to make some slight change in my dress, when the bell sounded for *table d'hôte*.

The guests were already seated when I entered, but a place had been reserved for me, which completed the table. I was a young—perhaps after reading a little farther you'll say a "*very young*" traveller at the time, but was soon struck by the quiet and decorous style in which the dinner was conducted The servants were prompt, silent, and observant; the guests easy and affable; the equipage of the table was even elegant; and the cookery, Biennais'. I was the only Englishman present, the party being made up of Germans and French; but all spoke together like acquaintances, and before the dinner had proceeded far, were polite enough to include me in the conversation.

At the head, sat a large and strikingly handsome man, of about eight-and-thirty or forty years of age; his dress a dark frock, richly braided, and ornamented by the decorations of several foreign orders; his forehead was high and narrow, the temples strongly indented, his nose arched and thin, and his upper lip covered by a short black moustache raised at either extremity, and slightly curled, as we see occasionally in a Vandyk picture; indeed, his dark brown features, somewhat sad in their expression, his rich hazel eyes and long waving hair, gave him all the character that great artist loved to perpetuate on his canvas; he spoke seldom, but, when he did, there was something indescribably pleasing in the low, mellow tones of his voice ; a slight smile too lit up his features at these times, and his manner had in it—I know not what—some strange power it seemed, that made whoever he addressed feel pleased and flattered by his notice of them, just as we see a few words spoken by a sovereign caught up and dwelt upon by those around.

At his side sat a lady, of whom when I first came into the room I took little notice. Her features seemed pleasing, but no more ; but gradually, as I watched her, I was struck by the singular delicacy of traits that rarely make their impression at first sight. She was about twenty-five, perhaps twenty-six, but of a character of looks that preserves something almost childish in their beauty. She was pale, and with brown hair—that light sunny brown that varies in its hue with every degree of light upon it, her face oval and inclined to plumpness ; her eyes large, full, and lustrous, with an expression of softness and candour that won on you wonderfully the longer you looked at them ; her nose was short, perhaps faultily so, but beautifully chiselled, and fine as a Greek statue ; her mouth, rather large, displayed, however, two rows of teeth beautifully regular, and of snowy whiteness ; while her chin, rounded and dimpled, glided by an easy transition into a throat large and most gracefully formed Her figure, as well as I could judge, was below the middle size, and inclined to *embonpoint ,* and her dress, denoting some national peculiarity of which I was ignorant, was a velvet bodice laced in front and ornamented with small silver buttons, which terminated in a white muslin skirt ; a small cap, something like what Mary Queen of Scots is usually represented in, sat on the back of her head and fell in deep lace folds on her shoulders Lastly, her hands were small, white, and dimpled, and displayed on her taper and rounded fingers several rings of apparently great value

I have been somewhat lengthy in my description of these two persons, and can scarcely ask my reader to accompany me round the circle ; however, it is with them principally I have to do. The others at table were remarkable enough. There was a leading member of the Chamber of Deputies —an ex-minister, a tall, dark-browed, ill-favoured man,

with a retiring forehead and coal-black eyes; he was a
man of great cleverness, spoke eloquently and well, and
singularly open and frank in giving his opinion on the
politics of the time.   There was a German or two, from
the grand-duchy of something, somewhat proud, reserved
personages, as all the Germans of petty states are; they
talked little, and were evidently impressed with the power
they possessed of tantalizing the company by not divulg-
ing the intention of the "Gross Herzog of Hoch Donner-
stadt" regarding the present prospects of Europe.

There were three Frenchmen and two French ladies, all
pleasant, easy, and conversable people; there was a doctor
from Louvain, a shrewd intelligent man; a Prussian major
and his wife, well-bred, quiet people, and, like all Prussians,
polite without inviting acquaintance; an Austrian secretary of legation, a wine merchant from Bordeaux, and a
celebrated pianist completed the party.

I have now put my readers in possession of information
which I only obtained after some days myself; for, though
one or other of these personages was occasionally absent
from *table d'hôte*, I soon perceived that they were all frequenters of the house, and well known there.

If the guests were seated at table wherever chance or
accident might place them, I could perceive that a tone
of deference was always used to the tall man, who invariably maintained his place at the head; and an air of
even greater courtesy assumed towards the lady beside
him, who was his wife.   He was always addressed as
Monsieur le Comte, and her title of Countess was never
forgotten in speaking to her.   During dinner, whatever
little chit-chat or gossip was the talk of the day, was
specially offered up to her.

The younger guests occasionally ventured to present a
bouquet, and even the rugged minister himself, accomplished a more polite bow in accosting her, than he could
have summoned up for his presentation to royalty.   To
all these little attentions she returned a smile, or a look,
or a word, or a gesture with her white hand, never exciting jealousy by any undue degree of favour, and distributing her honours with the practised equanimity of
one accustomed to it.

Dinner over and coffee, a handsome britzka, drawn by two splendid dark bay horses, would drive up, and Madame la Comtesse, conducted to the carriage by her husband, would receive the homage of the whole party, as they stood to let her pass. The Count would then linger some twenty minutes or so, and take his leave, to wander for an hour about the park, and afterwards to the theatre, where I used to see him in a private box with his wife.

Such was the little party at "The France" when I took up my residence there in the month of May, and gradually one dropped off after another as the summer wore on. The Germans went back to "sauer kraut" and "kreutzer" whist; the secretary of legation was on leave; the wine merchant was off to St. Petersburgh, the pianist was in the bureau he once directed, and so on, leaving our party reduced to the count and madame, a stray traveller, a deaf abbé, and myself.

The dog-days in a continental city are, every one knows, stupid and tiresome enough. Every one has taken his departure either to his chateau, if he has one, or to the watering-places; the theatre has no attraction, even if the heat permitted one to visit it; the streets are empty, parched, and grass-grown; and except the arrival and departure of that incessant locomotive, John Bull, there is no bustle or stir anywhere.

Hapless, indeed, is the condition then of the man who is condemned from any accident to toil through this dreary season; to wander about in solitude the places he has seen filled by pleasant company, to behold the park and promenades given up to Flemish *bonnes* or Norman nurses, where he was wont to glad his eye with the sight of bright eyes and trim shapes, flitting past in all the tasty elegance of Parisian toilette, to see the lazy *frotteur* sleeping away his hours at the *porte-cochère*, which, a month before, thundered with the deep roll of equipage coming and going—all this is very sad, and disposes one to become dull and discontented too.

For what reason I was detained at Brussels it is unnecessary to inquire: some delay ↑in remittances, if I remember aright, had their share in the cause. Who ever travelled without having cursed his banker, or his agent, or his uncle, or his guardian, or somebody in short, who had a deal of money belonging to him in his hands, and would not send it forward? In all my long experience of travelling and travellers, I don't remember meeting with one person, who, if it were not for such mischances, would not have been amply supplied with cash. Some, with a knowing wink, throw the blame on the "Governor;" others, more openly indignant, confound Coutts and Drummond; a stray Irishman will now and then damn the "tenantry that haven't paid up the last November;" but none, no matter how much their condition bespeaks that out-o'-elbows habit which a "ways-and-means" style of life contracts, will ever confess to the fact that their expectations are as blank as their banker's book, and that the only land they are ever to pretend to, is a post-obit right in some six-feet-by-two in a church-yard. And yet the world is full of such people—well-informed, pleasant, good-looking folk, who inhabit first-rate hotels—drink, dine, and dress well; frequent theatres and promenades, spend their winters at Paris, Florence, or Rome; their summers at Baden, Ems, or Interlachen; have a strange half intimacy with men in the higher circles; occasionally dine with them; are never heard of in any dubious or unsafe affair; are reputed safe fellows to talk to; know every one—from the horse-dealer who will give credit to the Jew who will advance cash; and notwithstanding that they neither gamble, nor bet, nor speculate, yet contrive to live—ay, and well, too—without any known resources whatever. If English—and they are for the most part so—they usually are called by some well-known name of aristocratic reputation in England · they are thus, Villiers, or Paget, or Seymour, or Percy, which on the Continent is already a kind of half nobility at once; and the question which seemingly needs no reply— *Ah, vous êtes parent de mi lord!* is a receipt in full for rank anywhere.

These men—and who that knows anything of the Continent has not met such everywhere?—are the great riddles of our century; and I'd rather give a reward for their secret than all the discoveries about perpetual motion, or longitude, or North-west Passages, that ever were heard of; and strange it is, too, no one has ever blabbed. Some have emerged from this misty state to inherit large fortunes and live in the best style, yet I have never heard tell of a single man having turned king's evidence on his fellows. And yet what a talent theirs must be, let any man confess who has waited three posts for a remittance without any tidings of its arrival; think of the hundred and one petty annoyances and ironies to which he is subject he fancies that the very waiters know he is "*à sec;*" that the landlord looks sour, and the landlady austere, the very clerk in the post-office appears to say "No letter for you, sir," with a gibing and impertinent tone. From that moment, too, a dozen expensive tastes that he never dreamed of before, enter his head he wants to purchase a hack, or give a dinner party, or bet at a racecourse, principally because he has not got a sou in his pocket, and he is afraid it may be guessed by others; such is the fatal tendency to strive or pretend to something, which has no other value in our eyes than the effect it may have on our acquaintances, regardless of what sacrifices it may demand the exercise.

Forgive, I pray, this long digression, which although, I hope, not without its advantages, should scarcely have been entered into were it not *à propos* to myself: and to go back—I began to feel excessively uncomfortable at the delay of my money. My first care every morning was to repair to the post-office; sometimes 1 arrived before it was open, and had to promenade up and down the gloomy "Rue de l'Evecque" till the clock struck; sometimes the mail would be late—a foreign mail is generally late when the weather is peculiarly fine and the roads good—but always the same answer came—"*Rien pour vous, Monsieur O'Leary;*" and at last I imagined from the way the fellow spoke, that he had set the response to a tune, and sang it.

Béranger has celebrated in one of his very prettiest lyrics "How happy one is at twenty in a garret" I have no doubt, for my part, that the vicinity of the slates and the poverty of the apartment would have much contributed to my peace of mind at the time I speak of. The fact of

a magnificently furnished *salon*, a splendid dinner every
day, champagne and Seltzer promiscuously, cab fares and
theatre tickets innumerable, being all scored against me,
were sad dampers to my happiness! and from being one of
the cheeriest and most light-hearted of fellows, I sank into
a state of fidgety and restless impatience, the nearest thing
I ever remember to low spirits

Such was I one day when the post, which I had been
watching anxiously from mid-day, had not arrived at five
o'clock. Leaving word with the commissionaire, to wait
and report to me at the hotel, I turned back to the *table
d'hôte* By accident, the only guests were the count and
madame ; there they were, as accurately dressed as ever ;
so handsome and so happy-looking ; so attached, too, in
their manner towards each other—that nice balance
between affection and courtesy, which before the world is
so captivating Disturbed as were my thoughts, I could
not help feeling struck by their bright and pleasant looks.

"Ah, a family party!" said the count, gaily, as I
entered, while madame bestowed on me one of her very
sweetest smiles.

The restraint of strangers removed, they spoke as if
I had been an old friend—chatting away about everything
and everybody, in a tone of frank and easy confidence
perfectly delightful ; occasionally deigning to ask if I did
not agree with them in their opinions, and seeming to
enjoy the little I ventured to say, with a pleasure I felt to
be most flattering.

The count's quiet and refined manner—the easy flow
of his conversation, replete as it was with information
and amusement, formed a most happy contrast with the
brilliant sparkle of madame's lively sallies, for she seemed
rather disposed to indulge a vein of slight satire, but so
tempered with good feeling and kindliness withal, that
you would not for the world forego the pleasure it afforded.
Long—long before the dessert appeared, I ceased to think
of my letter or my money, and did not remember that
such things as bankers, agents, or stockbrokers were in
the universe Apparently they had been great travellers ;
had seen every city in Europe, and visited every court ;
knew all the most distinguished people, and many of the

sovereigns intimately; and little stories of Metternich, *bon mots* of Talleyrand, anecdotes of Goethe and Chateaubriand, seasoned the conversation with an interest, which, to a young man like myself, was all-engrossing. Suddenly the door opened, and the commissionaire called out—" No letter for Monsieur O'Leary." I suddenly became pale and faint; and though the count was too well bred to take any direct notice of what he saw was caused by my disappointment, he contrived adroitly to direct some observation to madame, which relieved me from any burden of the conversation.

" What hour did you order the carriage, Duischka ? " said he.

" At half-past six. The forest is so cool, that I like to go slowly through it."

" That will give us ample time for a walk, too," said he; " and if Monsieur O'Leary will join us, the pleasure will be all the greater."

I hesitated, and stammered out an apology about a headache, or something of the sort

" The drive will be the best thing in the world for you," said madame; " and the strawberries and cream of Boitsfort will complete the cure."

" Yes, yes," said the count, as I shook my head, halfsadly—" La comtesse is infallible as a doctor."

" And, like all the faculty, very angry when her skill is called in question," said she.

" Go then, and find your shawl, madame," said he, " and, meanwhile, monsieur and I will discuss our liqueur, and be ready for you."

Madame smiled gaily, as if having carried her point, and left the room.

The door was scarcely closed, when the count drew his chair closer to mine, and, with a look of kindliness and good nature I cannot convey, said, " I am going, Monsieur O'Leary, to take a liberty—a very great liberty indeed— with you, and perhaps you may not forgive it." He paused for a minute or two, as if waiting some intimation on my part. I merely muttered something intended to express my willingness to accept of what he hinted, and he resumed. " You are a very young man; I not a very

old, but a very experienced one. There are occasions in
life, in which such knowledge as I possess of the world
and its ways may be of great service. Now, without
for an instant obtruding myself on your confidence, or
inquiring into affairs which are strictly your own, I wish
to say, that my advice and counsel, if you need either,
are completely at your service. A few minutes ago I
perceived that you were distressed at hearing there was
no letter for you——"

"I know not how to thank you," said I, "for such
kindness as this; and the best proof of my sincerity is, to
tell you the position in which I am placed."

"One word, first," added he, laying his hand gently
on my arm—"one word. Do you promise to accept of
my advice and assistance when you have revealed the
circumstances you allude to? If not, I beg I may not
hear it."

"Your advice I am most anxious for," said I, hastily.

"The other was an awkward word and I see that your
delicacy has taken the alarm. But come, it is spoken
now, and can't be recalled. I must have my way; so
go on."

I seized his hand with enthusiasm, and shook it
heartily. "Yes," said I, "you shall have your way. I have
neither shame nor concealment before you." And then,
in as few words as I could explain such tangled and
knotted webs as envelope all matters where legacies, and
lawyers, and settlements, and securities, and mortgages
enter, I put him in possession of the fact, that I had come
abroad with the assurance from my man of business of a
handsome yearly income, to be increased, after a time, to
something very considerable; that I was now two months
in expectation of remittances, which certain forms in
Chancery had delayed and deferred; and that I watched
the post each day with an anxious heart for means to relieve me from certain trifling debts I had incurred, and
enable me to proceed on my journey.

The count listened with the most patient attention to
my story, only interfering once or twice, when some difficulty demanded explanation, and then suffering me to
proceed to the end ; when, leisurely withdrawing a pocket-

book from the breast of his frock, he opened it slowly. "My dear young friend," said he, in a measured and almost solemn tone, "every hour that a man is in debt, is a year spent in slavery. Your creditor is your master; it matters not whether a kind or a severe one, the sense of obligation you incur saps the feeling of manly independence which is the first charm of youth. and, believe me, it is always through the rents in moral feeling that our happiness oozes out quickest. Here are five thousand francs, take as much more as you want. With a friend —and I insist upon you believing me to be such—these things have no character of obligation · you accommodate me to-day; I do the same for you to-morrow. And now, put these notes in your pocket. I see madame is waiting for us."

For a second or two I felt so overpowered I could not speak. The generous confidence and friendly interest of one so thoroughly a stranger were too much for my astonished and gratified mind. At last I recovered myself enough to reply, and assuring my worthy friend that when I spoke of my debts they were in reality merely trifling ones, that I had still ample funds in my banker's hands for all necessary outlay, and that by the next post, perhaps, my long-wished-for letter might arrive.

"And if it should not?" interposed he, smiling.

"Why then the next day——"

"And if not then," continued he, with a half-quizzing look at my embarassment.

"Then your five thousand francs shall tremble for it."

"That's a hearty fellow!" cried he, grasping my hand in both of his. "And now I feel I was not deceived in you. My first meeting with Metternich was very like this. I was at Presburg in the year 1804, just before the campaign of Austerlitz opened——"

"You are indeed most gallant, messieurs," said the countess, opening the door, and peeping in. "Am I to suppose that cigars and maraschino are better company than mine?"

We rose at once to make our excuses; and thus I lost the story of Prince Metternich, in which I already felt an uncommon interest, from the similarity of the adventure

to my own, though whether I was to represent the prince
or the count I could not even guess.

I was soon seated beside the countess in the luxurious
britzka; the count took his place on the box, and away
we rattled over the stones through the Porte de Namur,
and along the pretty suburbs of Etterbech, where we left
the high road, and entered the Bois de Cambre by that
long and beautiful *allée* which runs on for miles, like some
vast aisle in a Gothic cathedral—the branches above
bending into an arched roof, and the tall beech stems
standing like the pillars.

The pleasant odour of the forest, the tempered light,
the noiseless roll of the carriage, gave a sense of luxury to
the drive I can remember vividly to this hour. Not that
my enjoyment of such was my only one; far from it. The
pretty countess talked away about everything that came
uppermost, in that strain of spirited and lively chit-chat
that needs not the sweetest voice and the most fascinating
look to make it most captivating. I felt like one in a
dream, the whole thing was fairy land; and whether I
looked into the depths of the leafy wood, where some
horsemen might now and then be seen to pass at a gallop,
or my eyes fell upon that small and faultless foot that
rested on the velvet cushion in the carriage, I could not
trust the reality of the scene, and could only mutter to
myself—"What hast thou ever done, Arthur O'Leary, or
thy father before thee, to deserve happiness like this?"

Dear and kind reader, it may be your fortune to visit
Brussels; and although not exactly under such circumstances as I have mentioned here, let me advise you, even
without a beautiful Polonaise for your companion, to make
a trip to Boitsfort, a small village in the wood of Soignies.
Of course your nationality will lead you to Waterloo; and
equally of course, if you have any tact—which far be it from
me not to suppose you gifted with—you'll not dine there,
the little miserable cabarets that are called " restaurants "
being wretched beyond description ; you may have a glass
of wine, and if so, take champagne, for they cannot adul-
terate it, but don't venture on a dinner, if you hope to
enjoy one again for a week after. Well then, " having
done your Waterloo," as the cockneys say, seen Sergeant

Cotton and the church, La Haye Sainte, Hougoumont, and Lord Anglesey's boot, take your road back, not by that eternal and noisy *chaussée* you have come by, but turn off to the right, as if going to Wavre, and enter the forest by an earth road, where you'll neither meet wagons, nor postilions, nor even a "'pike." Your coachman will say, "Where to?" Reply "Boitsfort,"—which, for safety, pronounce "Boshfort,"—and lie back and enjoy yourself. About six miles of a delightful drive, all through forest, will bring you to a small village beside a little lake, surrounded by hills, not mountains, but still waving and broken in outline, and shaded with wood. The red-tiled roofs, the pointed gables, the green *jalousies*, and the background of dark foliage, will all remind you of one of Berghem's pictures, and if a lazy Fleming or so are seen lounging over the little parapet next the water, they'll not injure the effect. Passing over the little bridge, you arrive in front of a long, low, two-storied house, perforated by an arched door-way leading into the court; over the door is an inscription, which at once denotes the object of the establishment, and you read—" *Monsieur Dubos fait noces et festins.*"* Not that the worthy individual officiates in any capacity resembling the famed Vulcan of the North; as far be it from him to invade the prerogative of others, as for any to rival him in his own peculiar walk. No; Monsieur D.'s functions are limited to those delicate devices which are deemed the suitable diet of newly-married couples—those *petits plats* which are, like the orange-flower, only to be employed on great occasions. And as such he is unrivalled; for notwithstanding the simple and unpretending exterior, this little rural tavern can boast the most perfect cook, and the best-stored cellar. Here may be found the earliest turkey of the year, with a dowry of truffles; here, the first peas of spring, the newest strawberries, and the richest cream, iced Champagne and grapy Hermitage, Steinberger and Johannisberg, are all at your orders. You may dine in the long *salon*, *en cabinet*, in the garden, or in the summer-house over the lake, where the carp is flapping his tail in the

* M. Dubos provides wedding breakfasts and other entertainments.

clear water, the twin-brother of him at table ; the garden beneath sends up its delicious odours from beds of every brilliant hue ; the sheep are moving homeward along the distant hills to the tinkle of the faint bell , the plash of an oar disturbs the calm water as the fisherman skims along the lake, and the subdued murmurs of the little village all come floating in the air—pleasant sounds, and full of home thoughts. Well, well ; to be sure 1 am a bachelor, and know nothing of such matters ; but it strikes me I should like to be married now and then, and go eat my wedding-dinners at Boitsfort!

And, now once more, let me come back to my narrative ; for leaving which I should ask your pardon, were it not that the digression is the best part of the whole, and I should never forgive myself if I had not told you not to stop at Brussels without dining at Boitsfort.

When we reached Boitsfort, a waiter conducted us at once to a little table in the garden where the strawberries and the iced champagne were in waiting. Here and there, at some distance, were parties of the Brussels bourgeoisie enjoying themselves at their coffee, or with ice ; while a large *salon* that occupied one wing of the building was given up to some English travellers, whose loud speech and boisterous merriment bespoke them of that class one is always ashamed to meet with out of England.

" Your countrymen are very merry yonder," said the countess, as a more uproarious burst than ever broke from the party.

" Yes," said the count, perceiving that I felt uncomfortable at the allusion : " Englishmen always carry London about with them wherever they go   Meet them in the Caucasus, and you'll find that they'll have some imitation of a Blackwall dinner, or a Greenwich party."

" How comes it," said I, amazed at the observation, " that you know these places you mention ? "

" Oh, my dear sir, I have been very much about the world in my time, and have always made it my business to see each people in their own peculiar haunts. If at Vienna, I dine not at the ' Wilde Man,' but at the ' Fuchs ' in the Leopoldstadt. If in Dresden, I spend my evening in the Grun-Garten, beyond the Elbe. The bourgeoisie alone, of any nation, preserved traits marked enough for a stranger's appreciation : the higher classes are pretty much alike everywhere, and the nationality of the peasant takes a narrow range, and offers little to amuse."

"And the count is a quick observer," remarked madame, with a look of pleasure sparkling in her eyes.

"I flatter myself," rejoined he, "I seldom err in my guesses—I knew my friend here tolerably accurately without an introduction."

There was something so kind in the tone he spoke in, I could have no doubt of his desire to compliment me.

"Independently, too, of speaking most of the languages of Europe, I possess a kind of knack for learning a patois," continued he. "At this instant, I'll wager a cigar with you, I'll join that little knot of sober Belgians yonder, and by the magic of a few words of genuine Brussels French, I'll pass muster as a Boss."

The countess laughed heartily at the thought, and I joined in her mirth most readily.

"I take the wager," cried I, "and hope sincerely to lose it."

"Done," said he, springing up and putting on his hat, while he made a short circuit in the garden, and soon afterwards appeared at the table with the Flemings, asking permission, as it seemed, to light a cigar from a lantern attached to the tree under which they sat.

If we were to judge from the merriment of the little group, his success was perfect, and we soon saw him seated amongst them, busily occupied in concocting a bowl of flaming "ponche," of which it was clear by his manner he had invited the party to partake.

"Now Gustav is in his delight," said the countess, in a tone of almost pique; "he is a strange creature, and never satisfied if not doing something other people never think of. In half an hour he'll be back here, with the whole history of Mynheer van Houdendrochen and his wife, and their fourteen 'mannikins;' all their little absurdities and prejudices he'll catch them up, and for a week to come we shall hear nothing but Flemish French, and the habitudes of the Montagne de la Cour."

For a few seconds I was vastly uncomfortable; a

L

thought glanced across me—what if it were for some absurd feature in me, in *my* manner, or *my* conversation, that he had deigned to make my acquaintance ? Then came the recollection of his generous proposal, and I saw at once that I was putting a somewhat high price on my originality, if I valued it at five thousand francs.

"What ails you ?" said the countess, in a low soft voice, as she lifted her eyes, and let them fall upon me with a most bewitching expression of interest. "I fear you are ill, or in low spirits."

I endeavoured to rally and reply, when she went on.

"We must see you oftener. Gustav is so pleasant and so gay, he will be of great use to you. When he really takes a liking, he is delightful , and he has in your case, I assure you."

I knew not what to say, nor how look my gratitude for such a speech, and could only accomplish some few and broken words of thanks.

"Besides, you are about to be a traveller," continued she ; "and who can give you such valuable information of every country and people as the count ? Do you intend to make a long absence from England ?"

"Yes, at least some years. I wish to visit the East."

"You'll go into Poland ?" said she, quickly, without noticing my reply.

"Yes, I trust so; Hungary and Poland have both great interest for me."

"You know that we are Poles, don't you ?"

"Yes."

"We are both from beyond Varsovie. Gustav was there ten years ago. I have never seen my native country since I was a child."

At the last words her voice dropped to a whisper, and she leaned her head upon her hand, and seemed lost in thought.

I did not dare break in upon the current of recollections I saw were crowding upon her, and was silent. She looked up at length, and by the faint light of the moon, just risen, I saw that her eyes were tearful, and her cheeks still wet with weeping.

What, said I to myself, and has sorrow come even here

—here, where I imagined if ever the sunny path of life existed, it was to be found?

"Should you like to hear a sad story?" said she, smiling faintly, with a look of indefinable sweetness

"If it were yours, it would make my heart ache," said I, carried away by my feelings at the instant.

"I'll tell it to you one of these days, then—not now—not now though—I could not here—and there comes Gustav—how he laughs!"

And true enough, the merry sounds of his voice were heard through the garden as he approached, and strangely too, they seemed to grate and jar upon my ear, with a very different impression from what before they brought to me.

Our way back to Brussels led again through the forest, which now was wrapped in the shade, save where the moon came peeping down through the leafy branches, and falling in bright patches on the road beneath. The countess spoke a little at first, but gradually relapsed into perfect silence. The stillness and calm about seemed only the more striking from the hollow tramp of the horses, as they moved along the even turf. The air was mild and sweet, and loaded with that peculiar fragrance which a wood exhales after nightfall; and all the influences of the time and place were of that soothing, lulling kind that wraps the mind in a state of dreamy reverie. But one thought dwelt within me. It was of her who sat beside me, her head cast down, and her arms folded. She was unhappy—some secret sorrow was preying upon that fair bosom—some eating care corroding her very heart. A vague, shadowy suspicion shot through me, that her husband might have treated her cruelly and ill; but why suspect such—was not everything I witnessed the very reverse of such a fact? What could surpass the mutual kindliness and good feeling that I saw between them! and yet their dispositions were not at all alike—she seemed to hint as much. The very waywardness of his temperament—the incessant demand of his spirit for change, excitement, and occupation—how could it harmonize with her gentle and more constant nature? From such thoughts I was awakened by her saying, in a low, faint voice—

"You must forget what I said to-night. There are moments when some strong impulse will force the heart to declare the long-buried thoughts of years—perhaps some secret instinct tells us that we are near to those who can sympathise and feel for us—perhaps these are the overflowings of grief, without which the heart would grow full to bursting. Whatever they be, they seem to calm and soothe us, though afterwards we may sorrow for having indulged in them. You will forget it all, won't you?"

"I will do my best," said I, timidly, "to do all you wish; but I cannot promise you what may be out of my power· the few words you spoke have never left my mind since—nor can I say when I shall cease to remember them."

"What do you think, Duischka?" said the count, as he flung away the fragment of his cigar, and turned round on the box. "What do you think of an invitation to dinner I have accepted for Tuesday next?"

"Where, pray?" said she, with an effort to seem interested.

"I am to dine with my worthy friend Van Houdicamp, Rue de Lacken, number twenty-eight—a very high mark, let me tell you—his father was burgomaster at Alost, and he himself has a great sugar bakery, or salt 'raffinerie,' or something equivalent, at Scharbeck."

"How can you find any pleasure in such society, Gustav?"

"Pleasure you call it—delight is the word. I shall hear all the gossip of the Basse Ville—quite as amusing, I'm certain, as of the Place and the Boulevards; besides, there are to be some half-dozen Echevins, with wives and daughters, and we shall have a round game for the most patriarchal stakes. I have also obtained permission to bring a friend—so you see, Monsieur O'Leary——"

"I'm certain," interposed madame, "he has much better taste than to avail himself of your offer."

"I'll bet my life on it he'll not refuse."

"I say he will," said the lady.

"I'll wager that pearl ring at Mertan's, that if you leave him to himself, he says 'yes.'"

"Agreed," said madame—" I accept the bet. We Poles are as great gamblers as yourselves, you see," added she, turning to me. "Now, Monsieur, decide the question —will you dine with Van Hottentot on Tuesday next—— or, with *me ?* "

The last three words were spoken in so low a tone as made me actually suspect that my imagination alone had conceived them.

" Well," cried the count, " what say you ? "

" I pronounce for the —— Hotel de France," said I, fearing in what words to accept the invitation of the lady.

" Then I have lost my bet," said the count, laughing; " and worse still, have found myself mistaken in my opinion."

" And I," said madame, in a faint whisper, " have won mine, and found my impressions more correct."

Nothing more occurred worth mentioning on our way back ; when we reached the hotel in safety, and separated with many promises to meet early next day.

From that hour my intimacy took a form of almost friendship. I visited the count, or the countess, if he was out, every morning ; chatted over the news of the day ; made our plans for the evening, either for Boitsfort or Lacken, or occasionally the *allée verte*, or the theatre, and sometimes arranged little excursions to Antwerp, Louvain, or Ghent.

It is indeed a strange thing, to think of what slight materials happiness is made up. The nest that incloses our greatest pleasure is a thing of straws and feathers, gathered at random or carried towards us by the winds of fortune. If you were to ask me now, what I deemed the most delightful period of my whole life, I don't hesitate to say I should name this. In the first place, the great requisite of happiness I possessed—every moment of my whole day was occupied; each hour was chained to its fellow by some slight but invisible link; and whether I was hammering away at my Polish grammar, or sitting beside the pianoforte while the countess sang some of her country's ballads, or listening to legends of Poland in its times of greatness, or galloping along at her side through

the forest of Soignies, my mind was ever full—no sense
of weariness or *ennui* ever invaded me ; while a consciousness of a change in myself—I knew not what it was
—suggested a feeling of pleasure and delight I cannot
account for or convey ; and this, I take it—though
speaking in ignorance and merely from surmise—this, I
suspect, is something like what people in love experience,
and what gives them the ecstasy of the passion.   There is
sufficient concentration in the admiration of the loved
object to give the mind a decided and firm purpose, and
enough of change in the various devices to win her praise,
to impart the charm of novelty.   Now for all this, my
reader, fair or false as she or he may be, must not suspect
that anything bordering on love was concerned in the
present case.

To begin—the countess was married, and I was brought
up at an excellent school at Bangor, where the catechism,
Welsh and English, was flogged into me until every com-
mandment had a separate welt of its own on my back.
No ; I had taken the royal road to happiness ; I was
delighted without stopping to know why, and enjoyed
myself without ever thinking to inquire wherefore.   New
sources of information and knowledge were opened to me
by those who possessed vast stores of acquirement, and I
learned how the conversation of gifted and accomplished
persons may be made a great agent in training and
forming the mind, if not to the higher walks of knowledge, at least to those paths in which the greater part of
life is spent, and where it imports each to make the road
agreeable to his fellows.   I have said to you I was not
in love—how could I be, under the circumstances ?—but
still I own that the regular verbs of the Polish grammar
had been but dry work, if it had not been for certain
irregular glances at my pretty mistress ; nor could I ever
have seen my way through the difficulties of the declen-
sions if the light of her eyes had not lit up the page, and
her taper finger pointed out the place.

And thus two months flew past, during which she never
even alluded most distantly to our conversation in the
garden at Boitsfort, nor did I learn any one particular
more of my friends than on the first day of our meeting.

Meanwhile, all ideas of travelling had completely left me; and although I had now abundant resources in my banker's hands for all the purposes of the road, I never once dreamed of leaving a place where I felt so thoroughly happy.

Such, then, was our life, when I began to remark a slight change in the count's manner—an appearance of gloom and pre-occupation which seemed to increase each day, and against which he strove, but in vain, to combat. It was clear something had gone wrong with him, but I did not dare to allude to, much less ask him on the subject. At last, one evening, just as I was preparing for bed, he entered my dressing-room, and closing the door cautiously behind him, sat down. I saw that he was dressed as if for the road, and looking paler and more agitated than usual.

"O'Leary," said he, in a tremulous voice, "I am come to place in your hands the highest trust a man can repose in another—am I certain of your friendship?" I shook his hand in silence, and he went on. "I must leave Brussels to-night secretly. A political affair, in which the peace of Europe is involved, has just come to my knowledge; the government here will do their best to detain me; orders are already given to delay me at the frontier—perhaps send me back to the capital, in consequence, I must cross the boundary on horse back, and reach Aix-la-Chapelle by to-morrow evening. Of course, the countess cannot accompany me." He paused for a second. "You must be her protector. A hundred rumours will be afloat the moment they find I have escaped, and as many reasons for my departure announced in the papers. However, I'm content if they amuse the public and occupy the police, and meanwhile I shall obtain time to pass through Prussia unmolested. Before I reach St. Petersburgh, the countess will receive letters from me, and know where to proceed to; and I count on your friendship to remain here until that time—a fortnight, three weeks at farthest. If money is any object to you——"

"Not in the least; I have far more than I want."

"Well, then, may I conclude that you consent?"

"Of course, you may," said I, overpowered by a rush

of sensations I must leave to my reader to feel, if it has
ever been his lot to have been placed in such circumstances, or to imagine for me if he has not.

"The countess is, of course, aware——"

"Of everything," interrupted he, "and bears it all
admirably. Much, however, is attributable to the arrangement with you, which I promised her was completed,
even before I asked your consent—such was my confidence in your friendship."

"You have not deceived yourself," was my reply, while
I puzzled my brain to think how I could repay such
proofs of his trust. "Is there anything, then, more," said
I—"can you think of nothing in which I may be of
service?"

"Nothing, dear friend, nothing," said he. "Probably we
shall meet at St. Petersburgh."

"Yes, yes," said I; "that is my firm intention."

"That's all I could wish for," rejoined he. "The
grand-duke will be delighted to acknowledge the assistance your friendship has rendered us, and Potoski's house
will be your own." So saying, he embraced me most
affectionately, and departed, while I sat to muse over the
singularity of my position, and wonder if any other man
was ever similarly situated.

When I proceeded to pay my respects to the countess
the next morning, I prepared myself to witness a state of
great sorrow and depression. How pleasantly was I disappointed at finding her gay—perhaps gayer than ever—
and evidently enjoying the success of the count's scheme!

"Gustav is at St. Tron by this," said she, looking at the
map; "he'll reach Liège two hours before the post; fresh
horses will then bring him rapidly to Battiste. Oh, here
are the papers. Let us see the way his departure is
announced." She turned over one journal after another
without finding the wished-for paragraph, until at last,
in the corner of the "Handelsblad," she came upon the
following:—

"Yesterday morning an express reached the minister
for the home affairs, that the celebrated *escroc*, the Chevalier Duguet, whose famous forgery on the Neapolitan
bank may be in the memory of our readers, was actually

practising his art under a feigned name in Brussels, where, having obtained his *entrée* among some respectable families of the lower town, he has succeeded in obtaining large sums of money under various pretences; his skill at play is, they say, the least of his many accomplishments."

She threw down the paper in a fit of laughter at these words, and called out—"Is it not too absurd? That's Gustav's doing—anything for a quiz—no matter what. He once got himself and Prince Carl of Prussia brought up before the police for hooting the king."

"But Duguet," said I,—"what has he to do with Duguet?"

"Don't you see that's a feigned name," replied she,— "assumed by him as if he had half a dozen such? Read on, and you'll learn it all"

I took the paper, and continued where she ceased reading:—

"This Duguet is then, it would appear, identical with a very well-known Polish Count Czaroviski, who, with his lady, had been passing some weeks at the Hotel de France. The police have, however, received his '*signalement*,' and are on his track."

"But why, in Heaven's name, should he spread such an odious calumny on himself?" said I.

"Dear me, how very simple you are! I thought he had told you all. As a mere '*escroc*,' money will always bribe the authorities to let him pass; as a political offender, and as such the importance of his mission would proclaim him, nothing would induce the officials to further his escape— their own heads would pay for it. Once over the frontier, the '*ruse*' will be discovered, the editors obliged to eat their words and be laughed at, and Gustav receive the Black Eagle for his services. But see, here's another."

"Among the victims at play of the well-known Chevalier Duguet, or, as he is better known here, the Count Czaroviski, is a simple Englishman, resident at the Hotel de France, and from whom it seems he has won every louis-d'or he possessed in the world. This miserable dupe, whose name is O'Learie, or O'Leary——"

At these words she leaned back on the sofa, and laughed immoderately.

"Have you, then, suffered so deeply ?" said she, wiping her eyes—"has Gustav really won all your louis-d'ors ? "

"This is too bad—far too bad," said I, "and I really cannot comprehend how any intrigue could induce him so far to asperse his character in this manner; I, for my part, can be no party to it."

As I said this, my eyes fell on the latter part of the paragraph, which ran thus —

"This poor boy—for we understand he is no more—has been lured to his ruin by the beauty and attraction of Madame Czaroviski."

I crushed the odious paper without venturing to see more, and tore it in a thousand pieces, and, not waiting an instant, hurried to my room and seized a pen; burning with indignation and rage, I wrote a short note to the editor, in which I not only contradicted the assertions of his correspondent, but offered a reward of a hundred louis for the name of the person who had invented the infamous calumny

It was some time before I recovered my composure sufficiently to return to the countess, whom I now found greatly excited and alarmed at my sudden departure She insisted with such eagerness on knowing what I had done, that I was obliged to confess everything, and show her a copy of the letter I had already despatched to the editor. She grew pale as death as she read it, flushed deeply, and then became pale again, while she sank faint and sick into a chair.

" This is very noble conduct of yours," said she, in a low hollow voice ; " but I see where it will lead to—Czaroviski has great and powerful enemies ; they will become yours also."

" Be it so," said I, interrupting her. " They have little power to injure me—let them do their worst."

"You forget, apparently," said she, with a most bewitching smile, " that you are no longer free to dispose of your liberty—that, as *my* protector, you cannot brave dangers and difficulties which may terminate in a prison."

" What, then, would you have me do ? "

" Hasten to the editor at once ; erase so much of your letter as refers to the proposed reward ; the information could be of no service to you if obtained—some 'miserable,' perhaps some spy of the police, the slanderer What could you gain by his punishment, save publicity? A mere denial of the facts alleged is quite sufficient; and even that," continued she, smiling, "how superfluous is it after all! a week—ten days at farthest, and the whole mystery is unveiled. Not that I would dissuade you from a course I see your heart is bent upon, and which, after all, is a purely personal consideration."

"Yes," said I, after a pause, "I'll take your advice; the letter shall be inserted without the concluding paragraph."

The calumnious reports on the count prevented madame dining that day at the *table-d'hôte ;* and I remarked, as I took my place at table, a certain air of constraint and reserve among the guests, as though my presence had interdicted the discussion of a topic which occupied all Brussels Dinner over, I walked into the park to meditate on the course I should pursue under present circumstances, and deliberate with myself how far the habits of my former intimacy might or might not be admissible, during her husband's absence. The question was solved for me sooner than I anticipated, for a waiter overtook me with a short note, written with a pencil; it ran thus —

"They play the Zauberflötte to-night at the Opera; I shall go at eight—perhaps you would like a seat in the carriage.

"DUISCHKA."

Whatever doubts I might have conceived about my conduct, the manner of the countess at once dispelled them. A tone of perfect ease, and almost sisterly confidence, marked her whole bearing; and while I felt delighted and fascinated by the freedom of our intercourse, I could not help thinking how impossible such a line of acting would have been in my own more rigid country, and to what cruel calumnies and aspersions it would have subjected her. Truly, thought I, if they manage these things—as Sterne says they do—" better in France," they also far excel in them in Poland; and so my Polish grammar, and the canzonettes, and the drives to Boitsfort, all went on as usual, and my dream of happiness, interrupted for a moment, flowed on again in its former channel with increased force.

A fortnight had now elapsed without any letter from the count, save a few hurried lines written from Magdeburg; and I remarked that the countess betrayed at times a degree of anxiety and agitation I had not observed in her before. At last the secret cause came out. We were sitting together in the park, eating ice after dinner, when she suddenly rose, and prepared to leave the place.

"Has anything happened to annoy you?" said I, hurriedly. "Why are you going?"

"I can bear it no longer!" cried she, as she drew her veil down and hastened forward, and, without speaking another word, continued her way towards the hotel. On reaching her apartments, she burst into a torrent of tears, and sobbed most violently.

"What is it?" said I, maddened by the sight of such sorrow. "For Heaven's sake tell me. Has any one dared——"

"No, no," replied she, wiping the tears away with her handkerchief; "nothing of the kind. It is the state of doubt—of trying, harassing uncertainty I am reduced to here, is breaking my heart. Don't you see that, whenever I appear in public, by the air of insufferable impudence of the men, and the still more insulting looks of the women, how they dare to think of me? I have borne it as well as I was able hitherto, I can do so no longer."

"What!" cried I, impetuously, "and shall one dare to——"

"The world will always dare what may be dared in safety," interrupted she, laying her hand on my arm. "They know that you could not make a quarrel on my account without compromising my honour; and such an occasion to trample on a poor weak woman could not be lost. Well, well, Gustav may write to-morrow or next day. A little more patience; and it is the only cure for these evils."

There was a tone of angelic sweetness in her voice as she spoke these words of resignation, and never did she seem more lovely in my eyes.

"Now, then, as I shall not go to the opera, what shall we do to pass the time? You are tired—I know you are —of Polish melodies and German ballads. Well, well, then I am. I have told you that we Poles are as great gamblers as yourselves. What say you to a game at picquet?"

"By all means," said I, delighted at the prospect of anything to while away the hours of her sorrowing.

"Then you must teach me," rejoined she, laughing, "for I don't know it. I'm wretchedly stupid about all these things, and never could learn any game but *écarté*."

"Then *écarté* be it," said I; and in a few minutes more I had arranged the little table, and down we sat to our party.

"There," said she, laughing, and throwing her purse on the table, "I can only afford to lose so much; but you may win all that, if you're fortunate." A rouleau of louis escaped at the instant, and fell about the table.

"Agreed," said I, indulging the quiz. "I am an inveterate gambler, and play always high. What shall be our stakes?"

"Fifty, I suppose," said she, still laughing: "we can increase our bets afterwards."

After some little *badinage*, we each placed a double louis-d'or on the board, and began. For a while the game employed our attention; but gradually we fell into conversation, the cards gradually dropped listlessly from our hands, the tricks remained unclaimed, and we could never decide whose turn it was to deal.

"This wearies you, I see," said she; "perhaps you'd like to stop?"

"By no means," said I. "I like the game, of all things." This I said rather because I was a considerable winner at the time, than from any other motive; and so we played on till eleven o'clock, at which hour I usually took my leave; and by this time my gains had increased to some seventy louis.

"Is it not fortunate," said she, laughing, "that eleven

has struck? You'd certainly have won all my gold; and now you must leave off in the midst of your good fortune: and so, *bon soir, et à revanche.*"

Each evening now saw our little party at *écarté* usurp the place of the drive and the opera, and though our successes ran occasionally high at either side, yet, on the whole, neither was a winner, and we jested about the impartiality with which fortune treated us both.

At last, one evening, eleven struck when I was a greater winner than ever, and I thought I saw a little pique in her manner at the enormous run of luck I had experienced throughout.

" Come," said she, laughing, "you have really wounded a national feeling in a Polish heart—you have asserted a superiority at a game of skill   I must beat you," and with that she placed five louis on the table. She lost. Again the same stake followed, and again the same fortune—notwithstanding that I did all in my power to avoid winning—of course without exciting her suspicions.

"And so," said she, as she dealt the cards, " Ireland is really so picturesque as you say?"

" Beautifully so," replied I, as, warmed up by a favourite topic, I launched forth into a description of the mountain scenery of the south and west. the rich emerald green of the valleys, the wild fantastic character of the mountains, the changeful skies, were all brought up to make a picture for her admiration; and she did indeed seem to enjoy it with the highest zest, only interrupting me in my harangue by the words, " *Je marque le Roi,*" to which circumstance she directed my attention by a sweet smile, and a gesture of her taper finger. And thus hour followed hour; and already the grey dawn was breaking, while I was just beginning an eloquent description of " The Killeries," and the countess suddenly looking at her watch, cried out,—

"How very dreadful! only think of three o'clock!"

True enough, it was that hour. and I started up to say " Good-night," shocked at myself for so far transgressing, and yet secretly flattered that my conversational powers had made time slip by uncounted.

" And the Irish are really so clever—so gifted as you

say?", said she, as she held out her hand to wish me good-night.

"The most astonishing quickness is theirs," replied I, half-reluctant to depart: "nothing can equal their intelligence and shrewdness."

"How charming! *Bon soir*," said she, and I closed the door.

What dreams were mine that night! What delightful visions of lake scenery and Polish countesses,—and mountain gorges and blue eyes,—of deep ravines and lovely forms! I thought we were sailing up Lough Corrib; the moon was up, spangling and flecking the rippling lake; the night was still and calm, not a sound save the cuckoo was heard breaking the silence; as I listened I started, for I thought, instead of her wonted note, her cry was ever, "*Je marque le Roi.*"

Morning came at last, but I could not awake, and endeavoured to sink back into the pleasant realm of dreams, from which daylight disturbed me. It was noon when at length I succeeded in awaking perfectly

"A note for monsieur," said a waiter, as he stood beside the bed.

I took it eagerly. It was from the countess: its contents were these·—

"My dear Sir,—A hasty summons from Count Czaroviski has compelled me to leave Brussels without wishing you good-bye, and thanking you for all your polite attentions. Pray accept these hurried acknowledgments, and my regret that circumstances do not enable me to visit Ireland, in which, from your description, I must ever feel the deepest interest.

"The count sends his most affectionate greetings.

"Yours ever sincerely,

"Duischka Czaroviski née Gutzlaff."

"And is she gone?" said I, starting up in a state of frenzy.

"Yes, sir; she started at ten o'clock."

"By what road?" cried I, determined to follow her on the instant.

" Louvain was the first stage."

In an instant I was up, and dressed; in ten minutes more I was rattling over the stones to my banker's.

" I want three hundred Napoleons—at once," said I to the clerk

" Examine Mr. O'Leary's account," was the dry reply of the functionary.

" Overdrawn by fifteen hundred francs," said the other

" Overdrawn? impossible!" cried I, thunderstruck. " I had a credit for six hundred pounds."

"Which you drew out by cheque this morning," said the clerk. " Is not that your handwriting?"

" It is," said I faintly, as I recognized my own scrawl, dated the evening before.

I had lost above seven hundred, and had not a sou left to pay post-horses.

I sauntered back sadly to " The France," a sadder man than ever in my life before; a thousand tormenting thoughts were in my brain, and a feeling of contempt for myself, somehow, occupied a very prominent place. Well, well; it's all past and gone now, and I must not awaken buried griefs.

I never saw the count and countess again; and though I have since that been in St. Petersburg, the " Grand-Duke " seems to have forgotten my services, and a very pompous-looking porter in a bear-skin did not look exactly the kind of person to whom I should wish to communicate my impression about " Count Potoski's house being my own."

CHAPTER X.

FOREST LIFE.

SOON after my Polish adventure—I scarcely like to be more particular in my designation of it—I received a small remittance from England, and started for Namur. My uncle Toby's recollections had been an inducement for

the journey, had I not the more pleasant one in my wish
to see the Meuse, of whose scenery I had already heard
so much.

The season was a delightful one—the beginning of
autumn; and truly the country far surpassed all my anti-
cipations. The road to Dinant led along by the river—
the clear stream rippling at one side; at the other, the
massive granite rocks, rising to several hundred feet,
frowned above you; some gnarled oak or hardy ash, clinging to the steep cliffs, and hanging their drooping leaves
above your head; on the opposite bank, meadows of
emerald green, intersected with ash rows and tall poplars,
stretched away to the background of dense forest that
bounded the view to the very horizon.

Here and there a little farm-house framed in wood, and
painted in many a gaudy colour, would peep from the
little inclosure of vines and plum-trees, more rarely still,
the pointed roof and turreted gable of a venerable château
would rise above the trees. How often did I stop to gaze
on these quaint old edifices, with their balustrades and
terraces—on which a solitary peacock walked proudly to
and fro : the only sound that stirred, the hissing plash of
the *jet d'eau*, whose sparkling drops came pattering on the
broad water lilies; and as I looked, I wondered within
myself what kind of life they led who dwelt there The
windows were open to the ground, bouquets of rich flowers
stood on the little tables. These were all signs of habitation, yet no one moved about—no stir nor bustle denoted
that there were dwellers there. How different from the
country life of our great houses in England, with trains
of servants and equipages hurrying hither and thither;
all the wealth and magnificence of the great capital trans-
ported to some far-off county—that ennui and fastidious-
ness, fatigue and lassitude, should lose none of their
habitual aids. Well, for *my* part, the life among green
trees and flowers, where the thrush sings, and the bee goes
humming by, can scarcely be too homely for *my* taste It
is in the peaceful aspect of all Nature, the sense of calm
that breathes from every leafy grove and rippling stream,
that I feel the soothing influence of the country. I could
sit beside the trickling stream of water, clear, but brown,

M

that comes drop by drop from some fissure in the rocky cliff, and falls into the little well below, and dream away for hours. These slight and simple sounds, that break the silence of the calm air, are all fraught with pleasant thoughts. The unbroken stillness of a prairie is the most awful thing in all Nature.

Unoppressed in heart, I took my way along the river's bank, my mind revolving the quiet, pleasant thoughts silence and lovely scenery are so sure to suggest. Towards noon I sat myself down on a large flat rock beside the stream, and proceeded to make my humble breakfast— some bread and a few cresses, washed down with a little water, scarce flavoured with brandy, followed by my pipe; and I lay watching the white bubbles that flowed by me, until I began to fancy I could read a moral lesson in their course. Here was a great swollen fellow, rotund and full, elbowing out of his way all his lesser brethren, jostling and pushing aside each he met with; but at last bursting from very plethora, and disappearing as though he had never been · there were a myriad of little bead-like specks, floating past noiselessly, and yet having their own goal and destination some uniting with others, grew stronger and hardier, and braved the current with bolder fortune; while others vanished ere you could see them well. A low murmuring plash against the reeds beneath the rock drew my attention to the place, and I perceived that a little boat, like a canoe, was fastened by a hay-rope to the bank, and surged with each motion of the stream against the weeds. I looked about to see the owner, but no one could I detect—not a living thing seemed near, nor even a habitation of any kind. The sun at that moment shone strongly out, lighting up all the rich landscape on the opposite side of the river, and throwing long gleams into a dense beech wood, where a dark, grass-grown alley entered. Suddenly, the desire seized me to enter the forest by that shady path. I strapped on my knapsack at once, and stepped into the little boat. There was neither oar nor paddle, but as the river was shallow, my long staff served as a pole to drive her across, and I reached the shore safely. Fastening the craft securely to a branch, I set forward towards the wood. As I

approached, a little board, nailed to a tree, drew my eye
towards it, and I read the nearly-effaced inscription,
"*Route des Ardennes*." What a thrill did not these words
send through my heart: and was this, indeed, the forest
of which Shakespeare told us—was I really "under the
greenwood tree," where fair Rosalind had rested, and
where melancholy Jaques had mused and mourned? and
as I walked along, how instinct with his spirit did each
spot appear. There was the oak,

> "Whose antique root peeps out
> Upon the brook that brawls along the wood."

A little farther on I came upon

> "The bank of osiers by the murmuring stream."

What a bright prerogative has genius, that thus can
people space with images which time and years erase not;
making to the solitary traveller a world of bright thoughts
even in the darkness of a lonely wood! And so to me
appeared, as though before me, the scenes he pictured.
Each rustling breeze that shook the leafy shade, seemed
like impetuous passion of the devoted lover—the chirping
notes of the wood-pigeon, like the flippant raillery of
beauteous Rosalind—and in the low ripple of the brook I
heard the complaining sounds of Jaques himself.

Sunk in such pleasant fancies I lay, beneath a spreading
sycamore ; and with half-closed lids invoked the shades of
that delightful vision before me, when the tramp of feet,
moving across the low brushwood, suddenly aroused me.
I started up on one knee, and listened. The next moment
three men emerged from the wood into the path ; the two
foremost, dressed in blouses, were armed with carbines
and a sabre ; the last carried a huge sack on his shoulders,
and seemed to move with considerable difficulty.

" *Ventre du diable*," cried he passionately, as he placed his
burden on the ground ; " don't hasten on this way—they'll
never follow us so far, and I am half dead with fatigue."

" Come, come, Gros Jean," said one of the others, in a
voice of command ; " we must not halt before we reach
the three elms."

" Why not bury it here ? " replied the first speaker, " or
else take your share of the labour ? "

M 2

"So I would," retorted the other, violently, "if *you* could take *my* place when we are attacked ; but, *parbleu*, you are more given to running away than fighting."

During this brief colloquy my heart rose to my mouth. The ruffianly looks of the party, their arms, their savage demeanour, and their secret purpose, whatever it was, to which I was now to a certain extent privy, filled me with terror; and I made an effort to draw myself back on my hands into the brushwood beneath the tree. The motion unfortunately discovered me, and with a spring, the two armed fellows bounded towards me, and levelled their pistols at my head.

"Who are you? What brings you here?" shouted they both in a breath

"For heaven's sake! Messieurs," said I, "down with your pistols. I am only a traveller—a poor inoffensive wanderer—an Englishman, an Irishman, rather—a good Catholic"—Heaven forgive me if I meant an equivocation here—"lower the pistols, I beseech you."

"Shoot him through the skull, he's a spy," roared the fellow with the sack.

"Not a bit of it," said I; "I'm a mere traveller, admiring the country, and an——"

"And why have you tracked us out here?" said one of the first speakers.

"I did not; I was here before you came. Do put down the pistols, for the love of Mary; there's no guarding against accidents, even with the most cautious."

"Blow his brains out," reiterated he of the bag, louder than before

"Don't, Messieurs—don't mind *him;* he's a coward—you are brave men, and have nothing to fear from a poor devil like me."

The two armed fellows laughed heartily at this speech, while the other, throwing the sack from him, rushed at me with clenched hands.

"Hold off, Gros Jean," said one of his companions; "if he never tells a heavier lie than that, he may make an easy confession on Sunday;" and with that he pushed him rudely back, and stood between us. "Come, then," cried he, "take up that sack and follow us."

My blood curdled at the order; there was something fearful in the very look of the long bag as it lay on the ground. I thought I could actually trace the outline of a human figure. Heaven preserve me, I believed I saw it move

"Take it up," cried he, sternly, "there's no fear of its biting you."

"Ah," said I to myself, "the poor fellow is dead, then."

Without more ado they placed the bag on my shoulders, and ordered me to move forward.

I grew pale and sick, and tottered at each step

"Is it the smell affects you?" said one, with a demoniac sneer.

"Pardon, Messieurs," said I, endeavouring to pluck up courage, and seem at ease; "I never carried a——a thing like this before"

'Step out briskly," cried he; "you've a long way before you;" and with that he moved to the front, while the others brought up the rear.

As we proceeded on our way, they informed me that if by any accident they should be overtaken by any of my friends or associates, meaning thereby any of the human race that should chance to walk that way, the first thing they would do would be to shoot me dead—a circumstance that considerably damped all my ardour for a rescue, and made me tremble lest, at any turn of the way, some faggot-gatherer might appear in sight Meanwhile, never did a man labour more strenuously to win the favour of his company.

I began by protesting my extreme innocence—vowed that a man of more estimable and amiable qualities than myself never did, nor never would exist. To this declaration they listened with manifest impatience if not with actual displeasure. I then tried another tack. I abused the rich and commended the poor—I harangued, in round terms, on the grabbing monopoly of the great, who enjoyed all the good things of this life, and would share none with their neighbours. I even hinted a sly encomium on those public-spirited individuals, whose gallantry and sense of justice led them to risk their lives in endeavours to equalize somewhat more fairly this world's wealth;

and who were so ungenerously styled robbers and high-waymen, though they were in reality benefactors and heroes. But they only laughed at this; nor did they show any real sympathy with my opinions till, in my general attack on all constituted authorities—kings, priests, statesmen, judges, and gendarmes, by chance I included revenue officers. The phrase seemed like a spark on gunpowder.

"Curses be on the wretches—they are the plague-spots of the world," cried I, seeing how they caught at the bait; "and thrice honoured the brave fellows who would relieve suffering humanity from the burden of such odious oppression."

A low whispering now took place among my escort, and at length he who seemed the leader stopped me short, and, placing his hand on my shoulder, cried out—

"Are you sincere in all this? Are these your notions?"

"Can you doubt me?" said I. "What reasons have I for speaking them? How do I know but you are revenue officers that listen to me."

' Enough, you shall join us. We are going to pass this sack of cigars."

"Ho! these are cigars, then," said I, brightening up. "It is not a——a——eh?"

"They are Dutch cigars, and the best that can be made," said he, not minding my interruption. "We shall pass them over the frontier by Sedan to-morrow night, and then we return to Dinant, where you shall come with us."

"Agreed," said I, while a faint chill ran through my limbs, and I could scarcely stand—images of galley life, irons with cannon shot, and a yellow uniform, all flitting before me. From this moment they became extremely communicative, detailing for my amusement many pleasing incidents of their blameless life—how they burned a custom-house here, and shot an inspector there; and, in fact, displaying the advantages of my new profession, with all its attractions, before me. How I grinned with mock delight at atrocities that made my blood curdle, and chuckled over the roasting of a revenue officer as though he had been a chestnut. I affected to see drollery in cruelties that deserved the gallows, and laughed till the tears came at horrors that nearly made me faint. My concurrence and sympathy absolutely delighted the devils, and we shook hands a dozen times over.

It was evening, when tired and weary, I was ready to drop with fatigue, my companions called a halt.

" Come, my friend," said the chief, " we'll relieve you now of your burden. You would be of little service to us at the frontier, and must wait for us here till our return."

It was impossible to make any proposal more agreeable to my feelings. The very thought of being quit of my friends was ecstasy. I did not dare, however, to vent my raptures openly, but satisfied myself with a simple acquiescence.

" And when," said I, " am I to have the pleasure of seeing you again, gentlemen ? "

" By to-morrow forenoon. at farthest."

By that time, thought I, I shall have made good use of my legs, please Heaven.

" Meanwhile," said Gros Jean, with a grin that showed he had neither forgotten nor forgiven my insults to his courage—" meanwhile we'll just beg leave to fasten you to this tree ;" and with the words, he pulled from a great canvas pocket he wore at his belt, a hank of strong cord, and proceeded to make a slip noose on it.

" It's not your intention, surely, to tie me here for the whole night ? " said I, in horror.

" And why not ? " interposed the chief. " Do you think there are bears or wolves in the Ardennes forest in September ? "

" But I shall die of cold or hunger. I never endured such usage before."

" You'll have plenty worse when you've joined us, I promise you," was the short reply, as, without further loss of time, they passed the cord round my waist, and began, with a dexterity that bespoke long practice, to fasten me to the tree. I protested in all form against the proceeding—I declaimed loudly about the liberty of the sub-

ject—vowed that England would take a frightful measure
of retribution on the whole country, if a hair of my head
were injured—and even went so far in the fervour of my
indignation, as to threaten the party with future consequences from the police.

The word was enough.   The leader drew his pistol from
his belt, and slapping down the pan, shook the priming
with his hand.

"So," cried he, in a harsh and savage voice, unlike his
former tone, "you'd play the informer, would you ? Well,
it's honest at least to say as much.   Now then, my man,
a quick shrift and a short prayer, for I'll send you where
you'll meet neither gendarmes nor revenue officers, or if
you do, they'll have enough of business on their hands not
to care for yours."

"Spare my life, most amiable Monsieur," said I, with
uplifted hands.   "Never shall I utter one word about you,
come what will.   I'll keep all I've seen a secret.   Don't kill
the father of eight children.   Let me live this time, and
I'll never wander off a turnpike road, three yards, as long
as I breathe."

They actually screamed with laughter at the terror of
my looks ; and the chief, seemingly satisfied with my pro-
testation, replaced his pistol in his belt, and kneeling
down on the ground, began leisurely to examine my
knapsack, which he coolly unstrapped and emptied on the
grass.

"What are these papers ? " said he, as he drew forth a
most voluminous roll of manuscript from a pocket.

"They are notes of my travels," said I, obsequiously—
"little pen sketches of men and manners in the countries
I've travelled in.   I call them 'Adventures of Arthur
O'Leary.'   That's my name, gentlemen—at your service."

"Ah! indeed.   Well, then, we've given you a very
pretty little incident for your journal this evening," said
he, laughing, "in return for which I'll ask leave to bor-
row these memoranda for wadding for my gun.   Believe
me, Monsieur O'Leary, they'll make a greater noise in the
world under *my* auspices than under yours;" and with
that he opened a rude clasp knife and proceeded to cut my
valued manuscript into pieces about an inch square.   This

done, he presented two of my shirts to each of his followers, reserving three for himself; and having made a most impartial division of my other effects, he pocketed the purse I carried, with its few gold pieces, and then, rising to his feet, said—

"Antoine, let us be stirring now—the moon will be up soon. Gros Jean, throw that sack on your shoulder and move forward · and now, Monsieur, I must wish you a good night; and as in this changeful life we can never answer for the future, let me commend myself to your recollection hereafter, if, as may be, we should not meet again. Adieu, adieu," said he, waving his hand.

"Adieu," said I, with a great effort to seem at ease—"a pleasant journey, and every success to your honest endeavours."

"You are a fine fellow," said he, stopping and turning about suddenly; "a superb fellow, and I can't part from you without a '*gage d'amitié*' between us;" and with the word he took my handsome travelling cap from my head and placed it on his own, while he crowned me with a villanous straw thing, that nothing save my bondage prevented me from hurling at his feet

He now hurried forward after the others, and in a few minutes I was in perfect solitude. Well, thought I—it was my first thought—it might all have been worse; the wretches might have murdered me—and such reckless devils as practise their trade, care little for human life. Murder, too, would only meet the same punishment as smuggling, or nearly so—a year more, or a year less at the galleys: and, after all, the night is fine; and if I mistake not, he said something about the moon I wondered where was the pretty countess—travelling away, probably, as hard as extra post could bring her. Ah! she little thought of my miserable plight now! Then came a little interval of softness—and then a little turn of indignation at my treatment—that I, an Englishman, should be so barbarously molested—a native of the land where freedom was the great birthright of every one. I called to mind all the fine things Burke used to say about liberty—and if I had not begun to feel so cold, I'd have tried to sing "Rule Britannia," just to keep up my

spirits; and then I fell asleep—if sleep it could be called
—that frightful nightmare of famished wolves howling
about me, tearing and mangling revenue officers ; and
grisly bears running backward and forward with smuggled
tobacco on their backs.   The forest seemed peopled by
every species of horrible shapes—half men, half beast—
but all with straw hats on their heads, and leather
gaiters on their legs.   However, the night passed over,
and the day began to break—the purple tint, pale and
streaky, that announces the rising sun, was replacing the
cold grey of the darker hours.   What a different thing it
is, to be sure, to get out of your bed deliberately, and
rubbing your eyes for two or three minutes with your
fingers, as you stand at the half-closed curtain, and then,
through the mist of your sleep, look out upon the east,
and think you see the sun rising, and totter back to the
comfortable nest again—the whole incident not breaking
your sleep, but merely being interwoven with your
dreams—a thing to dwell on among other pleasant fancies,
and to be boasted of the whole day afterwards—what a
different thing it is, I say, from the sensations of him who has
been up all night in the mail—shaken, bruised, and cramped
—sat on by the fat man, and kicked by the lean one ; still
worse of him who spends his night *dos à dos* to an oak in
a forest, cold, chill, and comfortless—no property in his
limbs beneath the knees, where all sensation terminates
—and his hands as benumbed as the heart of a poor-law
guardian.

If I have never, in all my after life, seen the sun rise
from the Rigi, from Snowdon, or the Pic du Midi, or
any other place which seems especially made for this sole
purpose, I owe it to the experience of this night, and am
grateful therefore.   Not that I have the most remote
notion of throwing disrespect on the glorious luminary—
far from it   I cut one of my oldest friends for speaking
lightly of the equator; but I hold it that the sun looks
best—as every one else does—when he's up and dressed
for the day.   It's a piece of prying, impertinent curiosity,
to peep at him when he's rising and at his toilet—he has
not rubbed the clouds out of his eyes, or you dared not
look at him, and you feel it too.   The very way you

steal out to catch a glimpse shows the sneaking, contemptible sense you have of your own act. Peeping Tom was a gentleman compared to your early riser.

The whole of which digression simply seems to say—I by no means enjoyed the rosy-fingered morning's blushes, the more for having spent the preceding night in the open air. I need not worry myself, still less my reader, by recapitulating the various frames of mind which succeeded each other every hour of my captivity. At one time, my escape with life served to console me for all I endured; at another, my bondage excited my whole wrath—I vowed vengeance on my persecutors too, and meditated various schemes for their punishment—my anger rising as their absence was prolonged, till I thought I could calculate my indignation by an algebraical formula, and make it exactly equal to the "squares of the distance" of my persecutors : then I thought of the delight I should experience in regaining my freedom, and actually made a bold effort to see something ludicrous in the entire adventure—but no ; it would not do ; I could not summon up a laugh. At last—it might have been towards noon —I heard a merry voice chanting a song, and a quick step coming up the *allée* of the wood. Never did my heart beat with such delight : the very mode of progression had something joyous in it—it seemed a hop, and a step and a spring, suiting each motion to the tune of the air—when suddenly the singer, with a long bound, stood before me. It would, indeed, have been a puzzling question which of us more surprised the other : however, as I can render no accurate account of *his* sensations on seeing me, I must content myself with recording mine on beholding him, and the best way to do so is to describe him. He was a man, or a boy—Heaven knows which —of something under the middle size, dressed in rags of every colour and shape—his old white hat was crushed and bent into some faint resemblance of a chapeau, and decorated with a cockade of dirty ribands and a cock's feather—a little white jacket, such as men-cooks wear in the kitchen, and a pair of flaming crimson plush shorts, cut above the knee, and displaying his naked legs, with sabots, formed his costume. A wooden sword was attached to an old belt round his waist, an ornament of which he seemed vastly proud, and which from t me to time he regarded with no small satisfaction.

"Holloa!" cried he, starting back, as he stood some six paces off, and gazed at me with most unequivocal astonishment; then recovering his self-possession long before I could summon mine, he said—"*Bonjour, bon jour, camarade*—a fine day for the vintage."

"No better," said I; "but come a little nearer, and do me the favour to untie these cords."

"Ah! are you long fastened up there?"

"The whole night," said I, in a lamentable accent, hoping to move his compassion the more speedily.

"What fun," said he, chuckling. "Were there many squirrels about?"

"Thousands of them. But come—be quick and undo this, and I'll tell you all about it."

"Gently, gently," said he, approaching with great caution about six inches nearer me "When did the rabbits come out?—Was it before day?"

"Yes, yes, an hour before. But I'll tell you everything when I'm loose. Be alive now, do."

"Why did you tie yourself so fast?" said he, eagerly, but not venturing to come closer.

"Confound the fellow," said I, passionately. "I didn't tie myself; it was the—the——"

"Ah! I know—it was the Maire, old Pierre Bogout. Well, well, he knows best when you ought to be set free. *Bonjour*," and with that he began once more his infernal tune and set out on his way as if nothing had happened; and though I called, prayed, swore, promised, and threatened with all my might, he never turned his head, but went on capering as before, and soon disappeared in the dark wood. For a full hour, passion so completely mastered me, that I could do nothing but revile fools and idiots of every shade and degree—inveighing against mental imbecility as the height of human wickedness, and wondering why no one had ever suggested the propriety of having "naturals" publicly whipped. I am shocked at myself now, as I call to mind the extravagance of my anger; and I grieve to say, that had I been, for that short interval, the proprietor of a private madhouse, I fear I should have been betrayed into the most unwarrantable cruelties towards the patients ; indeed, what is technically called " moral government," would have formed no part of my system.

Meanwhile time was moving on, if not pleasantly, at least steadily ; and already the sun began to decline somewhat, and his rays, that before came vertical, were now slanting as they fell upon the wood For a while, my attention was drawn off from my miseries by watching the weasels as they played and sported about me, in the confident belief that I was at best only a kind of fungus—an excrescence on an oak tree. One of them used to come actually to my feet, and even ran across my instep in his play. Suddenly the thought ran through me—and with terror—how soon may it be thus, and that I shall only be a miserable skeleton, pecked at by crows, and nibbled by squirrels. The idea was too dreadful ; and, as if the hour had actually come, I screamed out to frighten off the little creatures, and sent them back scampering into their dens.

"Holloa there! what's the matter?" shouted a deep mellow voice from the middle of the wood ; and before I could reply, a fat, rosy-cheeked man, of about fifty, with a pleasant countenance terminating in a row of double chins, approached me, but still with evident caution, and halting when about five paces distant, stood still

" Who are you?" said I, hastily, resolving this time at least to adopt a different method of effecting my liberation

" What's all this ?" quoth the fat man, shading his eyes with his palm, and addressing some one behind him, whom I now recognised as my friend the fool who visited me in the morning.

" I say, sir," repeated I, in a note of command somewhat absurd from a man in my situation—"who are you, may I ask ? "

"The Maire of Givét," said he, pompously, as he drew himself up, and took a large pinch of snuff with an imposing gravity, while his companion took off his hat in the most reverent fashion, and bowed down to the ground.

"Well, Monsieur le Maire, the better fortune mine to fall into such hands. I have been robbed and fastened here, as you see, by a gang of scoundrels,"—I took good care to say nothing of smugglers—"who have carried away everything I possessed.   Have the goodness to loosen these confounded cords, and set me at liberty"

"Were there many of them?" quoth the Maire, without budging a step forward.

"Yes, a dozen at least.   But untie me at once.   I'm heartily sick of being chained up here."

"A dozen at least!" repeated he, in an accent of wonderment.   "*Ma foi*, a very formidable gang.   Do you remember any of their names?"

"Devil take their names! how should I know them? Come, cut these cords will you?   We can talk just as well when I'm free."

"Not so fast, not so fast," said he, admonishing me with a bland motion of his hand.   "Everything must be done in order.   Now, since you don't know their names, we must put them down as 'parties unknown.'"

"Put them down whatever you like; but let me loose."

"All in good time.   Let us proceed regularly.   Who are your witnesses?"

"Witnesses!" screamed I, overcome with passion.— "You'll drive me distracted.   I tell you I was waylaid in the wood by a party of scoundrels, and you ask me for their names, and then for my witnesses.   Cut these cords, and don't be so infernally stupid.   Come, old fellow, look alive, will you?"

"Softly, softly, don't interrupt public justice," said he, with a most provoking composure.   "We must draw up the *procès verbal*."

"To be sure," said I, endeavouring to see what might be done by concurrence with him—"nothing more natural. But let me loose first; and then we'll arrange the *procès*"

"Not at all; you're all wrong," interposed he.   "I must have two witnesses first, to establish the fact of your present position—ay, and they must be of sound mind, and able to sign their names."

"May heaven grant me patience, or I'll burst," said I to myself, while he continued in a regular sing-song tone—

"Then we'll take the depositions in form.   Where do you come from?"

"Ireland," said I, with a deep sigh, wishing I were up

to the neck in a bog-hole there, in preference to my actual misfortune.

"What language do you usually speak?"

"English."

"There now," said he, brightening up—"there's an important fact already in the class No. 1, identity, which speaks of 'all traits, marks, and characteristic signs by which the plaintiff may be known.' Now we'll set you forth as 'an Irishman that speaks English.'"

"If you go on this way a little longer, you may put me down as 'insane,' for I vow to heaven I'm becoming so."

"Come, Bobeche," said he, turning towards the natural, who stood in mute admiration at his side—"go over to Claude Gueirans, at the mill, and see if the '*Notaire*' be up there : there was a marriage of his niece this morning, and I think you'll find him ; then cross the bridge, and make for Papalot's, and ask him to come up here and bring some stamped paper to take informations with him. You may tell the curé as you go by, that there's been a dreadful crime committed in the forest, and that '*la justice s'informe*'"—these last words were pronounced with an accent of the most magniloquent solemnity.

Scarcely had the fool set out on his errand when my temper, so long restrained, burst all bounds, and I abused the Maire in the most outrageous manner. There was no insult I could think of I did not heap on his absurdity, his ignorance, his folly, and stupidity ; and never ceased till actually want of breath completely exhausted me. To all this the worthy man made no reply, nor paid even the least attention. Seated on the stump of a beech-tree, he looked steadily at vacancy, till at length I began to doubt whether the whole scene were real, and that he was not a mere creature of my imagination. I verily believe I'd have given five *louis d'ors* to have been free one moment, if only to pelt a stone at him. Meanwhile, the shadow of coming night was falling on the forest ; the crows came cawing home to their dwelling in the tree tops ; the sounds of insect life were stilled in the grass ; and the odours of the forest, stronger as night closed in, filled the air. Gradually the darkness grew thicker and thicker, and at last all I could distinguish was the stems of the trees near me, and a massive black object I judged to be the Maire.

I called out to him in accents intended to be most apologetic. I begged forgiveness for my warmth of temper; protested my regrets, and only asked for the pleasure of his entertaining society till the hour of my liberation should arrive. But no answer came; not a word, not a syllable in reply—I could not even hear him breathing. Provoked at this uncomplying obstinacy, I renewed my attacks on all constituted authorities; expressed the most lively hopes that the gang of robbers would some day or other burn down Givét and all it contained, not forgetting the Maire and the notary; and, finally, to fill up the measure of insult, tried to sing the "*ça ira*," which, in good monarchical Holland, was, I knew, a dire offence; but I broke down in the melody, and had to come back to prose. However, it came just to the same—all was silent. When I ceased speaking, not even an echo returned me a reply. At last I grew wearied; the thought that all my anathemas had only an audience of weasels and woodpeckers damped the ardour of my eloquence, and I fell into a musing fit on Dutch justice, which seemed admirably adapted to those good old times when people lived to the age of eight or nine hundred years, and when a few months were as the twinkling of an eye. Then I began a little plan of a tour from the time of my liberation, cautiously resolving never to move out of the most beaten tracks, and to avoid all districts where the Maire was a Dutchman. Hunger, and thirst, and cold, by this time began to tell upon my spirits too, and I grew sleepy from sheer exhaustion.

Scarcely had I nodded my head twice in slumber, when a loud shout awoke me. I opened my eyes, and saw a vast mob of men, women, and children, carrying torches, and coming through the wood at full speed, the procession being led by a venerable-looking old man on a white pony, whom I at once guessed to be the curé, while the fool, with a very imposing branch of burning pine, walked beside him.

"Good evening to you, Monsieur," said the old man, as he took off his hat, with an air of courtesy.

"You must excuse the miserable plight I'm in, Monsieur le Curé," said I, "if I can't return your politeness—but I'm tied."

"Cut the cords at once," said the good man to the crowd that now pressed forward.

"Your pardon, Father Jacques," said the Maire, as he sat up in the grass and rubbed his eyes, which sleep seemed to have almost obliterated; "but the *procès verbal* is——"

"Quite unnecessary here," replied the old man. "Cut the rope, my friends."

"Not so fast," said the Maire, pushing towards me. "I'll untie it. That's a good cord, and worth eight sous."

And so, notwithstanding all my assurances that I'd give him a crown piece to use more despatch, he proceeded leisurely to unfasten every knot, and took at least ten minutes before he set me at liberty

"Hurrah!" said I, as the last coil was withdrawn, and I attempted to spring into the air, but my cramped and chilled limbs were unequal to the effort, and I rolled headlong on the grass.

The worthy curé, however, was at once beside me, and after a few directions to the party to make a litter for me, he knelt down to offer up a short prayer for my deliverance; the rest followed the act with implicit devotion, while I took off my hat in respect, and sat still where I was.

"I see," whispered he, when the *ave* was over—"I see you are a Protestant. This is a fast day with us; but we'll get you a poulet at my cottage, and a glass of wine will soon refresh you."

With many a thankful speech, I soon suffered myself to be lifted into a large sheet, such as they use in the vineyards; and, with a strong cortége of the villagers carrying their torches, we took our way back to Givet.

*   *   *   *   *

The circumstances of my adventure, considerably exaggerated, of course, were bruited over the country; and before I was out of bed next morning, a chasseur, in a very showy livery, arrived with a letter from the lord of the manor, entreating me to take my abode for some days

N

at the Château de Rochepied, where I should be received with a perfect welcome, and every endeavour made to recover my lost effects. Having consulted with the worthy curé, who counselled me by all means to accept this flattering invitation—a course I was myself disposed to—I wrote a few lines of answer, and despatched a messenger by post to Dinant, to bring up my heavy baggage which I had left there.

Towards noon the count's carriage drove up to convey me to the château, and having taken an affectionate farewell of my kind host, I set out for Rochepied. The wicker conveniency in which I travelled, all alone, was, albeit not the thing for Hyde Park, easy and pleasant in its motion; the fat Flemish mares, with their long tails tastefully festooned over a huge cushion of plaited straw on their backs, went at a fair steady pace; the road led through a part of the forest abounding in pretty vistas of woodland scenery; and everything conspired to make me feel that even an affair with a gang of smugglers might not be the worst thing in life, if it were to lead to such pleasant results afterwards.

As we jogged along, I learned from the fat Walloon coachman that the château was full of company; the count had invited numerous guests for the opening of the *chasse*, and that there were French, and Germans, and English, and, for aught he knew, Chinese expected to "assist" at the ceremony. I confess the information considerably damped the pleasure I at first experienced. I was in hopes to see real country life, the regular course of château existence, in a family quietly domesticated on their own property. I looked forward to a peep at that *vie intime* of Flemish household, of which all I knew was gathered from a Wenix picture—I wanted to see the thing in reality. The good vrow, with her high cap and her long waist, her pale features lit up with eyes of such brown as only Vandyck ever caught the colour of; and the daughters, prim and stately, with their stiff, quaint courtesy, moving about the terraced walks, like figures stepping from an ancient canvas, with bouquets in their white and dimpled fingers, or mayhap a jess-hawk perched upon their wrist; and then the Mynheer Baron—I pic-

tured him as a large and portly Fleming, with a slouched
beaver, and a short trim moustache, deep of voice, heavy
of step, seated on a grey Cuyp-like horse, with a flowing
mane, and a huge tassel of a tail, flapping lazily his brawny
flanks, or slapping with heavy stroke the massive jack-
boots of his rider.

Such were my notions of a Dutch household. The unchanged looks of the dwellings, which for centuries were
the same, in part suggested these thoughts. The quaint
old turrets, the stiff and stately terraces, the fosse, stagnant
and sluggish, the carved tracery of the massive doorway,
were all as we see them in the oldest pictures of the land;
and when the rind looks so like, it is hard to imagine the
fruit with a different flavour.

It was then with considerable regret I learned that I
should see the family *en gala*, that I had fallen upon a
time of feasting and entertainment, and had it not been
too late, I should have beaten my retreat, and taken up
my abode for another day with the Cure of Givet; as it
was, I resolved to make my visit as brief as possible, and
take to the road with all convenient despatch.

As we neared the château, the Walloon remembered a
number of apologies with which the count charged him to
account for his not having gone himself to fetch me,
alleging the claims of his other guests, and the unavoid-
able details which the forthcoming *ouverture de chasse*
demanded at his hands. I paid little attention to the
mumbled and broken narrative, interrupted by impreca-
tions on the road, and exhortations to the horses; for
already we had entered the precincts of the demesne, and
I was busy in noting down the appearance of the place.
There was, however, little to remark the transition from
the wide forest to the park was only marked by a little
improvement in the road; there was neither lodge nor
gate—no wall, no fence, no inclosure of any kind. The
trim culture, which in our country is so observable around
the approach of a house of some consequence, was here
totally wanting; the avenue was partly of gravel, partly
of smooth turf; the brushwood of prickly holly was let
grow wild, and straggled in many places across the road;
the occasional views that opened seemed to have been

N 2

made by accident, not design; and all was rank vegetation and rich verdure, uncared for—uncultivated, but
like the children of the poor, seeming only the healthier
and more robust, because left to their own unchecked, un-
tutored impulses. The rabbits played about within a few
paces of the carriage tracks; the birds sat motionless on
the trees as we passed, while here and there, through the
foliage, I could detect the gorgeous colouring of some
bright peacock's tail, as he rested on a bough and held
converse with his wilder brethren of the air, just as if the
remoteness of the spot and its seclusions led to intimacies
which in the ordinary routine of life had been impossible.
At length the trees receded farther and farther from the
road, and a beautiful expanse of waving lawn, dotted with
sheep, stretched before the eye. In the distance, too, I
could perceive the château itself—a massive pile in the
shape of a letter L, bristling with chimneys, and pierced
with windows of every size and shape; clumps of flowering shrubs and fruit trees were planted about, and little
beds of flowers spangled the even turf like stars in the
expanse of heaven. The Meuse wound round the château
on three sides, and perhaps thus saved it from being
inflicted by a ditch, for without water a Dutchman can no
more exist than a mackerel.

"Fine! isn't it?" said the Walloon, as he pointed with
his finger to the scene before me, and seemed to revel with
delight in my look of astonishment, while he plied his
whip with renewed vigour, and soon drew up at a wide
flight of stone steps, where a row of orange trees mounted
guard on each side, and filled the place with their fragrance.

A servant in the strange *mélange* of a livery, where the
colours seemed chosen from a bed of ranunculuses just
near, came out to let down the steps and usher me into
the house. He informed me that the count had given
orders for my reception, but that he and all his friends
were out on horseback, and would not be back before din-
ner-time. Not sorry to have a little time to myself, I
retired to my room, and threw myself down on a most
comfortable sofa, excessively well satisfied with the locality
and well disposed to take advantage of my good fortune.

The little bed, with its snow-white curtains and gilded canopy; the brass dogs upon the hearth, that shone like gold; the cherry-wood table, that might have served as a mirror; the modest book-shelf, with its pleasant row of volumes; but, better than all, the open window, from which I could see for miles over the top of a dark forest, and watch the Meuse as it came and went, now shining, now lost in the recesses of the wood—all charmed me; and I fully confessed what I have had very frequently to repeat in life, that "Arthur O'Leary was born under a lucky planet."

CHAPTER XI.

CHÂTEAU LIFE.

STRETCHED upon a large old-fashioned sofa, where a burgomaster might have reclined with "ample room and verge enough," in all the easy abandonment of dressing-gown and slippers—the cool breeze gently wafting the window-blind to and fro, and tempering the lulling sounds from wood and water—the buzzing of the summer insects, and the far-off carol of a peasant's song—I fell into one of those delicious sleeps in which dreams are so faintly marked as to leave us no disappointment on waking: flitting, shadow-like, before the mind, they live only in a pleasant memory of something vague and undefined, and impart no touch of sorrow for expectations unfulfilled—for hopes that are not to be realized. I would that my dreams might always take this shape. It is a sad thing when they become tangible—when features and looks, eyes, hands, words, and signs, live too strongly in our sleeping minds—and that we awake to the cold reality of our daily cares and crosses, tenfold less endurable from very contrast. No! give me rather the faint and waving outline; the shadowy perception of pleasure, than the vivid picture, to end only in the conviction that I am but

Christopher Sly after all ; or what comes pretty much to the same, nothing but—Arthur O'Leary.

Still, I would not have you deem me discontented with my lot; far from it. I chose my path early in life, and never saw reason to regret the choice. How many of you can say as much? I felt that while the tender ties of home and family—the charities that grow up around the charmed circle of a wife and children—are the great prizes of life, there are also a thousand lesser ones in the wheel, in the kindly sympathies with which the world abounds ; that to him who bears no ill-will at his heart—nay, rather loving all things that are lovable, with warm attachments to all who have been kind to him, with strong sources of happiness in his own tranquil thoughts—the wandering life would offer many pleasures.

Most men live, as it were, with one story of their lives, the traits of childhood maturing into manly features, their history consists of the development of early character in circumstances of good or evil fortune. They fall in love, they marry, they grow old, and they die— each incident of their existence bearing on that before and that after, like link upon link of some great chain. He, however, who throws himself like a plank upon the waters, to be washed hither and thither, as wind or tide might drive him, has a very different experience. To him, life is a succession of episodes, each perfect in itself; the world is but a number of tableaux, changing with climate and country; his sorrows in France have no connection with his joys in Italy ; his delights in Spain live apart from his griefs on the Rhine. The past throws no shadow on the future—his philosophy is, to make the most of the present, and he never forgets La Bruyère's maxim—"Il faut rire avant d'être heureux, *de peur de mourir sans avoir ri.*"

Now, if you don't like my philosophy, set it down as a dream, and here I am awake once more.

And certainly I claim no great merit on the score of my vigilance; for the tantararara that awoke me would have aroused the Seven Sleepers themselves. Words are weak to convey the most distant conception of the noise : it seemed as though ten thousand peacocks had congre-

gated beneath my window, and with brazen throats were
bent on giving me a hideous concert. The fiend-chorus
in "Robert le Diable" was a psalm-tune compared to it.
I started up and rushed to the casement; and there, in
the lawn beneath, beheld some twenty persons costumed
in hunting fashion—their horses foaming and splashed,
their coats stained with marks of the forest; but the uproar was soon comprehensible, owing to some half-dozen
of the party who performed on that most diabolical of
all human inventions, the *cor de chasse*.

Imagine, if you can, and thank your stars that it is
only a work of imagination, some twenty feet of brass
pipe, worn belt-fashion over one shoulder, and under the
opposite arm—one end of the aforesaid tube being a
mouth-piece, and the other expanding itself into a huge
trumpet-mouth; then conceive a Fleming—one of Rubens' cherubs, immensely magnified, and decorated with
a beard and moustaches—blowing into this, with all the
force of his lungs, perfectly unmindful of the five other
performers, who at five several and distinct parts of the
melody are blasting away also; treble and bass, contralto
and soprano, shake and sostenuto—all blending into one
crash of hideous discord, to which the Scotch bagpipe,
in a pibroch, is a soothing, melting melody. A deaf-and-
dumb institution would capitulate in half an hour.
Truly, the results of a hunting expedition ought to be of
the most satisfactory kind, to make the "Retour de Chasse"
—it was this they were blowing—at all sufferable to
those who were not engaged in the concert; as for the
performers, I can readily believe they never heard a note
of the whole.

Even Dutch lungs grow tired at last; having blown
the establishment into ecstasies, and myself into a furious
headache, they gave in; and now an awful bell announced the time to dress for dinner. While I made my
toilet, I endeavoured, as well as my throbbing temples
would permit me, to fancy the host's personal appearance, and to conjecture the style of the rest of the party.
My preparations over, I took a parting look in the glass,
as if to guess the probable impression I should make
below stairs, and sallied forth.

Cautiously stealing along over the well-waxed oors, slippery as ice itself, I descended the broad oak stair into a great hall, wainscoted with dark walnut, and decorated with antlers and stags' heads, cross-bows and arquebusses, and, to my shuddering horror, various *cors de chasse*, now happily, however, silent on the walls. I entered the drawing-room, conning over to myself a little speech in French, and preparing myself to bow for the next fifteen minutes ; but, to my surprise, no one had yet appeared. All were still occupied dressing, and probably taking some well-merited repose after their exertions on the wind instruments. I had now time for a survey of the apartment ; and, generally speaking, a drawing-room is no bad indication of the tastes and temperament of the owners of the establishment.

The practised eye speedily detects in the character and arrangement of a chamber, something of its occupant In some houses, the absence of all decoration—the simple puritanism of the furniture, bespeaks the life of quiet souls, whose days are as devoid of luxury as their dwellings. You read in the cold grey tints,, the formal stiffness, the unrelieved regularity around the Quaker-like flatness of their existence In others, there is an air of ill-done display, a straining after effect, which shows itself in costly but ill-assorted details—a mingling of all styles and eras, without repose or keeping. The bad pretentious pictures, the faulty bronzes, meagre casts of poor originals, the gaudy china, are safe warranty for the vulgarity of their owners ; while the humble parlour of a village inn can be, as I have seen it, made to evidence the cultivated tastes and polished habits of those who have made it the halting-place of a day. We might go back and trace how much of our knowledge of the earliest ages is derived from the study of the interior of their dwellings ; what a rich volume of information is conveyed in a mosaic ; what a treatise does not lie in a frescoed wall.

The room in which I now found myself was a long, and, for its length, a narrow apartment ; a range of tall windows, deeply sunk in the thick wall, occupied one side, opposite to which was a plain wall, covered with pictures from floor to cornice, save where, at a considerable distance from each other, were two splendidly-carved chimney-pieces of black oak, one representing "The Adoration of the Shepherds," and the other "The Miraculous Draught of Fishes,"—the latter done with a relief, a vigour, and a movement I have never seen equalled. Above these were some armorial trophies of an early date, in which, among the maces and battle-axes, I could recognize some weapons of Eastern origin, which, by the family, I learned, were ascribed to the periods of the Crusades.

Between the windows were placed a succession of carved oak cabinets of the seventeenth century, beautiful specimens of art, and, for all their quaintness, far handsomer objects of furniture than our modern luxury has introduced among us. Japan vases of dark blue and green were filled with rare flowers; here and there small tables of costly buhl invited you to the window recesses, where the downy ottomans, pillowed with Flemish luxury, suggested rest, if not sleep. The pictures, over which I could but throw a passing glance, were all by Flemish painters, and of that character which so essentially displays their chief merits, richness of colour and tone—Gerard Dow and Ostade, Cuyp, Van der Meer, and Terburg; those admirable groupings of domestic life, where the nation is, as it were, miniatured before you; that perfection of domestic quiet, which bespeaks an heirloom of tranquillity, derived whole centuries back. You see at once, in those dark brown eyes and placid features, the traits that have taken ages to bring to such perfection; and you recognize the origin of those sturdy burgomasters and bold burghers, who were at the same time the thriftiest merchants and the hautiest princes of Europe.

Suddenly, and when I was almost on my knees, to examine a picture by Memling, the door opened, and a small, sharp-looking man, dressed in the last extravagance of Paris mode, resplendent in waistcoat, and glistening in jewellery, tripped lightly forward. "Ah, mi Lor O'Leary!" said he, advancing towards me with a bow and a slide.

It was no time to discuss pedigree; so gulping the

promotion, I made my acknowledgments as best I could; and by the time that we met, which, on a moderate calculation, might have been two minutes after he entered, we shook hands very cordially, and looked delighted to see each other. This ceremony, I repeat, was only accomplished after his having bowed round two tables, an ottoman, and an oak "armoire," I having performed the like ceremony behind a Chinese screen, and very nearly over a vase of the original "green dragon," which actually seemed disposed to spring at me for my awkwardness.

Before my astonishment—shall I add, disappointment ? —had subsided, at finding that the diminutive, over-dressed figure before me was the representative of those bold barons I had been musing over, for such he was, the room began to fill. Portly ladies of undefined dates sailed in and took their places—stiff, stately, and silent as their grandmothers on the walls; heavy-looking gentlemen, with unpronounceable names, bowed and wheeled, and bowed again; while a buzz of "*votre serviteur*," Madame, or Monsieur, swelled and sank amid the murmur of the room, with the scraping of feet on the glazed *parquet*, and the rustle of silk, whose plentitude bespoke a day when silkworms were honest.

The host paraded me around the austere circle, where the very names sounded like an incantation ; and the old ladies shook their bugles and agitated their fans, in recognition of my acquaintance. The circumstances of my adventure were the conversation of every group ; and although, I confess, I could not help feeling that even a small spice of malice might have found food for laughter in the absurdity of my durance, yet not one there could see anything in the whole affair, save a grave case of smuggled tobacco, and a most unwarrantable exercise of authority on the part of the curé who liberated me. Indeed, this latter seemed to gain ground so rapidly, that once or twice I began to fear they might remand me and sentence me to another night in the air, " till justice should be satisfied." I did the worthy Maire de Givét foul wrong, said I to myself; these people here are not a whit better.

The company continued to arrive at every moment; and now I remarked that it was the veteran battalion who led the march, the younger members of the household only dropping in as the hour grew later. Among these was a pleasant sprinkling of Frenchmen, as easily recognizable among Flemings as is an officer of the "Blues" from one of the new police. A German baron, a very portrait of his class—fat, heavy-browed, sulky-looking, but in reality a good-hearted, fine-tempered fellow, two Americans; an English colonel, with his daughters twain; and a Danish *chargé d'affaires*—the minor characters being what, in dramatic phrase, are called *premiers* and *premières*, meaning thereby young people of either sex, dressed in the latest mode, and performing the part of lovers. the ladies, with a moderate share of good looks, being perfect in the freshness of their toilette, and a certain air of ease and gracefulness, almost universal abroad, the men, a strange mixture of silliness and savagery—a bad cross— half hairdresser, half hero.

Before the dinner was announced, I had time to perceive that the company was divided into two different and very opposite currents—one party consisting of the old Dutch or Flemish race, quiet, plodding, peaceable souls, pretending to nothing new, enjoying everything old; their souvenirs referring to some event in the time of their grandfathers. the other section were the younger portion, who, strongly imbued with French notions on dress, and English on sporting matters, attempted to bring Newmarket and the "Boulevards des Italiens" into the heart of the Ardennes.

Between the two, and connecting them with each other, was a species of *pont du diable*, in the person of a little, dapper, olive-complexioned man of about forty; his eyes black as jet, but with an expression soft and subdued, save at moments of excitement, when they flashed like glow-worms; his plain suit of black, with deep cambric ruffles—his silk shorts and buckled shoes, had something of the ecclesiastic—and so it was: he was the Abbé van Praet, the cadet of an ancient Belgian family, a man of considerable ability, highly informed on most subjects—a linguist, a musician, a painter of no small pretensions, who spent his life in the "*far niente*" of chateau existence; now devising a party of pleasure, now inventing a madrigal—now giving directions to the *chef* how to make an *omelette à la curé*, now stealing noiselessly along some sheltered walk, to hear some fair lady's secret confidence,—for he was privy counsellor in all affairs of the heart, and, if the world did not wrong him, occasionally pleaded his own cause, when no other petitioner offered.

I was soon struck by this man, and by the tact with which, while he preserved his ascendancy over the minds of all, he never admitted any undue familiarity, yet affected all the ease and *insouciance* of the veriest idler. I was flattered, also, by his notice of me, and by the politeness of his invitation to sit next him at table.

The distinctions I have hinted at already made the dinner conversation a strange medley of Flemish history and sporting anecdotes—of reminiscences of the times of Maria Theresa, and dissertations on weights and ages—of the genealogies of Flemish families, and the pedigrees of English race-horses. The young English ladies, both pretty and delicate-looking girls, with an air of good breeding and tone in their manner, shocked me not a little by the intimate knowledge they displayed on all matters of the turf and the stable; their acquaintance with the details of hunting, racing, and steeple-chasing, seeming to form the most wonderful attraction to the moustached counts and whiskered barons who listened to them. The colonel was a fine, mellow-looking old gentleman, with a white head and a red nose, and with that species of placid expression one sees in the people who perform those parts in Vaudeville theatres, called *pères nobles;* he seemed, indeed, as if he had been daily in the habit of bestowing a lovely daughter on some happy, enraptured lover, and invoking a blessing on their heads   There was a rich unction in his voice, an almost imperceptible quaver, that made it seem kind and affectionate; he finished his shake of the hand with a little parting squeeze, a kind of "one cheer more," as they say now-a-days, when some misguided admirer calls upon a meeting for enthusiasm they don't feel. The Americans were—and one description will serve for both, so like were they—sallow, high-boned, silent men, with a species of quiet caution in their manner, as if they were learning, but had not yet completed, a European education, as to habits and customs, and were studiously careful not to commit any solecisms which might betray their country.

As dinner proceeded, the sporting characters carried the day. The "ouverture de chasse," which was to take place the following morning, was an all-engrossing topic, and I found myself established as judge on a hundred points of English jockey etiquette, of which as my ignorance was complete, I suffered grievously in the estimation of the company, and, when referred to, could neither apportion the weight to age, nor even tell the number of yards in a "distance."

It was, however, decreed that I should ride the next day—the host had the "very horse to suit me;" and, as the abbé whispered me to consent, I acceded at once to the arrangement.

When we adjourned to the drawing-room, Colonel Muddleton came towards me with an easy smile and an outstretched snuff-box, both in such perfect keeping—the action was a finished thing.

"Any relation, may I ask, of a very old friend and brother-officer of mine, General Mark O'Leary, who was killed in Canada?" said he.

"A very distant one only," replied I.

"A capital fellow—brave as a lion—and pleasant. By Jove, I never met the like of him! What became of his Irish property?—he was never married, I think?"

"No, he died a bachelor, and left his estates to my uncle; they had met once by accident, and took a liking to each other."

"And so your uncle has them now?"

"No, my uncle died since: they came into my possession some two or three years ago."

"Eh—ah—upon my life!" said he, with something of surprise in his manner; and then, as if ashamed of his exclamation, and with a much more cordial vein than at first, he resumed—"What a piece of unlooked-for good fortune to be sure! Only think of my finding my old friend Mark's nephew!"

"Not his nephew. I was only——"

"Never mind, never mind; he was a kind of an uncle, you know, any man might be proud of him. What a

glorious fellow ! full of fun—full of spirit and animation.
Ah, just like all your countryman ! I've a little Irish
blood in my veins myself; my mother was an O'Flaherty,
or an O'Neil, or something of that sort; and there's
Laura—you don't know my daughter ? "

" I have not the honour."

" Come along, and I'll introduce you to her—a little
reserved or so," said he, in a whisper, as if to give me the
carte du pays—" rather cold, you know, to strangers; but
when she hears you are the nephew of my old friend
Mark—Mark and I were like brothers. Laura, my love,"
said he, tapping the young lady on her white shoulder, as
she stood with her back towards us, " Laura, dear—the
son of my oldest friend in the world, General O'Leary."
The young lady turned quickly round, and, as she drew
herself up somewhat haughtily, dropped me a low curtsey, and then resumed her conversation with a very much
whiskered gentleman near.

The colonel seemed, despite all his endeavours to overcome it, rather put out by his daughter's hauteur to the
son of his old friend; and what he should have said or
done I know not, when the abbé came suddenly up, and
with a card invited me to join a party at whist. The
moment was so awkward for all, that I would have accepted an invitation even to *écarté* to escape from the
difficulty, and I followed him into a small boudoir where
two ladies where awaiting us. I had just time to see
that they were both pleasing-looking, and of that time of
life when women, without forfeiting any of the attractions
of youth, are much more disposed to please by the attractions of manner and *esprit* than by mere beauty, when we
sat down to our game. La Baronne de Meer, my partner,
was the younger and the prettier of the two; she was one
of those Flemings into whose families the race of Spain
poured the warm current of southern blood, and gave
them the dark eye and the olive skin, the graceful figure
and the elastic step, so characteristic of their nation.

" *A la bonne heure*," said she, smiling; " have we
rescued one from the enchantress ? "

" Yes," replied the abbé, with an affected gravity; " in
another moment he was lost."

"If you mean me," said I, laughing, "I assure you I ran no danger whatever; for whatever the young lady's glances may portend, she seemed very much indisposed to bestow a second on me."

The game proceeded with its running fire of chit-chat, in which I could gather that Mademoiselle Laura was a most established man-killer, no one ever escaping her fascinations, save when by some strange fatality they preferred her sister Julia, whose style was, to use the abbé's phrase, her sister's "diluted."

There was a tone of pique in the way the ladies criticized the colonel's daughters, which, since that, I have often remarked in those who, accustomed to the attentions of men themselves, without any unusual effort to please on their part, are doubly annoyed when they perceive a rival making more than ordinary endeavours to attract admirers. They feel as a capitalist would, when another millionaire offers money at a lower rate of interest. It is, as it were, a breach of conventional etiquette, and never escapes being severely criticized.

As for me, I had no personal feeling at stake, and looked on at the game of all parties with much amusement.

"Where is the Count D'Espagne to-night, said the baronne to the abbé—has he been false?"

"Not at all; he was singing with mademoiselle when I was in the *salon*."

"You'll have a dreadful rival there, Monsieur O'Leary," said she, laughingly; he "is the most celebrated swordsman and the best shot in Flanders."

"It is likely he may rust his weapons if he have no opportunity for their exercise till I give it," said I.

"Don't you admire her, then?" said she.

"The lady is very pretty, indeed," said I.

"The heart led," interrupted the abbé, suddenly, as he touched my foot beneath the table—"play a heart."

Close beside my chair, and leaning over my cards, stood Mademoiselle Laura herself at the moment.

"You have no heart," said she, in English, and with a singular expression on the words, while her downcast eye shot a glance—one glance—through me.

"Yes, but I have though," said I, discovering a card

that lay concealed behind another; "it only requires a little looking for."

"Not worth the trouble, perhaps," said she, with a toss of her head, as I threw the deuce upon the table; and before I could reply she was gone.

"I think her much prettier when she looks saucy," said the baronne, as if to imply that the air of pique assumed was a mere piece of acting got up for effect.

I see it all, said I to myself. Foreign women can never forgive English for being so much their superior in beauty and loveliness. Meanwhile our game came to a close, and we gathered around the buffet.

There we found the old colonel, with a large silver tankard of mulled wine, holding forth over some campaigning exploit, to which no one listened for more than a second or two, and thus the whole room became joint-stock hearers of his story. Laura stood eating her ice with the Count D'Espagne, the black-whiskered cavalier already mentioned, beside her. The Americans were prosing away about Jefferson and Adams. The Belgians talked agriculture and genealogy; and the French, collecting into a group of their own, in which nearly all the pretty women joined, discoursed the ballet, the "Chambre," the court, the coulisses, the last mode, and the last murder; and all in the same mirthful and lively tone. And truly, let people condemn as they will this superficial style of conversation, there is none equal to it. It avoids the prosaic flatness of German, and the monotonous pertinacity of English, which seems more to partake of the nature of discussion than dialogue. French chit-chat takes a wider range; anecdotic, illustrative, and discursive by turns. It deems nothing too light, nothing too weighty for its subject. It is a gay butterfly, now floating with gilded wings above you, now tremulously perched upon a leaf below, now sparkling in the sunbeam, now loitering in the shade; embodying not only thought, but expression, it charms by its style as well as by its matter. The language, too, suggests shades and "nuances" of colouring that exist not in other tongues, you can give to your canvas the precise tint you wish, for when mystery would prove a merit, the equivoque is there ready to your hand, that means so much, yet asserts so little. For my part I should make my will in English, but I'd rather make love in French. But while thus digressing, I have forgotten to mention that people are running back and forward with bedroom candles; there is a confused hum of *bon soir* on every side; and, with many a hope of a fine day for the morrow, we separate for the night

I lay awake some hours thinking of Laura, and then of the baronne—they were both arch ones; the abbé too crossed my thoughts, and once or twice the old colonel's roguish leer; but I slept soundly for all that, and did not wake till eight o'clock the next morning. The silence of the house struck me forcibly as I rubbed my eyes and looked about. Hang it, thought I, have they gone off to the *chasse* without me? I surely could never have slept through the uproar of their trumpets I drew aside the window curtains, and the mystery was solved: such rain never fell before; the clouds, actually touching the tops of the beech trees, seemed to ooze and squash like squeezed sponges The torrent came down in that splashing stroke as if some force behind momentarily propelled it stronger; and the long-parched ground seethed and smoked like a heated cauldron Pleasant this, was reflection number one, as I endeavoured to peer through the mist, and beheld a haze of weeping foliage. Pleasant to be immured here during Heaven knows how many days, without the power to escape. Lucky fellow, Arthur, was my second thought, capital quarters you have fallen into better far the snug comforts of a Flemish château than the chances of a wayside inn; besides, here is a goodly company met together, there will needs be pleasant people among them. I wish it may rain these three weeks; château life is the very thing I'm curious about—how do they get through the day? There's no "Times" in Flanders—no one cares a farthing about who's in and who's out, there's no "Derby," no trials for murder · what can they do ? was the question I put to myself a dozen times over. No matter, I have abundant occupation—my journal has never been posted up since—since—alas, I can scarcely tell!

It might be from reflections like these, or perhaps because I was less of a sportsman than my companions, but certainly whatever the cause, I bore up against the disappointment of the weather with far more philosophy, and dispersed a sack of proverbs about patience, hope, equanimity, and contentment Sancho Panza himself might have envied, until at length no one ventured a malediction on the day in my presence, for fear of eliciting a hailstorm of moral reflections. The company dropped down to breakfast by detachments. The elated looks and flashing eyes of the night before, saddened and overcast at the unexpected change. Even the elders of the party seemed discontented; and except myself and an old gentleman with the gout, who took an airing about the hall and the drawing-room in a wheel-chair, all seemed miserable.

Each window had its occupant posted against the glass, vainly endeavouring to catch one bit of blue amid the dreary waste of cloud. A little group, sulky and silent, were gathered around the weather-glass; a literary inquirer sat down to con over the predictions of the almanac; but you might as well have looked for sociability among the inhabitants of a private madhouse as here. The weather was cursed in every language from Cherokee to Sanscrit; all agreed that no country had such an abominable climate. The Yankee praised the summers of America, the Dane upheld his own, and I took a patriotic turn, and vowed I had never seen such rain in Ireland ! The master of the house could scarcely show amid this torrent of abusive criticism, and when he did by chance appear, looked as much ashamed as though he himself had pulled out the spigot, and deluged the whole land with water.

Meanwhile, none of those I looked for appeared. Neither the colonel's daughter nor the baronne came down; the abbé, too, did not descend to the breakfast-room, and I was considerably puzzled and put out by the disappointment.

After then enduring a good hour's boredom from the old colonel on the subject of my late lamented parent, Mark O'Leary; after submitting to a severe cross-exami-

nation from the Yankee gentleman as to the reason of my
coming abroad, what property and expectations I had,
my age, and birth-place, what my mother died of, and
whether I did not feel very miserable from the abject
slavery of submitting to an English government—I
escaped into the library, a fine comfortable old room, which
I rightly conjectured I should find unoccupied.

Selecting a quaint-looking quarto with some curious
illuminated pages for my companion, I drew a great deep
leather chair into a recess of one window, and hugged
myself in my solitude. While I listlessly turned over the
leaves of my book, or sat lost in reflection, time crept
over, and I heard the great clock of the château strike
three · at the same moment a hand fell lightly on my
shoulder; I turned about—it was the abbé.

" I half suspected I should find you here," said he.
" Do I disturb you, or may I keep your company?"

" But too happy," I replied, " if you'll do me the
favour."

"I thought," said he, as he drew a chair opposite to me
—" I thought you'd scarcely play dominoes all day, or
discuss waistcoats."

" In truth, I was scarcely better employed—this old
volume here which I took down for its plates——"

" *Ma foi*, a most interesting one ; it is Guchardi's History of Mary of Burgundy. Those quaint old processions,
those venerable councils, are admirably depicted. What
rich stores for a romance writer lie in the details of these
old books ;—their accuracy as to costume, the little traits
of everyday life so *naively* told ; every little domestic
incident is so full of its characteristic era. I wonder when
the springs are so accessible, men do not draw more frequently from them, and more purely also."

'· You forget Scott."

" No ; far from it. He is the great exception ; and
from his intimate acquaintance with this class of reading,
is he so immeasurably superior to all other writers of his
style. Not merely tinctured, but deeply imbued with the
habits of the feudal period, the traits by which others
attempt to paint the time, with him were mere accessories in the picture; costume and architecture he used to

o 2

heighten, not to convey his impressions; and while no one knew better every minute particular of dress, or arms, that betokened a period or a class, none more sparingly used such aid. He felt the same delicacy certain ancient artists did as to the introduction of pure white into their pictures, deeming such an unfair exercise of skill—— But why venture to speak of your countryman to you, save that genius is above nationality, and Scott's novels at least are European"

After chatting for some time longer, and feeling struck with the extent and variety of the abbé's attainments, I half dropped a hint expressive of my surprise that one so cultivated as he was, could apparently so readily comply with the monotonous routine of a château life, and the little prospect it afforded of his meeting congenial associates.

Far from feeling offended at the liberty of my remark, he replied at once with a smile—

"You are wrong there, and the error is a common one; but when you have seen more of life, you will learn that a man's own resources are the only real gratifications he can count upon. Society, like a field-day, may offer the occasion to display your troops and put them through their manœuvres, but, believe me, it is a rare and a lucky day when you go back richer by one recruit, and the chance is, that even he is a cripple, and must be sent about his business. People, too, will tell you much of the advantage to be derived from associating with men of distinguished and gifted minds. I have seen something of such in my time, and give little credit to the theory. You might as well hope to obtain credit for a thousand pounds, because you took off your hat to a banker"

The abbé paused after this, and seemed to be occupied with his own thoughts; then raising his head suddenly, he said—

"As to happiness, believe me, it lives only in the extremes of perfect vacuity, or true genius. Your clever fellow, with a vivid fancy and glowing imagination, strong feeling, and strong power of expression, has no chance of it. The excitement he lives in is alone a bar to the tranquil character of thought necessary to happiness; and however cold a man may feel, he should never warm himself through a burning glass."

There seemed through all he said something like a retrospective tone, as though he were rather giving the fruit of past personal experiences than merely speculating on the future; and I could not help throwing out a hint to this purport.

"Perhaps you are right," said he; then, after a long silence, he added—"It is a fortunate thing after all, when the faults of a man's temperament are the source of some disappointment in early life, because then they rarely endanger his subsequent career. Let him only escape the just punishment, whatever it be, and the chances are they embitter every hour of his after-life; his whole care and study being not correction, but concealment, he lives a life of daily duplicity; the fear of detection is over him at every step he takes: and he plays a part so constantly that he loses all real character at last in the frequency of dissimulation. Shall I tell you a little incident with which I became acquainted in early life? If you have nothing better to do, it may wile away the hours before dinner."

CHAPTER XII.

THE ABBE'S STORY.

"Without tiring you with any irrelevant details of the family and relatives of my hero, if I dare call him such, I may mention that he was the second son of an old Belgian family of some rank and wealth, and that in accordance with the habits of his house, he was educated for the career of diplomacy; for this purpose, a life of travel was deemed the best preparation—foreign languages being the chief requisite, with such insight into history, national law, and national usages, as any young man with moderate capacity and assiduity, can master in three or four years.

" The chief of the Dutch mission at Frankfort was an
old diplomate of some distinction, but who, had it not
been from causes purely personal towards the king, would
not have quitted the Hague for any embassy whatever.
He was a widower with an only daughter, one of those
true types of Dutch beauty which Terburg was so fond
of painting. There are people who can see nothing but
vulgarity in the class of features I speak of, and yet
nothing in reality is farther from it. Hers was a mild,
placid face, a wide, candid-looking forehead, down either
side of which two braids of sunny brown hair fell; her
skin, fair as alabaster, had the least tinge of colour, but
. her lips were full, and of a violet hue, that gave a character of brilliancy to the whole countenance; her figure
inclined to *embonpoint*, was exquisitely moulded, and in
her walk there appeared the composed and resolute
carriage of one whose temperament, however mild and
unruffled, was still based on principles too strong to be
shaken. She was indeed a perfect specimen of her nation,
embodying in her character the thrift, the propriety, the
high sense of honour, the rigid habits of order, so emi-
nently Dutch; but withal there ran through her nature
the golden thread of romance, and beneath that mild
eyebrow there were the thoughts and hopes of a highly
imaginative mind.

" The mission consisted of an old secretary of embassy,
Van Dohein, a veteran diplomate of some sixty years,
and Edward Norvins, the youth I speak of. Such was
the family party, for you are aware that they all lived in
the same house, and dined together every day; the
attachés of the mission being specially entrusted to the
care and attention of the head of the mission, as if they
were his own children. Norvins soon fell in love with
the pretty Marguerite—how could it be otherwise? they
were constantly together; he was her companion at
home, her attendant at every ball; they rode out together,
walked, read, drew, and sang together, and in fact very
soon became inseparable. In all this there was nothing
which gave rise to remark   The intimate habits of a
mission permitted such, and as her father, deeply immersed in affairs of diplomacy, had no time to busy him-

self about them, no one else did. The secretary had
followed the same course at every mission for the first
ten years of his career, and only deemed it the ordinary
routine of an *attaché's* life.

"Such then was the pleasant current of their lives,
when an event occurred which was to disturb its even
flow, ay, and alter the channel for ever A despatch
arrived one morning at the mission, informing them that
a certain Monsieur van Halsdt, a son of one of the ministers, who had lately committed some breach of discipline
in a cavalry regiment, was about to be attached to the
mission Never was such a shock as this gave Margaret
and her lover. To her the idea of associating with a wild,
unruly character like this was insupportable. To him it
was misery; he saw at once all his daily intimacy with her
interrupted, he perceived how their former habits could
no longer be followed, that with his arrival must cease
the companionship that made him the happiest of men.
Even the baron himself was indignant at the arrangement to saddle him with a "*vaurien*" to be reclaimed—
but then he was the minister's son The King himself
had signed the appointment, and there was no help for it.

"It was indeed with anything but feelings of welcome
they awaited the coming of the new guest. Even in the
short interval between his appointment and his coming,
a hundred rumours reached them of his numerous scrapes
and adventures, his duels, his debts, his gambling, and
his love exploits. All of course were duly magnified.
Poor Marguerite felt as though an imp of Satan was
about to pay them a visit, and Norvins dreaded him with
a fear that partook of a presentiment.

"The day came, and the dinner hour, in respect for
the son of the great man, was delayed twenty minutes in
expectation of his coming, and they went to table at last
without him, silent and sad. The baron, annoyed at the
loss of dignity he should sustain by a piece of politeness
exercised without result, the secretary fretting over the
entrées that were burned, Marguerite and Edward mourning over happiness never to return Suddenly a calèche
drove into the court at full galop, the steps rattled, and a
figure wrapped in a cloak sprang out. Before the first

surprise permitted them to speak, the door of the *salle* opened, and he appeared.

"It would, I confess, have been a difficult matter to have fixed on that precise character of looks and appearances which might have pleased all the party. Whatever were the sentiments of others I know not, but Norvin's wishes would have inclined to see him short and ill-looking, rude in speech and gesture—in a word, as repulsive as possible. It is indeed a strange thing—you must have remarked it I'm certain—the disappointment we feel at finding people we desire to like, inferior to our own conceptions of them, is not one-half so great as is our chagrin at discovering those we are determined to dislike, very different from our preconceived notions, with few or none of the features we were prepared to find fault with, and, in fact, altogether unlike the bugbear we had created for ourselves. One would suppose that such a revulsion in feeling would be pleasurable rather than otherwise. Not so, however; a sense of our own injustice adds poignancy to our previous prejudice, and we dislike the object only the more for lowering us in our own esteem.

"Van Halsdt was well calculated to illustrate my theory. He was tall and well made; his face, dark as a Spaniard's—his mother was descended from a Catalonian family—was manly looking and frank, at once indicating openness of temperament, and a dash of heroic daring, that would like danger for itself alone; his carriage had the easy freedom of a soldier, without anything bordering on coarseness or effrontery. Advancing with a quiet bow, he tendered his apologies for being late, rather as a matter he owed to himself, to excuse his want of punctuality, than from any sense of inconvenience to others, and ascribed the delay to the difficulty of finding post-horses —'While waiting, therefore,' said he, 'I resolved to economise time, and so dressed for dinner at the last stage.'

"This apology at least showed a desire on his part to be in time, and at once disposed the secretary in his favour. The baron himself spoke little, and as for Marguerite, she never opened her lips to him the whole time of dinner, and Norvins could barely get out the few common-places of table, and sat eyeing him from time to time with an increasing dislike.

"Van Halsdt could not help feeling that his reception was of the coldest; yet either perfectly indifferent to the fact, or resolved to overcome their impressions against him, he talked away unceasingly of everything he could think of—the dinners at court, the theatres, the diplomatic *soirées*, the news from foreign countries—all of which he spoke of with knowledge and intimacy. Yet nothing could he extract in return. The old baron retired, as was his wont, immediately after dinner; the secretary dropped off soon after; Marguerite went to take her evening drive on the Boulevards; and Norvins was left alone with his new comrade. At first he was going to pretend an engagement. Then the awkwardness of the moment came forcibly before him, and he sat still, silent and confused.

"'Any wine in that decanter?' said Van Halsdt, with a short abrupt tone, as he pointed to the bottle beside him. 'Pray pass it over here. I have only drank three glasses. I shall be better aware to-morrow how soon your party breaks up here.'

"'Yes,' said Edward, timidly, and not well knowing what to say. 'The baron retires to his study every evening at seven.

"'With all my heart,' said he, gaily; 'at six, if he prefer it, and he may even take the old secretary with him. But the mademoiselle, shall we see any more of her during the evening—is there no *salon*? Eh, what do you after dinner?'

"'Why, sometimes we drive, or we walk out on the Boulevards; the other ministers receive once or twice a week, and then there's the opera.'

"'Devilishly slow you must find all this,' said Van Halsdt, filling a bumper, and taking it off at a draught. 'Are you long here?'

"'Only three months.'

"'And well sick of it, I'll be sworn.'

"'No, I feel very happy—I like the quiet.'

"'Oh dear! oh dear!' said he with a long groan, 'what is to become of *me*?'

"Norvins heartily wished he could have replied to the question in the way he would have liked, but said nothing.

"'It's past eight,' said he, as he perceived him stealing a look at his watch. 'Never mind me, if you've any appointment—I'll soon learn to make myself at home here Perhaps you'd better ring for some more claret, however, before you go—they don't know me yet.'

"Edward almost started from his chair at this speech —such a liberty had never before been heard of as to call for more wine; indeed it was not their ordinary habit to consume half what was placed on the table, but so taken by surprise was he, that he actually arose and rang the bell, as he was desired.

"'Some claret. Johann,' said he with a gulp, as the old butler entered.

"The man started back, and fixed his eyes on the empty decanter.

"'And I say, ancient,' said Van Halsdt, 'don't decant it—you shook the last bottle confoundedly It's old wine, and won't bear that kind of usage.'

"The old man moved away with a deep sigh, and returned in about ten minutes with a bottle from the cellar.

"'Didn't Providence bless you with two hands, friend?' said Van Halsdt. 'Go down for another.'

"Go, Johann,' said Norvins, as he saw him hesitate, and not knowing what his refusal might call forth; and then, without waiting for further parley, he arose and withdrew.

"Well, thought he, when he was once more alone, if he is a good-looking fellow, and there's no denying *that*, one comfort is, he is a confirmed drunkard. Marguerite will never be able to endure him; for such, in his secret heart, was the reason of his premature dislike and dread of his new companion; and as he strolled along he meditated on the many ways he should be able to contrast his own acquirements with the other's deficiencies, for such he set them down at once, and gradually reasoned himself into the conviction that the fear of all rivalry from him was mere folly; and that whatever success his handsome face and figure might have elsewhere, that Marguerite was not the girl to be caught by such attractions, when coupled with an unruly temper, and an uneducated mind.

"And he was right. Great as his own repugnance was towards him, hers was far greater. She not only avoided him on every occasion, but took pleasure, as it seemed, in marking the cold distance of her manner to him, and contrasting it with her behaviour to others. It is true he appeared to care little for this; and only replied to it by a half-impertinent style of familiarity—a kind of jocular intimacy most insulting to a woman, and horribly tantalizing for those to witness who are attached to her.

"I don't wish to make my story a long one; nor could I without entering into the details of every-day life, which now became so completely altered. Marguerite and Norvins met only at rare intervals, and then less to cultivate each other's esteem than expatiate on the many demerits of him who had estranged them so utterly. All the reports to his discredit that circulated in Frankfort were duly conned over; and though they could lay little to his charge of their own actual knowledge, they only imagined the more, and condemned him accordingly.

"To Norvins he became hourly more insupportable. There was in all his bearing towards him the quiet, measured tone of a superior to an inferior—the patronizing protection of an elder to one younger and less able to defend himself; and which, with the other's consciousness of his many intellectual advantages over him, added double bitterness to the insult. As he never appeared in the bureau of the mission, nor in any way concerned himself with official duties, they rarely met save at table; there, his appearance was the signal for constraint and reserve—an awkwardness that made itself felt the more, as the author of it seemed to exult in the dismay he created.

"Such, then, was the state of events when Norvins received his nomination as secretary of legation at Stuttgardt. The appointment was a surprise to him, he did not even hear of the vacancy. The position, however, and the emoluments were such as to admit of his marrying, and he resolved to ask the baron for his daughter's hand, to which the rank and influence of his own family permitted him to aspire without presumption.

" He gave his willing consent; Marguerite accepted;
and the only delay was now caused by the respect for an
old Dutch custom—the bride should be at least eighteen,
and Marguerite yet wanted three months of that age.
This interval Norvins obtained leave to pass at Frankfort;
and now they went about to all public places together as
betrothed; paid visits in company, and were recognized
by all their acquaintances as engaged to each other.

" Just at this time a French cuirassier regiment marched
into garrison in the town—they were on their way to the
south of Germany, and only detained in Frankfort to make
up their full complement of horses.   In this regiment was
a young Dutch officer, who once belonged to the same
regiment as Van Halsdt, and who was broke by the court-
martial for the same quarrel.   They had fought twice with
swords, and only parted with the dire resolve to finish the
affair at the next opportunity.   This officer was a man of
an inferior class, his family being an obscure one of North
Holland, and thus, when dismissed the service, had no
other resource than to enter the French army, at that time
at war with Austria.   He was said to be a man of over-
bearing temper and passion, and it was not likely that the
circumstance of his expatriation and disgrace had improved
him.   However, some pledge Van Halsdt had made to his
father decided him in keeping out of the way.   The report
ran that he had given a solemn promise never to challenge
nor accept any challenge from the other on any pretext
whatsoever.   Whatever the promise, certain it was he
left Frankfort the same day the regiment marched into
town, and retired to Wiesbaden.

" The circumstance soon became the subject of town
gossip, and plenty there were most willing to attribute
Van Halsdt's departure to prudential motives, rather than
to give so wild a character any credit for filial ones.
Several who felt offended at his haughty, supercilious
manner, now exulted in this, as it seemed, fall to his
pride; and Norvins, unfortunately, fell into the same track,
and by many a sly innuendo, and half allusion to his
absence, gave greater currency to the report, that his
absence was dictated by other considerations than those
of parental respect.

"Through all the chit-chat of the time, Marguerite showed herself highly indignant at Van Halsdt's conduct. The quiet timid girl, who detested violence, and hated crime in any shape, felt disgusted at the thought of his poltroonery, and could not hear his name mentioned without an expression of contempt All this delighted Edward. It seemed to be the just retribution on the former insolence of the other, and he longed for his return to Frankfort to witness the thousand slights that awaited him. Such a strange and unaccountable thing is our triumph over others, for the want of those qualities in which we see ourselves deficient None are so loud in decrying dishonesty and fraud as the man who feels knave in his own heart. Who can censure female frailty like her who has felt its sting in her own conscience? You remember the great traveller, Mungo Park, used to calculate the depths of rivers in Africa, by rolling heavy stones over their banks and watching the air-bubbles that mounted to the surface, so, oftentimes, may you measure the innate sense of a vice by the execration some censor of morals bestows upon it. Believe me, these heavy chastisements of crime are many times but the cries of awakened conscience. I speak strongly, but I feel deeply on this subject. But to my story.—It was the custom for Marguerite and her lover each evening to visit the theatre, where the minister had a box, and as they were stepping into the carriage one night, as usual, Van Halsdt drove up to the door, and asked if he might accompany them. Of course, a refusal was out of the question—he was a member of the mission —he had done nothing to forfeit his position there, however much he had lost in the estimation of society generally, and they acceded to his request, still with a species of cold courtesy that would, by any other man, have been construed into a refusal.

"As they drove along in silence, the constraint increased at every moment, and had it not been for the long-suppressed feeling of hated rivalry, Norvins could have pitied Van Halsdt as he sat, no longer with his easy smile of self-satisfied indifference, but with a clouded heavy brow, mute and pale As for Marguerite, her features expressed a species of quiet cold disdain, whenever she looked towards him, far more terrible to bear than anything like an open reproach. Twice or thrice he made an effort to start some topic of conversation, but in vain, his observations were either unreplied to, or met a cold distant assent more chilling still. At length, as if resolved to break through their icy reserve towards him, he asked in a tone of affected indifference—

" ' Any changes in Frankfort, mademoiselle, since I had the pleasure of seeing you last? '

" ' None, sir, that I know of, save that the French cuirassier regiment marched this morning for Baden, *of which, however, it is more than probable you are aware already.*'

" On each of these latter words she laid an undue stress, fixing her eyes steadfastly on him, and speaking in a slow measured tone. He grew deeply red, almost black for a moment or two, his moustache seemed almost to bristle with the tremulous convulsion that shook his upper lip, then as suddenly he became lividly pale, while the great drops of perspiration stood on his brow, and fell upon his cheek. Not another word was spoken. They soon reached the theatre, when Norvins offered Marguerite his arm, Van Halsdt slowly following them up stairs.

" The play was one of Lessing's, and well acted, but somehow Norvins could pay no attention to the performance, his whole soul was occupied by other thoughts. Marguerite appeared to him in a different light from what he had ever seen her ; not less to be loved, but altogether different. The staid, placid girl, whose quiet thoughts seemed never to rest on topics of violent passion or excitement; who fled from the very approach of anything bordering on overwrought feeling, now appeared carried away by her abhorrence of a man, to the very extreme of hatred, for conduct, which Norvins scarcely thought she should have considered even faulty. If, then, his triumph over Van Halsdt brought any pleasure to his heart, a secret sense of his own deficiency in the very quality for which she condemned him, made him shudder.

" While he reflected thus, his ear was struck with a conversation in the box next his, in which were seated a large party of young men, with two or three ladies, whose air, dress, and manners were, at least, somewhat equivocal.

"'And so, Alphonse, you succeeded after all?' said a youth, to a large, powerful, dark-moustached man, whose plain blue frock could not conceal the soldier.

"'Yes,' replied he, in a deep sonorous voice, 'our doctor managed the matter for me—he pronounced me unable to march before to-morrow; he said that my old wound in the arm gave symptoms of uneasiness, and required a little more rest; but, by St. Denis, I see little benefit in the plan, after all This "white feather" has not ventured back, and I must leave in the morning without meeting him.'

"These words, which were spoken somewhat loudly, could be easily heard in any part of the adjoining box, and scarcely were they uttered when Van Halsdt, who sat the entire evening far back, and entirely concealed from view, covered his face with both his hands, and remained in that posture for several minutes. When he withdrew them, the alteration in his countenance was actually fearful Though his cheeks were pale as death, his eyes were bloodshot, and the lids swelled and congested; his lips, too, were protruded, and trembled like one in an ague, and his clasped hands shook against the chair.

"Norvins would have asked him if he were ill, but was afraid even to speak to him; while again his attention was drawn off by the voices near him.

"'Not got a bouquet?' said the large man to a lady beside him, 'pardie, that's too bad. Let me assist you. I perceive that this pretty damsel, who turns her shoulder so disdainfully towards us, makes little use of hers, and so avec permission, Mademoiselle!' With that he stood up, and leaning across the division into their box, stretched over his hand and took the bouquet that lay before Marguerite, and handed it to the lady at his side.

"Marguerite started back, as her eyes flashed with offended pride, and then turned them on her lover. He stood up, not to resent the insult, but to offer her his arm to leave the box. She gave him a look—never in a glance was there read such an expression of withering contempt

—and, drawing her shawl around her, said in a low voice, 'the carriage.' Before he could open the box door to permit her to pass out, Van Haldst sprang to the front of the box, and stretched over—then came a crash—a cry —a confused shout of many voices together—and the word '*polisson*,' above all; but hurrying Marguerite along, Norvins hastened down the stairs and assisted her into the carriage. As she took her place, he made a gesture, as if to follow, but she drew the door towards her, and with a shuddering expression—'No'—leaned back, and closed the door. The calèche moved on, and Norvins was alone in the street.

"I shall not attempt to describe the terrific rush of sensations that came crowding on his brain. Coward as he was, he would have braved a hundred deaths rather than endure such agony. He turned towards the theatre, but his craven spirit seemed to paralyze his very limbs; he felt as if though his antagonist were before him he would not have had energy to speak to him. Marguerite's look was ever before him—it sank into his inmost soul— it was burning there like a fire, that no memory nor after sorrow should ever quench.

"As he stood thus, an arm was passed hastily through his, and he was led along. It was Van Halsdt, his hat drawn over his brows, and a slight mark of blood upon his cheek. He seemed so overwhelmed with his own sensations as not to be cognizant of his companion's.

"'I struck him,' said he, in a thick guttural voice, the very breathings of vengeance, 'I struck him to my feet. It is now *à la mort* between us, and better it should be so at once.' As he spoke thus he turned towards the Boulevard, instead of the usual way towards the embassy.

"'We are going wrong,' said Norvins—'this leads to the *Breiten gasse*.'

"'I know it,' was the brief reply; 'we must make for the country; the thing was too public not to excite measures of precaution. We are to rendezvous at Katznach'

"'With swords?'

"'No; pistols, *this time*,' said he, with a fiendish emphasis on the last words.

"They walked on for above an hour, passing through the gate of the town, and reached the open country, each silent and lost in his own thoughts.

"At a small *cabaret* they procured horses and a guide to Katznach, which was about eleven miles up the mountain. The way was so steep that they were obliged to walk their horses, and frequently to get down and lead them, yet not a word was spoken on either side. Once, only, Norvins asked ' how he was to get his pistols from Frankfort ? ' to which the other answered merely, ' *they* provide the weapons!' and they were again silent.

"Norvins was somewhat surprised, and offended also, that his companion should have given him so little of his confidence at such a moment; gladly, indeed, would he have exchanged his own thoughts for those of any one else, but he left him to ruminate in silence on his unhappy position, and to brood over miseries that every minute seemed to aggravate.

"'They're coming up the road yonder; I see them now,' said Van Halsdt, suddenly, as he aroused the other from a deep train of melancholy thoughts. 'Ha, how lame he walks!' cried he, with savage exultation.

"In a few minutes the party, consisting of four persons, dismounted from their horses, and entered the little burial-ground beside the chapel. One of them advancing hastily towards Van Halsdt, shook him warmly by the hand, and whispered something in his ear. The other replied, when the first speaker turned towards Norvins, with a look of ineffable scorn, and then passed over to the opposite group. Edward soon perceived that this man was to act as Halsdt's friend ; and though really glad that such an office fell not to his share, was deeply offended on being thus, as it were, passed over. In this state of dogged anger, he sat down on a tombstone, and, as if having no interest whatever in the whole proceedings, never once looked towards them.

"He did not notice that the party now took the path towards the wood, nor was he conscious of the flight of time, when suddenly the loud report of two pistols, so close together as to be almost blended, rang through his ears. Then he sprang up, a dreadful pang piercing his

P

bosom; some terrible sense of guilt he could neither fathom nor explain, flashing across him; at the same instant the brushwood crashed behind him, and Van Halsdt and his companion came out, the former with his eyes glistening and his cheek flushed, the other pale and dreadfully agitated. He nodded towards Edward significantly, and Van Halsdt said—' Yes.'

" Before Norvins could conjecture what this meant, the stranger approached him, and said—

" ' I am sorry, sir, the sad work of this morning cannot end here; but of course you are prepared to afford my friend the only reparation in your power.'

" ' Me — reparation — what do you mean? — afford whom ? '

" ' Monsieur van Halsdt,' said he, coolly; and with a slight emphasis of contempt as he spoke.

" ' Monsieur van Halsdt! he never offended me—I never insulted, never injured him,' said he, trembling at every word.

" ' Never injured me !' cried Van Halsdt. 'Is it nothing that you have ruined me for ever—that your cowardice to resent an affront offered to one who should have been dearer than your life, a hundred times told, should have involved me in a duel with a man I swore never to meet, never to cross swords, nor exchange a shot with ? Is it nothing that I am to be disgraced by my king, disinherited by my father—a beggar, an exile at once ? is it nothing, sir, that the oldest name of Friesland is to be blotted from the nobles of his nation ? Is it nothing that for you I should be *what I now am !*'

" The last words were uttered in a voice that made Norvins' very blood run cold ; but he could not speak, he could not mutter a word in answer.

" ' What !' said Van Halsdt, in an accent of cutting sarcasm, ' I thought that perhaps in the suddenness of the moment, your courage, unprepared for an unexpected call, might not have stood your part ; but can it be true that you are a coward ? Is this the case ?'

" Norvins hung down his head—the sickness of death was on him. The dreadful pause was broken at last; it was Van Halsdt who spoke—

"'Adieu, sir; I grieve for you. I hope we may never meet again: yet let me give you a counsel ere we part. There is but one coat men can wear with impunity, when they carry a malevolent and a craven spirit; you can be a——' "

"Monsieur l'Abbé, the dinner is on the table," said a servant, entering at this moment of the story.

"*Ma foi*, and so it is," said he, looking gaily at his watch, as he rose from his chair.

"But, mademoiselle," said I, "what became of her ?"

"Ah, Marguerite ; she was married to Van Halsdt in less than three months ; the cuirassier fortunately recovered from his wounds ; the duel was shown to be a thing forced by the stress of consequences. As for Van Halsdt, the King forgave him, and he is now ambassador at Naples."

"And the other, Norvins ? though I scarcely feel any interest in him."

"I'm sorry for it," said he, laughing ; "but won't you move forward ?"

With that he made me a polite bow to precede him towards the dinner room, and followed me with the jaunty step and the light gesture of an easy and contented nature.

I need scarcely say that I did not sit next the abbé that day at dinner ; on the contrary, I selected the most stupid-looking old man I could find for my neighbour, hugging myself in the thought, that where there is little agreeability, Nature may kindly have given in recompense some traits of honesty, and some vestiges of honour. Indeed, such a disgust did I feel for the amusing features of the pleasantest part of the company—and so inextricably did I connect repartee with rascality, that I trembled at every good thing I heard, and stole away early to bed, resolving never to take sudden fancies to agreeable people as long as I lived—an oath which a long residence in a certain country, that shall be nameless, happily permits me to keep, with little temptation to transgress.

The next morning was indeed a brilliant one—the earth refreshed by rain—the verdure more brilliant—the mountain streams grown fuller: all the landscape seemed

to shine forth in its gladdest features. I was up and
stirring soon after sunrise; and with all my prejudices
against such a means of "lengthening one's days," sat at
my window, actually entranced with the beauty of the
scene. Beyond the river there rose a heath-clad mountain,
along which misty masses of vapour swept hurriedly, dis-
closing as they passed some tiny patch of cultivation,
struggling for life amid granite rocks and abrupt preci-
pices. As the sun grew stronger, the grey tints became
brown, and the brown grew purple, while certain dark
lines that tracked their way from summit to base, began
to shine like silver, and showed the course of many a
mountain torrent, tumbling and splashing towards that
little lake that lay calm as a mirror below. Immediately
beneath my window was the garden of the château—a
succession of terraces descending to the very river—the
quaint yew hedges carved into many a strange device—
the balustrades half hidden by flowering shrubs and
creepers—the marble statues peeping out here and there,
trim and orderly as they looked, were a pleasant feature
of the picture, and heightened the effect of the desolate
grandeur of the distant view. The very swans that sailed
about on the oval pond told of habitation and life, just
as the broad expanded wing that soared above the mountain peak spoke of the wild region where the eagle was
king.

My musings were suddenly brought to a close by a
voice on the terrace beneath. It was that of a man who
was evidently, from his pace, enjoying his morning's promenade under the piazza of the château, while he hummed
a tune to pass away the time :—

> " Why, soldiers, why
> Should we be melancholy, boys ;
> Why, soldiers, why ?
> Whose business——

Holloa, there, François, ain't they stirring yet ? why, it's
past six o'clock "

The person addressed was a serving man, who, in the
formidable attire of an English groom—in which he was
about as much at home as a coronation champion feels in

plate armour—was crossing the garden towards the stables.

"No, sir; the count won't start before eight."

"And when do we breakfast ? "

"At seven, sir."

"The devil—another hour—

"Why, soldiers, why,
Should we be——

I say, François, what horse do they mean for Mademoiselle Laura to-day ? "

"The mare she rode on Wednesday, sir. Mademoiselle liked her very much."

"And what have they ordered for the stranger that came the night before last ? The gentleman who was robbed——"

"I know, I know, sir ; the roan, with the cut on her knee."

"Why, she's a mad one—she's a run-away."

"So she is, sir, but then monsieur is an Englishman, and the count says he'll soon tame the roan filly."

"Why, soldiers, why," hummed the old colonel, for it was Muddleton himself ; and the groom pursued his way without further questioning. Whereupon two thoughts took possession of my brain : one of which was, what peculiar organization it is which makes certain old people who have nothing to do early risers ; the other, what offence had I committed to induce the master of the château to plot my sudden death.

The former has been a puzzle to me all my life. What a blessing should sleep be to that class of beings who do nothing when awake , how they should covet those drowsy hours that give, as it were, a sanction to indolence , with what anxiety they ought to await the fall of day, as announcing the period when they become the equals of their fellow-men ; and with what terror they should look forward to the time when the busy world is up and stirring, and their incapacity and slothfulness only become more glaring from contrast. Would not any one say that such people would naturally cultivate sleep as their comforter ? Should they not hug their pillow as the friend of their bosom? On the contrary, these are invariably your early risers: every house where I have ever been on a visit, has had at least one of these troubled and troublesome spirits; the torment of Boots—the horror of housemaids. Their chronic cough forms a duet with the inharmonious crowing of the young cock, who, for lack of better knowledge, proclaims day a full hour before his time. Their creaking shoes are the accompaniment to the scrubbing of brass fenders and the twigging of carpets, the jarring sounds of opening shutters, and the cranking discord of a hall-door chain; their heavy step sounds like a nightmare's tread, through the whole sleeping house; and what is the object of all this? What new fact have they acquired? what difficult question have they solved? whom have they made happier, or wiser, or better? Not Betty, the cook, certainly, whose morning levée of beggars they have most unceremoniously scattered and scared; not Mary, the housemaid, who, unaccustomed to be caught *en déshabille,* is cross the whole day after, though he was "only an elderly gentleman, and wore spectacles:" not Richard, who cleaned their shoes by candle-light· nor the venerable butler, who, from shame sake, is up and dressed, but who, still asleep, stands with his corkscrew in his hand, under the vague impression that it is a late supper party.

These people, too, have always a consequential, self-satisfied look about them; they seem to say, as though they knew a "thing or two" others had no wot of; as though the day, more confidential when few were by, told them some capital secrets the sleepers never heard of; and they made this pestilential habit a reason for eating the breakfast of a Cossack, as if the consumption of victuals was a cardinal virtue.

Civilized differs from savage life as much by the regulation of time as by any other feature. I see no objection to your red man, who, probably, can't go to breakfast till he has caught a bear, being up betimes; but for the gentleman who goes to bed with the conviction that hot rolls and coffee, tea and marmalade, bloaters and honey, ham, muffins, and eggs await him at ten o'clock; for him, I say, these absurd vagabondisms are an insufferable affectation, and a most unwarrantable liberty with the peace and privacy of a household

Meanwhile, old Colonel Muddleton is parading below; and here we must leave him for another chapter.

CHAPTER XIII.

THE CHASE.

ALL the world was to figure on horseback. The horses themselves no bad evidence of the exertions used to mount the party. Here was a rugged pony from the Ardennes, with short neck and low shoulder; his head broad as a bull's, and his counter like the bow of a Dutch galliot; there, a great Flemish beast, seventeen hands high, with a tail festooned over a straw " bustle," and even still hanging some inches on the ground—straight in the shoulder, and straighter in the pasterns—giving the rider a shock at every motion that, to any other than a Fleming, would lead to concussion of the brain. Here stood an English thoroughbred, sadly " shook " before, and with that tremulous quivering of the fore-legs that betokens a life of hard work; still, with all his imperfections, and the mark of a spavin behind, he looked like a gentleman among a crowd of low fellows—a reduced gentleman it is true—but a gentleman still His mane was long and silky; his coat was short and glossy; his head finely formed, and well put on his long, taper, and well-balanced neck. Beside him was a huge Holsteiner, flapping his broad flanks with a tail like a weeping ash— a great massive animal, that seemed from his action as if he were in the habit of ascending stairs, and now and then got the shock one feels when they come to a step too few. Among the mass there were some " Limousins "—pretty, neatly-formed little animals, with great strength for their appearance, and showing a deal of Arab breeding; and an odd Schimmel or two from Hungary, snorting and pawing like a war-horse. But the staple was a collection

of such screws as every week are to be seen at Tattersall's
auction, announced as "first-rate weight-carriers with
any fox-hounds—fast in double and single harness, and
'believed' sound by the owner." Well, what credulous
people are the proprietors of horses! These are the
great exports to the Low Countries, repaid in mock
Vandycks, apocryphal Rembrandts, and fabulous Hob-
bimas; for the exhibition of which, in our dining-rooms
and libraries, we are as heartily laughed at as they are
for their taste in manners equine! and in the same way
exactly as we insist upon a great name with our landscape
or our battle, so your Fleming must have a pedigree
with his hunter. There must be "dam to Louisa," and
"own brother to Ratcatcher" and Titus Oates, that won
the "Levanter Handicap" in —— no matter where. Oh
dear, oh dear! when shall we have sense enough to go
without Snyders and Ostade? and when will Flemings be
satisfied to ride on beasts which befit them—strong of
limb, slow of gait, dull of temper, and not over-fastidious
in feeding; whose parentage has had no registry, and whose
blood relations never were chronicled?

Truly, England is the land of "turn-out." All the
foreign imitations of it are most ludicrous, from Prince
Max of Bavaria, who brought back with him to Munich
a lord-mayor's coach, gilding, emblazonry, wigs, and all,
as the true type of a London equipage—down to those
strange merry-andrew figures in orange plush breeches
and sky-blue frocks, that one sees galloping after their
masters along the Champs Elysées, like insane comets
taking an airing on horseback. The whole thing is
absurd: they cannot accomplish it, do what they will;
there's no success in the endeavour. It is like our miserable failures to get up a *petit diner* or a *soirée*. If, then,
French, Italians, and Germans, fail so lamentably, only
think, I beseech you, of Flemings— imagine Belgium *à
cheval!* The author of "Hudibras" discovered years ago
that these people were fish—that their land life was a
little bit of distraction they permitted themselves to take
from time to time; but that their real element was a dyke
or a canal. What would he have said if he saw them on
horseback?

Now I am free to confess that few men have less hope to win the world by deeds of horsemanship than Arthur O'Leary. I have ever looked upon it as a kind of pre sumption in me to get into the saddle I have regarded my taking the reins as a species of duplicity on my part— a tacit assumption that I had any sort of control over the beast; I have appeared to myself guilty of a moral mis-demeanour—the "obtaining a ride under false pretences." Yet when I saw myself astride of the "roan with the cut on her knee," and looked around me at the others, I fancied that I must have taken lessons from Franconi without knowing it; and even among the moustached heroes of the evening before, I bore myself like a gallant cavalier

"You sit your horse devilish like your father; he had just the same easy *dégagé* way in his saddle," said the old colonel, tapping his snuffbox, and looking at me with a smile of marked approval , while he continued in a lower tone, " I've told Laura to get near you if the mare becomes troublesome : the Flemings, you know, are not much to boast of as riders."

I acknowledged the favour as well as I could, for already my horse was becoming fidgety. Every one about me thinking it essential to spur and whip his beast into the nearest approach to mettle, and caper about like so many devils, while they cried out to each other—

"Regardez, Charles, comment il est vif ce 'Tear away.' C'est une bête du diable. Ah tiens—tiens, vois donc ' Albert.' Le voilà, c'est 'All-in-my-eye,' fils de ' Charles l'ox,' frère de ' Sevins-de-main'——"

" Ah, marquis, how goes it ?—Il est beau votre cheval."

"Oui, parbleu; he is frère aîné of ' Kiss-mi-ladi,' qui a gagné le handicap à l'Ile du Dogs."

And thus did these miserable imitators of Ascot and Doncaster, of Leamington and the Quorn, talk the most insane nonsense, which had been sold to them by some London horsedealer, as the pedigree of their hackneys.

It was really delightful amid all this to see the two English girls, who sat their horses so easily and so grace-fully—bending slightly with each curvet, they only yielded to the impulse of the animal as much as served to keep their own balance; the light but steady finger on the bridle, the air of quiet composure, uniting elegance with command. What a contrast to the distorted gesture, the desperate earnestness, and the fearful tenacity of their much-whiskered companions. And yet it was to please and fascinate these same pinchbeck sportsmen, these girls were then there. If they rode over everything that day —fence or rail, brook or bank—it was because the *chasse* to them was less *au cerf* than *au mari*.

Such was the case. The old colonel had left England because he preferred the Channel to the Fleet. The glorious liberty which Englishmen are so proud of would have been violated in his person had he remained. His failing, like many others, was that he had lived, "not wisely, but too well;" and, in short, however cold the climate, London would have proved too hot for him, had he stayed another day in it.

What a deluge of such people float over the Continent, living well and what is called "most respectably;" dining at embassies, and dancing at courts ; holding their heads very high, too—most scrupulous about acquaintances, and exclusive in all their intimacies. They usually prefer foreign society to that of their countrymen, for obvious reasons. Few Frenchmen read the *Gazette* I never heard of a German who knew anything about the list of outlaws. Of course they have no more to say to English preserves, and so they take out a license to shoot over the foreign manors; and though a marquis or a count are but "small deer," it's the only game left, and they make the best of it.

At last the host appeared, attired in a scarlet frock, and wearing a badge at his buttonhole, something about the shape and colour of a new penny-piece. He was followed by above a dozen others, similarly habited, minus the badge ; and then came about twenty more, dressed in green frocks, with red collars and cuffs, a species of smaller deities, who, I learned, were called " Aspirants," though to what they aspired, where it was, or when they hoped for it, nobody could inform me. Then there were piquers, and grooms, and whippers-in, without number, all noisy and all boisterous; about twenty couple of fox-hounds

giving tongue, and a due proportion of the scarlet folk
blowing away at that melodious pipe—the *cor de chasse.*

With this goodly company I moved forward, " alone,
but in a crowd ," for, unhappily, my want of tact as a
sporting character the previous evening had damaged me
seriously with the hunting youths, and Mademoiselle Laura
showed no desire to accept the companionship her worthy
father had selected for her. No matter, thought I, there's
a great deal to see here, and I can do without chatting in
so stirring a scene as this.

Her companion was the Comte D'Espagne, an admirable
specimen of what the French call " Tigre ," for be it
known that the country which once obtained a reputation little short of ludicrous for its excess of courtesy and
the surplusage of its ceremony, has now, in the true spirit
of reaction, adopted a degree of abruptness we should
call rudeness, and a species of cold effrontery we might
mistake for insolence. The disciples of this new school
are significantly called " Young France," and distinguished for length of hair and beard—a look of frowning
solemnity and mock pre-occupation, very well-fitting garments, and yellow gloves. These gentlemen are sparing
of speech, and more so of gesture. They give to understand that some onerous deed of regeneration is expected
at their hands—some revival of the old spirit of the
nation. Though in what way it is to originate in curled
moustaches and lacquered boots, is still a mystery to the
many; but enough of them now. Of these was the
Comte D'Espagne.

I had almost forgotten to speak of one part of our
cortége, which should certainly not be omitted. This was
a wooden edifice on wheels, drawn by a pair of horses at
a brisk rate at the tail of the procession. At first it
occurred to me that it might be an ambulant dog-kennel,
to receive the hounds on their return. Then I suspected
it to be a walking hospital for wounded sportsmen ; and
certainly I could not but approve of the idea, as I called
to mind the position of any unlucky chasseur, in the event
of a fall, with his fifteen feet of " metal main" around
him; and I only hoped that a plumber accompanied the
expedition. My humanity, however, led me astray. The

pagoda was destined for the accommodation of a stag, who always assisted at the *chasse*, whenever no other game could be started. This venerable beast, some five-and-twenty years in the service, was like a stock piece in the theatres, which, always ready, could be produced without a moment's notice. Here was no rehearsal requisite; if a prima donna was sulky, or a tenor was drunk —if the fox wouldn't show, or the deer were shy—there was the stag, perfectly prepared for a pleasant canter of a few miles, and ready, if no one was intemperately precipitate, to give a very agreeable morning's sport. His perfections, however, went farther than this; for he was trained to cross the high road at all convenient thoroughfares, occasionally taking the main streets of a village, or the market-place of a bourg, swimming whenever the water was shallow enough to follow him on horseback, and giving up the ghost at the blast of a grand maître's bugle, with an accuracy as unerring as though he had performed at Franconi's.

Unhappily for me, I was not fated to witness an exhibition of his powers; for scarcely had we emerged from the wood when the dogs were laid on, and soon after found a fox

For some time the scene was an animated one, as every Fleming seemed to pin his faith on some favourite dog; and it was rather amusing to witness the eagerness with which each followed the movements of his adopted animal, cheering him on, and encouraging him to the top of his bent. At last the word "Away!" was given, and suddenly the dogs broke cover, and made across the plain in the direction of a great wood, or rather forest, above a mile off. The country, happily for most of us—I know it was so for me—was an open surface of gentle undulation, stubble and turnips the only impediments, and clay soft enough to make a fall easy.

The sight was so far exhilarating, that red coats in a gallop have always a pleasant effect; besides which, the very concourse of riders looks well. However, even as unsportsmanlike an eye as mine could detect the flaws in jockeyship about me—the fierce rushings of the gentlemen who pushed through the deepest ground, with a loose rein, flogging manfully the while; the pendulous motions of others between the mane and the haunches with every stride of the beast. But I had little time for such speculations, the hour of my own trial was approaching; the roan was getting troublesome, the pace was gradually working up her mettle, and she had given three or four preparatory bounds, as though to see whether she'd part company with me before she ran away or not. My own calculations at the moment were not very dissimilar— I was meditating a rupture of the partnership too The matrix of a full-length figure of Arthur O'Leary in red clay was the extent of any damage I could receive, and I only looked for a convenient spot where I might fall unseen. As I turned my head on every side, hoping for some secluded nook, some devil of a hunter, by way of directing the dogs, gave a blast of his brass instrument, about a hundred yards before me—the thing was now settled, the roan gave a whirl of her long vicious tail, plunged fearfully, and throwing down her head and twisting it to one side, as if to have a peep at my confusion, away she went. From having formed one of the rear guard, I now closed up with the main body—" aspirants," all—through whom I dashed like a catapult, and notwithstanding repeated shouts of " Pull in, sir !" " hold back!" &c., continued my onward course; a few seconds more and I was in the thick of the scarlet coats, my beast at the stretch of her speed, and caring nothing for the bridle. Amid a shower of " *sacrés*" that fell upon me like hail, I sprung through them, making the " red ones " " black" with every stroke of my gallop. Leaving them far behind, I flew past the grand maitre himself, who rode in the van, almost upsetting him by a side spring, as I passed, a malediction reached me as I went, but the forest soon received me in its dark embrace, and I saw no more

It was at first a source of consolation to me to think that every stride removed me from the reach of those whose denunciations I had so unfortunately incurred— grand maitre, chasseurs, and aspirants—they were all behind me. Ay, for that matter, so were the dogs, and the piquers, and, for aught I knew, the fox with them.

When I discovered, however, that the roan continued
her speed, still unabated, 1 began to be somewhat discon-
certed. It was true the ground was perfectly smooth and
safe · a long *allée* of the wood, with turf shorn close as a
pleasure ground. I pulled and sawed the bit, I jerked the
bridle, and performed all the manual exercise I could remember, as advised in such extremities, but to no use It
seemed to me that some confounded echo started the beast,
and incited her to increased speed. Just as this notion
struck me, I heard a voice behind cry out—"Do hold in—
try and hold in, Mr. O'Leary!" I turned my head, and
there was Laura, scarce a length behind, her thoroughbred
straining every sinew to come up. No one else was in
sight, and there we were, galloping like mad, with the
wood all to ourselves.

I can very well conceive why the second horse in a race
does his best to get foremost, if it were only the indulgence
of a very natural piece of curiosity to see what the other
has been running for , but why the first one only goes the
faster, because there are others behind him, that is a dead
puzzle to me. But so it was ; my ill-starred beast never
seemed to have put forth her full powers till she was
followed. "*Ventre à terre*," as the French say, was now
the pace, and though from time to time Laura would cry
out to me to hold back, I could almost swear I heard her
laughing at my efforts Meanwhile the wood was becoming
thicker and closer, and the *allée* narrower and evidently less
travelled ; still it seemed to have no end or exit. Scarcely
had we rounded one turn when a vista of miles would seem
to stretch away before us, passing over which, another, as
long again, would appear.

After about an hour's hard galloping, if I dare form any
conjecture as to the flight of time, I perceived with a
feeling of triumph that the roan was relaxing somewhat
in her stride, and beginning to evince, by an up-and-down
kind of gait, what sailors call a "fore-and-aft" motion,
that she was getting enough of it. I turned and saw
Laura about twenty yards behind : her thoroughbred dead
beat, and only able to sling along at that species of lobbing
canter blood cattle can accomplish, under any exigency.
With a bold effort I pulled up short, and she came along-

side of me, and before I could summon courage to meet the reproaches 1 expected for having been the cause of her runaway, she relieved my mind by a burst of as merry and good-tempered laughter as ever I listened to. The emotion was contagious, and so I laughed too, and it was full five minutes before either of us could speak.

" Well, Mr. O'Leary! 1 hope you know where we are," said she, drying her eyes, where the sparkling drops of mirth were standing, " for I assure you I don't."

" Oh, perfectly," replied I, as my eye caught a board nailed against a tree, on which some very ill-painted letters announced, " *La route de Bouvigne* "—" we are on the high road to Bouvigne, wherever that may be."

" Bouvigne ! " exclaimed she, in an accent of some alarm — " why it's five leagues from the château, I travelled there once by the high road. How are we ever to get back ? "

That was the very question I was then canvassing in my own mind, without a thought of how it was to be solved. However, I answered with an easy indifference— " Oh, nothing easier—we'll take a calèche at Bouvigne."

" But they've none."

" Well, then, fresh horses."

" There's not a horse in the place; it's a little village near the Meuse, surrounded with tall granite rocks, and only remarkable for its ruined castle, the ancient schloss of Philip de Bouvigne ? "

" How interesting ! " said I, delighted to catch at any-thing which should give the conversation a turn ; " and who was Philip de Bouvigne ? "

" Philip," said the lady, " was the second or third count, I forget which, of the name. The chronicles say that he was the handsomest and most accomplished youth of the time. Nowhere could he meet his equal at joust or tour-nament ; while his skill in arms was the least of his gifts ; he was a poet and a musician. In fact, if you were only to believe his historians, he was the most dangerous person for the young ladies of those days to meet with. Not that he ran away with them, *sur la grande route.*" As she said this a burst of laughing stopped her, and it was one I could really forgive, though myself the object of it. "However," resumed she, "I believe he was just as bad Well, to pursue my story, when Philip was but eighteen, it chanced that a party of warriors, bound for the Holy Land, came past the Castle of Bouvigne, and, of course, passed the night there. From them, many of whom had already been in Palestine, Philip heard the wondrous stories the crusaders ever brought back of combats and encounters, of the fearful engagements with the infidels, and the glorious victories of the Cross. And at length, so excited did his mind become by the narrations, that he resolved on the spot to set out for the Holy Land, and see with his own eyes the wonderful things they had been telling him

"This resolution could not fail of being applauded by the rest, and by none was it met with such decided approval as by Henri de Bethune, a young Liègeois, then setting out on his first crusade, who could not help extolling Philip's bravery, and above all, his devotion in the great cause, in quitting his home, and his young and beautiful wife; for I must tell you, as indeed I ought to have told you before, he had been but a few weeks married to the lovely Alice de Franchemont, the only daughter of the old Graf de Franchemont, of whose castle you may see the ruins near Chaude Fontaine."

I nodded assent, and she went on.

"Of course you can imagine the dreadful grief of the young countess when her husband broke to her his determination. If I were a novelist I'd tell you of tears and entreaties, and sighs and faintings, of promises and pledges, and vows, and so forth; for, indeed, it was a very sorrowful piece of business, and she didn't at all fancy passing some three or four years alone in the old keep at Bouvigne, with no society, not one single friend to speak to. At first, indeed, she would not hear of it, and it was only at length, when Henri de Bethune undertook to plead for him,—for he kindly remained several days at the château, to assist his friend at this conjuncture,—that she gave way, and consented. Still her consent was wrung from her against her convictions, and she was by no means satisfied that the arguments she yielded to were a whit too sound; and this, let me remark, *en passant*, is a most dangerous species of assent, when given by a lady—and one she always believes to be something of the nature of certain Catholic vows, which are only binding while you believe them reasonable and just."

"Is that really so?" interrupted I. "Do you, indeed, give me so low a standard of female fidelity as this?"

"If women are sometimes false," replied she, "it is because men are never true; but I must go on with my tale. Away went Count Philip, and with him his friend De Bethune. The former, if the fact were known, just as low-spirited, when the time came, as the countess herself. But, then, he had the double advantage—that he had a friend to talk with, and make participator of his sorrows, besides being the one leaving, not left."

"I don't know," interrupted I at this moment, "that you are right there; I think that the associations which cling to the places where we have been happy are a good requital for the sorrowful memories they may call up. I'd rather linger around the spot consecrated by the spirit of past pleasure, and dream over again, hour by hour, day by day, the bliss I knew there, than break up the charm of such memories by the vulgar incidents of travel, and the common-place adventures of a journey"

"There, there I differ from you completely," replied she. "All your reflections and reminiscences, give them as fine names as you will, are nothing but sighings and repinings for what cannot come back again; and such things only injure the temper, and spoil the complexion; whereas,—— but what are you laughing at?"

"I was smiling at your remark, which has only a feminine application."

"How teasing you are! I declare I'll argue no more with you. Do you want to hear my story?"

"Of all things—I'm greatly interested in it."

"Well, then, you must not interrupt me any more. Now, where was I? You actually made me forget where I stopped."

"You were just at the point where they set out, Philip and his friend, for the Holy Land."

"You must not expect from me any spirit-stirring narrative of the events in Palestine. Indeed, I'm not aware

Q

if the *Chronique de Flandre*, from which I take my tale,
says anything very particular about Philip de Bouvigne's
performances.   Of course, they were in accordance with
his former reputation : he killed his Saracens, like a true
knight—that there can be no doubt of.   As for Henri de
Bethune, before the year was over, he was badly wounded,
and left on the field of battle, where some said he expired
soon after ; others averring that he was carried away to
slavery   Be that as it might, Philip continued his career
with all the enthusiasm of a warrior and a devotee, a
worthy son of the church, and a brave soldier, unfortunately, however, forgetting the poor countess he had
left behind him, pining away her youth at the barred
casements of the old château ; straining her eyes from day
to day along the narrow causeway that led to the castle,
and where no charger's hoof re-echoed, as of old, to tell
of the coming of her lord.   Very bad treatment, you'll
confess ; and so, with your permission, we'll keep her
company for a little while.   Madame la Comtesse de
Bouvigne, as some widows will do, only became the prettier from desertion.   Her traits of beauty, mellowed by a
tender melancholy, without being marked too deeply by
grief, assumed an imaginative character, or what men
mistake for it "

"Indeed ! " said I, catching at the confession.

" Well, I'm sure it is so," replied she.   " In the great
majority of cases you are totally ignorant of what is
passing in a woman's mind.   The girl that seemed all
animation to-day, may have an air of deep depression to-
morrow, and of downright wildness the next—simply by
changing her *coiffure* from ringlets to braids, and from a
landeau to a state of dishevelled disorder.   A little flattery
of yourselves, artfully and well done, and you are quite
prepared to believe anything.   In any case, the countess
was very pretty, and very lonely.

" In those good days, when gentlemen left home, there
were neither theatres nor concerts to amuse their poor
neglected wives ; they had no operas, nor balls, nor *soirées*,
nor promenades.   No ; their only resource was to work
away at some huge piece of landscape embroidery, which,
begun in childhood, occupied a whole life, and transmitted

a considerable labour of background and foliage to the next generation. The only pleasant people in those times, it seems to me, were the jongleurs and the pilgrims; they went about the world fulfilling the destinies of newspapers; they chronicled the little events of the day, births, marriages, deaths, &c., and must have been a great comfort on a winter's evening.

" Well, it so chanced, that as the countess sat at her window one evening, as usual, watching the sun go down, she beheld a palmer coming slowly along up the causeway, leaning on his staff, and seeming sorely tired and weary——"

" But see," cried Laura, at this moment, as we gained the crest of a gentle acclivity, "yonder is Bouvigne; it is a fine thing even yet."

We both reined in our horses, the better to enjoy the prospect, and certainly it was a grand one. Behind us, and stretching for miles in either direction, was the great forest we had been traversing, the old Ardennes had been a forest in the times of Cæsar; its narrow pathways had echoed to the tread of Roman legions. In front was a richly cultivated plain, undulating gently towards the Meuse, whose silver current wound round it like a garter; the opposite bank being formed by an abrupt wall of naked rocks of grey granite, sparkling with its brilliant hues, and shining doubly in the calm stream at its foot. On one of the highest cliffs, above an angle of the river, and commanding both reaches of the stream for a considerable way, stood Bouvigne; two great squaret owers, rising above a battlemented wall, pierced with long loopholes, stood out against the clear sky; one of them, taller than the other, was surmounted by a turret at the angle, from the top of which something projected laterally, like a beam

" Do you see that piece of timber yonder? " said Laura.

" Yes," said I, " it's the very thing I've been looking at, and wondering what it could mean."

" Carry your eye downward," said she, " and try if you can t make out a low wall, connecting two masses of rock together; far, far down; do you see it ? "

" I see a large archway, with some ivy over it."

" That's it; that was the great entrance to the schloss; before it is the fosse—a huge ditch cut in the solid rock, so deep as to permit the water of the Meuse, when flooded, to flow into it. Well, now, if you look again, you'll see that the great beam above hangs exactly over that spot. It was one of the rude defences of the time, and intended, by means of an iron basket, which hung from its extremity, to hurl great rocks and stones upon any assailant. The mechanism can still be traced by which it was moved back and loaded ; the piece of rope which opened the basket at each discharge of its contents was there not many years ago. There's a queer, uncouth representation of the *panier de morte* as it is called, in the *Chronique*, which you can see in the old library at Rochepied. But here we are already at the ferry."

As she spoke we had just reached the bank of the Meuse, and in front was a beautifully situated little village, which, escarped in the mountain, presented a succession of houses, at different elevations, all looking towards the stream. They were mostly covered with vines and honeysuckles, and with the picturesque outlines of gable and roof, diamond windows and rustic porches, had a very pleasing effect.

As I looked, I had little difficulty in believing that they were not a very equestrian people : the little pathways that traversed their village being inaccessible, save to foot-passengers, frequently ascending by steps' cut in the rock, or rude staircases of wood, which hung here and there over the edge of the cliff in anything but a tempting way; the more so, as they trembled and shook with every foot that passed over them. Little mindful of this, the peasants might now be seen leaning over their frail barriers, and staring at the unwonted apparition of two figures on horseback ; while I was endeavouring, by signs and gestures, to indicate our wish to cross over.

At last a huge raft appeared to move from beneath the willows of the opposite bank, and by the aid of a rope fastened across the stream, two men proceeded slowly to ferry the great platform over.

Leading our horses cautiously forward, we embarked in this frail craft, and landed safely in Bouvigne.

CHAPTER XIV.

A NARROW ESCAPE.

" WILL you please to tell me, Mr. O'Leary," said Laura, in the easy tone of one who asked for information's sake, " what are your plans here? for up to this moment I only perceive that we have been increasing the distance between us and Rochepied."

"Quite true," said I; " but you know we agreed it was impossible to hope to find our way back through the forest Every *allée* here has not only its brother, but a large family, so absolutely alike no one could distinguish between them; we might wander for weeks without extricating ourselves."

" I know all that," said she, somewhat pettishly; " still my question remains unanswered; what do you mean to do here?"

" In the first place," said I, with the affected precision of one who had long since resolved on his mode of pro- ceeding, " we'll dine.'

I stopped here, to ascertain her sentiments on this part of my arrangement. She gave a short nod and I pro- ceeded—

' Having dined," said I, " we'll obtain horses and a calèche, if such can be found, for Rochepied."

" I've told you already there are no such things here; they never see a carriage of any kind from year's end to year's end, and there is not a horse in the whole village."

'· Perhaps, then, there may be a château near, where, on making known our mishap, we might be able——"

" Oh, that's very simple, as far as you're concerned," said she, with a saucy smile; " but I'd just as soon not have this adventure published over the whole country."

Ha! by Jove, thought I, there's a consideration com- pletely overlooked by me: and so I became silent and thoughtful, and spoke not another word, as we led our horses up the little rocky causeway towards the Toison d'Or. If we did not admire the little auberge of the Golden Fleece, truly the fault was rather our own, than from any want of merit in the little hostel itself. Situated on a rocky promontory on the river, it was built actually over the stream, the door fronting it, and approachable by a little wooden gallery, along which a range of orange-trees and arbutus was tastefully disposed, scenting the whole air with their fragrance As we walked along we caught glimpses of several rooms within, neatly and even handsomely furnished; and one *salon* in particular, where books and music lay scattered on the tables, with that air of habitation so pleasant to look on.

So far from our appearance in a neighbourhood thus remote and secluded creating any surprise, both host and hostess received us with the most perfect ease, blended with a mixture of cordial civility, very acceptable at the moment.

" We wish to dine at once," said I, as I handed Laura to a chair.

" And to know in what way we can reach Rochepied," said she; " our horses are weary and not able for the road "

" For the dinner, mademoiselle, nothing is easier; but as to getting forward to-night——"

" Oh, of course I mean to-night—at once."

" Ah, voilà," said he, scratching his forehead in bewilderment; " we're not accustomed to that, never. People generally stop a day or two ; some spend a week here, and have horses from Dinant to meet them."

" A week here! " exclaimed she; " and what in heaven's name can they do here for a week ? "

" Why, there's the château, mademoiselle; the château of Philip de Bouvigne, and the gardens terraced in the rock; and there's the well of St. Sèvres, and the Ile de Notre Dame aux bois ; and then there's such capital fishing in the stream—abundance of trout."

" Oh, delightful, I'm sure," said she, impatiently, " but we wish to get on: so just set your mind to that, like a worthy man."

" Well, we'll see what can be done," replied he; " and

before dinner's over, perhaps I may find some means to forward you."

With this he left the room, leaving mademoiselle and myself *téte-à-téte.* And here let me confess, never did any man feel his situation more awkwardly than I did mine at that moment; and before any of my younger and more ardent brethren censure me, let me at least " show cause " in my defence. First, I myself, however unintentionally, had brought Mademoiselle Laura into her present embarrassment, but for me and the confounded roan she had been at that moment cantering away pleasantly with the Comte D'Espagne beside her, listening to his *fleurettes,* and receiving his attentions. Secondly, I was, partly from bashfulness, partly from fear, little able to play the part my present emergency demanded, which should either have been one of downright indifference and ease, or something of a more tender nature, which indeed the very pretty companion of my travels might have perfectly justified.

" Well," said she, after a considerable pause, " this is about the most ridiculous scrape I've ever been involved in. What *will* they think at the château ? "

" If they saw your horse when he bolted——."

" Of course they did," said she ; " but what could they do ? The Comte D'Espagne is always mounted on a slow horse : *he* couldn't overtake me ; then the maîtres couldn't pass the grand maître."

" What ? " cried I, in amazement ; " I don't comprehend you perfectly."

" It's quite clear, nevertheless," replied she , " but I see you don't know the rules of the *chasse* in Flanders "

With this she entered into a detail of the laws of the hunting-field, which more than once threw me into fits of laughter. It seemed, then, that the code decided that each horseman who followed the hounds should not be left to the wilfulness of his horse, or the aspirings of his ambition, as to the place he occupied in the chase. It was no momentary superiority of skill or steed, no display of jockeyship, no blood, that decided this momentous question. No, that was arranged on principles far less vacillating and more permanent, at the commencement of the

hunting season, by which it was laid down as a rule certain
that the grand maître was always to ride first. His pace
might be fast or it might be slow, but his place was there.
After him came the maîtres, the people in scarlet, who, in
right of paying double subscription, were thus costumed
and thus privileged; while the aspirants in green followed
last, their smaller contribution only permitting them to
see so much of the sport as their respectful distance
opened to them; and thus that indiscriminate rush, so
observable in our hunting-fields, was admirably avoided
and provided against. It was no headlong piece of reckless daring—no impetuous dash of bold horsemanship;
on the contrary, it was a decorous and stately canter, not
after hounds, but after an elderly gentleman in a red coat
and a brass tube, who was taking a quiet airing in the
pleasing delusion that he was hunting an animal unknown.

Woe unto the man who forgot his place in the procession; you might as well walk into dinner before your host,
under the pretence that you were a more nimble pedestrian. Besides this, there were subordinate rules to no
end—certain notes on the *cor de chasse* were royalties of
the grand maître, the maîtres possessed others as *their*
privileges, which no aspirant dare venture on There
were quavers for one, and semiquavers for the other; and,
in fact, a most complicated system of legislation compre-
hended every incident, and, I believe, every accident of
the sport, so much that 1 can't trust my memory as
to whether the wretched aspirants were not limited to
tumbling in one particular direction, which, if so, must
have been somewhat of a tyranny, seeing they were but
men, and Belgians.

"This might seem all very absurd and very fabulous,
if I referred to a number of years back; but when I say
that the code exists still, in the year of grace, 1856, what
will they say at Melton or Grantham? So you may
imagine," said Laura, on concluding her description, which
she gave with much humour, "how manifold your trans-
gressions have been this day; you have offended the grand
maître, maîtres, and aspirants, in one *coup;* you have
broken up the whole ' order of their going.' "

"And run away with the belle of the château," added I.

She did not seem half to relish my jest, however; and gave a little shake of the head, as though to say—

"You're not out of *that* scrape yet."

Thus did we chat over our dinner, which was really excellent; the host's eulogy on the Meuse trout being admirably sustained by their merits; nor did his flask of Haut-Brion lower the character of his cellar. Still no note of preparation seemed to indicate any arrangements for our departure; and although, sooth to say, I could have reconciled myself wonderfully to the inconvenience of the Toison D'Or for the whole week if necessary, Laura was becoming momentarily more impatient, as she said—

"*Do* see if they are getting anything like a carriage ready, or even horses; we can ride, if they'll only get us animals."

As I entered the little kitchen of the inn, I found my host stretched at ease in a wicker chair, surrounded by a little atmosphere of smoke, through which his great round face loomed like the moon in the grotesque engravings one sees in old spelling-books So far from giving himself any unnecessary trouble about our departure, he had never ventured beyond the precincts of the stove, contenting himself with a wholesome monologue on the impossibility of our desires; and that great Flemish consolation, that however we might chafe at first, time would calm us in the end.

After a fruitless interrogation about the means of proceeding, I asked if there were no château in the vicinity where horses could be borrowed?

He replied, "No, not one for miles round."

"Is there no Maire in the village—where is he?"

"I am the Maire," replied he, with a conscious dignity.

Alas! thought I, as the functionary of Givet crossed my mind, why did I not remember that the Maire is always the most stupid of the whole community.

"Then I think," said I, after a brief silence, "we had better see the Curé at once."

"I thought so," was the sententious reply.

Without troubling my head why he "thought so," I begged that the Curé might be informed that a gentleman at the inn begged to speak with him for a few minutes.

"The Père José, I suppose?" said the host, significantly

"With all my heart," said I; "José or Pierre, it's all alike to me."

"He is there in waiting this half-hour," said the host, pointing with his thumb to a small *salon* off the kitchen.

"Indeed!" said I; "how very polite the attention. I'm really most grateful."

With which, without delaying another moment, I pushed open the door, and entered.

The Père José was a short, ruddy, astute-looking man of about fifty, dressed in the canonical habit of a Flemish priest, which, from time and wear, had lost much of its original freshness. He had barely time to unfasten a huge napkin, which he had tied around his neck during his devotion to a great mess of vegetable soup, when I made my bow to him.

"The Père José, I believe?" said I, as I took my seat opposite to him.

"That unworthy priest!" said he, wiping his lips, and throwing up his eyes with an expression not wholly devotional.

"Père José," resumed I, "a young lady and myself, who have just arrived here with weary horses, stand in need of your kind assistance." Here he pressed my hand gently, as if to assure me I was not mistaken in my man, and I went on:—"We must reach Rochepied to-night; now will you try and assist us at this conjuncture? we are complete strangers."

"Enough, enough!" said he. "I'm sorry you are constrained for time. This is a sweet little place for a few days' sojourn. But if," said he, "it can't be, you shall have every aid in my power. I'll send off to Poil de Vache for his mule and car. You don't mind a little shaking," said he, smiling.

"It's no time to be fastidious, Père, and the lady is an excellent traveller."

"The mule is a good beast, and will bring you in three hours, or even less." So saying, he sat down and wrote a few lines on a scrap of paper, with which he despatched a boy from the inn, telling him to make every haste. "And now, Monsieur, may I be permitted to pay my respects to Mademoiselle ?"

" Most certainly, Père José ; she will be but too happy to add her thanks to mine for what you have done for us."

" Say rather, for what I am about to do," said he, smiling.

" The will is half the deed, Father."

" A good adage, and an old," replied he, while he proceeded to arrange his drapery, and make himself as presentable as the nature of his costume would admit.

" This was a rapid business of yours," said he, as he smoothed down his few locks at the back of his head.

" That it was, Père,—a regular runaway."

" I guessed as much," said he. " I said so, the moment I saw you at the ferry."

The Padre is no bad judge of horse-flesh, thought I, to detect the condition of our beasts at that distance.

" ' There's something for me,' said I to Madame Guyon. ' Look yonder ! See how their cattle are blowing ! They've lost no time, and neither will I.' And with that I put on my gown and came up here."

" How considerate of you, Père ; you saw we should need your help."

" Of course I did," said he, chuckling. " Of course I did. Old Gregoire, here, is so stupid and so indolent that I have to keep a sharp look-out myself. But he's the Maire, and one can't quarrel with him."

" Very true," said I. " A functionary has a hundred opportunities of doing civil things, or the reverse."

" That's exactly the case," said the Père. " Without him we should have no law on our side. It would be all *sous la cheminée*, as they say."

The expression was new to me, and I imagined the good priest to mean, that without the magistrature, respect for the laws might as well be " up the chimney." " And now, if you allow me, we'll pay our duty to the lady," said the Père José, when he had completed his toilette to his satisfaction.

When the ceremonial of presenting the Père was over I informed Laura of his great kindness in our behalf, and the trouble he had taken to provide us with an equipage.

" A sorry one, I fear, Mademoiselle," interposed he, with a bow. " But I believe there are few circumstances in life where people are more willing to endure sacrifices."

" Then Monsieur has explained to you our position ? " said Laura, half blushing at the absurdity of the adventure.

" Everything, my dear young lady—everything. Don't let the thought give you any uneasiness, however. I listen to stranger stories every day."

" Taste that Haut-Brion, Père," said I, wishing to give the conversation a turn, as I saw Laura felt uncomfortable, " and give me your opinion of it. To my judgment it seems excellent."

" And your judgment is unimpeachable in more respects than that," said the Père, with a significant look, which fortunately was not seen by Mademoiselle.

Confound him, said I to myself; I must try another tack. " We were remarking, Père José, as we came along that very picturesque river, the Château de Bouvigne—a fine thing in its time, it must have been."

" You know the story, I suppose ? " said the Père.

" Mademoiselle was relating it to me on the way, and indeed I am most anxious to hear the *dénouement.*"

" It was a sad one," said he, slowly. " I'll show you the spot where Henry fell—the stone that marks the place."

" O Père José," said Laura, " I must stop you—indeed I must—or the whole interest of my narrative will be ruined. You forget that Monsieur has not heard the tale out "

" Ah ? *ma foi,* I beg pardon—a thousand pardons. Mademoiselle, then, knows Bouvigne ? "

" I've been here once before, but only part of a morning. I've seen nothing but the outer court of the château and the *fosse du traître.*"

" So, so; you know it all, I perceive," said he, smiling pleasantly. " Are you too much fatigued for a walk that far ? "

" Shall we have time ? " said Laura; " that's the question."

"Abundance of time. Jocot can't be here for an hour yet, at soonest And, if you allow me, I'll give all the necessary directions before we leave, so that you'll not be delayed ten minutes on your return"

While Laura went in search of her hat, I again proffered my thanks to the kind Père for all his good nature, expressing the strong desire I felt for some opportunity of requital

"Be happy," said the good man, squeezing my hand affectionately, "that's the way you can best repay me."

"It would not be difficult to follow the precept in your society, Père José," said I, overcome by the cordiality of the old man's manner.

"I have made a great many so, indeed," said he "The five-and-thirty years I have lived in Bouvigne have not been without their fruit."

Laura joined us here, and we took the way together towards the château, the priest discoursing all the way on the memorable features of the place, its remains of ancient grandeur, and the picturesque beauty of its site.

As we ascended the steep path which, cut in the solid rock, leads to the château, groups of pretty children came flocking about us, presenting bouquets for our acceptance, and even scattering flowers in our path This simple act of village courtesy struck us both much, and we could not help feeling touched by the graceful delicacy of the little ones, who tripped away ere we could reward them; neither could I avoid remarking to Laura on the perfect good understanding that seemed to subsist between Père José and the children of his flock—the paternal fondness on one side, and the filial reverence on the other. As we conversed thus, we came in front of a great arched doorway, in a curtain wall connecting two massive fragments of rock. In front lay a deep fosse, traversed by a narrow wall, scarce wide enough for one person to venture on. Below, the tangled weeds and ivy concealed the dark abyss, which was full eighty feet in depth.

"Look up, now," said Laura, "you must bear the features of this spot in mind to understand the story. Don't forget where that beam projects—do you mark it well?"

"He'll get a better notion of it from the tower," said the Père. "Shall I assist you across?"

Without any aid, however, Laura trod the narrow pathway, and hasted along up the steep and time-worn steps of the old tower. As we emerged upon the battlements we stood for a moment, overcome by the splendour of the prospect. Miles upon miles of rich landscape lay beneath us, glittering in the red, brown, and golden tints of autumn,—that gorgeous livery which the year puts on, ere it dons the sad-coloured mantle of winter. The great forest, too, was touched here and there with that light brown, the first advance of the season; while the river reflected every tint in its calm tide, as though it also would sympathize with the changes around it.

While the Père José continued to point out each place of mark or note in the vast plain, interweaving in his descriptions some chance bit of antiquarian or historic lore, we were forcibly struck by the thorough intimacy he possessed with all the features of the locality, and could not help complimenting him upon it.

"Yes, *ma foi*," said he, "I know every rock and crevice, every old tree and rivulet for miles round In the long life I have passed here, each day has brought me among those scenes with some traveller or other; and albeit they who visit us here have little thought for the picturesque, few are unmoved by this peaceful and lovely valley. You'd little suspect, Mademoiselle, how many have passed through my hands here, in these five-and-thirty years. I keep a record of their names, in which I must beg you will kindly inscribe yours"

Laura blushed at the proposition which should thus commemorate her misadventure; while I mumbled out something about our being mere passing strangers, unknown in the land.

"No matter for that," replied the inexorable Father, "I'll have your names—ay, autographs too!"

"The sun seems very low," said Laura, as she pointed to the west, where already a blaze of red golden light was spreading over the horizon: "I think we must hasten our departure."

"Follow me, then," said the Père, "and I'll conduct

you by an easier path than we came up by." With that
he unlocked a small postern in the curtain wall, and led
us across a neatly-shaven lawn to a little barbican, where,
again unlocking the door, we descended a flight of stone
steps into a small garden terraced in the native rock.
The labour of forming it must have been immense, as
every shovelful of earth was carried from the plain beneath ; and here were fruit-trees and flowers, shrubs and
plants, and in the midst, a tiny *jet d'eau*, which, as we
entered, seemed magically to salute us with its refreshing
plash. A little bench, commanding a view of the river
from a different aspect, invited us to sit down for a
moment. Indeed, each turn of the way seduced us by
some beauty, and we could have lingered on for hours.
As for me, forgetful of the past, careless of the future, I
was totally wrapt up in the enjoyment of the moment,
and Laura herself seemed so enchanted by the spot that
she sat, silently gazing on the tranquil scene, and
apparently lost in delighted reverie. A low, faint sigh
escaped her as she looked, and I thought I could see a
tremulous motion of her eyelid, as though a tear were
struggling within it : my heart beat powerfully against
my side. I turned to see where was the Père. He had
gone. I looked again, and saw him standing on a point
of rock far beneath us, and waving his handkerchief as a
signal to some one in the valley. Never was there such a
situation as mine—never was mortal man so placed. I
stole my hand carelessly along the bench till it touched
hers, but she moved not away—no, her mind seemed quite
pre-occupied. I had never seen her profile before, and
truly it was very beautiful. All the vivacity of her
temperament calmed down by the feeling of the moment,
her features had that character of placid loveliness which
seemed only wanting to make her perfectly handsome. I
wished to speak, and could not. I felt that if I could have
dared to say " Laura," I could have gone on bravely afterwards,—but it would not come. " Amen stuck in my
throat." Twice I got half-way, and covered my retreat
by a short cough. Only think what a change in my
destiny another syllable might have caused ! It was
exactly as my second effort proved fruitless, that a deli-

cious sound of music swelled up from the glen beneath, and floated through the air—a chorus of young voices singing what seemed to be a hymn. Never was anything more charming. The notes, softened as they rose on high, seemed almost like a seraph's song—now raising the soul to high and holy thoughts—now thrilling within the heart with a very ecstasy of delight.

At length they paused, the last cadence melted slowly away, and all was still—we did not dare to move—when Laura touched my hand gently, and whispered—

"Hark! there it is again." and at the instant the voices broke forth, but into a more joyous measure. It was one of those sweet peasant-carollings which breathe of the light heart and the simple life of the cottage.

The words came nearer and nearer as we listened, and at length I could trace the *refrain* which closed each verse:

"Puisque l'herbe et la fleur parlent mieux que les mots,
Puisque un aveu d'amour s'exhale de la rose,
Que le ' ne m'oublie pas ' de souvenir s'arrose,
Que le laurier dit Gloire! et cyprés sanglots."

At last the wicket of the garden slowly opened, and a little procession of young girls, all dressed in white, with white roses in their hair, and carrying bouquets each in their hands, entered, and with steady step came forward. We watched them attentively, believing that they were celebrating some little devotional pilgrimage, when, to our surprise, they approached where we sat, and, with a low courtesy, each dropped her bouquet at Laura's feet, whispering in a low silver voice as they passed, " May thy feet always tread upon flowers !"

Ere we could speak our surprise and admiration of this touching scene—for it was such, in all its simplicity—they were gone, and the last notes of their chant were dying away in the distance.

"How beautiful — how very beautiful!" said Laura; "I shall never forget this."

"Nor I," said I, making a desperate effort at I know not what avowal, which the appearance of the Père at once put to flight. He had just seen the boy returning along the river-side with the mule and cart, and came to apprise us that we had better descend.

"It will be very late indeed before we reach Dinant; we shall scarcely get there before midnight."

"Oh, you'll be there much earlier; it is now past six; in less than ten minutes you can be *en route*. I shall not cause you much delay."

Ah, thought I, the good Father is still dreaming about his album; we must indulge his humour, which, after all, is but a poor requital for all his politeness.

As we entered the parlour of the Toison D'Or, we found the host in all the bravery of his Sunday suit, with a light brown wig, and stockings blue as the heaven itself, standing waiting our arrival. The hostess, too, stood at the other side of the door, in the full splendour of a great quilted *jupe*, and a cap, whose ears descended half-way to her waist. On the table, in the middle of the room, were two wax-candles, of that portentous size that we see in chapels Between them there lay a great open volume, which at a glance I guessed to be the priest's album. Not comprehending what the worthy host and hostess meant by their presence, I gave a look of interrogation to the Père, who quickly whispered—

"Oh, it is nothing, they are only the witnesses."

I could not help laughing outright at the idea of this formality, nor could Laura refrain either when I explained to her what they came for. However, time passed; the jingle of the bells on the mules' harness warned us that our equipage waited; and I dipped the pen in the ink and handed it to Laura

"I wish he could excuse me from performing this ceremony," said she, holding back; "I really am quite enough ashamed already."

"What says Mademoiselle?" inquired the Père, as she spoke in English.

I translated her remark, when he broke in—

"Oh, you must comply; it's only a formality, but still every one does it."

"Come, come," said I, in English, "indulge the old man; he is evidently bent on this whim, and let us not leave him disappointed."

"Be it so, then," said she; "on your head, Mr. O'Leary, be the whole of this day's indiscretion;" and so saying,

R

she took the pen and wrote her name, "Laura Alicia Muddleton."

"Now, then, for my turn," said I, advancing; but the Père took the pen from her fingers, and proceeded carefully to dry the writing with a scrap of blotting-paper.

"On this side, Monsieur," said he, turning over the page; "we do the whole affair in orderly fashion, you see, put your name there, with the date and the day of the week.'

"Will that do?" said I, as I pushed over the book towards him, where certainly the least imposing specimen of caligraphy the volume contained now stood confessed.

"What a droll name!" said the priest, as he peered at it through his spectacles. "How do you pronounce it?"

While I endeavoured to indoctrinate the Father into the mystery of my Irish appellation, the mayor and the mayoress had both appended their signatures on either page.

"Well, I suppose now we may depart at last," said Laura; "it's getting very late."

"Yes," said I, aloud; "we must take the road now; there is nothing more, I fancy, Père José?"

"Yes; but there is though," said he, laughing——

But, at the same moment, the galloping of horses and the crash of wheels were heard without, and a carriage drew up in the street. Down went the steps with a crash —several people rushed along the little gallery, till the very house shook with their tread. The door of the salon was now banged wide, and in rushed Colonel Muddleton, followed by the count, the abbé, and an elderly lady.

"Where is he?"—"Where is she?"—"Where is he?" —"Where is she?"—Where are they?" screamed they, in confusion, one after the other.

"Laura! Laura!" cried the old colonel, clasping his daughter in his arms; "I didn't expect this from you!"

"Monsieur O'Leary, vous êtes un——"

Before the count could finish, the abbé interposed between us, and said—

"No, no! Everything may be arranged. Tell me, in one word, is it over?"

"Is what over?" said I, in a state two degrees worse than insanity—"is what over?"

"Are you married?" whispered he.

" No, bless your heart; never thought of it."

" Oh, the wretch!" screamed the old lady, and went off into strong kickings on the sofa.

" It's a bad affair," said the abbé, in a low voice, " take my advice—propose to marry her at once "

" Yes, *parbleu!*" said the little count, twisting his moustaches in a fierce manner; " there is but one road to take here."

Now, though unquestionably but half an hour before, when seated beside the lovely Laura in the garden of the château, such a thought would have filled me with delight; now, the same proposition, accompanied by a threat, stirred up all my indignation and resistance.

" Not on compulsion," said Sir John; and truly there was reason in the speech.

But, indeed, before I could reply, the attentions of all were drawn towards Laura herself, who, from laughing violently at first, had now become hysterical, and continued to laugh and cry at intervals; and as the old lady continued her manipulations with a candlestick on an oak table near, while the colonel shouted for various unattainable remedies at the top of his voice, the scene was anything but decorous; the abbé, who alone seemed to preserve his sanity, having as much as he could do to prevent the little count from strangling me with his own hands; such, at least, his violent gestures seemed to indicate. As for the priest, and the Maire, and the she Maire, they had all fled long before. There appeared now but one course for me, which was to fly also. There was no knowing what intemperance the count might not commit under his present excitement. It was clear they were all labouring under a delusion, which nothing at the present moment could elucidate. A nod from the abbé and a motion towards the open door decided my wavering resolution I rushed out, over the gallery, and down the road, not knowing whither, nor caring.

I might as well try to chronicle the sensations of my raving intellect, in my first fever in boyhood, as convey any notion of what passed through my brain for the next two hours. I sat on a rock beside the river, vainly endeavouring to collect my scattered thoughts, which only presented to me a vast chaos of a wood and a crusader, a priest and a lady, veal cutlets and music, a big book, an old lady in fits, and a man in sky-blue stockings. The rolling of a carriage with four horses near me aroused me for a second, but I could not well say why, and all was again still, and I sat there alone.

"He must be somewhere near this," said a voice, as I heard the tread of footsteps approaching; "this is his hat. Ah, here he is." At the same moment the abbé stood beside me.

"Come along, now; don't stay here in the cold," said he, taking me by the arm. "They've all gone home two hours ago. I have remained to ride back the nag in the morning."

I followed without a word.

"*Ma foi!*" said he, "it is the first occasion in my life where I could not see my way through a difficulty. What, in Heaven's name, were you about? What was your plan?"

"Give me half an hour in peace," said I, "and if I'm not deranged before it's over, I'll tell you."

The abbé complied, and I fulfilled my promise—though, in good sooth, the shouts of laughter with which he received my story caused many an interruption. When I had finished, he began, and leisurely proceeded to inform me that Bouvigne's great celebrity was as a place for runaway couples to get married; that the inn of the Golden Fleece was known over the whole kingdom, and the Père José's reputation wide as the Archbishop of Ghent's; and as to the phrase "*sous la cheminée*," it is only applied to a clandestine marriage, which is called a "*mariage sous la cheminée.*"

"Now I," continued he, "can readily believe every word you've told me, yet there's not another person in Rochepied would credit a syllable of it. Never hope for an explanation. In fact, before you were listened to, there are at least two duels to fight—the count first, and then D'Espagne. I know Laura well—she'll let the affair have all its *éclat* before she will say a word about it; and, in fact, your executors may be able to clear your character—you'll never do so in your lifetime.

Don't go back there," said the abbé, "at least for the present."

" I'll never set eyes on one of them," cried I, in desperation; "I'm nigh deranged as it is—the memory of this confounded affair——"

" Will make you laugh yet," said the abbé. " And now, good night, or rather good-bye—I start early to-morrow morning, and we may not meet again."

He promised to forward my effects to Dinant, and we parted.

" Monsieur will have a single bed ? " said the house-maid, in answer to my summons

" Yes," said I, with a muttering, I fear very like an oath.

Morning broke in, through the half-closed curtains, with the song of birds, and the ripple of the gentle river. A balmy air stirred the leaves, and the sweet valley lay in all its peaceful beauty before me.

" Well, well," said I, rubbing my eyes, " it was a queer adventure ; and there's no saying what might have happened, had they been only ten minutes later. I'd give a napoleon to know what Laura thinks of it now. But I must not delay here—the very villagers will laugh at me."

I ate my breakfast rapidly, and called for my bill. The sum was a mere trifle, and I was just adding something to it, when a knock came to the door.

" Come in," said I, and the Père entered.

" How sadly unfortunate," began he, when I interrupted him at once, assuring him of his mistake ; that we were no runaway couple at all, had not the most remote idea of being married, and in fact owed our whole disagreeable adventure to his ridiculous misconception.

" It's very well to say that *now*," growled out the Père, in a very different accent from his former one. " You may pretend what you like, but—"and he spoke in a determined tone—" you'll pay *my* bill."

" *Your* bill ! " said I, waxing wroth. " What have I had from you—how am I your debtor ? I should like to hear."

" And you shall," said he, drawing forth a long document from a pocket in his cassock. "Here it is." He handed me the paper, of which the following is a transcript.—

Noces de Mi Lord O'Leary et Mademoiselle Mi Lady de Muddleton.

	FRANCS	
Two conversations—preliminary, admonitory, and consolatory	10	0
Advice to the young couple, with moral maxims interspersed	3	0
Soirée, and society at wine	5	0
Guide to the Château, with details, artistic and antiquarian	12	0
Eight Children with flowers, at half a franc each	4	0
Fees at the Château	2	0
Chorus of Virgins, at one franc per virgin	10	0
Roses for Virgins	2	10
M. le Maire et Madame "en grande tenue"	1	0
Book of Registry, setting forth the date of the Marriage—		

"The devil take it!" said I; "it was no marriage at all."
"Yes, but it was, though," said he. "It's your own fault if you can't take care of your wife."

The noise of his reply brought the host and hostess to the scene of action; and though I resisted manfully for a time, there was no use in prolonging a hopeless contest, and, with a melancholy sigh, I disbursed my wedding expenses, and with a hearty malediction on Bouvigne,—its château—its inn—its Père—its Maire—and its virgins,—I took the road towards Namur, and never lifted my head till I had left the place miles behind me.

CHAPTER XV.

A MOUNTAIN ADVENTURE.

IT was growing late on a fine evening of autumn, as, a solitary pedestrian, I drew near the little town of Spa. From the time of my leaving Chaude Fontaine, I lingered along the road, enjoying to the utmost the beautiful valley of the Vesdre, and sometimes half hesitating whether I would not loiter away some days in one of the little villages I passed, and see if the trout, whose circling eddies marked the stream, might not rise as favourably to my fly as to the vagrant insect that now flitted across the water.

In good sooth, I wished for rest, and I wished for solitude; too much of my life latterly had been passed in *salons* and *soirées*—the peaceful habit of my soul, the fruit of my own lonely hours—had suffered grievous inroads by my partnership with the world; and I deemed it essential to be once more apart from the jarring influences and distracting casualties which every step in life is beset by, were it only to recover again my habitual tranquillity—to refit the craft ere she took the sea once more.

I wanted but little to decide my mind, the sight of an inn, some picturesque spot, a pretty face—anything, in short—would have sufficed; but somehow I suppose I must have been more fastidious than I knew of, for I continued to walk onward, and at last, leaving the little hamlet of Pepinsterre behind me, set out with brisker pace towards Spa.

The air was calm and balmy; no leaf stirred; the river beside the road did not even murmur, but crept silently along its gravelly bed, fearful to break the stillness. Gradually the shadows fell stronger and broader, and at length mingled into one broad expanse of gloom, and in a few minutes more it was night.

There is something very striking, I had almost said saddening, in the sudden transition from day to darkness, in those countries where no twilight exists. The gradual change by which road and mountain, rock and cliff, mellow into the hues of sunset, and grow grey in the "gloaming," deepening the shadows, and by degrees losing all outline in the dimness around, prepares us for the gloom of night. We feel it like the tranquil current of years, marking some happy life, where childhood and youth, and manhood and age, succeed in measured time. Not so the sudden and immediate change, which seems rather like the stroke of some fell misfortune, converting the cheerful hours into dark brooding melancholy. Years may, they do, fall lightly on some; they creep with noiseless step, and youth and age glide softly into each other, without any shock to awaken the thought that says—Adieu to this!—Farewell to that for ever!

Thus was I musing, when suddenly I found myself at the spot where the road branched off in two directions. No house, not a living thing was near, from whom I could ask the way. I endeavoured, by the imperfect light of the stars—for there was no moon—to ascertain which road seemed most frequented and travelled, judging that Spa was the most likely resort of all journeying in these parts; but, unhappily, I could detect no difference to guide me; there were wheel-tracks in both, and ruts and stones tolerably equitably adjusted, each had a pathway, too, the right-hand road enjoying a slight superiority over the other, in this respect, as its path was more even.

I was completely puzzled. Had I been mounted, I had left the matter to my horse; but, unhappily, my decision had not a particle of reason to guide it. I looked from the road to the trees, and from the trees to the stars, but they looked down as tranquilly as though either way would do—all save one—a sly little brilliant spangle in the south, that seemed to wink at my difficulty. "No matter," said I, "one thing is certain; neither a supper nor a bed will come to look for me here, and so now for the best pathway, as I begin to feel foot-sore."

My momentary embarrassment about the road completely routed all my musings, and I now turned my thoughts to the comforts of the inn, and the pleasant little supper I promised myself on reaching it. I debated about what was in season, and what was not; I spelled October twice to ascertain if oysters were in, and there came a doubt across me whether the Flemish name for the month might have an *r* in it, and then I laughed at my own bull; afterwards I disputed with myself as to the relative merits of Chablis and Hochheimer, and resolved to be guided by the *garçon*. I combated long a weakness I felt growing over me—for a pint of mulled claret, as the air was now becoming fresh; but I gave in at last, and began to hammer my brain for the French words for cloves and nutmeg.

In these innocent ruminations did an hour pass by, and yet no sign of human habitation, no sound of life, could I perceive at either side of me. The night, 'tis true, was brighter as it became later, and there were stars in thousands in the sky; but I would gladly have exchanged Venus for the chambermaid of the humblest aubeige, and given the Great Bear himself for a single slice of bacon. At length, after about two hours' walking, I remarked that the road was becoming much more steep; indeed, it had presented a continual ascent for some miles, but now the acclivity was very considerable, particularly at the close of a long day's march; I remembered well that Spa lay in a valley, but, for the life of me, I could not think whether a mountain was to be crossed to arrive there. "That comes of travelling by post," said I to myself, "had I walked the road, I had never forgotten so remarkable a feature." While I said this, I could not help confessing that I had as lieve my present excursion had been also in a conveyance. "Forwarts! fort, und Immer fort!" hummed I, remembering Körner's song, and taking it for my motto, and on I went at a good pace. It needed all my powers as a pedestrian, however, to face the mountain—for such I could see it was that I was now ascending—the pathway, too, less trodden than below, was encumbered with loose stones, and the trees which lined the way on either side gradually became thinner and rarer, and at last ceased altogether, exposing me to the cold blast, which swept from time to time across the barren heath with a chill that said October was own brother to November. Three hours and a half did I toil along, and at last the conviction came before me that I must have taken the wrong road. This could not possibly be the way to Spa; indeed, I had great doubts that it led anywhere: I mounted upon a little rock, and took a survey of the bleak mountain side; but nothing could I see that indicated that the hand of man had ever laboured in that wild region. Fern and heath, clumps of gorse and misshapen rocks, diversified the barren surface on every side, and I now seemed to have gained the summit, a vast table-land spreading away for miles. I sat down to con-

sider what was best to be done; the thought of retracing
so many leagues of way was very depressing, and yet what
were my chances if I went forward ?

Ah! thought I, why did not some benevolent individual think of erecting lighthouses inland ? What a
glorious invention would it have been !—just think of the
great mountain districts which lie in the very midst of
civilization, pathless, trackless, and unknown—where a
benighted traveller may perish, within the very sound of
succour, if he but knew where to seek it How cheering to the wayworn traveller as he plodded along his
weary road, to lift from time to time his eyes to the guide-
star in the distance! Had the monks been in the habit
of going out in the dark, there's little doubt they'd have
persuaded some good Catholics to endow some institutions
like this. How well they knew how to have their
chapels and convents erected! I'm not sure but I'd vow
a little lighthouse myself to the Virgin, if I could only
catch a glimpse of a gleam of light this moment.

Just then, I thought I saw something twinkle, far
away across the heath · I climbed up on the rock, and
looked steadily in the direction—there was no doubt of it
—there was a light—no Jack-o'-Lantern either,—but a
good, respectable light, of domestic habits, shining steadily
and brightly. It seemed far off, but there is nothing so
deceptive as the view over a flat surface. In any case, I
resolved to make for it, and so, seizing my staff, I once
more set forward; unhappily, however, I soon perceived
that the road led off in a direction exactly the reverse of
the object I sought, and I was now obliged to make
my choice of quitting the path or abandoning the
light; my resolve was quickly made, and I started off
across the plain, with my eyes steadily fixed upon my
beacon.

The mountain was marshy and wet, that wearisome
surface of spongy hillock, and low, creeping brushwood,
the most fatal thing to a tried walker, and I made but
slow progress; besides, frequently, from inequalities of
the soil, I would lose sight of the light for half an hour
together, and then, on its reappearing suddenly, discover
how far I had wandered out of the direct line. These

little aberrations did not certainly improve my temper, and I plodded along, weary of limb, and out of spirits.

At length I came to the verge of a declivity: beneath me lay a valley, winding and rugged, with a little torrent brawling through rocks and stones—a wild and gloomy scene, by the imperfect light of the stars. On the opposite mountain stood the coveted light, which now I could discover, proceeding from a building of some size, at least so far as I could pronounce from the murky shadow against the background of sky.

I summoned up one great effort, and pushed down the slope; now sliding on hands and feet, now trusting to a run of some yards where the ground was more feasible. After a fatiguing course of two hours, I reached the crest of the opposite hill, and stood within a few hundred yards of the house—the object of my wearisome journey.

It was indeed in keeping with the deserted wildness of the place. A ruined tower, one of those square keeps which formerly were intended as frontier defences, standing on a rocky base, beside the edge of a steep cliff, had been made a dwelling of by some solitary herdsman, for so the sheep, collected within a little inclosure, bespoke him. The rude efforts to make the place habitable were conspicuous in the door formed of wooden planks nailed coarsely together, and the window, whose panes were made of a thin substance, like parchment, through which, however, the blaze of a fire shone brightly without.

Creeping carefully forward to take a reconnoissance of the interior before I asked for admission, I approached a small aperture, where a single pane of glass permitted a view a great heap of blazing furze that filled the old chimney of the tower, lit up the whole space, and enabled me to see a man who sat on a log of wood beside the hearth, with his head bent upon his knees. His dress was a coarse blouse of striped woollen, descending to his knees, where a pair of gaiters of sheepskin were fastened by thongs of untanned leather—his head was bare, and covered only by a long mass of black hair, that fell in tangled locks down his back, and even over his face, as he bent forward. A shepherd's staff, and a broad hat of felt, lay on the ground beside him; there was neither

chair nor table, nor, save some fern in one corner, anything that might serve as a bed; a large earthenware
jug, and a metal pot, stood near the fire, and a knife, such
as butchers kill with, beside them. Over the chimney,
however, was suspended, by two thongs of leather, a
sword, long and straight, like the weapon of the heavy
cavalry of France; and, higher again, I could see a great
piece of printed paper was fastened to the wall. As I
continued to scan, one by one, these signs of utter poverty,
the man stretched out his limbs and rubbed his eyes for a
minute or two, and then with a start sprang to his feet,
displaying, as he did so, the proportions of a most powerful and athletic frame. He was, as well as I could guess,
about forty-five years of age; but hardship and suffering
had worn deep lines about his face, which was sallow and
emaciated. A black moustache, that hung down over
his lip, and descended to his chin, concealed the lower
part of his face—the upper was bold and manly, the forehead high and well developed; but his eyes—and I could
mark them well as the light fell on him—were of an unnatural brilliancy—their sparkle had the fearful gleam of
a mind diseased, and in their quick, restless glances
through the room I saw that he was labouring under
some insane delusion. He paced the room with a steady
step, backwards and forwards, for a few minutes, and
once, as he lifted his eyes above the chimney, he stopped
abruptly, and carried his hand to his forehead in a military salute, while he muttered something to himself; the
moment after he threw open the door, and stepping outside, gave a long, shrill whistle; he paused for a few
seconds, and repeated it, when I could hear the distant
barking of a dog replying to his call Just then he
turned abruptly, and, with a spring, seized me by the
arm

"Who are you—what do you want here? " said he, in
a voice tremulous with passion.

A few words—it was no time for long explanations—
told him how I had lost my way in the mountain, and was
in search of shelter for the night.

"It was a lucky thing for you that one of my lambs
was astray," said he, with a fierce smile. "If Tête-noire

had been at home, he'd have made short work of you—come in."

With that he pushed me before him into the tower, and pointed to the block of wood, where he had been sitting previously, while he threw a fresh supply of furze upon the hearth, and stirred up the blaze with his foot.

"The wind is moving round to the south'ard," said he; "we'll have a heavy fall of rain soon."

'The stars look very bright, however——"

"Never trust them. Before day breaks, you'll see the mountain will be covered with mist."

As he spoke, he crossed his arms on his breast, and recommenced his walk up and down the chamber. The few words he spoke surprised me much by the tones of his voice—so unlike the accents I should have expected from one of his miserable and squalid appearance—they were mild, and bore the traces of one who had seen very different fortunes from his present ones.

I wished to speak and induce him to converse with me; but the efforts I made seemed only to excite his displeasure, and I abandoned the endeavour with a good grace; and having disposed my knapsack as a pillow, stretched myself full length before the hearth, and fell sound asleep.

When I awoke, the shepherd was not to be seen; the fire, which blazed brightly, showed, however, that he had not long been absent, a huge log of beech had recently been thrown upon it. The day was breaking, and I went to the door to look out; nothing, however, could I see; vast clouds of mist were sweeping along before the wind, that sighed mournfully over the bleak mountains, and concealed everything a few yards off, while a thin rain came slanting down, the prelude to the storm the shepherd had prophesied.

Never was there anything more dreary, within or without, the miserable poverty of the ruined tower was scarcely a shelter from the coming hurricane. I returned to my place beside the fire, sad and low in heart. While I was conjecturing within myself what distance I might be from Spa, and how I could contrive to reach it, I chanced to fix my eyes on the sabre above the chimney, which I took down to examine. It was a plain straight weapon, of the kind carried by the soldiery; its only sign of inscription was the letter " N " on the blade. As I replaced it, I caught sight of the printed paper, which, begrimed with smoke, and partly obliterated by time, was nearly illegible. After much pains, however, I succeeded in deciphering the following; it was headed in large letters—

" Ordre du Jour, de l'Armée Française.
" Le 9 Thermidor."

The lines which followed immediately were covered by another piece of paper pasted over them, where I could just here and there detect a stray word, which seemed to indicate that the whole bore reference to some victory of the republican army. The last four lines, much clearer than the rest, ran thus :—

" Le citoyen Aubuisson, chef de bataillon de Grenadiers, de cette demi-brigade, est entré le premier dans la redoute. Il a eu son habit criblé de balles." *

I read and re-read the lines a dozen times over; indeed, to this hour are they fast fixed in my memory. Some strange mystery seemed to connect them with the poor shepherd—otherwise, why were they here ? I thought over his figure, strong and well-knit, as I saw him stand upright in the room, and of his military salute ; and the conviction came fully over me that the miserable creature, covered with rags and struggling with want, was no other than the citizen Aubuisson.

Yet, by what fearful vicissitude had he fallen to this ? The wild expression of his features at times did indeed look like insanity ; still, what he said to me was both calm and coherent. The mystery excited all my curiosity, and I longed for his return, in the hope of detecting some clue to it.

The door opened suddenly ; a large dog, more mastiff than sheep-dog, dashed in ; seeing me, he retreated a step, and, fixing his eyes steadily upon me, gave a fearful howl.

---

* The citizen Aubuisson, chef-de-bataillon of Grenadiers, of this brigade, was the first to enter the redoubt. His coat was riddled with bullets.

I could not stir from fear. I saw that he was preparing for a spring, when the voice of the shepherd called out, "Couche-toi, Tête-noire, couche!" The savage beast at once slunk quietly to a corner, and lay down, still never taking his eyes from me, and seeming as if his services would soon be in request in my behalf; while his master shook the rain from his hat and blouse, and came forward to dry himself at the fire. Fixing his eyes steadfastly on the red embers as he stirred them with his foot, he muttered some few and broken words, among which, although I listened attentively, I could but hear, "Pas un mot—silence—silence, à la mort!"

"You were not wrong in your prophecy, shepherd; the storm is setting in already," said I, wishing to attract his attention.

"Hush!" said he, in a low whisper, while he motioned me with his hand to be still, "hush—not a word!"

The eager glare of madness was in his eye as he spoke, and a tremulous movement of his pale cheek betokened some great inward convulsion. He threw his eyes slowly around the miserable room, looking below and above with the scrutinizing glance of one resolved to let nothing escape his observation; and then kneeling down on one knee beside the blaze, he took a piece of dry wood, and stole it quietly among the embers.

"There, there!" cried he, springing to his legs, while he seized me rudely by the shoulder, and hurried me to the distant end of the room. "Come—quickly—stand back—stand back there—see—see," said he, as the crackling sparks flew up and the tongued flame rose in the chimney, "there it goes!" Then, putting his lips to my ear, he muttered, "Not a word!—silence—silence to the death!"

As he said this, he drew himself up to his full height, and, crossing his arms upon his breast, stood firm and erect before me, and certainly—covered with rags the meanest poverty would have rejected, shrunk by famine, and chilled by hunger and storm—there was still remaining the traits of a once noble face and figure. The fire of madness, unquenched by every misery, lit up his dark eye, and even on his compressed lip there was a curl of pride.

Poor fellow! some pleasant memory seemed to flit across
him; he smiled, and as he moved his hair from his forehead he bowed his head slightly, and murmured, "Oui,
sire!" How soft, how musical that voice was then!
Just at this instant the deep bleating of the sheep was
heard without, and Tête-noire, springing up, rushed to the
door, and scratched fiercely with his fore-paws. The
shepherd hastened to open it, and to my surprise I beheld
a boy, about twelve years of age, poorly clad and drip-
ping with wet, who was carrying a small canvas bag on
his back.

"Has the lamb been found, Lazare?" said the child, as
he unslung his little sack.

"Yes; 'tis safe in the fold."

"And the spotted ewe? You don't think the wolves
could have taken her away so early as this——"

"Hush, hush!" said the shepherd, with a warning gesture to the child, who seemed at once to see that the lunatic's vision was on him; for he drew his little blouse close
around his throat, and muttered a "Bon jour, Lazare," and
departed.

"Couldn't that boy guide me down to Spa, or some village near it?" said I, anxious to seize an opportunity of
escape.

He looked at me without seeming to understand my
question. I repeated it more slowly, when, as if suddenly
aware of my meaning, he replied quickly—

"No, no; little Pierre has a long road to go home; he
lives far away in the mountains; I'll show you the way
myself."

With that, he opened the sack, and took forth a loaf of
coarse wheaten bread, such as the poorest cottagers make,
and a tin flask of milk. Tearing the loaf asunder, he
handed me one half, which, more from policy than hunger,
though I had endured a long fast, I accepted. Then,
passing the milk towards me, he made a sign for me to
drink, and when I had done, seized the flask himself, and,
nodding gaily with his head, cried, "A vous, camarade."
Simple as the gesture, and few the words, they both convinced me that he had been a soldier once; and each
moment only strengthened me in the impression that I

had before me in the shepherd Lazare an officer of the
Grande Armée—one of those heroes of a hundred fights,
whose glory was the tributary stream in the great ocean
of the Empire's grandeur.

Our meal was soon concluded, and in silence; and
Lazare, having replenished his fire, went to the door and
looked out.

" It will be wilder ere night," said he, as he peered into
the dense mist, which, pressed down by rain, lay like a
pall upon the earth, " if you are a good walker, I'll take
you by a short way to Spa."

" I'll do my best," said I, " to follow you."

" The mountain is easy enough ; but there may be a
stream or two swollen by the rains. They are sometimes
dangerous."

" What distance are we then from Spa ? "

"Four leagues and a half by the nearest route—seven
and a half by the road. Come, Tête-noire—bonne bête,"
said he, patting the savage beast, who, with a rude gesture
of his tail, evinced his joy at the recognition. "Thou
must be on guard to-day—take care of these for me—that
thou wilt, old fellow—farewell, good beast, good-bye!"
The animal, as if he understood every word, stood with
his red eyes fixed upon him till he had done, and then
answered by a long, low howl. Lazare smiled with
pleasure, as he waved his hand towards him, and led the
way from the tower.

I had but time to leave two louis-d'ors on the block of
wood, when he called out to me to follow him. The pace
he walked at, as well as the rugged course of the way he
took, prevented my keeping at his side ; and I could only
track him as he moved along through the misty rain, like
some genius of the storm, his long locks flowing wildly
behind him, and his tattered garments fluttering in the
wind.

It was a toilsome and dreary march, unrelieved by
aught to lessen the fatigue. Lazare never spoke one word
the entire time—occasionally he would point with his
staff to the course we were to take, or mark the flight of
some great bird of prey, soaring along near the ground, as
if fearless of man in regions so wild and desolate save:

s

at these moments, he seemed buried in his own gloomy
thoughts. Four hours of hard walking brought us at last
to the summit of a great mountain, from which, as the
mist was considerably cleared away, I could perceive a
number of lesser mountains surrounding it, like the waves
of the sea. My guide pointed to the ground, as if recom-
mending a rest, and I willingly threw myself on the heath,
damp and wet as it was.

The rest was a short one : he soon motioned me to
resume the way, and we plodded onward for an hour
longer, when we came to a great table-land of several
miles in extent, but which still I could perceive was on a
very high level. At last we reached a little grove of
stunted pines, where a rude cross of stone stood—a mark
to commemorate the spot where a murder had been committed, and to entreat prayers for the discovery of the
murderers. Here Lazare stopped, and pointing to a
little narrow path in the heather, he said,—

" Spa is scarce two leagues distant—it lies in the valley
yonder—follow this path, and you'll not fail to reach it."

While I proffered my thanks to him for his guidance, I
could not help expressing my wish to make some slight
return for it. A dark, disdainful look soon stopped me
in my speech, and I turned it off, in a desire to leave some
souvenir of my night's lodging behind me, in the old
tower. But even this he would not hear of, and when I
stretched out my hand to bid him good-bye, he took it with
a cold and distant courtesy, as though he were condescending to a favour he had no fancy for.

"Adieu, monsieur," said I, still tempted, by a last
effort of allusion to his once condition, to draw something
from him ; "adieu !"

He approached me nearer, and with a voice of tremulous eagerness, he muttered—

"Not a word yonder—not a syllable—pledge me your
faith in that ! "

Thinking now that it was merely the recurrence of his
paroxysm, I answered carelessly—

" Never fear, I'll say nothing."

" Yes, but swear it," said he, with a fixed look of his
dark eye; " swear it to me now—so long as you are

below there"—he pointed to the valley—"you never speak of me."

I made him the promise he required, though with great unwillingness, as my curiosity to learn something about him was becoming intense.

"Not a word!" said he, with a finger on his lip, "that's the *consigne.*"

"Not a word!" repeated I, and we parted.

CHAPTER XVI.

THE BORE—A SOLDIER OF THE EMPIRE.

Two hours after I was enjoying the pleasant fire of the Hotel de Flandre, where I arrived in time for *table d'hôte*, not a little to the surprise of the host and six waiters, who were totally lost in conjectures to account for my route, and sorely puzzled to ascertain the name of my last hotel in the mountains

A watering-place at the close of a season is always a sad-looking thing. The barricades of the coming winter already begin to show—the little statues in public gardens are assuming their great coats of straw against the rigours of frost—the *jet-d'eaux* cease to play, or perform with the unwilling air of actors to empty benches—the *table d'hôtes* present their long dinner-rooms unoccupied, save by a little table at one end, where some half-dozen shivering inmates still remain, the débris of the mighty army who flourished their knives there but six weeks before. These usually consist of a stray invalid or two, completing his course of the waters—he has a fortnight of sulphuretted hydrogen before him yet, and he dare not budge till he has finished his "heeltap" of abomination. Then there's the old half-pay major, that has lived in Spa, for aught I know, since the siege of Namur, and who passes his nine months of winter shooting quails and playing dominoes; and there's an elderly

s 2

lady, with spectacles, always working at a little embroidery frame, who speaks no French, nor seems to be aware of anything going on around her. No one can guess why she is there—I wager she does not know herself; and lastly, there is a very distracted-looking young gentleman, with a shooting jacket, and young moustaches, who having been " cleaned out " at *rouge et noir*, is waiting in the hope of a remittance from some commiserating relative in England.

The theatre is closed—its little stars, dispersed among the small capitals, have shrunk back to their former proportions of third and fourth-rate parts—for though butterflies in July, they are mere grubs in December. While the clink of the croupier's mace no longer is heard, revelling amid the five-franc pieces, all is still and silent in that room which so late the conflict of human passion, hope, envy, fear, and despair, had made a very hell on earth.

The donkeys, too—who but the other day were decked in scarlet trappings—are now despoiled of their gay panoply, and condemned to the mean drudgery of the cart. Poor beasts! their drooping ears and fallen heads seem to show some sense of their changed fortunes. No longer bearing the burden of some fair-cheeked girl, or laughing boy, along the mountain side—they are brought down to the daily labour of the cottage; and a cutlet is no more like a mutton chop, than is a donkey like an ass. So does everything suffer a " sea-change." The " modiste," whose pretty cap with its gay ribbons was itself an advertisement of her wares, has taken to a close bonnet and a woollen shawl—a metamorphosis as complete as is the misshapen mass of cloaks and mud-boots of the agile " danseuse," who flitted between earth and air, a few moments before. Even the doctor—and what a study is the doctor of a watering-place!—even he has laid by his smiles and his soft speeches, folded up in the same drawer with his black coat, for the winter. He has not thrown physic to the dogs, because he is fond of sporting, and would not injure the poor beasts, but he has given it an " au revoir," and as grouse come in with autumn, and blackcock in November, so does he feel chalybeates are in season on the first of May. Exchang-

ing his cane for a Manton, and his mild whisper for a
dog-whistle, he takes to the pursuit of the lower animals,
leaving men for the warmer months.

All this disconcerts one, you hate to be present at those
" déménagements," where the curtains are taking down,
and the carpet is taking up; where they are nailing
canvas across pictures, and storing books into pantries.
These smaller revolutions are all very detestable, and you
gladly escape into some quiet and retired spot and wait
till the fussing be over. So felt I. Had I came a month
later, this place would have suited me perfectly, but this
process of human moulting is horrible to witness, and so,
say I once more—*en route*.

Like a Dutchman who took a run of three miles to
jump over a hill, and then sat down tired at the foot of it,
I flurried myself so completely in canvassing all the possible places I might, could, would, should, or ought to pass
the winter in, that I actually took a fortnight to recover
my energies before I could set out. Meanwhile I had
made a close friendship with a dyspeptic countryman of
mine, who went about the Continent with a small port-
manteau and a very large medicine chest, chasing health
from Naples to Paris, and from Aix-la-Chapelle to Wild-
bad, firmly persuaded that every country had only one month
in the year at most wherein it were safe to live there—Spa
being the appropriate place to pass the October. He cared
nothing for the ordinary topics that engross the attention
of mankind—kings might be dethroned and dynasties
demolished—states might revolt and subjects be rebellious
—all he wanted to know was, not what changes were
made in the code but in the pharmacopœia. The liberty
of the press was a matter of indifference to him; he cared
little for what men might say, but a great deal for what it
was safe to swallow, and looked upon the inventor of blue
pill as the greatest benefactor of mankind. He had the
analysis of every well and spring in Germany at his finger's end, and could tell you the temperature and atomic
proportions like his alphabet. But his great system was a
kind of reciprocity treaty between health and sickness, by
which a man could commit any species of gluttony he
pleased when he knew the peculiar antagonist principle;

and thus he ate—I was going to say like a shark, but let me
not in my ignorance calumniate the fish—for I know not
if anything that ever swam could eat a soup with a cus-
tard pudding, followed by beef and beetroot, stewed mackerel and treacle, pickled oysters and preserved cherries,
roast hare and cucumber, venison, salad, prunes, hashed
mutton, omelettes, pastry ; and finally, to wind up with
effect, a sturgeon baked with brandy-peaches in his abdo-
men—a thing to make a cook weep and a German blessed.
Such was my poor friend, Mr. Bartholomew Cater, the
most thin, spare, emaciated, and miserable-looking man
that ever sipped at Schwalbach or shivered at Kissingen.

To permit these extravagancies in diet, however, he had
concocted a code of reprisals, consisting in the various
mineral waters of Germany, and the poisonous metals of
modern pharmacy ; and having established the fact that
" bitter wasser " and " Carlsbad," the " Powon " and
" Pilnitz," combined with blue pill, were the natural enemies of all things eatable, he swallowed these freely, and
then left the matter to the rebellious ingredients, pretty
much as the English used to govern Ireland in times gone
by, set both parties by the ears and wait the result in
peace, well aware that a slight derangement of the balance,
from time to time, would keep the contest in motion.
Such was the state policy of Mr. Cater, and I can only say
that *his* " constitution " survived it, though that of Ireland
seems to suffer grievously from the experiment.

This lively gentleman was then my companion; indeed,
with that cohesive property of your true bore, he was ever
beside me, relating some little interesting anecdote of a
jaundice or a dropsy, a tertian or a typhus, by which agreeable souvenirs he preserved the memory of Athens or
Naples, Rome or Dresden, fresh and unclouded in his mind.
Not satisfied, however, with narration, like all enthusiasts,
he would be proselytizing , and whether from the force of
his arguments or the weakness of *my* nature, found a ready
victim in me—insomuch, that under his admirable instruction I was already beginning to feel a dislike and disgust to
all things eatable, with an appetite only grown more raven-
ous ; while my reverence for all springs of unsavoury taste
and smell—once, I must confess, at a deplorably low ebb—

was gradually becoming more developed. It was only by the accidental discovery that my waistcoat could be made to fit, by putting it twice round me, and that my coat was a dependency, of which I was scarcely the nucleus, that I really became frightened.

What! thought I, can this be that Arthur O'Leary whom men jested on his rotundity? Is this me, around whom children ran, as they would about a pillar or a monument, and thought it exercise to circumambulate? Arthur, this will be the death of thee; thou wert a happy man and a fat before thou knewest Koch brunnens and thermometers; run while it is yet time, and be thankful at least that thou art in racing condition.

With noiseless step and cautious gesture, I crept down stairs one morning at daybreak. My enemy was still asleep. I heard him muttering as I passed his door; doubtless he was dreaming of some new combination of horrors, some infernal alliance of cucumbers and quinine. I passed on in silence; my very teeth chattered with fear —happy was I to have them to chatter—another fortnight of his intimacy, and they would have trembled from blue pill as well as panic.

With a heavy sigh I paid my bill, and crossed the street towards the diligence office. One place only remained vacant, it was in the banquette. No matter, thought I, anywhere will do at present

"Where is monsieur going? for there will be a place vacant in the coupé at——"

"I have not thought of that yet," said I; "but when we reach Vervier we'll see"

"Allons, then," said the conducteur, while he whispered to the clerk of the office a few words I could not catch. "You are mistaken, friend," said I; "it's not creditors, they are only chalybeates I'm running from;" and so we started.

Before I follow out any further my own ramblings, I should like to acquit a debt I owe my reader—if I dare flatter myself that he cares for its discharge—by returning to the story of the poor shepherd of the mountains, and which I cannot more seasonably do than at this place; although the details I am about to relate were furnished to me a great many years after this, and during a visit I paid to Lyons in 1828.

In the Café de la Coupe d'Or, so conspicuous in the Place des Terreaux, where I usually resorted to pass my evenings, and indulge in the cheap luxuries of my coffee and cheroot, I happened to make a bowing acquaintance with a venerable elderly gentleman, who each night resorted there to read the papers, and amuse himself by looking over the chess-players, with which the room was crowded. Some accidental interchange of newspapers led to a recognition, and that again advanced to a few words each time we met, till one evening, chance placed us at the same table, and we chatted away several hours, and parted in the hope, mutually expressed, of renewing our acquaintance at an early period.

I had no difficulty in interrogating the Dame du Café about my new acquaintance. He was a striking and remarkable-looking personage, tall, and military-looking, with an air of "Grand Seigneur," which in a Frenchman is never deceptive; certainly I never saw it successfully assumed by any who had no right to it. He wore his hair "en queue," and in his dress evinced, in several trifling matters, an adherence to the habitudes of the old régime; so, at least, I interpreted his lace ruffles and silk stockings, with his broad buckles of brilliants in his shoes, the ribbon of St. Louis, which he wore unostentatiously on his waistcoat, was his only decoration.

"That is the Vicomte de Berlemont, ancien colonel-en-chef," said she, with an accent of pride at the mention of so distinguished a frequenter of the café; "he has not missed an evening here for years past"

A few more words of inquiry elicited from her the information that the Vicomte had served in all the wars of the Empire up to the time of the abdication—that on the restoration of the Bourbons he had received his rank in the service from them, and, faithful to their fortunes, had followed Louis XVIII. in exile to Ghent.

"He has seen a deal of the world, then, Madame, it would appear?"

"That he has, and loves to speak about it, too; time was when they reckoned the Vicomte the pleasantest

persons in Lyons ; but they say he has grown old now,
and contracted a habit of repeating his stories. I can't
tell how that may be, but I think him always *aimable*."
A delightful word that same *aimable* is ! and so thinking,
I wished Madame good-night, and departed.

The next evening I lay in wait for the old colonel, and
was flattered to see that he was taking equal pains to
discover me. We retired to a little table, ordered our
coffee and chatted away till midnight. Such was the commencement, such the course, of one of the pleasantest
intimacies I ever formed.

The Vicomte was unquestionably the most agreeable
specimen of his nation I had ever met; easy and unaffected in his manner ; he had seen much, and observed
shrewdly ; not much skilled in book learning, but deeply
read in mankind , his views of politics were of that
unexaggerated character which are so often found correct ;
while of his foresight I can give no higher token, than that
he then predicted to me the events of the year 1830, only
erring as to the time, which he deemed might not be so
far distant. The Empire, however, and Napoleon, were
his favourite topics. Bourbonist as he was, the splendour
of France in 1810 and 1811, the greatness of the mighty
man whose genius then ruled its destinies, had captivated
his imagination, and he would talk for hours over the
events of Parisian life at that period, and the more brilliant incidents of the campaigns.

It was in one of our conversations, prolonged beyond
the usual time, in discussing the characters of those immediately about the person of the Emperor, that I felt somewhat struck by the remark he made, that, while " Napoleon did meet unquestionably many instances of deep
ingratitude from those whom he had covered with honours
and heaped with favours, still nothing ever equalled the
attachment the officers of the army generally bore to his
person, and the devotion they felt for his glory and his
honour.

" It was not a sentiment, it was a religious belief among
the young men of my day, that the Emperor could do no
wrong. What you assume in your country by courtesy,
we believed *de facto*. So many times had events, seeming

most disastrous, turned out pregnant with advantage and success, that a dilemma was rather a subject of amusing speculation amongst us, than a matter of doubt and despondency.

"There came a terrible reverse to all this, however," said he, as his voice fell to a lower and sadder key; "a fearful lesson was in stoie for us. Poor Aubuisson——"

"Aubuisson!" said I, starting; "was that the name you mentioned?"

"Yes," said he, in amazement; "have you heard the story, then?"

"No," said I, "I know of no story; it was the name alone struck me. Was it not one of that name who was mentioned in one of Bonaparte's despatches from Egypt?"

"To be sure it was, and the same man, too; he was the first in the trenches at Alexandria; he carried off a Mameluke chief his prisoner, at the battle of the Pyramids."

"What manner of man was he?"

"A powerful fellow, one of the largest of his regiment, and they were a Grenadier battalion; he had black hair and black moustache, which he wore long and drooping, in Egyptian fashion."

"The same—the very same!" cried I, carried away by my excitement.

"What do you mean?" said the colonel; "you've never seen him, surely, he died at Charenton the same year Waterloo was fought."

"No such thing," said I, feeling convinced that Lazare was the person. "I saw him alive long since;" and with that I related the story I have told my reader, detailing minutely every little particular which might serve to confirm my impression of the identity.

"No, no," said the Vicomte, shaking his head, "you are mistaken; Aubuisson was a patient at Charenton for ten years, when he died. The circumstances you mention are certainly both curious and strange, but I cannot think they have any connection with the fortunes of poor Gustave; at all events, if you like to hear the story, come home with me, and I'll tell it; the café is about to close now, and we must leave."

I gladly accepted the offer, for whatever doubts *he* had concerning Lazare's identity with Aubuisson, *my* convictions were complete, and I longed to hear the solution of a mystery over which I had pondered many a day of march, and many a sleepless night.

I could scarcely contain my impatience during supper. The thought of Lazare absorbed everything in my mind, and I fancied the old colonel's appetite knew no bounds when the meal had lasted about a quarter of an hour. At last he finished, and having devised his modest glass of weak wine and water, began the story, of which I present the leading features to my readers, omitting, of course, those little occasional digressions and reflections by which the narrator himself accompanied his tale.

CHAPTER XVII.

THE RETREAT FROM LEIPSIC.

THE third day of the disastrous battle of Leipsic was drawing to a close, as the armies of the coalition made one terrible and fierce attack, in concert, against the Imperial forces. Never was anything before heard like the deafening thunder, as three hundred guns of heavy artillery opened their fire at once, from end to end of the line, and three hundred thousand men advanced, wildly cheering, to the attack.

Wearied, worn out, and exhausted, the French army held their ground, like men prepared to die before their Emperor, but never desert him, when the fearful intelligence was brought to Napoleon, that in three days the army had fired ninety-five thousand cannon balls,* that the reserve ammunition was entirely consumed, and but sixteen thousand cannon balls remained, barely sufficient

* Historical.

to maintain the fire two hours longer! What was to be done? No resources lay nearer than Magdeburg or Erfurt. To the latter place the Emperor at once decided on retiring, and at seven o'clock the order was given for the artillery waggons and baggage to pass the defile of Lindenau, and retreat over the Elster; the same order being transmitted to the cavalry and the other corps of the army. The defile was a long and difficult one, extending for two leagues, and traversing several bridges. To accomplish the retreat in safety, Napoleon was counselled to hold the allies in check by a strong force of artillery, and then set fire to the faubourg; but the conduct of the Saxon troops, however deserving of his anger, could not warrant a punishment so fearful on the monarch of that country, who, through every change of fortune, had stood steady in his friendship · he rejected the course at once, and determined on retreating as best he might.

The movement was then begun at once, and every avenue that led to the faubourg of Lindenau was crowded by troops of all arms, eagerly pressing onward—a fearful scene of confusion and dismay, for it was a beaten army who fled, and one which until now never had thoroughly felt the horrors of defeat. From seven until nine the columns came on at a quick step, the cavalry at a trot; defiling along the narrow gorge of Lindenau, they passed a mill at the roadside, where, at a window, stood one with arms crossed and head bent upon his bosom. He gazed steadfastly at the long train beneath, but never noticed the salutes of the general officers as they passed along. It was the Emperor himself! pale and careworn, his low chapeau pressed down far on his brows, and his uniform splashed and travel-stained. For above an hour he stood thus silent and motionless, then throwing himself upon a bed he slept. Yes! amid all the terrible events of that disastrous retreat, when the foundations of the mighty empire he had created were crumbling beneath him, when the great army he had so often led to victory was defiling beaten before him, he laid him wearied upon a pillow and slept!

A terrible cannonade, the fire of seventy large guns, brought to bear upon the ramparts, shook the very earth,

and at length awoke him, who through all the din and
clamour slept soundly and tranquilly.

" What is it, Duroc ? " said he, raising himself upon
one arm, and looking up.

" It is Swartzenberg's attack, sire, on the rampart of
Halle "

" Ha! so near ? " said he, springing up and approaching
the window, from which the bright flashes of the artillery
were each moment discernible in the dark sky. At the
same moment an aide-de-camp galloped up, and dismounted at the door : in another minute he was in the
room.

The Saxon troops, left by the Emperor as a guard of
honour and protection to the unhappy monarch, had
opened a fire on the retreating columns, and a fearful
confusion was the result. The Emperor spoke not a word.
Macdonald's corps and Poniatowski's division were still in
Leipsic , but already they had commenced their retiring
movement on Lindenau Lauriston's brigade was also
rapidly approaching the bridge over the Elster, to which
now the men were hurrying madly on, intent alone on
flight. The bridge—the only one by which the troops
could pass—had been mined, and committed to the charge
of Colonel Montfort, of the Engineers, with directions to
blow it up when the enemy appeared, and thus gain time
for the baggage to retreat.

As the aide-de-camp stood awaiting Napoleon's orders
to a few lines written in pencil by the Duke of Tarento,
another staff officer arrived, breathless, to say that the
allies had carried the rampart, and were already in Leipsic.

Napoleon became deadly pale ; then, with a motion of
his hand, he signed to the officer to withdraw. " Duroc,"
said he, when they were alone, " where is Nansouty ? "

" With the eighth corps, sire. They have passed an
hour since."

' Who commands the picquet without ? "

" Aubuisson, sire "

" Send him to me, and leave us alone."

In a few moments Colonel Aubuisson entered. His
arm was in a sling from a sabre wound he had received
the morning before, but which did not prevent his remain-

ing on duty. The stout soldier seemed as unconcerned and fearless in that dreadful moment as though it were a day of gala manœuvres, and not one of disaster and defeat.

"Aubuisson," said the Emperor, "you were with us at Alexandria?"

"I was, sire," said he, as a deeper tinge coloured his bronzed features.

"The first in the rampart—I remember it well," said Napoleon; "the *ordre du jour* commemorates the deed. It was at Moscowa you gained the cross, I believe?" continued he, after a slight pause.

"I never obtained it, sire," replied Aubuisson, with a struggle to repress some disappointment in his tone.

"How—never obtained it!—you, Aubuisson, an ancient 'brave' of the Pyramids. Come, come, there has been a mistake somewhere—we must look to this. Meanwhile, *General* Aubuisson, take mine."

With that he detached his cordon from the breast of his uniform, and fastened it on the coat of the astonished officer, who could only mutter the words, "Sire—sire!" in reply.

"Now, then, for a service you must render me, and speedily, too," said Napoleon, as he laid his hand on the general's shoulder.

The Emperor whispered for some seconds in his ear, then looked at him fixedly in the face. "What!" cried he, "do you hesitate?"

"Hesitate, sire!" said Aubuisson, starting back. "Never! If your majesty had ordered me to the mouth of a mortar—but I wish to know——"

Napoleon did not permit him to conclude, but drawing him closer, whispered again a few words in his ear. "And, mark me," said he, aloud, as he finished, "mark me, Aubuisson—silence, *pas un mot*—silence, *à la mort!*"

"*A la mort*, sire!" repeated the general, while at the same moment Duroc hurried into the room, and cried out—

"They are advancing towards the Elster—Macdonald's rear-guard is engaged——"

A motion of Napoleon's hand towards the door, and a look at Aubuisson, was the only notice he took of the intelligence, and the officer was gone.

While Duroc continued to detail the disastrous events the last arrived news had announced, the Emperor approached the window, which was still open, and looked out. All was in darkness towards that part of the city near the defile. The attack was on the distant rampart, near which the sky was red and lurid. Still it was towards that dark and gloomy part Napoleon's eyes were turned, and not in the direction where the fight was still raging. Peering into the dense blackness, he stood without speaking, when suddenly a bright gleam of light shot up from the gloom, and then came three tremendous reports, so rapidly, one after the other, as almost to seem like one The same instant a blaze of fire flashed upwards towards the sky, and glittering fragments of burning timber were hurled into the air. Napoleon covered his eyes with his hand, and leaned against the side of the window.

"It is the bridge over the Elster!" cried Duroc, in a voice half-wild with passion. "They've blown up the bridge before Macdonald's division have crossed."

"Impossible!" said the Emperor. "Go see, quickly, Duroc, what has happened."

But before the general could leave the room, a wounded officer rushed in, his clothes covered with the marks of recent fire.

"The Sappers, sire—the Sappers——"

"What of them?" said the Emperor.

"They've blown up the bridge, and the fourth corps are still in Leipsic."

The next moment Napoleon was on his horse, surrounded by his staff, and galloping furiously towards the river.

Never was a scene more awful than that which now presented itself there Hundreds of men had thrown themselves headlong into the rapid river, where masses of burning timber were falling on every side—horse and foot all mixed up in fearful confusion, struggled madly in the stream, mingling their cries with the shouts of those who came on from behind, and who discovered for the first time that the retreat was cut off. The Duke of Tarento crossed, holding by his horse's mane. Lauriston had nearly reached the bank, when he sunk to rise no more ; and Poniatowski, the chivalrous Pole, the last hope of his nation, was seen for an instant, struggling with the waves, and then disappeared for ever.

Twenty thousand men, sixty great guns, and above two hundred waggons, were thus left in the power of the enemy. Few who sought refuge in flight ever reached the opposite bank, and for miles down, the shores of the Elster were marked by the bodies of French soldiers, who thus met their death on that fearful night.

Among the disasters of this terrible retreat, was the fate of Reynier, of whom no tidings could be had, nor was it known whether he died in battle, or fell a prisoner into the hands of the enemy. He was the personal friend of the Emperor, who in his loss deplored not only the brave and valorous soldier, but the steady adherent to his fortunes, through good and evil.

No more striking evidence of the amount of this misfortune can be had, than the bulletin of Napoleon himself. That document, usually devoted to the expression of vainglorious and exaggerated descriptions of the triumphs of the army—full of those highflown narratives by which the glowing imagination of the Emperor conveyed the deeds of his soldiers to the wondering ears of France, was now a record of mournful depression and sad reverse of fortune.

"The French army," said he, "continues its march on Erfurt—a beaten army ; after so many brilliant successes, it is now in retreat."

Every one is already acquainted with the disastrous career of that army, the greatest that ever marched from France. Each step of their return, obstinately contested against overwhelming superiority of force, however it might evidence the chivalrous spirit of a nation who would not confess defeat, brought them only nearer to their own frontiers, pursued by those whose countries they had violated, whose kings they had dethroned, whose liberties they had trampled on

The fearful Nemesis of war had come, the hour was arrived when all the wrongs they had wreaked on others were to be tenfold inflicted on themselves—when the

plains of that " belle France," of which they were so
proud, were to be trampled beneath the feet of insulting
conquerors—when the Cossack and the Hulan were to
bivouac in that capital which they so arrogantly styled
" the centre of European civilization."

I need not dwell on these things, I will but ask you to
accompany me to Erfurt where the army arrived five
days after. A court-martial was there summoned for the
trial of Colonel Montfort, of the Engineers, and the party
under his command, who, in violation of their orders, had
prematurely blown up the bridge over the Elster, and
were thus the cause of that fearful disaster, by which so
many gallant lives were sacrificed, and the honour of a
French army so grievously tarnished.

Contrary to the ordinary custom, the proceedings of
that court-martial were never made known,* the tribunal
sat with closed doors, accessible only to the Emperor himself and the officers of his personal staff. On the fourth
day of the investigation, a messenger was despatched to
Braunach, a distant outpost of the army, to bring up
General Aubuisson, who, it was rumoured, was somehow
implicated in the transaction.

The general took his place beside the other prisoners,
in the full uniform of his " grade." He wore on his breast
the cross the Emperor himself had given him, and he
carried at his side the sabre of honour he had received on
the battle-field of Eylau. Still, they who knew him well
remarked that his countenance no longer wore its frank
and easy expression, while in his eye there was a restless,
anxious look as he glanced from side to side, and seemed
troubled and suspicious.

An order, brought by one of the aides-de-camp of the
Emperor, commanded that the proceedings should not be
opened that morning before his Majesty's arrival, and
already the court had remained an hour inactive, when
Napoleon entered suddenly, and saluting the members of
the tribunal with a courteous bow, took his place at the
head of the table. As he passed up the hall he threw
one glance upon the bench where the prisoners sat, it

* The Vicom'e's assertion is historically correct.

T

was short and fleeting, but there was one there who felt it in his inmost soul, and who in that rapid look read his own fate for ever.

"General Aubuisson," said the President of the court-martial, "you were on duty with the peloton of your battalion on the evening of the 18th?"

A short nod of the head was the only reply. "It is alleged," continued the President, "that a little after nine o'clock you appeared on the bridge over the Elster, and held a conversation with Colonel Montfort, the officer commanding the post; the court now desires that you will recapitulate the circumstances of that conversation, as well as inform it generally on the reasons of your presenting yourself at a post so remote from your duty?"

The general made no reply but fixed his eyes steadfastly on the face of the Emperor, whose cold glance met his own, impassive and unmoved.

"Have you heard the question of the court?" said the President, in a louder tone, "or shall I repeat it?"

The prisoner turned upon him a look of vacancy. Like one suddenly awakened from a frightful dream, he appeared struggling to remember something which no effort of his mind could accomplish. He passed his hand across his brow, on which now the big drops of sweat were standing, and then there broke from him a sigh, so low and plaintive, it was scarcely audible.

"Collect yourself, General," said the President, in a milder tone, "we wish to hear from your own lips your account of this transaction."

Aubuisson cast his eyes downwards, and with his hands firmly clasped, seemed to reflect. As he stood thus, his look fell upon the Cross of the Legion which he wore on his bosom, and with a sudden start he pressed his hand upon it, and drawing himself up to his full height, exclaimed, in a wild and broken voice—

"Silence!—silence à la mort!"

The members of the court-martial looked from one to the other in amazement, while, after a pause of a few minutes, the President repeated his question, dwelling patiently on each word, as if desirous to suit the troubled intellect of the prisoner.

"You are asked," said he, "to remember why you appeared at the bridge of the Elster."

"Hush!" replied the prisoner, placing his finger upon his lips, as if to instil caution; "not a word!"

"What can this mean?" said the President, "his mind appears completely astray."

The members of the tribunal leaned their heads over the table, and conversed for some moments in a low tone, after which the President resumed the interrogatory as before.

"Que voulez-vous?" said the Emperor, rising, while a crimson spot on his cheek evinced his displeasure; "Que voulez-vous, Messieurs! do you not see the man is mad?"

"Silence!" reiterated Aubuisson, in the same solemn voice, "à la mort—silence!"

There could no longer be any doubt upon the question. From whatever cause proceeding, his intellects were shaken, and his reason gone. Some predominant impression, some all-powerful idea, had usurped the seat of both judgment and memory, and he was a maniac.

In ten days after, the General Aubuisson—the distinguished soldier of the Republic, the "brave" of Egypt, and the hero of many a battle in Germany, Poland, and Russia—was a patient of Charenton. A sad and melancholy figure, wasted and withered like a tree reft by lightning, the wreck of his former self, he walked slowly to and fro; and though at times his reason would seem to return free and unclouded, suddenly a dark curtain would appear to drop over the light of his intellect, and he would mutter the words, "Silence! silence à la mort!" and speak not again for several hours after.

The Vicomte de Berlemont, from whom I heard this sad story, was himself a member of the court-martial on the occasion.

For the rest, I visited Paris about a fortnight after I heard it, and, determining to solve my doubts on a subject of such interest, paid an early visit to Charenton. On examining the registry of the institution, I found the name of " Gustave Guillaume Aubuisson, native of Dijon, aged thirty-two. Admitted at Charenton the 31st of October, 1813—Incurable."

And on another page was the single line—
"Aubuisson escaped from Charenton, June 16th, 1815
—supposed to have been seen at Waterloo on the 18th."

One more era remains to be mentioned in this sad
story. The old tower still stands, bleak and desolate, on
the mountains of the Vesdre; but it is now uninhabited;
the sheep seek shelter within its gloomy walls, and herd
in that spacious chimney. There is another change, too,
but so slight as scarcely to be noticed—a little mound of
earth, grass-grown, and covered with thistles, marks the
spot where "Lazare the shepherd" takes his last rest. It
is a lone and dreary spot, and the sighing night winds
as they move over the barren heath seem to utter his
last "consigne," and his requiem—"Silence! silence à la
mort!"

CHAPTER XVIII.

THE TOP OF A DILIGENCE.

"Summa diligentia," as we used to translate it at school,
"on the top of the diligence," I wagged along towards
the Rhine—a weary and a lonely way it is. Indeed, I half
believe a frontier is ever thus · a kind of natural barrier
to ambition on either side, where both parties stop short
and say, Well, there's no temptation there, anyhow!

Reader, hast ever travelled in the banquette of a diligence? I will not ask you, fair lady, for how could you
ever mount to that Olympus of trunks, carpet-bags, and
hat-boxes; but my whiskered friend with the cheroot
yonder, what says he? Never look angry, man, there was
no offence in my question; better men than either of us
have done it, and no bad place either.

First, if the weather be fine, the view is a glorious
thing; you are not limited, like your friends in the coupé,
to the sight of the conducteur's gaiters, or the leather
disc of the postilion's "continuations." No Your eye
ranges away at either side over those undulating plains

which the Continent presents, unbroken by fence or
hedge-row, vast corn-fields, great waving woods, inter-
minable tracts of yellowish pasture land, with here and
there a village spire, or the pointed roof of some château
rising above the trees. A yellow-earthy by-road tra-
verses the plain, on which a heavy waggon plods along,
the eight huge horses stepping as free as though no
weight restrained them; their bells are tinkling in the
clear air, and the merry chant of the waggoner chimes in
pleasantly with them. It is somewhat hard to fancy how
the land is ever tilled, you meet few villages; scarcely a
house is in sight: yet there are the fragrant fields, the
yellow gold of harvest tints the earth, and the industry of
man is seen on every side. It is peaceful, it is grand,
too, from its very extent; but it is not "homelike." No.
Our own happy land alone possesses that attribute. *It is*
the country of the hearth and home The traveller in
France or Germany catches no glances as he goes of the
rural life of the proprietors of the soil. A pale white
château, seemingly uninhabited, stands in some formal
lawn, where the hot sun darts down his rays unbroken,
and the very fountain seems to hiss with heat. No signs
of life are seen about, all is still and calm, as though the
moon were shedding her yellow lustre over the scene.
Oh! how I long for the merry school-boy's laugh, the
clatter of the pony's canter, the watch-dog's bark, the
squire's self breathing the morning air amid his woods,
that tell of England. How I fancy a peep into that large
drawing-room, whose windows open to the greensward,
letting in a view of distant mountains, and far-receding
foreground, through an atmosphere heavy with the rose
and the honeysuckle. Lovely as is the scene, with foliage
tinted in every hue, from the light sprayey hazel to the
dull pine or the dark copper beech; how I prefer to look
within where *they* are met who call this "home," and
what a Parad se is such a home!—but I must think no
more of these things. I am a lone and solitary man, my
happiness is cast in a different path, nor shall I mar it by
longings which never can be realized. While I sat thus
musing, my companion of the banquette, of whom I had
hitherto seen nothing but a blue cloth cloak and a tra-

velling-cap, came slap down on me with a snort that choked him, and aroused me.

"I ask your pardon, sir," said he in a voice that betrayed Middlesex most culpably. "Je suis—that is, j'ai——"

"Never mind, sir; English will answer every purpose," cried I. "You have had a sound sleep of it"

"Yes, heaven be praised! I get over a journey as well as most men. Where are we now—do you happen to know?"

"That old castle yonder, I suspect, is the Alten Burg," said I, taking out my guide-book and directory. "The Alten Burg was built in the year 1334, by Carl Ludwig Graf von Lowenstein, and is not without its historic associations——"

"D—n its historic associations," said my companion, with an energy that made me start. "I wish the devil and his imps had carried away all such trumpery, or kept them to torture people in their own hot climate, and left us free here. I ask pardon, sir—I beseech you to forgive my warmth; you would if you knew the cause, I'm certain."

I began to suspect as much myself, and that my neighbour, being insane, was in no wise responsible for his opinions, when he resumed—

"Most men are made miserable by present calamities: some feel apprehensions for the future; but no one ever suffered so much from either as I do from the past. No, sir," continued he, raising his voice, "I have been made unhappy from those sweet souvenirs of departed greatness guide-book people and tourists gloat over. The very thought of antiquity makes me shudder; the name of Charlemagne gives me the lumbago; and I'd run a mile from a conversation about Charles the Bold, or Philip van Artevelde. I see what's passing in your mind; but you're all wrong—I'm not deranged, not a bit of it—though, faith, I might be, without any shame or disgrace."

The caprices of men, of Englishmen in particular, had long ceased to surprise me; each day disclosed some new eccentricity or other. In the very last hotel I had left a

member of Parliament planning a new route to the Rhine
—avoiding Cologne, because in the coffee-room of the
Grossen Rheinberg there was a double door, that everybody banged when he went in or out, and so discomposed
the honourable and learned gentleman, that he was laid
up for three weeks with a fit of gout, brought on by pure
passion at the inconvenience.

I had not long to wait for the explanation in this case.
My companion appeared to think he owed it to himself to
" show cause why " he was not to be accounted a lunatic,
and after giving me briefly to understand that his means
enabled him to retire from active pursuits and enjoy his
ease, he went on to recount that he had come abroad to
pass the remainder of his days in peace and tranquillity—
but I shall let him tell his own story in his own words.

" On the eighth day after my arrival at Brussels, I told
my wife to pack up, for, as Mr. Thysens, the lawyer, who
promised to write before that time, had not done so, we
had nothing to wait for. We had seen Waterloo, visited
the Musée, skated about in listen slippers, through the
Palais d'Orange, dined at Dubos's, ate ice at Velloni's,
bought half the old lace in the Rue de la Madelaine, and
almost caught an ague in the Allée Verte. This was,
certainly, pleasure enough for one week; so I ordered my
bill, and prepared 'to evacuate Flanders.' Lord help us,
what beings we are! Had I gone down to the railroad
by the Boulevards, and not by the Montagne de la Cour,
what miseries might I not have been spared. Mr. Thysens' clerk met me, just as I emerged from the Place
Royale, with a letter in his hand.

" I took it—opened—and read.—

" 'Sir,—I have just completed the purchase of the
beautiful Château of Vanderstradentendonk, with all its
gardens, orchards, pheasantries, piscinæ, prairies, and
forest rights, which are now your property. Accept my
most respectful congratulations upon your acquisition of
this magnificent seat of ancient grandeur, rendered doubly
precious by its having been once the favourite residence
and château of the great Vandyck.'

" Here followed a long encomium upon Rubens and his
school, which I did not half relish, knowing it was charged

to me in my account; the whole winding up with a press-ing recommendation to hasten down at once to take possession, and enjoy the partridge shooting, then in great abundance.

"My wife was in ecstasy to be the Frow Vanderstra-dentendonk, with a fish-pond before the door, and twelve gods and goddesses in lead around it.   To have a brace of asthmatic peacocks on a terrace, and a dropsical swan on an island, were strong fascinations; not to speak of the straight avenues leading nowhere, and the winds of heaven blowing everywhere.   A house with a hundred and thirty windows, and half as many doors, none of which would shut close; a garden, with no fruit but crab-apples ; and a nursery, so called, because the play-ground of all the brats for a league round us.   No matter, I had resolved to live abroad for a year or two ; one place would do just as well as another ; at least, I should have quietness ; that was something : there was no neighbourhood, no town, no high road, no excuse for travelling acquaintances to drop in, or rambling tourists to bore one with letters of introduction.   Thank God! there was neither a battle-field, a cathedral, a picture, nor a great living poet, for ten miles on every side.

"Here, thought I, I shall have that peace Piccadilly cannot give.   Cincinnatus-like, I'll plant my cabbages, feed my turkeys, let my beard grow, and nurse my rental.   Solitude never bored me ; I could bear anything but intrusive impertinence, and so far did I carry this feeling, that on reading Robinson Crusoe, I laid down the volume in disgust on the introduction of his man Friday.

"It mattered little, therefore, that the *couleur de rose* picture the lawyer had drawn of the château, had little existence out of his own florid imagination : the quaint old building, with its worn tapestries and faded furniture, suited the habit of my soul, and I hugged myself often in the pleasant reflection that my London acquaintances would be puzzling their brains for my whereabouts, with-out the slightest clue to my detection.   Now, had I settled in Florence, Frankfort, or Geneva, what a life I must have led !   There is always some dear Mrs. Somebody going to

live in your neighbourhood, who begs you'll look out for a
house for her: something very eligible; eighteen rooms
well furnished, a southern aspect, in the best quarter; a
garden indispensable; and all for some forty pounds a
year or some other dear friend who desires you'll find a
governess, with more accomplishments than Malibran, and
more learning than Porson, with the temper of five angels,
and a 'vow in heaven' to have no higher salary than a
college bed-maker.   Then there are the Thompsons passing through, whom you have taken care never to know
before; but who fall upon you now, as strangers in a
foreign land, and take the 'benefit' of the 'Alien Act' in
dinners at your house during their stay.   I stop not to
enumerate the crying wants of the more lately arrived
resident, all of which are refreshed for your benefit; the
recommendations to butlers who don't cheat, to moral
music-masters, grave dancing-masters, and doctors who
never take fees; every infraction by each of these individuals in his peculiar calling being set down as a just
cause of complaint against yourself, requiring an animated
correspondence in writing, and concluding with an abject
apology and a promise to cut the delinquent that day,
though you owe him a half-year's bill.

   " These are all pleasant—not to speak of the curse of
disjointed society, ill-assorted, ill-conceived, unreasonable
pretension, vulgar impertinence, and fawning toadyism on
every side, and not one man to be found to join you in
laughing at the whole thing, which would amply repay
one for any endurance.

   " No, thought I, I've had enough of this! I'll try my
bark in quieter waters, and though it's only a punt, yet
I'll hold the sculls myself, and that's something.

   " So much for the self-gratulation I indulged in, as the
old chaise de poste rattled over the heavy pavement, and
drew up short at the portico of my future dwelling.   My
wife was charmed with the procession of villagers who
awaited us on the steps, and, although an uglier population
never trod their mother earth in wooden slippers, fancied
she could detect several faces of great beauty and much
interest in the crowd.   I saw nothing but an indiscriminate
haze of cotton nightcaps, striped jackets, blouses, black

petticoats and *sabots* . so, pushing my way through them,
I left the bazoon and the burgomaster, to the united
delights of their music and eloquence, and, shutting the
hall door, threw myself on a seat, and thanked Heaven
that my period of peace and tranquillity was at length to
begin

"Peace and tranquillity! What airy visions! Had I
selected the post of cad to an omnibus, a steward to a
Greenwich steamer, were I a guide to the Monument, or
a waiter at Long's, my life had been one of dignified repose,
in comparison with my present existence

"I had not been a week in the château, when a
travelling Englishman sprained his ankle, within a short
distance of the house. As a matter of course he was
brought there, and taken every care of for the few days of
his stay. He was fed, housed, leeched, and stuped, and
when at length he proceeded upon his journey, was profuse in his acknowledgments for the services rendered him ;
and yet, what was the base return of the ungrateful man ?
. . . I have scarcely temper to record it. During the
very moment when we were most lavish in our attention
to him, he was sapping the very peace of his benefactors.
He learned from the Flemish servants of the house that
it had formerly been the favourite residence of Vandyck ;
that the very furniture then there was unchanged since
his time ; the bed, the table, the chair he sat on were all
preserved. The wretch—am I not warranted in calling
him so?—made notes of all this, and before I had been
three weeks in my abode, out came a 'Walk in Flanders,'
in two volumes, with a whole chapter about me, headed
'CHÂTEAU DE VANDYCK.' . . . There we were, myself and
my wife, in every window of the Row—Longman, Hurst,
Rees, Orme, Brown, Green, and Blue, had bought us at a
price, and paid for us : there we were—we, who courted
solitude and retirement, to be read of by every puppy in
the West End, and every apprentice in Cheapside. Our
hospitality was lauded, as if I kept open house for all
comers, with 'hot chops and brown gravy' at a moment's
notice. The antiquary was bribed to visit me by the
fascinations of a spot, 'sacred to the reveries of genius ;'
the sportsman, by the account of my 'preserves,' the

idler, to say he had been there, and the guide-book-maker and historical biographer, to vamp up details for a new edition of ' Belgium as it was,' or ' Vandyck and his Contemporaries.'

" From the hour of the publication of that horrid book I never enjoyed a moment's peace or ease. The whole tide of my travelling countrymen—and what a flood it is ! —came pouring into Ghent. Post horses could not be found sufficient for half the demand; the hotels were crowded; respectable peasants gave up their daily employ to become guides to the château ; and little busts of Vandyck were hawked about the neighbourhood by children of four years old. The great cathedral of Ghent—Van Scamp's pictures—all the historic remains of that ancient city, were at a discount ; and they who formerly exhibited them, as a livelihood, were now thrown out of bread. Like the dancing-master who has not gone up to Paris for the last ' pirouette,' or the physician who has not taken up the stethoscope, they were reputed old-fashioned and *passé;* and, if they could not describe the Château de Vandyck, were voted among the bygones.

" The impulse once given, there was no stopping ; the current was irresistible ; the double lock on the gate of the avenue, the bulldog at the hall door, the closed shut-ters, the cut-away bell-rope, announced a firm resolution in the fortress not to surrender ; but we were taken by assault, escaladed, and starved out in turns.

" Scarcely was the tea-urn on the breakfast-table, when they began to pour in ; old and young, the halt, the one-eyed, the fat, the thin, the melancholy, the merry, the dissipated, the dyspeptic, the sentimental, the jocose, the blunt, the ceremonious, the courtly, the rude, the critical, and the free and easy : one came forty miles out of his way, and pronounced the whole thing an imposition, and myself a ' humbug;' another insisted upon my getting up at dinner, that he might sit down in my chair, char-acterized by the confounded guides as ' le fauteuil de Vandyck ; ' a third went so far as to propose lying down in our great four-post bed, just to say he had been there, though my wife was then in it. I speak not of the miserable practice of cutting slices off all the furniture as

relics. John Murray took an inventory of the whole contents of the house for a new edition of his Guide-book;
and Holman, the blind traveller, *felt* me all over with his
hand as I sat at tea with my wife, and last of all, a
respectable cheesemonger from the Strand, after inspecting
the entire building from the attics to the cellar, pressed
sixpence into my hand at parting, and said, 'Happy to see
you, Mr. Vandyck, if you come into the City!'

"Then the advice and counsel I met with, oral and
written, would fill a volume, and did, for I was compelled
to keep an album in the hall for the writers' names

"One suggested that my desecration of the temple of
genius would be less disgusting if I dined in my kitchen,
and left the ancient dining-room as the great artist had
left it.

"Another hinted that my presence in my own house
destroyed all the illusion of its historic associations.

"A third, a young lady—to judge by the writing—proposed my wearing a point beard and lace ruffles, with
trunk hose and a feather in my hat, probably to favour
the 'illusion' so urgently mentioned by the last writer,
and, perhaps, to indulge visitors like my friend the cheesemonger

"Many pitied me—well might they!—as one insensible
to the associations of the spot; while my very servants,
regarding me only as a show part of the establishment,
neglected their duties on every side, and betook themselves
to ciceroneship, each allocating his peculiar territory to
himself, like the people who show the lions and the armour
in the Tower.

"No weather was either too hot or too cold, too sultry
or too boisterous, no hour too late or too early, no day was
sacred. If the family were at prayers, or at dinner, or at
breakfast, or in bed, it mattered not? they had come
many miles to see the château, and see it they would.

"'Alas!' thought I, 'if, as some learned persons suppose, individuals be recognizable in the next world, what
a melancholy time of it will be yours, poor Vandyck! If
they make all this hubbub about the house you lived in,
what will they do about your fleshy tabernacle?'

"As the season advanced, the crowds increased, and as

autumn began, the conflicting currents to and from the Rhine all met in my bedroom.   There took place all the *rendezvous* of Europe.   Runaway daughters there first repented in papa's arms, and profligate sons promised amendment for the future.   Myself and my wife were passed by unnoticed and disregarded amid this tumult of recognition and salutation.   We were emaciated like skeletons; our meals we ate when we could, like soldiers on a retreat; and we slept in our clothes, not knowing at what moment the enemy might be upon us.   Locks, bolts, and bars were ineffectual; our resistance only increased curiosity, and our garrison was ever open to bribery.

"It was to no purpose that I broke the windows to let in the north wind and acute rheumatism: to little good did I try an alarm of fire every day about two, when the house was fullest; and I failed signally in terrifying my torturers when I painted the gardener's wife sky-blue, and had her placed in the hall, with a large label over the bed, 'collapsed cholera.'   Bless your heart! the tourist cares for none of these; and I often think it would have saved English powder and shot to have exported half a dozen of them to the East for the siege of Seringapatam. Had they been only told of an old picture, a tea-pot, a hearth-brush, or a candlestick that once belonged to Godfrey de Bouillon or Peter the Hermit, they would have stormed it under all the fire of Egypt!   Well, it's all over at last, human patience could endure no longer.   We escaped by night, got away by stealth to Ghent, took post horses in a feigned name, and fled from the Château de Vandyck, as from the plague.   Determined no longer to trust to chances, I have built a cottage myself, which has no historic associations further back than six weeks ago; and fearful even of being known as the *ci-devant* possessor of the château, never confess to have been in Ghent in my life, and if Vandyck be mentioned, ask if he is not the postmaster at Tervueren.

"Here, then, I conclude my miseries.   I cannot tell what may be the pleasure that awaits the *live* 'lion,' but I envy no man the delights that fall to his lot who inhabits the den of the *dead* one."

CHAPTER XIX.

BONN AND STUDENT LIFE.

WHEN I look at the heading of this chapter, and read
there the name of a little town upon the Rhine—which,
doubtless, there is not one of my readers has not visited
—and reflect on how worn the track, how beaten the path,
I have been guiding them on so long, I really begin to
feel somewhat faint-hearted. Have we not all seen
Brussels and Antwerp, Waterloo and Quatre Bras? Are
we not acquainted with Belgium, as well as we are with
Middlesex—don't we know the whole country, from its
cathedrals down to Sergeant Cotton—and what do we
want with Mr. O'Leary here? And the Rhine—bless the
dear man!—have we not steamed it up and down in every
dampschiffe of the rival companies? The Drachenfels and
St. Goar, the Caub and Bingen, are familiar to our eyes
as Chelsea and Tilbury Fort. True, all true, mesdames
and messieurs—I have been your fellow-traveller myself.
I have watched you pattering along, John Murray in
hand, through every narrow street and ill-paved square,
conversing with your commissionaire, in such French
as it pleased God, and receiving his replies in equivalent
English. I have seen you at *table d'hôte*, vainly in search
of what you deemed eatable—hungry and thirsty in the
midst of plenty; I have beheld you yawning at the opera,
and grave at the Vaudeville; and I knew you were
making your summer excursion of pleasure, "doing your
Belgium and Germany," like men who would not be
behind their neighbours. And still, with all this fatigue
of sea and land—this rough-riding and railroading—this
penance of short bed, and shorter board—though you
studied your handbook from the Scheldt to Schaffhausen,
you came back with little more knowledge of the Continent than when you left home. It is true, your son
Thomas, that lamb-like scion of your stock, with light eyes
and hair, has been initiated into the mysteries of *rouge-*

et-noir and *roulette*; "madame," your wife, has obtained a more extravagant sense of what is becoming in costume; your daughter has had her mind opened to the fascinations of a French *escroc*, or a "refugee Pole;" and you, yourself, somewhat the worse for your change of habits, have found the salads of Germany imparting a tinge of acidity to your disposition. These are, doubtless, valuable imports to bring back; not the less so, that they are duty free. Yet, after all, "joy's recollection is no longer joy;" and I doubt if the retrospect of your wanderings be a repayment for their fatigues.

It is one o'clock, and you can't do better than sit down to the *table d'hôte*—call it breakfast, if your prejudices run high, and take your place. I have supposed you at "Die Sterne," "The Star," in the little square of the town—and, *certes*, you might be less comfortably housed. The *cuisine* is excellent, both French and German, and the wines delicious. The company, at first blush, might induce you to step back, under the impression that you had mistaken the *salon*, and accidentally fallen upon a military mess. They are nearly all officers of the cavalry regiments garrisoned at Bonn, well-looking and well-dressed fellows—stout, bronzed, and soldier-like—and wearing their moustaches like men who felt hair on the upper lip a birthright. If a little too noisy and uproarious at table, it proceeds not from any quarrelsome spirit—the fault, in a great measure, lies with the language. German, except spoken by a Saxon Mädchen, invariably suggests the idea of a row, to an uninterested bystander; and if Goethe himself were to recite his ballads before an English audience, I'd venture long odds they'd accuse him of blasphemy. Welsh and Irish are soft zephyrs compared to it.

A stray Herr baron or two—large, portly, responsible-looking men, with cordons at their button-holes, and pipe-sticks projecting from their breast-pockets; and a sprinkling of students of the higher class—it is too dear for the others—make up the party. Of course, there are English—but my present business is not with them.

By the time you have arrived at the "Rae-braten, with capers," which—on a fair average, taken in the months of

spring and summer—may be after about an hour and a
half's diligent performance—you'll have more time to
survey the party, who by this time are clinking their
glasses, and drinking hospitably to each other in champagne—for there is always some newly returned comrade
to be fêted—or a colonel's birthday, or a battle, a poet, or
some sentimentalism about the Rhine or the Fatherland,
to be celebrated.   Happy, joyous spirits, removed equally
from the contemplation of vast wealth, or ignominious
poverty!   The equality so much talked of in France is
really felt in Germany, and, however the exclusives of
Berlin and Vienna, or the still more exalted coteries of
Baden or Darmstadt, rave of the fourteen quarterings,
which give the *entrée* to their *salons*, the nation has no
sympathy with these follies   The unaffected, simple-
minded, primitive German has no thought of assuming
an air of distance to one his inferior in rank   and I have
myself seen a sovereign prince take his place at *table
d'hôte*, beside the landlord, and hob-nob with him, cordially, during dinner.

I do not mean to say that the German has no respect
for rank, on the contrary, none more than he looks up
to aristocracy, and reveres its privileges, but he does so
from its association with the greatness of his Fatherland.
The great names of his nobles recall those of the heroes
and sages of whom the traditions of the country bear
record—they are the watchwords of German liberty, or
German glory—they are the monuments of which he feels
proudest.   His reverence for their descendants is not
tinged with any vulgar desire to be thought their equal
or their associate—far from it, he has no such yearnings.
His own position could never be affected by anything in
theirs.   The skipper of the fishing-craft might join convoy
with the great fleet—but he knows that he only commands a shallop after all.   And this, be it remarked, is a
very different feeling from what we occasionally see,
nearer home.   I have seen a good deal of student-life in
Germany, and never witnessed anything approaching that
process so significantly termed " tuft-hunting" with us;
perhaps it may be alleged in answer, that rank and riches,
so generally allied in this country, are not so there ; and,

consequently, much of what the world deems the *prestige* of condition, is wanting to create that respect.
Doubtless this is, to a certain extent, true; but I have
seen the descendants of the most distinguished houses in
Germany mixing with the students of a very humble
walk, on terms the most agreeable and familiar—assuming
nothing themselves, and, certainly, receiving no marks of
peculiar favour or deference from their companions.
When one knows something of German character, this
does not surprise. As a people, highly imaginative and
poetic in temperament—dreamy and contemplative—
falling back rather on the past than facing the future—
they are infinitely more assailable by *souvenirs* than promises; and in this wise, the ancient fame of a Hohen-
stauffen has a far firmer hold on the attachment of a
Prussian, than the hopes he may conceive from his successor. It was by recalling to the German youth the
once glories of the fatherland, that the beautiful Queen
of that country revived the drooping spirit of the nation.
It was over the tomb of the Great Frederick the monarch
swore to his alliance with Alexander, against the invading
legions of France. The songs of Uhland and Goethe, the
lyrics of Bürgher and Körner, have their source and spirit
in the heartfelt patriotism of the people. The great features of the land, and the more striking traits of national
character, are inextricably woven in their writings, as if
allied to each other; and the Rhine, and the male energy
of German blood, their native mountains, and their native
virtues, are made to reciprocate with one another; and
thus the eternal landmarks of Germany are consecrated
as the altars of its faithfulness and its truth.

The students are a means of perpetuating these notions.
The young German is essentially romantic. A poet and
a patriot, his dreams are of the greatness of his fatherland
—of its high mission among the nations of Europe; and
however he may exaggerate the claims of his country, or
over-rate his own efforts in her cause, his devotion is a
noble one; and, when sobered down by experience and
years, gives to Germany that race of faithful and high-
souled people—the best guardians of her liberty, and the
most attached defenders of her soil.

A great deal of *mauvaise plaisanterie* has been expended by French and English authors on the subject of the German student. The theme was perhaps an inviting one. Certainly nothing was easier than to ridicule absurdities in their manner, and extravagancies in their costume. Their long pipes and their long beards—their long skirts, and long boots, and long sabres—their love of beer, and their law-code of honour. Russell, in his little work on Germany—in many respects the only English book worth reading on that country—has been most unjustly severe upon them. As to French authors, one never expects truth from *them*, except it slip out, unconsciously, in a work of fiction. Still, they have displayed a more than common spirit of detraction when speaking of the German student. The truth is, they cannot forget the part these same youths performed, in repelling the French invasion of their country. The spirit evoked by Körner, and responded to from the Hartz to the Black Forest, was the death-note to the dominant tyranny of France. The patriotism which in the Basque provinces called into existence the wild Guerillas, and in the Tyrol created the Jager-bund; in more cultivated Germany elicited that race of poets and warriors whose war-songs aroused the nation from its sleep of slavery, and called them to avenge the injuries of their nation.

Laugh, then, if you will, at the strange figures, whose uncouth costumes of cap and jack-boot bespeak them a hybrid between a civilian and a soldier. The exterior is, after all, no bad type of what lies within—its contradictions are indeed scarcely as great. The spectacles and moustaches—the note-book beneath the arm, and the sabre at the side—the ink-bottle at the buttonhole, and the spurs jingling at the heels—are all the outward signs of that extraordinary mixture of patient industry and hot-headed enthusiasm—of deep thought and impetuous rashness—of matter-of-fact shrewdness and poetic fervour, and, lastly, of the most forgiving temper, allied to an unconquerable propensity for duelling. Laugh if you will at him—but he is a fine fellow for all that; and despite all the contrarieties of his nature, has the seed of those virtues which, in the peaceful life of his native country,

grow up into the ripe fruits of manly truth and
honesty.

I wish you then to think well of the Bursche, and forgive the eccentricities into which a college life, and a most
absurd doctrine of its ordinances, will now and then lead
him. That wild-looking youth, for all that he has a sabre-
wound across his cheek, and wears his neck bare, like a
Malay—despite his savage moustache and his lowering
look, has a soft heart, though it beats behind that mass of
nonsensical braiding. He could recite you, for hours long,
the ballads of Schiller, and the lyrics of Uhland; ah! and
sing for you, too, with no mean skill, the music of Spohr
and Weber, accompanying himself the while on the piano,
with a touch that would make your heart thrill; and I
am not sure that, even in his wildest moments of enthusiastic folly, he is not nearly as much an object of hope to
his country, as though he were making a "book" on the
"Derby," or studying "the odds" among the legs at
Tattersall's.

Above all things, I would beg of you, don't be too hasty
in judging him. Put not much trust in half what English
writers lay to his charge—believe not one syllable of any
Frenchman on the subject—no! not even that estimable
Alexandre Dumas, who represents the "Student" as
demanding alms on the high-road—thus confounding him
with the "Lehr-Junker"—the travelling apprentice—who,
by the laws of Germany, is obliged to spend two years in
wandering through different countries, before he is permitted to reside permanently in his own. The blunder
would have been too gross for anything but a Frenchman
and a Parisian; but the Rue St. Denis covers a multitude
of mistakes, and the Boulevard de Montmartre is a dis-
pensation to all truth.

Howitt, if you can read a heavy book, will tell you
nearly everything a *book* can tell; but setting a Quaker
to describe Burschen life, was pretty much like sending a
Hindoo to report at a county meeting.

Now all this time we have been wandering from Bonn,
and its gardens, sloping down into the very Rhine, and its
beautiful park, the once pleasure-ground of that palace
which now forms the building of the University. There

are few sweeter spots than this. You have escaped from
the long, low swamps of Holland—you have left behind
you the land of marsh and fog—and already the moun-
tainous region of Germany breaks on the view: the
Sieben Gebirge are in sight, and the bold Drachenfels,
with its ruined tower on its summit—an earnest of the
glorious scenery to come. The river itself looks brighter
and fresher—its eddies seem to sparkle with a lustre they
know not when circling along the swampy shores of
Nimmegen.

Besides, there is really something in a name, and the
sound of "Deutschland" is pleasanter than that of the
country of "dull fogs and dank ditches;" and although
I would not have you salute it, like Voltaire—

"Adieu ! canaille—canards—canaux !"

still be thankful for being where you are, take your coffee,
and let us have a ramble through the Park.

Alas! the autumn is running into the winter—each
breeze that sighs along the ground is the dirge over the
dead leaves that lie strewn around us. The bare branches
throw their gaunt arms to and fro as the cold grey clouds
flit past. The student, too, has donned his fur-lined
mantle, and strides along, with cap bent down, and hurried
step.

But a few weeks since and these alleys were crowded
by gay and smiling groups, lingering beneath the shadow
of tall trees, and listening to the Jäger band that played
in yonder pavilion. The grey-haired professor moved
slowly along, uncovering his venerable head as some
student passed, and respectfully saluting him; and there,
too, walked his fair daughters, the "fräuleins with the
yellow hair!" How calmly sweet their full blue eyes!
how gentleness is written in their quiet gait! Yet, see!
as each bar of the distant waltz is heard beating on the
ear, how their footsteps keep time and mark the measure.
Alas! the summer hours have fled, and with them those
calm nights, when, by the flickering moon, the pathways echoed to the steps of lingering feet now homeward
turning.

I never can visit a University town in Germany without

a sigh after the time when I was myself a Bursche, read myself to sleep each night with Ludwig Tieck, and sported two broadswords crosswise above my chimney.

I was a student of Göttingen—the Georgia Augusta— and in the days I speak of—I know not well what King Ernest has done since—it was rather a proud thing to be "ein Göttinger Bursche;" there was considered something of style to appertain to it above the other Universities, and we looked down upon a Heidelberger, or a Halle man as only something above a "Philister." The professors had given a great celebrity to the University too; there was Stromeyer in chemistry, and Hausman in philology, Behr in Greek; Shrader in botany; and, greater than all, old Blumenbach himself, lecturing four days each week on everything he could think of—natural philosophy, physics, geography, anatomy, physiology, optics, colours, metallurgy, magnetism, and the whale fishery in the South Seas—making the most abstruse and grave subjects interesting by the charm of his manner, and elevating trivial topics into consequence by their connection with weightier matters. He was the only lecturer I ever heard of who concluded his hour to the regret of his hearers, and left them longing for the continuation; anecdote and illustration fell from him with a profusion almost inconceivable and perfectly miraculous, when it is borne in mind that he rarely was known to repeat himself in a figure, and more rarely still in a story, and when he has detected himself in this latter he would suddenly stop short, with an "Ach Gott, I'm growing old," and immediately turn into another channel, and by some new and unheard-of history, extricate himself from his difficulty.

With all the learning of a Buffon and a Cuvier, he was simple and unaffected as a child. His little receptions in the summer months were held in his garden; I have him before me this minute, seated under the wide-spreading linden tree, with his little table before him, holding his coffee and a few books; his long hair, white as snow, escaping beneath his round cap of dark green velvet, falling loosely on his shoulders, and his large grey eyes, now widely opened with astonishment at some piece of intelligence a boy would have heard without amazement,

then twinkling with sly humour at the droll thoughts
passing through his mind; while around him sat his
brother professors and their families, chatting pleasantly
over the little news of their peaceful community—the
good Vraus knitting and listening, and the Frauleins
demurely sitting by, wearing a look of mock attention to
some learned dissertation, and ever and anon stealing a
sly glance at the handsome youth who was honoured by
an invitation to the *soirée*. How charming, too, to hear
them speak of the great men of the land as their old
friends and college companions! It was not the author
of "Wallenstein" and "Don Carlos," but Frederick
Schiller, the student of medicine, as they knew him in
his boyhood—bold, ardent, and ambitious—toiling along
a path he loved not, and feeling within him the working of
that great genius which, one day, was to make him the pride
of his fatherland; and Wieland—strange and eccentric—
old in his youth, with the innocence of a child and the
wisdom of a sage ; and Hoffman—the victim of his gloomy
imagination, whose spectral shapes and dark warnings
were not the forced efforts of his brain, but the companions of his wanderings—the beings of his sleep. How
did they jest with him on his half-crazed notions, and
laugh at his eccentricities. It was strange to hear them
tell of going home with Hummel, then a mere boy, and
how, as the evening closed in, he sat down to the pianoforte, and played and sung, and played again for hours
long, now exciting their wonder by passages of brilliant
and glittering effect, now knocking at their hearts by
tones of plaintive beauty. There was a little melody he
played the night they spoke of—some short and touching
ballad—the inspiration of the moment—made on the
approaching departure of some one amongst them, which,
many years after in "Fidelio," called down thunders of
applause ; mayhap the tribute of his first audience was a
sweeter homage after all

While thus they chatted on, the great world without
and all its mighty interests seemed forgotten by them.
France might have taken another choleric fit, and been in
march upon the Rhine ; England might have once more
covered the ocean with her fleets, and scattered to the

waves the wreck of another Trafalgar; Russia might be pouring down her hordes from the Don and Dnieper; little chance had they of knowing aught of these things! The orchards that surrounded the ramparts shut out the rest of Europe, and they lived as remote from all the collisions of politics and the strife of nations as though the University had been in another planet

I must not forget the old Hofrath Froriep, Ordentliche-Professor von—Heaven knows what. No one ever saw his collegium (lecture-room), no one ever heard him lecture. He had been a special tutor to the princes—as the Dukes of Cumberland and Cambridge were then called, about forty years ago—and he seemed to live upon the memory of those great days, when a "Royal Highness" took notes beside his chair, and when he addressed his class "Princes and Gentlemen!" What pride he felt in his clasp of the Guelph, and an autograph letter of the "Herzog von Clarence," who once paid him a visit at his house in Gottingen!

It was a strange thing to hear the royal family of England spoken thus of among foreigners, who neither knew our land, nor its language. One was suddenly recalled to the recollection of that Saxon stock, from which our common ancestry proceeded—the bond of union between us—the source from which so many of the best traits of English character take their origin. The love of truth, the manly independence, the habits of patient industry which we derived from our German blood, are not inferior to the enterprising spirit and the chivalrous daring of Norman origin.

But to return to the Hofrath, or Privy Councillor Froriep, for so was he most rigidly styled. I remember him so well as he used to come slowly down the garden-walk, leaning on his sister's arm. He was the junior by some years, but no one could have made the discovery now, the thing rested on tradition, however, and was not disputed. The Fraulein Martha von Froriep was the Daguerreotype of her brother. To see them sitting opposite each other was actually ludicrous; not only were the features alike, but the expressions tallied so completely, it was as if one face reflected the other. Did the professor look grave—the Fraulein Martha's face was serious. Did

he laugh—straightway her features took a merry cast. If
his coffee was too hot, or did he burn his fingers with his
pipe, the old lady's sympathies were with him still. The
Siamese twins were on terms of distant acquaintanceship,
compared with the instinctive relation these two bore
each other.

How was it possible, you will ask, that such an eternal
similarity should have marked their dispositions? The
answer is an easy one. The Fraulein was deaf—perfectly
destitute of hearing. The last recorded act of her auditory
nerves was on the occasion of some public rejoicing, when
twenty-four large guns were discharged in a few seconds
of time, and by the reverberation broke every window in
Göttingen ; the old lady, who was knitting at the time,
merely stopped her work and called out " Come in ! "
thinking it was a tap at the room-door. To her malady
was it then owing if she so perfectly resembled the professor, her brother. She watched him with an anxious
eye; his face was the dial that regulated every hour of
her existence; and as the telegraph repeats the signal that
is made to it, yet knows not the interpretation of the sign,
so did she signalize the passing emotions of his mind, long
perhaps after her own could take interest in the cause.

Nothing had a stranger effect, however, than to listen
to the professor's conversation, to which the assent of the
deaf old lady chimed in at short and regular intervals.
For years long she had been in the habit of corroborating
everything he said, and continued the practice now from
habit.   It was like a clock that struck the hour when
all its machinery had run down. And so, whether the
Hofrath descanted on some learned question of Greek
particles, some much-disputed fact of ancient history, or,
as was more often the case, narrated with German broad-
ness some little anecdote of his student life, the old lady's
" Ja! ja! den sah Ich, selbst, da! war Ich, auch! " " Yes,
yes, I saw it myself; I was there, too," bore testimony to
the truth of Tacitus or Heredotus, or, more precarious
still, to these little traits of her brother's youthful existence, which, to say the least, were as well uncorroborated.

The Hofrath had passed his life as a bachelor, a circumstance which could not fail to surprise, for his stories

were generally of his love adventures and perils; and all teemed with dissertations on the great susceptibility of his heart, and his devoted admiration of female beauty— weaknesses of which it was plain he felt vain, and loved to hear authenticated by his old associates. In this respect Blumenbach indulged him perfectly; now recall- ing to his memory some tender scene, or some afflicting separation, which invariably drew him into a story.

If these little reminiscences possessed not all the point and interest of more adventurous histories, to me, at least, they were more amusing by the force of truth, and by the singular look, voice, and manner of him who related them. Imagine, then, a meagre old man, about five feet two, whose head was a wedge with the thin side foremost, the nose standing abruptly out, like the cut- water of a man-o'-war gig; a large mouth, forming a bold semicircle, with the convexity downwards, the angles of which were lost in a mass of wrinkles on his withered cheeks; two fierce-looking, fiery, little grey eyes set slant- wise in his head without a vestige of eyelash over them; his hair, combed back with great precision, and tied behind into a queue, had, from long pulling, gradually drawn the eyebrows upwards to double their natural height, where they remained fixed, giving to this uncouth face an expression of everlasting surprise—in fact, he appeared as if he were perpetually beholding the ghost of somebody. His voice was a strange, unnatural, clattering sound, as though the machinery of speech had been left a long while without oiling, and could not work flippantly, but, to be sure, the language was German, and that may excuse much.

Such was the Herr Hofrath Froriep; once, if you were to believe himself, a lady-killer of the first water. Indeed, still, when he stretched forth his thin and twisted shanks, attired in satin shorts and black silk stockings, a gleam of conscious pride would light up his features, and he would seem to say to himself, "These legs might do some mis- chief yet."

Caroline Pichler, the novelist, had been one of his loves, and, if you believed himself, a victim to his fascinations. However, another version of the tale had obtained cur-

rency, and was frequently alluded to by his companions at
those moments when a more boastful spirit than they
deemed suitable animated his discourse ; and at such times
I remarked that the Hofrath became unusually sensitive,
and anxious to change the subject.

It was one evening, when we sat somewhat later than
our wont in the garden, tempted by the delicious fragrance
of the flowers and the mild light of a new moon, that at
last the Hofrath's Madchen made her appearance, lantern
in hand, to conduct him home. She carried on her arm a
mass of cloaks, shawls, and envelopes that would have
clothed a procession, with which she proceeded leisurely
and artistically to dress up the professor and his sister,
until the impression came over the bystanders that none
but she who hid them in that mountain of wearables would
ever be able to discover them again.

"Ach Gott," exclaimed the Hofrath, as she crowned
him with a quilted nightcap, whose jaws descended and
fastened beneath the chin, like an antique helmet, leaving
the miserable old face, like an uncouth pattern, in the
middle of the Berlin embroidery—"Ach Gott, but for
that!"

"But for that!" reiterated old Hausman, in a solemn
tone, as if he knew the secret grief his friend alluded to,
and gave him all his sympathy.

"Sit down again, Froriep," said Blumenbach ; "it is an
hour too soon for young folk like us to separate. We'll
have a glass of Rosenthaler, and you shall tell us that
story."

"Be it so," said the Hofrath, as he made signs to the
Mädchen that he would cast his skin. "Ich bin dabey!
I'm ready."

> "Wi' tippenny we fear nae evil,
> Wi' usquebaugh we'd face the devil,"

quoth Burns; and, surely, Tam's knowledge of human
nature took a wide circuit when he uttered the words.
The whole philosophy of temptation is comprised in the
distich, and the adage of coming up "to a man's price"
has no happier illustration ; and certainly, had the poet
been a Bursche in Germany, he could not have conveyed
the "sliding-scale" of professors' agreeability under a more

suitable formula. He, who would be civil with a pipe, becomes communicative with coffee,—brotherly with beer, —but opens every secret of his nature under the high-pressure power of a flask of Rhenish. The very smack of the Hofrath's lips, as he drained his glass to the bottom, and then exclaimed in a transport, " Er ist zum kissen, der Wein !" announced that the folding-doors of his heart stood wide open, and that he might enter who would.

" Rosenthaler was Goethe's favourite," quoth Stro-meyer ; " and he had a good taste in wine."

" Your great folk ever," said Hausman, " like to show some decided preference to one vintage above the rest, Napoleon adopted Chambertin, Joseph the Second drank nothing but Tokay, and Peter the Great found brandy the only fluid to his palate."

" A plague on their fancies," interrupted old Blumen-bach. " Let us have the story "

" Ah ! well, well," said the Hofrath, throwing up his eyes with an air of sentimentalism, " so you shall ' Love's young dream !' was sweet, after all ! We were in the Hartz," continued he, at once springing into his story with a true Demosthenic abruptness—" we were in the Hartz mountains, making a little tour, for it was ' semestre,' and all the classes were closed in the University. There was Tieck, and Feldtbourg the Dane, and Upsal, and old Lau-gendorf of Jena, and Gr̈otchen von Zobelschein, and Mina Upsal, and Caroline, and Martha there—she, poor thing, was getting deaf at the time, and could not take the same pleasure as the rest of us: she was always stupid, you know."

Here he looked over at her, when she immediately responded,—

" Ja, ja, what he says is true."

" Each morning we used to set off up the mountains, botanizing and hammering among the limestone rocks, and seeking for cryptogamia and felspar, lichens and jungermannia, and primitive rock; mingling our little diversions with pleasant talk about the poets, and reciting verses to one another from Hans Sachs and the old writers, and chatting away about Schiller—the ' Lager ' was just come out, and more than one among us could scarcely believe it was Frederick did it.

" Tieck and I soon found that we were rivals ; for before a week each of us was in love with Caroline. Now, Ludwig was a clever fellow, and had a thousand little ways of ingratiating himself with a pretty woman—and a poetess besides. He could come down every day to breakfast with some ode or sonnet, or maybe a dream ; and then he was ready after dinner with his bit of poetry, which sometimes, when he found a piano, he'd set to music; or maybe in the evening he'd invent one of those strange rigmarole stories of his, about a blue-bottle fly, dying for love of a white moth or some superannuated old drone bee, that retired from public life, and spent his days reviling the rest of the world. You know his nonsense well ; but, somehow, one could not help listening, and, what's worse, feeling interest in it. As for Caroline, she became crazed about gnats, and spiders, and fleas, and would hear for whole days long the stories of their loves and sorrows.

" For some time I bore up as well as I could. There was a limit, Heaven be thanked, to that branch of the creation, and as he had now got down to millepedes, I trusted that before the week was over he'd have reached mites—beyond which it was impossible he could be expected to proceed. Alas! I little knew the resources of his genius ; for one evening, when I thought him running fast aground, he sat down in the midst of us, and began a tale of the life and adventures of the Herr Baron von Beetroot, in search of his lost love, the Fraulein von Cucumber. This confounded narrative had its scene in an old garden in Silesia, where there were incidents of real beauty and interest interwoven, ay, and verses, that would make your heart thrill. Caroline could evidently resist no longer. The Baron von Beetroot was ever uppermost in her mind, and if she ate 'gurkin-salade,' it brought the tears into her eyes. In this sad strait, I wandered out alone one evening, and, without knowing it, reached the Rase Mühle, near Oltdorf. There I went in and ordered a supper ; but they had nothing but ' Thick milk '* and ' Kalte-schade.'   No matter, thought I; a man in such

* Thick milk ; a mess of sour cream thickened with sugar and crumbs of bread. " Kalte-schade," the same species of abomination, the only difference being beer, *vice* cream, for the fluid.

grief as mine need little care what he eats; and I ordered
both, that I might afterwards decide which I'd prefer.
They came, and were placed before me. Himmel! und
Erde! what did I do but eat the two! beer and cream,
cream and beer, pepper and sugar, brown bread and nutmeg! Such was my abstraction, that I never noticed what
I was doing till I saw the two empty bowls before me.
'I am a dead Hofrath before day breaks,' said I, 'and I'll
make my will;' but before I could put the plan into execution I became very ill, and they were obliged to carry me
to bed. From that moment my senses began to wander;
exhaustion, sour beer, and despair, were all working within
me, and I was mad. It was a brief paroxysm, but a
fearful one. A hundred and fifty thousand ridiculous
fancies went at racing speed through my mind, and I
spent the night alternately laughing and crying. My
pipe, that lay on the chair beside the bed, figured in nearly
every scene, and performed a part in many a strange
adventure.

" By noon the others learned where I was, and came
over to see me. After sitting for half an hour beside
me, they were going away, when I called Caroline and
Martha back. She blushed; but, taking Martha's arm,
she seated herself upon a sofa, and asked in a timid voice
what I wished for.

" 'To hear me before I die,' replied I; 'to listen to a
wonderful vision I have seen this night.'

" 'A vision,' said Caroline—'oh, what was it?'

" 'A beautiful and a touching one. Let me tell it to
you. I will call it, 'The never-to-be-lost-sight-of, though
not-the-less-on-that-account-to-be-concealed, Loves of the
Mug and the Meerschaum.'

" Caroline sprang to my side as I uttered these words,
and as she wiped the tears from her eyes she sobbed
forth,—

" 'Let me but hear it—let me but hear it!'

" 'Sit down,' said I, taking her hand and pressing it to
my lips—'sit down, and you shall.' With that I began
my tale. I suppose," continued the Hofrath, " you don't
wish to have the story?"

" Gott bewahr! Heaven forbid," broke in the whole

company in a breath. "Leave the Mug and the Meerschaum, and go on with Caroline."

"Well, from that hour her heart was mine. Ludwig
might call all the reptiles that ever crawled, every vegetable that ever grew, to his aid—the victory was with
me. He saw it, and, irritated by defeat, returned to
Berlin without bidding us even farewell, and we never
heard of him till we saw his new novel of 'Fortunio.'
But to go on; the day after Tieck left us was my birthday, and they all arranged to give me a little fête, and
truly nothing could be prettier. The garden of the inn
was a sweet spot, and there was a large linden like this,
where the table was spread; and there was a chair all
decked with roses and myrtle for me—Caroline herself
had done it; and they had composed a little hymn in
honour of me, wherein were sundry compliments to my
distinction in science and poesy—the gifts of my mind
and the graces of my person. Ach, ja! I was handsome
then.

"Well, well, I must close my tale—I cannot bear to
think of it even now. Caroline came forward, dressed in
white, with a crown of roses and laurel leaves intertwined,
and approached me gracefully, as I sat waiting to receive
her—all the rest ranged on either side of me.

> ' Auf seine stirne, wo, der licht——'
> ' Upon that brow where shines the light——'

said Caroline, raising the chaplet.

"'Ach Du Heiliger!' screamed Martha, who only that
instant saw I was bareheaded, 'the dear man will catch
his death of cold!' and with that she snatched this confounded nightcap from her pocket, and rushing forward,
clapped it on my head before I could know it was done.
I struggled and kicked, like one possessed, but it was
of no use; she had tied the strings in a black knot,
and they could neither be loosened nor broken. 'Be
still there,' said she; 'thou knowest well that at fifty-
three——' You can conceive," said the Hofrath in a
parenthesis, "that her passion obliterated her memory."
—'At fifty-three one can't play the fool like at twenty.'

"Ach, ja! it was over with me for ever. Caroline

screamed at the cap, first laughing, then crying, and then both—the rest nearly died of it, and so did I. Caroline would never look at me after, and I came back home, disappointed in my love—and all because of a woollen nightcap."

When the Hofrath concluded, he poured the remainder of the Rosenthaler into his glass, and bowing to each in turn, wished us good night, while, taking the Fraulein Martha's arm, they both disappeared in the shade, as the little party broke up and each wended his way homeward.

CHAPTER XX.

THE "STUDENT."

If I were not sketching a real personage, and retailing an anecdote once heard, I should pronounce the Hofrath von Floriep a fictitious character, for which reason I bear you no ill-will if you incline to that opinion. I have no witness to call in my defence. There were but two Englishmen in Göttingen, in *my* day—one of them is now no more. Poor fellow! he had just entered the army; his regiment was at Corfu, and he was spending the six months of his first leave in Germany. We chanced to be fellow-travellers, and ended by becoming friends. When he left me, it was for Vienna, from which, after a short stay, he departed for Venice, where he purchased a yacht, and with eight Greek sailors, sailed for a cruise through the Ionian Islands. He was never seen alive again; his body, fearfully gashed and wounded, was discovered on the beach at Zante. His murderers, for such they were, escaped with the vessel, and never were captured. Should any "61st" man throw his eye over these pages he will remember that I speak of one beloved by every one who knew him. With all the heroic daring of the stoutest heart, his nature was soft and gentle as a child's. Poor G——! some of the happiest moments of my life were spent with you—some of the saddest in thinking over your destiny.

You must take my word for the Hofrath, then, good reader. They who read the modern novels of Germany —the wild exaggerations of Fouqué and Hoffman, Museus and Tieck, will comprehend that the story of himself has no extravagance whatever. To ascribe language and human passions to the lower animals, and even to the inanimate creation, is a favourite German notion, the indulgence of which has led to a great deal of that mysticism we find in their writings; and the secret sympathies of cauliflowers and cabbages, for young ladies in love, is a constant theme among this class of novelists.

A word now of the students, and I have done. Whatever the absurdities in their code of honour, however ludicrous the etiquette of the "comment," as it is called, there is a world of manly honesty and trueheartedness among them. There is nothing mean or low, nothing dishonourable nor unworthy in the spirit of the Burschenschaft. Exaggerated ideas of their own importance—an overweening sense of their value to the Vaterland—there are in abundance, as well as a mass of crude, unsettled notions about liberty, and the regeneration of Germany. But, after all, these are harmless fictions; they are not allied to any evil passions at the time—they lead to no bad results for the future. The murder of Kotzebue, and the attempt on the life of Napoleon by Staps, were much more attributable to the mad enthusiasm of the period than to the principles of the student league. The spirit of the nation revolted at the tyranny they had so long submitted to, and these fearful crimes were the agonized expression of endurance pushed to madness. Only they who witnessed the frantic joy of the people, when the tide of fortune turned against Napoleon, and his baffled legions retreated through Germany, on their return from the Russian campaign, can understand how deeply stored were the wrongs for which they were now to exact vengeance. The "volker schlaght"—the "people's slaughter" —as they love to call the terrible fight of Leipsic, was the dreadful recompense of all their sufferings.

When the French Revolution first broke out, the Ger-

man students, like many wiser and more thinking heads
than theirs, in our own country, were struck with the
great movement of a mighty people in their march to
liberty; but when, disgusted with the atrocities that
followed, they afterwards beheld France the first to assail
the liberties and trample on the freedom of every other
country, they regarded her as a traitor to the cause she
once professed; and while their apathy, in the early wars
of the republican armies marked their sympathy with the
wild notions of liberty, of which Frenchmen affected to
be the apostles in Europe—yet, when they saw the lust of
conquest and the passion for dominion usurp the place
of those high-sounding virtues—*Liberté, Égalité,* the
reverse was a tremendous one, and may well excuse, if
excuse were needful, the proud triumph of the German
armies, when they bivouacked in the streets of Paris.

The changed fortunes of the Continent have of course
obliterated every political feature in the student life of
Germany; or, if such still exist, it takes the form merely
of momentary enthusiasm, in favour of some banished
professor, or a Burschen festival, in honour of some
martyr of the press. Still their ancient virtues survive,
and the German student is yet a type—one of the few
remaining—of the Europe of thirty years ago. Long may
he remain so, say I. Long may so interesting a land
have its national good faith and brotherly affection rooted
in the minds of its youth. Long may the country of
Schiller, of Wieland, and of Goethe, possess the race of
those who can appreciate their greatness, or strive to
emulate their fame.

1 leave to others the task of chronicling their beer
orgies. their wild festivals and their duels; and though
not disposed to defend them on such charges, I might,
were it not invidious, adduce instances, nearer home, of
practices little more commendable. At those same festivals, at many of which I have been present, I have heard
music that would shame most of our orchestras, and
listened to singing such as I have never heard surpassed,
except within the walls of a grand opera; and as to their
duelling, the practice is bad enough, in all conscience, but
still I would mention one instance, of which I myself

x

was a witness, and perhaps even in so little fertile a field we may find one grain of goodly promise.

Among my acquaintances in Gottingen were two students, both Prussians, and both from the same small town of Magdebourg. They had been school-fellows, and came together to the University, where they lived together on terms of brotherly affection, which, even there, where friendship takes all the semblance of a sacred compact, was the subject of remark. Never were two men less alike, however, than these. Eisendecker was a bold, hot-headed fellow, fond of all the riotous excesses of Burschen life; his face, seamed with many a scar, declared him a " hahn," as, in student phrase, a confirmed duellist is termed. He was ever foremost in each scheme of wild adventure, and continually brought up before the senate on some charge of insubordination. Von Mühry, his companion, was exactly the opposite. His *sobriquet*—for nearly every student had one—was " der Zahme—the gentle," and never was any more appropriate. His disposition was mildness itself. He was very handsome, almost girlish in his look, with large blue eyes, and fine, soft silky hair, which, German like, he wore upon 'his neck. His voice—the index of his nature—soft, low, and musical, would have predisposed you at once in his favour. Still, those disparities did not prevent the attachment of the two youths; on the contrary, they seemed rather to strengthen the bond between,—each, as it were, supplying to the other the qualities which nature had denied him. They were never separate in lecture-room, or at home, or in the *allée*—as the promenade was called —or in the garden, where, each evening, the students resorted to sup, and listen to the music of the Jäger band. Eisendecker and Mühry were names that no one ever heard separated, and when one appeared the other was never more than a few yards off.

Such was their friendship when an unhappy incident occurred to trouble its even course, and sow dissension between these who never had known a passing difference in their lives. The sub-rector of Göttingen was in the habit of giving little receptions every week, to which many of the students were invited, and to which Eisendecker and Mühry were frequently asked, as they both belonged to the professor's class. In the quiet world of a little University town, these *soirées* were great occasions, and the invited plumed themselves not a little on the distinction of a card which gave the privilege of bowing in the Herr professor's drawing-room, and kissing the hand of his fair daughter, the Frederica von Ettenheim, the belle of Göttingen. Frederica was the prettiest German girl I ever saw, for this reason, that having been partly educated at Paris, French *espièglerie* relieved what had been, otherwise, the too regular monotony of her Saxon features, and imparted a character of sauciness—or "*fierté*" is a better word—to that quietude which is too tame to give the varied expression, so charming in female beauty. The *esprit*, that delicious ingredient which has been so lamentably omitted in German character, she had imbibed from her French education; and in lieu of that plodding interchange of flat commonplaces which constitute the ordinary staple of conversation between the young of opposite sexes beyond the Rhine, she had imported the light, delicate tone of Parisian raillery—the easy and familiar gaiety of French society, so inexpressibly charming in France, and such a boon from heaven, when one meets it by accident, elsewhere.

Now, of all tongues ever invented by man, German is the most difficult and clumsy, for all purposes of conversation. You may preach in it—you may pray in it—you may hold a learned argument, or you may lay down some involved and intricate statement—you may, if you have the gift, even tell a story in it, provided the hearers be patient— and some have gone so far as to venture on expressing a humorous idea in German; but these have been bold men, and their venturous conduct is more to be admired than imitated. At the same time, it is right to add, that a German joke is a very wooden contrivance at best, and that the praise it meets with, is rather in the proportion of the difficulty of the manufacture, than of the superiority of the article—just as we admire those Indian toys carved with a rusty nail, or those fourth-string performances of Paganini and his followers.

And now to come back to the students, whom, mayhap,

x 2

you deem to have been forgotten by me all this time, but
for whose peculiar illustration my digression was intended; it being neither more nor less than to show that
if Frederica von Ettenheim turned half the heads in
Göttingen, Messrs. Eisendecker and Mühry were of the
number. What a feature it was of the little town, her
coming to reside in it! What a sweet atmosphere of
womanly gracefulness spread itself, like a perfume,
through those old *salons*, whose dusty curtains and moth-
eaten chairs looked like the fossils of some antediluvian
furniture! With what magic were the old ceremonials of
a professor's reception exchanged for the easier habits of a
politer world! The venerable dignitaries of the University felt the change, but knew not where it lay, and could
not account for the pleasure they now experienced in the
vice-rector's *soirées:* while the students knew no bounds
to the enthusiastic admiration; and " Die Ettenheim"
reigned in every heart in Göttingen.

Of all her admirers, none seemed to hold a higher
place in her favour than Von Mühry. Several causes
contributed to this, in addition to his own personal advantages, and the distinction of his talents, which were
of a high order. He was particularly noticed by the
vice-rector, from the circumstance of his father holding a
responsible position in the Prussian government, while
Adolphe himself gave ample promise of one day making
a figure in the world. He was never omitted in any invitation, nor forgotten in any of the many little parties
so frequent among the professors; and even where the
society was limited to the dignitaries of the college, some
excuse would ever be made by the vice-rector, to have him
present, either on the pretence of wanting him for something, or that Frederica had asked him without thinking.

Such was the state of this little world, when I settled
in it, and took up my residence at the Meissner Thor,
intending to pass my summer there. The first evening I
spent at the vice-rector's, the matter was quite clear to
my eyes. Frederica and Adolphe were lovers. It was to
no purpose, that when he had accompanied her on the
piano he retreated to a distant part of the room, when
she ceased to sing. It signified not, that he scarcely ever

spoke to her, and when he did, but a few words, hurriedly and in confusion. Their looks met once; I saw
them exchange one glance—a fleeting one, too—but I
read in it their whole secret, mayhap even more than
they knew themselves. Well had it been, if I alone had
witnessed this, but there was another at my side who
saw it also, and whispered in my ear, " Der Zahme is in
love." I turned round—it was Eisendecker: his face,
sallow and sickly, while large circles of dark olive surrounded his eyes, and gave him an air of deep suffering.
" Did you see that? " said he suddenly, as he leaned his
hand on my arm, where it shook like one in ague.
    " Did you see that? "
    " What?—the flower? "
    " Yes—the flower. It was she dropped it, when she
crossed the room. You saw him take it up—didn't
you? "
    The tone he spoke in was harsh, and hissing, as if he
uttered the words with his teeth clenched. It was clear
to me now, that he, too, was in love with Frederica, and
I trembled to think of the cruel shock their friendship
must sustain ere long.
    A short time after, when I was about to retire, Eisen-
decker took my arm, and said, "Are you for going home?
May I go with you? " I gave a willing assent, our
lodgings being near, and we spent much of every day in
each other's chambers. It was the first time we had ever
returned without waiting for Mühry; and fearing what a
separation, once begun, might lead to, I stopped suddenly
on the stairs, and said, as if suddenly remembering,—
    " By the bye, we are going without Adolphe."
    Eisendecker's fingers clutched me convulsively, and
while a bitter laugh broke from him, he said, " You
wouldn't tear them asunder—would you? " For the rest
of the way, he never spoke again, and I, fearful of awakening the expression of that grief, which, when avowed,
became confirmed, never opened my lips, save to say—
" Good-night."
    I never intended to have involved myself in a regular
story when I began this chapter, nor must I do so now,
though, sooth to say, it would not be without its interest,

to trace the career of these two youths, who now became gradually estranged from each other, and were no longer to be seen, as of old, walking with arms on each other's shoulder—the most perfect realization of true brotherly affection. Day by day the distance widened between them; each knew the secret of the other's heart, yet neither dared to speak of it. From distrust there is but a short step to dislike—alas! it is scarcely even a step. They parted.

Another change came over them, and a stranger still. Eisendecker, the violent youth, of ungovernable temper, and impetuous passion—who loved the wildest freak of student-daring, and ever was the first to lead the way in each mad scheme—had now become silent and thoughtful —a gentle sadness tempered down the fierce traits of his hot nature, and he no longer frequented his old haunts of the cellar and the fighting school, but wandered alone into the country, and spent whole days in solitude. Von Muhry, on the other hand, seemed to have assumed the castaway mantle of his once friend the gentle bearing, and almost submissive tone of his manner, were exchanged for an air of conscious pride—a demeanour that bespoke a triumphant spirit—and the quiet youth suddenly seemed changed to a rash, high-spirited boy, reckless from very happiness. During this time, Eisendecker had attached himself particularly to me; and although I had always hitherto preferred Von Muhry, the feeling of the other's unhappiness—a sense of compassion for suffering, which it was easy to see was great—drew me closer in my friendship towards him; and, at last, I scarcely saw Adolphe at all—and when we did meet, a mutual feeling of embarrassment separated and estranged us from each other. About this time I set off on an excursion to the Hartz Mountains, to visit the Brocken, and see the mines; my absence, delayed beyond what I first intended, was above four weeks, and I returned to Gottingen, just as the summer vacation was about to begin.

About five leagues from Gottingen, on the road towards Nordheim, there is a little village called Meissner, a favourite resort of the students, in all their festivals— while, at something less than a mile distant, stands a water-mill, on a little rivulet among the hills—a wild, sequestered spot, overgrown with stunted oak and brush-wood. A narrow bridle-path leads to it from the village, and this was the most approved place for settling all those affairs of honour whose character was too serious to make it safe to decide nearer the University; for, strangely enough—while, by the laws of the University, duelling was rigidly denounced, yet, whenever the quarrel was decided by the sword, the authorities never, or almost never, interfered—but if a pistol was the weapon, the thing at once took a more serious aspect.

For what reasons the mills have been always selected, as the appropriate scenes for such encounters, I never could discover; but the fact is unquestionable—and I never knew a University town that did not possess its "water privileges" in this manner.

Towards the mill I was journeying at the easy pace of my pony, early on a summer's morning, preferring the rural breakfast with the miller—for they are always a kind of innkeepers—to the fare of the village. I entered the little bridle-path that conducted to his door, and was sauntering listlessly along, dreaming pleasantly, as one does, when the song of the lark, and the heavy odour of dew-pressed flowers, steep the heart in happiness all its own—when, behind me, I heard the regular tramp of marching. I listened—had I been a stranger to the sound, I should have thought them soldiers—but I knew too well the measured tread of the student, and I heard the jingling of their heavy sabres, a peculiar clank a student's ear cannot be deceived in. I guessed at once the object of their coming, and grew sick at heart to think that the storm of men's stubborn passions, and the strife of their revengeful nature, should desecrate a peaceful spot like this. I was about to turn back, disgusted at the thought, when I remembered I must return by the same path, and meet them—but even this I shrunk from. The footsteps came nearer and nearer, and I had barely time to move off the path, into the brushwood, and lead my pony after, when they turned the angle of the way. They who walked first were muffled in their cloaks, whose high collars concealed their faces, but the caps of many a gaudy colour proclaimed them students. At a little distance behind, and with a slower step, came another party, among whom I noticed one who walked between two others, his head sunk on his bosom, and evidently overcome with emotions of deep sorrow. A movement of my horse, at this instant, attracted their attention towards the thicket—they stopped, and a voice called out my name. I looked round, and there stood Eisendecker before me. He was dressed in deep mourning, and looked pale and worn—his black beard and moustache deepening the haggard expression of features, to which the red borders of his eyelids, and his bloodless lips, gave an air of the deepest suffering. "Ah! my friend," said he, with a sad effort at a smile, "you are here quite *à-propos*. I am going to fight Adolphe this morning." A fearful presentiment that such was the case came over me the instant I saw him—but when he said so, a thrill ran through me, and I grew cold from head to foot.

"I see you are sorry," said he, tenderly, while he took my hand within both of his, "but you would not blame me—indeed you would not—if you knew all."

"What, then, was the cause of this quarrel? How came you to an open rupture?"

He turned round, and as he did so his face was purple, the blood suffused every feature, and his very eyeballs seemed like bursting with it. He tried to speak; but I only heard a rushing noise like a hoarse-drawn breath.

"Be calm, my dear Eisendecker," said I. "Cannot this be settled otherwise than thus?"

"No, no," said he, in the voice of indignant passion I used to hear from him long before, "never!" He waved his hand impatiently as he spoke, and turned his head from me. At the same moment one of his companions made a sign with his hand towards me.

"What!" whispered I, in horror—"a blow?"

A brief nod was the reply. Alas! from that minute all hope left me. Too well I knew the desperate alternative that awaited such an insult. Reconciliation was no longer to be thought of. I asked no more, but followed the group along the path towards the mill.

In a little garden, as it was called—we should rather
term it a close-shaven grass-plot—where some tables and
benches were placed, under the shade of large chestnut
trees, Adolphe von Muhry stood, surrounded by a number
of his friends. He was dressed in his costume as a member of the Prussian club of the Landsmanschaft—a kind of
uniform of blue and white, with a silver braiding on the
cuffs and collar, and looked handsomer than ever I saw
him. The change his features had undergone gave him
an air of manliness and confidence that greatly improved
him, and his whole carriage indicated a degree of self-
reliance and energy which became him perfectly. A faint
blush coloured his cheek as he saw me enter, and he lifted
his cap straight above his head and saluted me cour-
teously, but with an evident effort to appear at ease before
me. I returned his salute mournfully—perhaps reproachfully, too—for he turned away and whispered something
to a friend at his side.

Although I had seen many duels with the sword, it
was the first time I was present at an affair with pistols
in Germany; and I was no less surprised than shocked to
perceive that one of the party produced a dice-box and
dice, and placed them on a table.

Eisendecker all this time sat far apart from the rest,
and, with folded arms and half-closed eyelids, seemed to
wait in patience for the moment of being called on.

" What are they throwing for, yonder ? " whispered I
to a Saxon student near me.

" For the shot, of course," said he ; " not but that they
might spare themselves the labour. Eisendecker must fire
first; and as for who comes second after him——"

" Is he so sure as that ? " asked I in terror: for the
fearful vision of blood would not leave my mind.

" That is he. The fellow that can knock a bullet off a
champagne bottle at five-and-twenty paces may chance to
hit a man at fifteen."

" Muhry has it," cried out one of those at the table ;
and I heard the words repeated from mouth to mouth till
they reached Eisendecker, as he moved his cane listlessly
to and fro in the mill-stream.

" Remember Ludwig," said his friend, as he grasped

his arm with a strong clasp; "remember what I told you."

The other nodded carelessly, and merely said, "Is all ready?"

"Stand here, Eisendecker," said Muhry's second, as he dropped a pebble in the grass.

Mühry was already placed, and stood erect, his eyes steadily directed to his antagonist, who never once looked towards him, but kept his glance fixed straight in front.

"You fire first, sir," said Muhry's friend, while I could mark that his voice trembled slightly at the words "You may reserve your fire till I have counted twenty after the word is given."

As he spoke he placed the pistol in Eisendecker's hand, and called out,—

"Gentlemen, fall back, fall back ; I am about to give the word. Herr Eisendecker, are you ready?"

A nod was the reply.

"Now!" cried he, in a loud voice; and scarcely was the word uttered when the discharge of the pistol was heard. So rapid, indeed, was the motion, that we never saw him lift his arm ; nor could any one say what direction the ball had taken

"I knew it, I knew it," muttered Eisendecker's friend, in tones of agony. "All is over with him now."

Before a minute elapsed, the word to fall back was again given, and I now beheld Von Mühry standing with his pistol in hand, while a smile of cool but determined malice sat on his features.

While the second repeated the same words over to him, I turned to look at Eisendecker, but he evinced no apparent consciousness of what was going on about him ; his eyes, as before, were bent on vacancy; his pale face, unmoved, showed no signs of passion. In an instant the fearful "Now" rang out, and Mühry slowly raised his arm, and, levelling his pistol steadily, stood with his eye bent on his victim. While the deep voice of the second slowly repeated one—two—three—four—never was anything like the terrible suspense of that moment. It seemed as if the very seconds of human life were measuring out one by one. As the word "ten" dropped from his lips, I saw Mühry's hand shake. In his revengeful desire to kill his man, he had waited too long, and now he was growing nervous · he let fall his arm to his side, and waited for a few seconds, then raising it again, he took a steady aim, and at the word "nineteen" fired.

A slight movement of Eisendecker's head at this instant brought his face full front; and the bullet, which would have transfixed his head, now merely passed along his cheek, tearing a rude flesh-wound as it went.

A half-cry broke from Mühry: I heard not the word; but the accent I shall never cease to remember. It was now Eisendecker's time; and as the blood streamed down his cheek, and fell in great drops upon his neck and shoulders, I saw his face assume the expression it used to wear in former days. A terrible smile lit up his dark features, and a gleam of passionate vengeance made his eye glow like that of a maniac.

"I am ready—give the word," cried he, in frantic impatience.

But Mühry's second, fearful of giving way to such a moment of passion, hesitated; when Eisendecker again called out, "The word, sir, the word;" and the by-standers, indignant at the appearance of unfairness, repeated the cry.

The crowd fell back, and the word was given. Eisendecker raised his weapon, poised it for a second in his hand, and then, elevating it above his head, brought it gradually down, till, from the position where I stood, I could see that he aimed at the heart.

His hand was now motionless, as if it were marble; while his eye, rivetted on his antagonist, seemed to fix on one small spot, as though his whole vengeance was to be glutted there. Never was suspense more dreadful, and I stood breathless, in the expectation of the fatal flash, when, with a jerk of his arm, he threw up the pistol and fired above his head; and then, with a heart-rending cry of "Mein bruder, mein bruder," rushed into Mühry's arms, and fell into a torrent of tears.

The scene was indeed a trying one, and few could witness it unmoved. As for me, I turned away completely overcome; while my heart found vent in thankfulness that such a fearful beginning should end thus happily.

"Yes," said Eisendecker, as we rode home together that evening, when, after a long silence, he spoke; "yes, I had resolved to kill him; but when my finger was even on the trigger, I saw a look upon his features that reminded me of those earlier and happier days when we had but one home and one heart; and I felt as if I was about to become the murderer of my brother."

Need I add that they were friends for ever after?

But I must leave Göttingen and its memories too. They recall happy days, it is true; but they who made them so—where are they?

CHAPTER XXI.

THE TRAVELLING PARTY.

I HAVE already taken occasion to indoctrinate my reader on the subject of what I deem the most perfect species of *table d'hôte*. May I now beg of him, or her, if she will be kind enough, to accompany me to the *table-monstre* of Wiesbaden, Ems, or Baden-Baden? We are at the Cursaal or Shuberts, or the "Hof von Nassau" at Wiesbaden. Four hundred guests are assembled; their names indicative of every land of Europe, and no small portion of America; the mixture of language giving the impression of its being a grand banquet to the "operatives at Babel," but who, not satisfied with the chances of misunderstanding afforded by speaking their own tongues to foreigners, have adventured on the more certain project of endeavouring to be totally unintelligible, by speaking languages with which they are unacquainted; while in their dress, manner, and appearance, the great object seems to be an accurate imitation of some other country than their own.

Hence Frenchmen affect to seem English—English to
look like Prussians—Prussians to appear Poles—Poles
to be Calmucks. Your "elegant" of the Boulevard
de Ghent sports a "cut away" like a Yorkshire squire,
and rides in cords; your Londoner wears his hair on
his shoulders, and his moustaches like a Pomeranian
count; Turks find their way into tight trousers and
"Wellingtons;" and even the Yankees cannot resist the
soft impeachment, but take three inches off their hair
behind, and don't whittle before company.

Nothing is more amusing than these general congresses
of European vagrancy. Characters the most original
meet you at every step, and display most happily traits
you never have the opportunity to inspect at home. For
so it is, the very fact of leaving home, with most people,
seems like an absolution from all the necessities of sustaining a part. They feel as though they had taken off
the stage finery in which they had fretted away their
hours before, and stand forth themselves *in propriâ.* Thus
your grave Chancery lawyer becomes a chatty pleasant
man of the world, witty and conversable;—your abstruse
mathematician, leaving conic sections behind him, talks
away with the harmless innocence of a child about men and
politics; and even your cold "exclusive" bids a temporary
farewell to his "morgue," and answers his next neighbour
at table without feeling shocked at his obtrusion.

There must be some secret sympathy—of whose opera-
tions we know nothing—between our trunks and our
temperaments—our characters and our carpet-bags; and
that by the same law which opens one to the inspection of
an official at the frontier, the other must be laid bare when
we pass across it. How well would it have been for us, if
the analogy had been pushed a little farther, that the fiscal
regulations adopted in the former were but extended to the
latter, and that we had applied the tariff to the morals, as
well as to the manufactures, of the Continent.

It was in some such musing as this I sat in a window
of the Nassau, at Wiesbaden, during the height of the
season of ———. Strangers were constantly arriving,
and hourly was the reply "no room" given to the discon-
solate travellers, who peered from their carriages with the

road-sick look of a long journey. As for myself, 1 had
been daily and nightly transferred from one quarter of
the hotel to another—now sleeping in an apartment forty
feet square, in a bed generally reserved for royalty—now
bivouacking under the very slates; one night exposed to
the incessant din of the street beside my windows; the
next, in a remote wing of the building, where there were
no bells in the chambers, nor any waiter was ever known
to wander. In fact, I began to believe that they made
use of me to air the beds of the establishment, and was
seriously disposed to make a demand for some compensation in my bill, and if I might judge from the pains in
my bones I contracted in " Lit de Parade," I must have
saved her Majesty of Greece, who was my successor in it,
a notable attack of rheumatism. To this shuttlecock state
of existence the easiness of my nature made me submit
tamely enough, and I never dreamed of rebellion.

I was sitting conning over to myself the recollections
of some faces I had seen before, when the head waiter
appeared before me, with a request that I would be kind
enough to give up my place at the table, which was No. 14,
to a gentleman lately arrived, and who desired to sit
near his friends in that vicinity. " To be sure," said I at
once; " I have no acquaintance here, and 114 will do me
as well as 14—place me where you like." At the same
time, it rather puzzled me to learn what the individual
could be like who conceived such a violent desire to be in
the neighbourhood of some Hamburg Jews—for such were
the party around me—when the waiter began to make
room for a group that entered the room, and walked up to
the end of that table. A glance told they were English.
There was an elderly man, tall and well-looking, with the
air " gentleman " very legibly written on his quiet, composed features; the carriage of his head, and a something
in his walk, induced me to believe him military. A lady
leaned on his arm, some thirty years his junior—he was
about sixty-six or seven—whose dress and style were
fashionable, at the same time that they had not that perfect
type of unpretending legitimacy that belongs essentially
to but one class. She was, in fact, *trop bien mise* for a
table-d'hôte; for, although only a morning costume, there

was a display about it which was faulty in its taste; her features, without being handsome, were striking, as much for the carriage of her head as anything in themselves. There was an air of good looks, as though to say, " If you don't think me handsome, the fault is yours." Her eyes were of a bluish grey, large and full, with lightly-arched brows; but the mouth was the most characteristic feature —it was firm and resolute-looking, closely compressed, and with a slight protrusion of the lower lip, that said as plainly as words could say it, " I will, and that's enough." In walking, she took some pains to display her foot, which, with all the advantages of a Parisian shoe, was scarcely as pretty as she conceived it, but on the whole was well-formed, and rather erring on the score of size than symmetry.

They were followed by three or four young men, of whom I could only remark that they wore the uniform appearance of young Englishmen of good class, very clean-looking faces, well-brushed hair, and well-fitting frock-coats. One sported a moustache of a dirty-yellow colour, and whiskers to match, and by his manner, and a certain half-shut-eye kind of glance, proclaimed himself the knowing man of the party.

While they were taking their places—which they did at once on entering—I heard a general burst of salutations break from them in very welcome accent : " Oh, here he is—here he comes. Ah! I knew we should see him " At the same instant, a tall, well-dressed fellow leaned over the table and shook hands with them all in succession.

" When did you arrive ? " said he, turning to the lady.

" Only an hour ago ; Sir Marmaduke would stay at Frankfort yesterday, to see Duvernet dance, and so we were detained beyond our time."

The old gentleman half blushed at this charge, and while a look of pleasure showed that he did not dislike the accusation, he said,—

" No, no ; I stayed to please Calthorpe."

" Indeed ! " said the lady, turning a look of very peculiar, but unmistakable, anger at him of the yellow moustache. "Indeed, my lord ! "

" Oh,—ves, that is a weakness of mine," said he, in an

easy tone of careless banter, which degenerated to a
mutter, heard only by the lady herself.

" I ought to have a place somewhere here about," said
the tall man. "Number 14 or 15, the waiter said. Hallo,
garçon——"

At this he turned round, and I saw the well-remem-
bered face of my fellow-traveller, the Honourable Jack
Smallbranes. He looked very hard at me, as if he were
puzzled to remember where or when we had met, and then,
with a cool nod, said, "How d'ye do ?—over in England
lately ? "

" Not since I had the pleasure of meeting you at Rotterdam. Did you go far with the Alderman's daughters ? "

A very decided wink, and a draw down of the brows,
cautioned me to silence on that subject, but not before the
lady had heard my question, and looked up in his face
with an expression that said—" I'll hear more of that
affair before long."

" Monsieur has given you his place, sir," said the waiter,
arranging a chair at No. 14. " I have put *you* at 83."

" All right," replied Jack, as if no recognition were
called for on his part, and that he was not sorry to be
separated from one with an unpleasant memory.

" I am shocked, sir," said the lady, addressing me in her
blandest accents, " at our depriving you of your place, but
Mr Carrisbrook will, I'm sure, give you his."

While I protested against such a surrender, and Mr.
Carrisbrook looked very much annoyed at the proposal,
the lady only insisted the more, and it ended in Mr. Carrisbrook—one of the youths already mentioned—being
sent down to 83, while I took up my position in front of
the party in his place.

I knew to what circumstance I was indebted for this
favourable notice ; she looked up to me as a kind of king's
evidence, whenever the Honourable Jack should be called
up for trial, and already I had seen a great deal into the
history and relative position of all parties. Such was the
state of matters when the soup appeared.

And now. to impart to my readers, as is my wont, such
information as I possessed afterwards, and not to keep
him waiting for the order in which I obtained it, the party

before me consisted of Sir Marmaduke Lonsdall and his lady. He, an old general officer of good family and connections, who, with most unexceptionable manners and courtly address, had contrived to spend a very easy, good-for-nothing existence, without ever seeing an hour's service. His clubs and his dinner-parties filling up life tolerably well, with the occasional excitement arising from who was in and who was out, to season the whole. Sometimes a Lord of the Treasury, with a seat for a Government borough, and sometimes patriotically sitting among the opposition when his friends were out, he was looked upon as a very honourable straightforward person, who could not be "overlooked" when his party were distributing favours.

My Lady Lonsdall was a *soi-disant* heiress, the daughter of some person unknown, in the city, the greater part of whose fortune was unhappily embarked in Poyais Scrip— a fact only ascertained when too late, and, consequently, though discoursing most eloquently in a prospectus about mines of gold and silver, strata of pearl necklaces, and diamond earrings, all ready to put on, turned out an unfortunate investment, and only realized an article in the *Times* headed "ANOTHER BUBBLE SPECULATION." Still, however, she was reputed very rich, and Sir Marmaduke received the congratulations of his club on the event with the air of a conqueror. She married him simply because, having waited long and impatiently for a title, she was fain to put up at last with a baronet. Her ambition was to be in the fashionable world; to be among that sect of London elect who rule at Almack's and dictate at the West End, to occupy her portion of the *Morning Post*, and to have her name circulated among the illustrious few who entertain royalty, and receive archdukes at luncheon. If the Poyais investment, in its result, denied the means of these extravagances, it did not, unhappily, obliterate the taste for them, and my lady's ambition to be fashionable was never at a higher spring-tide than when her fortunes were at the ebb. Now, certes, there are two ways to London distinction—rank and wealth. A fair union of both will do much, but, without either, the pursuit is utterly hopeless. There is but one course, then, for these

Y

unfortunate aspirants of celebrity—it is to change the venue and come abroad. They may not, it is true, have the rank and riches which give position at home. Still, they are better off than most foreigners; they have not the wealth of the aristocracy, yet they can imitate their wickedness; their habits may be costly, but their vices are cheap, and thus they can assert their high position and their fashionable standing, by displaying the abandonment which is unhappily the distinctive feature of a certain set in the high world of London.

Followed, then, by a train of admirers, she paraded about the Continent, her effrontery exalted into beauty, her cold insolence assumed to be high breeding, her impertinence to women was merely exclusiveness, and her condescending manner to men the simple acknowledgment of that homage to which she was so unquestionably entitled.

Of her suite—they were animated by different motives. Some were young enough to be in love with any woman who, a great deal older than themselves, would deign to notice them. The noble Lord, who accompanied her always, was a ruined Baron, whose own wife had deserted him for another; he had left his character and his fortune at Doncaster and Epsom; and having been horsewhipped as a defaulter, and outlawed for debt, was of course in no condition to face his acquaintances in England. Still he was a Lord, there was no denying that; De Brett and Burke had chronicled his baptism, and the eighth Baron from Hugo de Colbrooke, who carried the helmet of his sovereign at Agincourt, was unquestionably of the best blood of the peerage. Like your true white feather, he wore a most *farouche* exterior; his moustaches seemed to bristle with pugnacity, and the expression of his eye was indescribably martial : he walked as if he was stepping out the ground, and in his salute he assumed the cold politeness with which a second takes off his hat to the opposite principal in a duel; even his valet seemed to favour the illusion, as he ostentatiously employed himself cleaning his master's pistols, and arranging the locks, as though there was no knowing at what moment of the day he might not be unexpectedly called on to shoot somebody.

He, I say, was a part of the household. Sir Marmaduke rather finding his society agreeable, and the lady
regarding him as the cork jacket on which she was to
swim into the ocean of fashion, at some remote period or
other of her existence.

As for the Honourable Jack Smallbranes, who was he
not in love with? or rather who was not in love with
him? Poor fellow! he was born, in his own estimation,
to be the destroyer of all domestic peace; he was created
to be the ruin to all female happiness; such a destiny
might well have filled any one with sadness and depression. Most men would have grieved over a lot which
condemned them to be the origin of suffering. Not so,
Jack, he felt he couldn't help it, that it was no affair of
his if he were the best-looking fellow in the world. The
thing was so palpable; women ought to take care of themselves; he sailed under no false flag. No, there he was,
the most irresistible, well-dressed, and handsomest fellow
to be met with; and if they didn't escape, or, to use his
own expression, "cut their lucky" in time, the fault was
all their own. If queens smiled, and archduchesses
looked kind upon him, let kings and archdukes look to it.
He took no unfair or underhand advantages, he made no
secret attacks, no dark advances, he carried every fortress
by assault, and in noonday. Some malicious people—the
world abounds in such—used to say, that Jack's gallantries
were something like Falstaff's deeds of prowess, and that
his victims were all "in buckram." But who could
believe it? Did not victory sit on his very brow? were
not his looks the signs of conquest? and, better than all,
who that ever knew him had not the assurance from his
own lips? With what a happy mixture of nonchalance
and self-satisfaction would he make these confessions!
how admirably blended was the sense of triumph, with
the consciousness of its ease! how he would shake his
ambrosial curls, and throw himself into a pose of elegance,
as though to say, "'Twas thus I did it; ain't I a sad dog?"

Well, if these conquests were illusions, they were certainly the pleasantest ever a man indulged in. They
consoled him at heart for the loss of fortune, country,
and position—they were his recompense for all the lost

glories of Crockford's and the Clarendon. Never was
there such a picture of perfect tranquillity and unclouded
happiness. Oh! let moralists talk as they will about the
serenity of mind derivable alone from a pure conscience—
the peaceful nature that flows from a source of true
honour, and then look abroad upon the world, and count
the hundreds whose hairs are never tinged with grey—
whose cheeks show no wrinkles—whose elastic steps
suffer no touch of age, and whose ready smile and cheerful laugh are the ever-present signs of their contentment.
Let them look on these, and reflect that of such are nine-
tenths of those who figure in lists of outlawry, whose
bills do but make the stamps they are written on of no
value—whose creditors are Legion, and whose credit is
at zero, and say which seems the happier. To see them,
one would opine that there must be some secret good in
cheating a coachmaker, or some hidden virtue in tricking
a jeweller—that hotel-keepers are a natural enemy to
mankind, and that a tailor has not a right even to a
decimal fraction of honesty. Never was Epicurean philosophy like theirs; they have a fine liberal sense of the
blackguardisms that a man may commit, and yet not
forfeit his position in society. They know the precise
condition in life when he may practise dishonesty, and
they see when he must be circumspect. They have one
rule for the city, and another for the club; and, better
than all, they have stored their minds with sage maxims
and wise reflections, which, like the philosophers of old,
they adduce on every suitable occasion, and many a
wounded spirit has been consoled by that beautiful sentiment, so frequent in their mouths, of—

"Go ahead, for what's the odds so long as you're happy!"

Such, my reader, was the clique in which, strangely
enough, I now found myself; and, were it not that such
characters abound in every part of the Continent—that
they swarm at spas, and infest whole cities—I would
scruple to introduce you among such company. It is as
well, however, that you should be put on your guard
against them, and that any amusement you may derive

from the study of eccentricity, should not be tarnished with the recollection of your being imposed upon.

There happened, on the day I speak of, to be a man of some rank at table, with whom I had a slight, a very slight acquaintance; but, in passing from the room, he caught my eye, came over, and conversed with me for a few minutes. From that moment Lady Lonsdall's manners underwent a great change in my regard. Not only did she venture to look at me without expressing any air of supercilious disdain, but even vouchsafed the ghost of a smile; and, as we rose from table, I overheard her ask the Honourable Jack for my name. I could not hear the first part of his reply, but the last was couched in that very classic slang, expressive of my unknown condition—

"I take it, he harn't got no friends !"

Notwithstanding this Foundling-Hospital sentence, Sir Marmaduke was instructed to invite me to take coffee, an honour which, having declined, we separated, as do people who are to speak when next they meet.

Meditating on the unjust impression foreigners must conceive of England and the English, by the unhappy specimens we " grind for exportation," I sat alone at a little table in the park. It was a sad subject, and it led me farther than I wished or knew of. I thought I could trace much of the animosity of foreign journals to English policy, in their mistaken notions of national character, and could well conceive how dubiously they must receive our claim to being high-spirited and honourable, when their own experiences would incline to a different conclusion; for, after all, the Fleet Prison, however fashionable its inmates, would scarcely be a flattering specimen of England, nor do I think Horsemonger Lane ought to be taken as a fair sample of the country. It is vain to assure foreigners that these people are not known, nor received at home, neither held in credit nor estimation; their conclusive reply is, " How is it, then, that they are admitted to the tables of your ambassadors, and presented at our courts ? Is it possible you would dare to introduce to our sovereigns those whom you could not present to your own ?" This answer is a fatal one. The fact is so; the most rigid censor of morals leaves his conscience at the Ship Hotel at Dover; he has no room for it on a voyage, or perhaps he thinks it might be detained by a revenue officer. Whatever the cause, he will know at Baden—ay, and walk with—the man he would cut in Bond Street, and drive with the party at Brussels he would pass to-morrow if he met in Hyde Park.

These be unpleasant reflections, Arthur, and I fear the coffee or the maraschino must have been amiss; in any case, away with them, and now for a stroll in the Cursaal.

CHAPTER XXII.

THE GAMBLING-ROOM.

ENGLISHMEN keep their solemnity and respectful deportment for a church; foreigners reserve theirs for a gambling-table. Never was I more struck than by the decorous stillness and well-bred quietness of the room in which the highest play went forward. All the animation of French character—all the bluntness of German—all the impetuosity of the Italian, or the violent rashness of the Russian—were calmed down and subdued beneath the influence of the great passion; and it seemed as though the devil would not accept the homage of his votaries, if not rendered with the well-bred manners of true gentlemen. It was not enough that men should be ruined; they should be ruined with easy propriety and thorough good breeding Whatever their hearts might feel, their faces should express no discomfiture; though their head should ache, and their hand should tremble, the lip must be taught to say " rouge " or " noir " without any emotion.

I do not scruple to own that all this decorum was more dreadful than any scene of wild violence or excitement. The forced calmness—the pent-up passion, might be kept from any outbreak of words; but no training could completely subdue the emotions which speak by the bloodshot eye, the quivering cheek, the livid lip.

No man's heart is consecrated so entirely to one passion as a gambler's. Hope, with him, usurps the place of every other feeling. Hope, however rude the shocks it meets from disappointment, however beaten and baffled, is still there: the flame may waste down to a few embers; but a single spark may live amid the ashes; but it is enough to kindle up into a blaze before the breath of fortune.

At first he lives but for moments like these; all his agonies, all his sufferings, all the torturings of a mind verging on despair, are repaid by such brief intervals of luck. Yet each reverse of fate is telling on him heavily; the many disappointments to his wishes are sapping by degrees his confidence in fortune. His hope is dashed with fear, and now commences within that struggle the most fearful man's nature can endure. The fickleness of chance, the waywardness of fortune, fill his mind with doubts and hesitations. Sceptical on the sources of his great passion, he becomes a doubter on every subject; he has seen his confidence so often at fault that he trusts nothing, and at last the ruling feature of his character is suspicion. When this rules paramount, he is a perfect gambler; from that moment he has done with the world and all its pleasures and pursuits; life offers to him no path of ambition, no goal to stimulate his energies. With a mock stoicism he affects to be superior to the race which other men are running, and laughs at the collisions of party, and the contests of politics. Society, art, literature, love itself, have no attractions for him then; all excitements are feeble compared with the alternations of the gaming-table; and the chances of fortune in real life are too tame and too tedious for the impatience of a gambler.

I have no intention of winding up these few remarks by any moral episode of a gambler's life, though my memory could supply me with more than one such, when the baneful passion became the ruin, not of a thoughtless, giddy youth, inexperienced and untried, but of one who had already won golden opinions from the world, and stood high in the ranks which lead to honour and distinction.

These stories have, unhappily, a sameness which mars the
force of their lesson; they are listened to like the "refrain"
of an old song, and, from their frequency, are disregarded.
No, I trust in the fact that education, and the tastes that
flow from it, are the best safeguards against a contagion of
a heartless, soulless passion, and would rather warn my
young countrymen at this place against the individuals
than the system.

"Am I in your way, sir?" said a short, somewhat over-
dressed man, with red whiskers, as he made room for me
to approach the play-table, with a politeness quite remarkable; "am I in your way, sir?"

"Not in the least; I beg you'll not stir."

"Pray take my seat; I request you will."

"By no means, sir; I never play. I was merely looking
on."

"Nor I either, or at least very rarely," said he, rising
with the air of a man who felt no pleasure in what was
going forward.

"You don't happen to know that young gentleman in
the light blue frock and white vest yonder?"

"No, I never saw him before."

"I'm sorry for it," said he, in a whisper; "he has just
lost seventy thousand francs, and is going the readiest way
to treble the sum by his play. I'm certain he is English
by his look and appearance, and it is a cruel thing, a very
cruel thing, not to give him a word of caution here."

The words, spoken with a tone of feeling, interested me
much in the speaker, and already I was angry with myself
for having conceived a dislike to his appearance, and a
prejudice against his style of dress.

"I see," continued he, after a few seconds' pause, "I see
you agree with me. Let us try if we can't find some one
who may know him. If Wycherley is here—you know
Sir Harry, I suppose?——"

"I have not that honour."

"Capital fellow—the best in the world. He's in the
Blues, and always about Windsor or St. James's. He
knows everybody, and if that young fellow be anybody,
he's sure to know him. Ah! how d'ye do, my Lord?"
continued he, with an easy nod, as Lord Colebrook passed.

" Eh, Crotty, how goes it ? " was the reply.

" You don't happen to know that gentleman yonder, my Lord, do you ? "

" Not I; who is he ? "

" This gentleman and I were both anxious to learn who he is ; he is losing a deal of money."

" Eh ! dropping his tin, is he ? and you'd rather save him, Crotty—all right and sportsmanlike," said his lordship, with a knowing wink, and walked on.

" A very bad one, indeed, I fear," said Crotty, looking after him ; " but I didn't think him so heartless as that. Let us take a turn, and look out for Wycherley."

Now, although I neither knew Wycherley nor his friend Crotty, I felt it a case where one might transgress a little on etiquette, and probably save a young man—he didn't look twenty—from ruin, and so, without more ado, I accompanied my new acquaintance through the crowded *salons*, elbowing and pushing along, amid the hundreds that thronged there. Crotty seemed to know almost every one of a certain class ; and as he went, it was a perpetual "Comment ça va," prince, count, or baron ? or, " How d'ye do, my Lord ?" or, " Eh, Sir Thomas, you here ? " &c ; when at length, at the side of a doorway leading into the supper-room, we came upon the Honourable Jack, with two ladies leaning upon his arms. One glance was enough ; I saw they were the Alderman's daughters Sir Peter himself, at a little distance off, was giving directions to the waiter for supper.

" Eh ! Crotty ; what are you doing to-night ? " said Jack, with a triumphant look at his fair companions, " any mischief going forward, eh ? "

" Nothing half so dangerous as your doings," said Crotty, with a very arch smile ; " have you seen Wycherley; is he here ? "

" Can't possibly say," yawned out Jack ; then, leaning over to me, he said in a whisper, " Is the Princess Von Hohenstauvenof in the rooms ? "

" I really don't know ; I'm quite a stranger."

" By Jove, if she is," said he, without paying any attention to my reply, " I'm floored, that's all; Lady Maude

Beverley has caught me already. I wish you'd keep the
Deverington girls in talk, will you ? "

" You forget, perhaps, I have no acquaintance here."

" Oh yes, by Jove, so I did ! Glorious fun you must have
of it ! what a pace I'd go along if I wasn't known, eh !—
wouldn't I ? "

" There's Wycherley—there he is," said Crotty, taking
me by the arm as he spoke, and leading me forward. " Do
me the favour to give me your name ; I should like you
to know Wycherley ; " and scarcely had I pronounced it,
when I found myself exchanging greetings with a large,
well-built, black-whiskered, and moustached man of about
forty. He was dressed in deep mourning, and looked in
his manner and air very much the gentleman.

" Have you got up the party yet, Crotty ? " said he,
after our first salutations were over, and with a half-glance
towards me.

"No, indeed," said Crotty, slowly ; "the fact is, I wasn't
thinking of it. There's a poor young fellow yonder losing
very heavily, and I wanted to see if you knew him ; it
would be only fair to——"

" So it would—where is he ? " interrupted the baronet,
as he pushed through the crowd towards the play-room.

" I told you he was a trump," said Crotty, as we followed him ; " the fellow to do a good-natured thing at
any moment."

While we endeavoured to get through after him, we
passed close beside a small supper-table, where sat the
Alderman and his two pretty daughters, the Honourable
Jack between them. It was evident from his boisterous
gaiety that he had triumphed over all his fears of detection by any of the numerous fair ones he spoke of ; his
great object at this instant appearing to be the desire to
attract every one's attention towards him, and to publish
his triumph to all beholders. For this, Jack conversed
in a voice audible at some distance off, surveying his victims from time to time with the look of the Great Mogul ;
while they, poor girls, only imagined themselves regarded
for their own attractions, which were very considerable,
and believed that the companionship of the distinguished
Jack was the envy of every woman about them. As for

the father, he was deep in the mysteries of a *vol au vent,* and perfectly indifferent to such insignificant trifles as Jack's blandishments and the ladies' blushes.

Poor girls! no persuasion in life could have induced them to such an exhibition in their own country, and in company with one their equal in class. But the fact of its being Germany! and the escort being an Honourable! made all the difference in the world; and they who would have hesitated with maiden coyness at the honourable proposals of one of their own class, felt no scruple at compromising themselves before hundreds to indulge the miserable vanity of a contemptible coxcomb.

I stood for a second or two beside the table, and thought within myself, " Is not this as much a case to call for the interference of friendly caution as that of the gambler yonder." But then, how was it possible?

We passed on and reached the play-table, where we found Sir Harry Wycherley in low and earnest conversation with the young gentleman. I could only catch a stray expression here and there, but even they surprised me; the arguments advanced to deter him from gambling being founded on the inconsiderate plan of his game, rather than on the immorality and vice of the practice itself.

" Don't you see," said he, throwing his eye over the card all dotted with pin holes—" don't you see, it's a run, a dead run? that you may bet on red, if you like, a dozen times, and only win once or twice? "

The youth blushed, and said nothing.

" I've seen forty thousand francs lost that way in less than an hour."

" I've lost *seventy* thousand!" muttered the young man, with a shudder like one who felt cold all over.

" Seventy!—not to-night, surely? "

" Yes, to-night," replied he ; " I won fourteen hundred Naps here when I came first, and didn't play for three weeks afterwards ; but unfortunately I strolled in here a few nights since, and lost the whole back, as well as some hundreds besides ; but this evening I came bent on winning back—that was all I desired—winning back my own."

As he said these words, I saw Sir Henry steal a glance at Crotty. The thing was as quick as lightning, but never did a glance reveal more; he caught my eye upon him, and, looking round fully at me, said, in a deep, ominous voice,—

"That's the confounded part of it; it's so hard to stop when you're losing."

"Hard!—impossible!" cried the youth, whose eyes were now rivetted on the table, following every card that fell from the banker's hands, and flushing and growing pale with every alternation of the game "See now, for all you've said, look if the red has not won, four times in succession."

"So it has," replied the Baronet, coolly; "but the previous run on black would have left your purse rather shallow, or you must have a devilish deep one, that's all."

He took up a pencil as he spoke, and began to calculate on the back of the card; then, holding it over, he said,—

"There's what you'd have lost if you went on betting."

"What!—two hundred and eighty thousand francs!"

"Exactly; look here;" and he went over the figures carefully before him.

"Don't you think you've had enough of it to-night?" said Crotty, with an insinuating smile; "what say you if we all go and sup together in the Saal?"

"Agreed," said Sir Harry, rising at once; "Crotty, will you look at the *carte* and do the needful? you may trust him, gentlemen," continued he, turning towards us with a smile; "old Crotty has a most unexceptionable taste in all that regards *cuisine* and *câve;* save a slight leaning towards expense, he has not a fault!"

I mumbled out something of an apology, which was unfortunately supposed by the Baronet to have reference to his last remark. I endeavoured to explain away the mistake, and ended like a regular awkward man, by complying with a request I had previously resolved to decline. The young man had already given his consent, and so we arose and walked through the rooms, while Crotty inspected the bill of fare and gave orders about the wine."

Wycherley seemed to know and be known by every one, and as he interchanged greetings with the groups that passed, declined several pressing invitations to sup. "The fact is," said he to one of his most anxious inviters, "the fact is"—and the words were uttered in a whisper I could just hear—"there's a poor young fellow here who has been getting it rather sharp at the gold table, and I mustn't lose sight of him to-night, or he'll inevitably go back there."

These few words dispelled any uneasiness I had already laboured under, from finding myself so unexpectedly linked with two strangers. It was quite clear Sir Harry was a fine-hearted fellow, and that his manly, frank countenance was no counterfeit. As we went along, Wycherley amused us with his anecdotes of the company, with whose private history he was conversant in its most minute details; and truly, low as had been my estimate of the society at first, it fell considerably lower as I listened to the private memoirs with which he favoured us.

Some were the common narratives of debt and desertion, protested bills, and so forth; others were the bit-by-bit details of extravagant habits pushed beyond all limits, and ending in expatriation for ever. There were faithless husbands, outraging all decency by proclaiming their bad conduct; there were as faithless wives, parading about in all the effrontery of wickedness. At one side sat the *roué* companion of George the Fourth, in his princely days, now a mere bloated *debauchée* with rouged cheeks, and dyed whiskers, living on the hackneyed anecdotes of his youthful rascality, and earning his daily bread by an affected epicurism, and a Sybarite pretension, which flattered the vulgar vanity of those who fed him; while the lion of the evening was a newly-arrived Earl, whose hunters were that very day sold at Tattersall's, and whose beautiful Countess, horror-stricken at the ruin so unexpectedly come upon them, was lying dangerously ill at her father's house in London. The young Peer, indeed, bore up with a fortitude that attracted the highest encomiums, and from an audience, the greater portion of which knew in their own persons most of the ills he suffered. He exchanged an easy nod, or a familiar shake of the hand, with several acquaintances, not seen before for many a day, and seemed to think that the severest blow fortune had dealt him, was the miserable price his stud would fetch at such a time of the year.

"The old story," said Wycherley, as he shook him by the hand, and told him his address   "The old story ; he thought twenty thousand a year would do anything, but it won't though. If men will keep a house in town, and another in Gloucestershire, with a pack of fox-hounds, and have four horses in training at Doncaster—not to speak of a yacht at Cowes, and some other fooleries—they must come to the Jews : and when they come to the Jews, the pace is faster than for the Derby itself Two hundred per cent. is sharp practice, and I can tell you, not uncommon either ; and then, when a man does begin to topple, his efforts to recover always ruin him. It's like a fall from your horse—make a struggle, and you're sure to break your leg or your collar-bone—take it kindly, and the chances are, that you get up all right again, after the first shock."

I did not like either the tone or the morality of my companion, but I well knew both were the conventional coinage of his set, and I suffered him to continue without interruption.

"There's Mosely Cranmer," said he, pointing to a slight effeminate-looking young man, with a most girlish soft- ness about his features. He was dressed in the very extreme of fashion, and displayed all that array of jewel- lery, in pins, diamond vest buttons, and rings, so fre- quently assumed by modern dandyism. His voice was a thin, reedy treble, scarcely deep enough for a child.

"Who is he, and what is he doing here ?" asked I.   .

"He is the heir to about eighty thousand per annum, to begin with," said Wycherley, "which he has already dipped beyond redemption. So far for his property. As to what he is doing here, you may have seen in the *Times* last week, that he shot an officer of the Guards in a duel —killed him on the spot : the thing was certain—Cran- mer's the best pistol-shot in England."

"Ah ! Wycherley, how goes it, old fellow ?" said the youth, stretching out two fingers of his well-gloved hand. "You see Edderdale is come over. Egad ! we shall have all England here soon,—leave the island to the Jews, I think !"

Sir Harry laughed heartily at the conceit, and invited him to join our party at supper, but he was already, I was rejoiced to find, engaged to the Earl of Edderdale, who was entertaining a select few, at his hotel, in honour of his arrival.

A waiter now came to inform us that Mr. Crotty was waiting for us, to order supper, and we immediately proceeded to join him in the Saal.

The Baronet's eulogium on his friend's taste in *gourmandaise*, was well and justly merited. The supper was admirable—the "potage printanière" seasoned to perfection—the "salmi des perdreaux, aux points d'asperges," delicious—and the "ortolans à la provençale," a dish for the gods; while the wines were of that *cru* and flavour that only favoured individuals ever attained to, at the hands of a landlord. As *plat* succeeded *plat*, each admirably selected in the order of succession, to heighten the enjoyment and gratify the palate of the guest, the conversation took its natural turn to matters gastronomic, and where, I must confess, I can dally with as sincere pleasure, as in the discussion of any other branch of the fine arts. Mr. Crotty's forte seemed essentially to lie in the tact of ordering and arranging a very admirable repast. Wycherley, however, took a higher walk: he was historically *gastronome*, and had a store of anecdotes about the dishes and their inventors, from Clovis to Louis Quatorze. He knew the favourite meats of many illustrious personages, and told his stories about them with an admirable blending of seriousness and levity.

There are excellent people, Arthur, who will call you sensualist, for all this. Good souls, who eat like Cossacks, and drink like camels in the desert, before whose masticatory powers joints become beautifully less in shortest space of time; and who, while devouring in greedy silence, think nothing too severe to say of him who, with more cultivated palate and discriminating taste, eats sparingly, but choicely, making the nourishment of his body the nutriment of his mind ; and while he supports nature, can stimulate his imagination, and invigorate his understanding. The worthy votaries of boiled mutton and turnips ! of ribs and roasts, believe themselves temperate and moderate eaters, while consuming at a meal the provender sufficient for a family; and when, after an hour's steady performance, they sit, with hurried breathing, and half-closed eyelids, sullen, stupid, and stertorous; drowsy and dull, saturated with stout, and stuffed with Stilton, they growl out a thanksgiving that they are not like other men—epicures and wine-bibbers. Out upon them, I say! Let me have my light meal—be its limits a cress, and the beverage that ripples from the rock beside me—but be it such that, while eating, there is no transfusion of the beast devoured, into the man, nor, when eaten, the semi-apoplectic stupor of a gorged boa!

Sir Harry did the honours of the table, and sustained the burden of the conversation, to which Crotty contributed but little, the young man and myself being merely non-effectives; nor did we separate until the garçon came to warn us that the Saal was about to close for the night.

CHAPTER XXIII.

A WATERING-PLACE DOCTOR.

NOTHING is more distinct than the two classes of people who are to be met with in the morning and the afternoon sauntering along the *allées* of a German watering-place. The former are the invalid portion, poured forth in numbers from hotel and lodging-house, attired in every absurdity of dressing-room toilette, with woollen nightcaps and flannel jackets, old-fashioned douillettes and morocco slippers, they glide along, glass in hand, to some sulphur spring, or to repose for an hour or two in the delights of a "mud bath." For the most, they are the old and the feeble, pale of face and tottering in step. The pursuit of health with them would seem a vain and fruitless effort; the machine appears to have run its destined time, and all the skill of man is unavailing to repair it. Still hope survives, when strength and youth have failed, and the very grouping together in their gathering places has its consolation; while the endless diversity of malady gives an interest in the eye of a sick man.

This may seem strange, but it is, nevertheless, perfectly true; there is something which predisposes an invalid to all narratives of illness; they are the topics he dwells on with most pleasure, and discourses about with most eagerness. The anxiety for the "gentleman next door" is neither philanthropy, nor is it common curiosity. No, it is perfectly distinct from either; it is the deep interest in the course of symptoms, in the ups and downs of chance. It is compounded of the feelings which animate the physician, and those which fill the invalid. And hence we see that the severest sufferings of their neighbours make less impression on the minds of such people than on those in full health. It is not from apathy nor selfishness they are seemingly indifferent, but simply because they regard the question in a different light; to take an illustration from the gaming-table, they have too deep an interest in the game itself to feel greatly for the players. The visit of the doctor is, to them, the brightest moment of the day. Not only the messenger of good tidings to the patient, he has a thousand little bits of sick-room gossip, harmless, pointless trifles, but all fraught with their own charm to the greedy ear of the sick man. It is so pleasant to know how Mrs W. bore her drive, or Sir Arthur liked his jelly, what Mrs. T. said when they ordered her to be bled, and whether dear Mr. H. would consent to the blister. And with what consummate tact your "Watering-place Doctor" doles out the infinitesimal doses of his morning's intelligence; how different his visit from the hurried flight of a West-end practitioner, who, while he holds his watch in hand, counts the minutes of his stay while he feels your pulse, and whose descent down stairs is watched by a cordon of the household, catching his directions as he goes, and learning his opinion as he springs into his chariot. Your Spa doctor has a very different mission; *his* are no heroic remedies, which, taken to-day, are to cure to-morrow; *his* character is tried by no subtle test of immediate success. His patients

z

come for a term, or, to use the proper phrase, for "a course of the waters." Then they are condemned to chalybeates for a quarter of the year, so many glasses per diem. With their health, properly speaking, he has no concern; his function is merely an inspection that the individual drinks his fluid regularly, and takes his mud like a man. The patient is invoiced to him, with a bill of lading from Bell or Brodie; he has full information of the merchandise transmitted, and the mode in which the consignee desires it may be treated; out of this ritual he must not move. The great physician of the West-end says, "Bathe and drink," and his *chargé d'affaires* at Wiesbaden takes care to see his orders obeyed. As well might a *forçat* at Brest or Toulon hope to escape the punishment described in the catalogue of prisoners, as for a patient to run counter to the remedies thus arranged, and communicated by post. Occasionally changes will take place in a sick man's condition *en route*, which alter the applicability of his treatment, but, then, what would you have? Brodie and Chambers are not prophets! divination and augury are not taught in the London and Middlesex Hospitals!

I remember, myself, a marquis of gigantic proportions, who had kept his prescription by him from the time of his being a stripling, till he weighed twenty stone. The fault here lay not with the doctor. The bath he was to take contained some powerful ingredient, a preparation of iron, I believe; well, he got into it, and immediately began swelling and swelling out, till, big as he was before, he was now twice the size, and at last, like an overheated boiler, threatened to explode with a crash. What was to be done? To lift him was out of the question, he fitted the bath like a periwinkle in its shell; and, in this dilemma, no other course was open than to decant him, water and all, which was performed, to the very considerable mirth of the bystanders.

The doctor, then, it will be seen, moves in a very narrow orbit. He must manage to sustain his reputation without the aid of the Pharmacopœia, and continue to be imposing without any assistance from the dead languages. Hard conditions! but he yields to them, like a man of nerve.

He begins, then, by extolling the virtues of the waters, which, by analysis of "his own making," and set forth in a little volume published by himself, contain very different properties from those ascribed to them by others He explains most clearly to his non-chemical listener, how "pure silica found in combination with oxide of iron, at a temperature of thirty-nine and a half of Fahrenheit," must necessarily produce the most beneficial effects on the knee-joint; and describes, with all the ardour of science the infinite satisfaction the nerves must experience when invigorated by "free carbonic gas," sporting about in the system. Day by day he indoctrinates the patient into some stray medical notion, giving him an interest in his own anatomy, and putting him on terms of familiar acquaintance with the formation of his heart, or his stomach. This flatters the sick man, and, better still, it occupies his attention. He himself thus becomes a "particeps" in the first degree to his own recovery, and the simplicity of treatment, which had at first no attractions for his mind, is now complicated with so many little curious facts about the "blood" and the "nerves," "mucous membranes," and "muscles," as fully to compensate for any lack of mystery, and is, in truth, just as unintelligible as the most involved inconsistency of any written prescription. Besides this, he has another object which demands his attention. Plain, common-sense people, who know nothing of physic or its mysteries, might fall into the fatal error of supposing that the wells so universally employed by the people of the country for all purposes of washing, bathing, and cooking, however impregnated by mineral properties, were still by no means so, in proportions of great power and efficacy, capable of effecting either very decided results, curative or noxious. The doctor must set his heel on this heresy at once; he must be able to show how a sip too much, or a half-glass too many, can produce the gravest consequences; and no summer must pass over without at least one death being attributed to the inconsiderate rashness of some insensate drinker. Woe unto him then who drinks without a doctor, you might as well, in an access of intense thirst, rush into the first apothecary's shop,

and take a strong pull at one of the vicious little phials
that fill the shelves, ignorant whether it might not be
aquafortis or Prussic acid.

Armed, then, with all the terrors of his favourite Spa
—rich in a following which is as much partisan as patient
—he has an admirable life of it. The severe and trying
cases of illness that come under the notice of other physicians fall not to his share. The very journey to the
waters is a trial of strength which guards against this.
His disciples are the dyspeptic diners out, in the great
worlds of London, Paris, or Vienna; the nervous and
irritable natures, cloyed with excess of enjoyment, and
palled with pleasure; the imaginary sick man, or the
self-created patient, who has dosed himself into artificial
malady; all, of necessity, belonging to the higher, or
at least the wealthier classes of mankind, with whom
management goes farther than medicine, and tact is a
hundred times better than all the skill of Hippocrates.
He had need, then, be a clever man of the world; he
may dispense with science, he cannot with *savoir faire*.
Not only must he be conversant with the broader traits
of national character, but he must be intimately acquainted with the more delicate and subtle workings of
the heart in classes and gradations of mankind; a keen
observer and a quick actor. In fact, to get on well, he
must possess in a high degree many of those elements,
any one of which would ensure success in a dozen other
walks in life.

And he must have all these virtues, as Swift says,
" for twenty pounds per annum," not literally, indeed,
but for a very inadequate recompense. These watering-
place seasons are brief intervals, in which he must make
hay while the sun shines. With the approach of winter
the tide turns, and the human wave retires faster than it
came. Silent streets, and deserted promenades, closed
shutters and hermetically-sealed cafés, meet him at every
step, and then comes the long, dreary time of hyberna-
tion; happy would it be for him if he could but imitate
the seal, and spend it in torpor; for, if he be not a sportsman, and in a country favourable to the pursuit, his life
is a sad one. Books are generally difficult to come at,

there is little society, there is no companionship, and so he has to creep along the tedious time silent and sad, counting over the months of his durance, and longing for spring.

Some there are who follow the stream, and retire each winter to the cities where their strongest connection lies; but this practice I should deem rather dictated by pleasure than profit. Your Spa Doctor without a Spa is like Liszt or Herz without a pianoforte. Give him but his instrument, and he will "discourse you sweet music," but deprive him of it and he is utterly helpless. The springs of Helicon did not suggest inspiration more certainly than do those of Nassau to their votaries; but the fount must run that the poet may rhyme. So your physician must have the odour of sulphurets in his nose; he must see the priestess ministering, glass in hand, to the shivering shades around her; he must have the long vista of the promenade, with its flitting forms in flannel cased, ere he feel himself "every inch a doctor." Away from these, and the piston of a steam-engine without a boiler is not more helpless. The fountain is, to use Lord Londonderry's phrase, the "fundamental feature on which his argument hinges," and he could no more exist without water than a fish.

Having said so much of the genus, let me be excused if I do not dilate on the species, nor, indeed, had I dwelt so long on the subject, but in this age of stomach, when every one has dyspepsia, it is as well to mention those who rule over our diets and destinies, and where so many are worshippers at the Temple, a word about the Priest of the Mysteries may not be unseasonable.

And now, to change the theme, who is it that, at this early hour of the morning, seems taking his promenade, with no trace of the invalid in his look or dress? He comes along at a smart walk; his step has the assured tramp of one who felt health, and knew the value of the blessing. What! is it possible, can it be, indeed? Yes, it is Sir Harry Wycherley himself, with two lovely children, a boy and a girl, the eldest scarcely seven years old, the boy a year or so younger. Never did I behold anything more lovely.

The girl's eyes were dark, shaded with long, deep fringe, that added to their depth, and tempered into softness the glowing sparkle of youth. Her features were of a pensive, but not melancholy character, and in her walk and carriage "gentle blood" spoke out in accents not to be mistaken. The boy, more strongly formed, resembled his father more, and in his broad forehead, and bold, dashing expression, looked like one who should become one day a man of nerve and mettle. His dress, too, gave a character to his appearance that well suited him; a broad hat, turned up at the side, and ornamented with a dark blue feather, that hung drooping over his shoulder; a blue tunic, made so as to show his chest in its full breadth, and his arms naked the whole way; a scarlet scarf, knotted carelessly at his side, hung down, with its deep fringe, beside his bare leg, tanned and bronzed with sun and weather; while even his shoes, with their broad silver buckles, showed that care presided over every part of his costume.

There was something intensely touching in the sight of this man of the world—for such I well knew he was—thus enjoying the innocence and fresh buoyancy of his children, turning from the complex web of men's schemes and plottings, their tortuous paths and deep designings, to relax in the careless gaiety of infant minds; now pursuing them along the walk, now starting from behind some tree where he lay in ambush, he gives them chase, and as he gains on them they turn short round, and spring into his arms, and clasp him round the neck. Arthur, thou hast had a life of more than man's share of pleasure; thou hast tasted much happiness, and known but few sorrows; but would not a moment like this outnumber them all? Where is love so full, so generous, so confiding? What affection comes so pure and unalloyed, not chilled by jealous doubts or fears, but warm and gushing; the incense of a happy heart, the outpourings of a guileless nature. Nothing can be more beautiful than the picture of maternal fondness, the gracefulness of woman thrown like a garment around her children; her look of love etherealized by the holiest sentiment of tenderness; her loveliness exalted above the earth by the contemplation of those, her own dear ones, who are but a "little lower than the angels," is a sight to make the eyes gush tears of happiness, and the heart swell with thankfulness to Heaven. Second alone to this is the unbending of man's stern nature before the charms of childhood, when, casting away the pride of manhood and the cold spirit of worldly ambition, he becomes like one among his children, the participator in their joys and sorrows, the companion of their games, the confidant of their little secrets. How insensibly does each moment thus passed draw him farther from the world and its cares, how soon does he forget disappointments, or learn to think of them less poignantly, and how by nature's own magnetism does the sinless spirit of the child mix with the subtle workings of the man, and lift him above the petty jarrings and discords of life! And thus, while he teaches *them* precepts of truth and virtue, *they* pour into his heart lessons of humility and forbearance. If he point out the future to them, with equal force they show the past to him, and a blessing rests on both. The "populus me sibilat" of the miser is a miserable philosophy compared to his who can retire from the rancorous assaults of enemies, and the dark treachery of false friends, to the bosom of a happy home, and feel his hearth a sanctuary where come no forms of malice to assail him!

Such were my musings as I saw the father pass on with his children, and never before did my loneliness seem so devoid of happiness.

* * * * * *

Would that I could stop here. Would that I might leave my reader to ponder over these things, and fashion them to his mind's liking ; but I may not. I have but one object in these notes of my loiterings; it is to present to those younger in the world, and fresher to its wiles than myself, some of the dangers as well as some of the enjoyments of foreign travel; and having surveyed the coast with much care and caution, I would fix a wreck-buoy here and there along the channel as a warning and a guide. And now to begin.

Let me take the character before me, one, of whom I hesitate not to say that only the name is derived from

invention.   Some may have already identified him ; many
more may surmise the individual meant : it is enough
that I say he still lives, and the correctness of the portrait
may easily be tested by any traveller Rhine-wards, but I
prefer giving him a chapter to himself.

CHAPTER XXIV.

SIR HARRY WYCHERLEY.

SIR HARRY WYCHERLEY was of an old Hampshire family,
who, entering the army when a mere boy, contrived,
before he came of age, so completely to encumber a very
large estate that his majority only enabled him to finish
the ruin he had so actively begun, and leave him penniless
at seven-and-twenty.   Before the wreck of his property
became matter of notoriety, he married an Earl's daughter
with a vast fortune, a portion of which was settled on any
children that might be born to their union.   She, poor
girl, scarcely nineteen when she married, (for it was a
love match,) died of a broken heart at three-and-twenty,
leaving Sir Harry, with two infant children, all but irre-
trievably ruined, nearly everything he possessed mort-
gaged beyond its value, and not even a house to shelter
him.   By the advice of his lawyer he left England
secretly, and came over to Paris, whence he travelled
through Germany down to Italy, where he resided some
time.   The interest of the fortune settled on the children
sufficed to maintain him in good style, and enabled him to
associate with men of his own rank, provided he incurred
no habits of extravagance.   A few years of such prudence
would, he was told, enable him to return with a moderate
income ; and he submitted.

This career of quiet, unobtrusive character was gradually
becoming more and more insupportable to him.   At first
the change from a life beset by duns and bailiffs—by daily

interviews with Jews, and consultations with scheming
lawyers—was happiness itself; the freedom he enjoyed
from pressing difficulties and contingencies which arose
with every hour, was a pleasure he never knew before,
and he felt like a schoolboy escaped from the drudgery of
the desk. But by degrees, as he mixed more with those
his former associates and companions—many of them
exiles on the same plea as himself—the old taste for past
pleasures revived; their conversation brought back London
with all its brilliant gaiety before him. Its clubs and
coteries—the luxurious display of the dinners at the
Clarendon, or the reckless extravagance of the nights at
Crockford's—the triumphs of the Derby, and the glories
of Ascot—passed all in review before him, heightened by
the recollection of the high spirits of his youth. He began
once more to hanker after the world he believed he had
quitted without regret; and a morbid anxiety to learn
what was doing and going forward in the circles he used
to move in, took possession of his mind. All the gossip
of Tattersall's, all the chit-chat of the Carlton, or the
scandal of Graham's, became at once indispensable to his
existence. Who was going it "fastest" among the rising
spirits of the day, and which was the favourite of "Scott's
lot," were points of vital interest to him, while he felt
the deepest anxiety about the fortunes of those who were
tottering on the brink of ruin, and spent many a sleepless
night in conjectures as to how they were to get through
this difficulty or that, and whether they could ever "come
round" again.

Not one of the actors in that busy scene—into whose
wild chaos fate mixes up all that is highest and everything the most depraved of human nature—ever took
the same interest in it as he did. He lived henceforth in
an ideal world, ignorant and careless of what was passing
around him; his faculties strained to regard events at a
distance, he became abstracted and silent. A year passed
over thus; twelve weary months, in which his mind dwelt
on home and country with all the ardour of a banished
man At last glad tidings reached him that a compromise
had been effected with his principal creditors; his most
pressing debts had been discharged; time obtained to

meet others of less moment; and no obstacle any longer
existed to his returning to England.

What a glorious thing it was to come back again once
more to the old haunts and scenes of pleasure; to revisit
the places of which his days and nights were filled with
the very memory; to be once again the distinguished
among that crowd who ruled supreme at the table and on
the turf, and whose fiat was decisive, from the Italian
Opera to Doncaster! Alas, and alas! the resumption of
old tastes and habits will not bring back the youth and
buoyancy which gave them all their bright colouring
There is no standing still in life; there is no resting-place
whence we can survey the panorama, and not move along
with it. Our course continues, and as changes follow
each other in succession without, so, within in our own
natures, are we conforming to the rule, and becoming
different from what we had been.   '

The dream of home, the ever-present thought to the
exile's mind, suffers the rude shock when comes the hour
of testing its reality; happy for him if he die in the
delusion. Early remembrances are hallowed by a light
that age and experience dissipate for ever, and as the
highland " tarn " we used to think grand in its wild
desolation in the hours of our boyhood, becomes to our
manhood's eye but a mere pond among the mountains, so
do we look with changed feelings on all about us, and
feel disappointment where we expected pleasure.

In all great cities these changes succeed with fearful
rapidity. Expensive tastes and extravagant habits are
hourly ruining hundreds who pass off the scene where
they shone and are heard of no more. The "lion" of
the season, whose plate was a matter of royal curiosity,
whose equipage gave the tone to the time, whose dinner
invitations were regarded as the climax of fashionable
distinction, awakes some morning to discover that an
expenditure of four times a man's income, continued for
several years, may originate embarrassment in his affairs.
He finds out that tailors can be uncivil, and coachmakers
rude; and, horror of horrors, he sees within the precincts of
his dressing-room the plebeian visage of a sheriff's officer,
or the calculating countenance of a West-end auctioneer.

He who was booked for Ascot now hurries away to Antwerp. An ambiguous paragraph in an evening paper informs London that one among the ranks of extravagance has fallen; a notice of "public competition" by the hand of George Robins comes next; a criticism, and generally a sharp one, on the taste of his furniture and the value of his pictures follows; the broad pages of the *Morning Post* become the winding-sheet of his memory, and the knock of the auctioneer's hammer is his requiem! The ink is not dried on his passport, ere he is forgotten. Fashionable circles have other occupations than regrets and condolences; so that the exile may be a proud man if he retain a single correspondent in that great world which yesterday found nothing better than to chronicle his doings.

When Sir Harry Wycherley then came back to London he was only remembered—nothing more. The great majority of his contemporaries had, like himself, passed off the boards during the interval; such of them as remained were either like vessels too crippled in action to seek safety in flight, or, adopting the philosophy of the devil when sick, had resolved on prudence when there was no more liking for dissipation. He was almost a stranger in his club; the very waiters at Mivart's asked his name; while the last new peer's son, just emerging into life, had never even heard of him before. So is it decreed—dynasties shall fall and others succeed them—Charles le Dix gives place to Louis Philippe, and Nugee occupies the throne of Stultz.

Few things men bear worse than this oblivion in the very places where once their sway was absolute. It is very hard to believe that the world has grown wiser and better, more cultivated in taste and more correct in its judgments than when we knew it of old; and a man is very likely to tax with ingratitude those who, superseding him in the world's favour, seem to be forgetful of claims which in reality they never knew of.

Sir Harry Wycherley was not long in England ere he felt these truths in all their bitterness, and saw that an absence of a few years teaches one's friends to do without them so completely that they are absolutely unwilling to open a new want of acquaintance, as though it were an expensive luxury they had learned to dispense with. Besides, Wycherley was decidedly "rococo" in all his tastes and predilections. Men did not dine now where they used in *his* day—Doncaster was going out—Goodwood was coming in—people spoke of Grisi, not Pasta—Mario more than Rubini. Instead of the old absolute monarchy of fashion, where one dictated to all the rest, a new school sprung up, a species of democracy, who thought Long Wellesley and D'Orsay were unclean idols, and would not worship anything save themselves.

Now of all the marks of progress which distinguish men in the higher circles, there is none in these latter days at all comparable with the signs of—to give it a mild name—increased "sharpness," distinguishable amongst them. The traveller by the heavy Falmouth mail whisked along forty miles per hour in the Grand Junction would see far less to astonish and amaze him than your shrewd man about town of some forty years back, could he be let down any evening among the youth at Tattersall's, or introduced among the rising generation just graduating at Graham's.

The spirit of the age is unquestionably to be "up and doing." A good book on the Oaks has a far higher preeminence, not to say profit, than one published in "the Row;" the "honours" of the crown are scarcely on a par with those scored at whist; and to predict the first horse in at Ascot would be a far higher step in the intellectual scale than to prophesy the appearance of a comet or an eclipse; the leader in the House can only divide public applause with the winner of the Leger, and even the versatile gyrations of Lord Brougham himself must yield to the more fascinating pirouettes of Fanny Ellsler. Young men leave Eton and Sandhurst now with more tact and worldly wit than their fathers had at forty, or their grandfathers ever possessed at all.

Short as Sir Harry Wycherley's absence had been, the march of mind had done much in all these respects. The babes and sucklings of fashion were more than his equals in craft and subtlety; none like *them* to ascertain what was wrong with the favourite, or why the "mare" would not start; few could compete with them in those difficult

walks of finance which consist in obtaining credit from
coachmakers, and cash from Jews. In fact, to that
generation who spent profusely to live luxuriously, had
succeeded a race who reversed the position, and lived
extravagantly in order to have the means of spending.
Wiser than their fathers, they substituted paper for cash
payments, and saw no necessity to cry "stop" while there
was a stamp in England

It was a sad thing for one who believed his education
finished to become a schoolboy once more, but there was
nothing else for it. Sir Harry had to begin at the bottom
of the class; he was an apt scholar it is true, but before
he had completed his studies he was ruined. High play
and high interest—Jews and jockeys—dinners and
danseuses—with large retinues of servants, will help a
man considerably to get rid of his spare cash; and however he may—which in most cases he must—acquire
some wisdom *en route*, his road is not less certain to lead
to ruin In two years from the time of his return. another
paragraph and another auction proclaimed that "Wycherley was cleaned out," and that he had made his "posi-
tively last appearance" in England.

The Continent was now to be his home for life. He
had lost his "means," but he had learned "ways" of
living, and from pigeon he became rook.

There is a class, possibly the most dangerous that exists,
of men, who without having gone so far as to forfeit
pretension to the society and acquaintance of gentlemen,
have yet involved their name and reputation in circumstances which are more than suspicious. Living expen-
sively, without any obvious source of income; enjoying
every luxury, and indulging every taste that costs dearly,
without any difficulty in the payment, their intimacy with
known gamblers and blacklegs exposes them at once to the
inevitable charge of confederacy. Rarely or never playing themselves, however, they reply to such calumnies by
referring to their habits; their daily life would indeed
seem little liable to reproval. If married, they are the
most exemplary of husbands. If they have children,
they are models for fathers. Where can you see such
little ones—so well-mannered—so well-dressed—with such

beautifully curled hair, and such perfectly good breeding —or, to use the proper phrase, " so admirably taken care of." They are liberal to all public charities—they are occasionally intimate with the chaplain of the Embassy too,—of whom, a word hereafter,—and, in fact, it would be difficult to find fault with any circumstance in their bearing before the world. Their connection by family with persons of rank and condition, is a kind of life-buoy of which no shipwreck of fortune deprives them, and long after less well-known people have sunk to the bottom, they are to be found floating on the surface of society. In this way they form a kind of " Pont de Diable" between persons of character and persons of none—they are the narrow isthmus, connecting the main land with the low reef of rocks beyond it.

These men are the tame elephants of the swindling world, who provide the game, though they never seem to care for the sport. Too cautious of reputation to become active agents in these transactions, they introduce the unsuspecting traveller into those haunts and among those where ruin is rife ; and as the sheriff consigns the criminal to the attentions of the hangman, so these worthies halt at the " drop," and would scorn, with indignation, the idea of exercising the last office of the law.

Far from this, they are eloquent in their denunciations of play. Such sound morality as theirs cannot be purchased at any price; the dangers that beset young men coming abroad—the risk of chance acquaintance—the folly of associating with persons not known—form the staple of their converse—which, lest it should seem too cynical in its attack on pleasure, is relieved by that admirable statement so popular in certain circles. " You' know a man of the world must see every thing for himself, so that though I say don't gamble, I never said, don't frequent the Cursaal—though I bade you avoid play, I did not say, shun blacklegs." It is pretty much like desiring a man not to take the yellow fever, but to be sure to pass an autumn on the coast of Africa !

Such, then, was the character of him who would once have rejected with horror the acquaintance of one like himself. A sleeping partner in swindling, he received his

share of the profits, although his name did not appear in
the firm. His former acquaintances continued to know
him, his family connections were large and influential, and
though some may have divined his practices, he was one
of those men that are never " cut." Some pitied him;
some affected to disbelieve all the stories against him ;
some told tales of his generosity and kindness, but scarcely
any one condemned him—" Ainsi va le monde? "

Once more I ask forgiveness, if I have been too prolix
in all this ; rather would I have you linger in pleasanter
scenes, and with better company, but—there must always
be a " but,"—but he is only a sorry pilot who would content himself with describing the scenery of the coast, and
expatiating on the beauty of the valleys and the boldness
of the headlands, while he let the vessel take her course
among reefs and rocks, and risk a shipwreck, while he
amused the passengers. Adieu, then, to Spas and their
visitors; the sick are seldom the pleasantest company;
the healthy at such places are rarely the safest.

" You are going, Mr. O'Leary? " said a voice from a
window opposite the Hotel, as my luggage was lifted into
a fiacre. I looked up. It was the youth who had lost so
deeply at the Cursaal.

" Only to Coblentz, for a few days," said I ; " I am weary
of gaiety and fine people. I wish for quiet just now."

" I would that I had gone some weeks ago," exclaimed
he, with a sigh. " May I walk with you as far as the
river ? "

I assented with pleasure, and in a moment after he was
by my side.

" I trust," said I, when we had walked together some
time, " I trust you have not been to the Cursaal again ? "

" Never since I met you ; that night was the last I ever
passed there!" He paused for some minutes, and then
added, " You were not acquainted with either of the gentlemen in whose company we supped ; I think you told me
so on the way home? "

" No, they were both strangers to me ; it was a chance
rencontre, and in the few weeks I passed at Wiesbaden, I
learned enough not to pursue the acquaintance farther.
Indeed, to do them justice, they seemed as well disposed

as myself to drop the intimacy ; I seldom play, never among strangers."

"Ah !" said he, in an accent of some bitterness, "that resolve would avail you little with *them ; they* can win without playing for it."

"How so ; what do you mean ? "

"Have you a mind for a short story ? it is my own adventure, and I can vouch for the truth." I assented, and he went on. "About a week ago, Mr. Crotty, with two others, one of whom was called Captain Jacob, came to invite me to a little excursion to Kreutznach. They were to go one day and return the following one. Sir Harry was to join the party also, and they spoke of Lord Edderdale and some others. But Wycherley only came down to the steamboat, when a messenger arrived with a pressing letter, recalling him to Wiesbaden, and the rest never appeared. Away we went, however, in good spirits ; the day was fine, and the sail down the Rhine, as you know, delightful. We arrived at Kreutznach to dinner—spent the evening in wandering about the pretty scenery, and came back by moonlight to a late supper. As usual with them, cards were produced after supper, but I had never touched a card, nor made a bet, since my unlucky night at the Cursaal, so I merely sat by the table and looked on at the game, of course taking that interest in it a man fond of play cannot divest himself of—but neither counselling any party, nor offering a bet to either side. The game gradually became interesting, deeply so, as well from the skill of the players, as the high stakes they played for. Large sums of money changed owners, and heavy scores were betted besides. Meanwhile, champagne was called for, and, as the night wore on, a bowl of smoking bishop, spiced and seasoned to perfection. My office was to fill the glasses of the party, and drink toasts with each of them in succession, as luck inclined to this side or that.

"The excitement of play needs not wine to make it near to madness ; but with it no mania is more complete. Although but a looker-on, my attention was bent on the game, and what with the odorous bowl of bishop, and the long-sustained interest, the fatigue of a day more than usually laborious, and a constitution never strong, I became so heavy that I threw myself upon a sofa, and fell fast asleep.

"How I reached my bed, and became undressed, I never knew since; but by noon the next day I was awakened from a deep slumber, and saw Jacob beside me.

"'Well, old fellow, you take it coolly,' said he, laughing; 'you don't know it's past twelve o'clock.'

"'Indeed!' said I, starting up, and scarce remembering where I was. 'The fact is, my wits are none of the clearest this morning — that bowl of bishop finished me.'

"'Did it, by Jove?' replied he, with a half saucy laugh; 'I'll wager a pony, notwithstanding, you never played better in your life.'

"'Played? why I never touched a card,' said I, in horror and amazement.

"'I wish you hadn't, that's all,' said he, while he took a pocket-book from his pocket, and proceeded to open it on the bed. 'If you hadn't, I should have been somewhat of a richer man this morning.'

"'I can only tell you,' said I, as I rubbed my eyes, and endeavoured to waken up more completely, 'I can only tell you that I don't remember anything of what you allude to, nor can I believe that I would have broken a firm resolve I made against play——'

"'Gently, sir, gently,' said he, in a low, smooth voice; 'be a little careful I beseech you—what you have just said amounts to something very like a direct contradiction of my words. Please to remember, sir, that we were strangers to each other yesterday morning. But to be brief—was your last bet a double or quit, or only a ten-pound note? for on that depends whether I owe you two hundred and sixty, or two hundred and seventy pounds. Can you set me right on that point—they made such a noise at the time, I can't be clear about it.'

"'I protest, sir,' said I, once more, 'this is all a dream to me; as I have told you already, I never played——'

"'You never played, sir?'

"'I mean, I never knew I played, or I have no remembrance of it now——'

"'Well, young gentleman, fortune treats *you* better

A A

when asleep than she does *me* with my eyes open, and as
I have no time to lose, for I leave for Bingen in half an
hour, I have only to say, here is your money. You may
forget what you have won; I have also an obligation, but
a stronger one, to remember what I have lost; and as for
the ten pounds, shall we say head or tail for it, as we
neither of us are quite clear about it ? '

" ' Say anything you like, for I firmly believe one or
other of us must be out of our reason.'

" ' What do you say, sir,—head or tail ? '

" ' Head ! ' cried I, in a frenzy, 'there ought to be *one*
in the party.'

" ' Won again, by Jove ! ' said he, opening his hand;
' I think you'll find that rouleau correct, and now, sir, *au
revoir*, I shall have my revenge one of these days.' He
shook my hand and went out, leaving me sitting up in
the bed, trying to remember some one circumstance of the
previous night, by which I could recall my joining the
play-table. But nothing of the kind; a thick haze was
over everything, through which I could merely recollect
the spicy bishop, and my continued efforts to keep their
glasses filled. There I sat, puzzled and confused, the bed
covered with bank-notes, which, after all, have some confounded magic in their faces, that makes our acceptance of
them a matter of far less repugnance than it ought While
I counted over my gains, stooping every instant to think
on the strange caprices of fortune, that wouldn't afford me
the gambler's pleasure of winning, while enriching me
with gain, the door opened, and in came Crotty.

" ' Not up yet! why we start in ten minutes ; didn't the
waiter call you ? '

" ' No. I am in a state of bewilderment this whole
morning——'

" ' Well, well, get clear of it for a few seconds, I advise
you, and let us settle scores——'

" ' What ! ' cried I, laughing, ' have I won from you
also ? '

" ' No, by Jove, it's the other way · you pushed me rather
sharply though, and if I took all your bets I should have
made a good thing of it. As it is,'—here he opened a
memorandum book and read out—'As it is, I have only

won seven hundred and twenty, and two hundred and fifty-eight,—nine hundred and seventy-eight, I believe; does not that make it ? '

" I shivered like one in the ague, and couldn't speak a word.

" ' Has Jacob booked up ? ' asked Crotty.

" ' Yes,' said I, pointing to the notes on the bed, that now looked like a brood of rattlesnakes to my eyes.

" ' All right,' continued he, ' Jacob is a most punctilious fellow; foolishly so, indeed, among friends—well, what are we to say about this ? are you strong in cash just now ? '

" ' No,' stammered I, with a sigh.

" ' Well, never mind—a short bill for the balance—I'll take what's here in part payment, and don't let the thing give you any inconvenience.'

" This was done in a good off-hand way. I signed the bill which he drew up in due form. He had a dozen stamps ready in his pocket-book. He rolled up the bank-notes carelessly stuffed them into his coat-pocket, and with a most affectionate hope of seeing me next day at Wiesbaden, left the room.

" The bill is paid—I released it in less than a week. My trip to Kreutznach just cost me seven hundred pounds, and 1 may be pardoned if I never like ' bishop ' for the rest of my life after."

" I should not wonder if you became a Presbyterian to-morrow," said I, endeavouring to encourage his own effort at good humour; " but here we are at the Rhine. Good-bye, I needn't warn you about——"

" Not a word, I beseech you; I'll never close my eyes as long as I live without a double lock on the door of my bed-room."

CHAPTER XXV.

THE RECOVERY HOUSE.

FRANKFORT is a German Liverpool, minus the shipping, and consequently has few attractions for the mere traveller. The statue of Ariadne, by the Danish sculptor Danncker, is almost its only great work of art. There are some, not first-rate, pictures in the Gallery and the Hotel de Ville, and the Town Library possesses a few Protestant relics—among others, a pair of Luther's slippers.

There is, however, little to delay a wanderer within the walls of the "Frey Stadt," if he have no peculiar sympathy with the Jews and money-changers. The whole place smacks of trade and traders, and seems far prouder of being the native city of Rothschild than the birthplace of Goethe

The happy indolence of a foreign city, the easy enjoyment of life so conspicuous in most continental towns, exists not here All is activity, haste, and bustle. The *tables d'hôte* are crowded to excess by eager individuals, eating away against time, and anxious to get back once more to the Exchange, or the counting-house. There is a Yankee abruptness in the manners of the men, who reply to you as though information were a thing not to be had for nothing; and as for the women, like the wives and daughters of all commercial communities, they are showy dressers and poor conversers; wear the finest clothes, and inhabit the most magnificent houses, but scarcely become the one, and don't know how to live in the other.

I certainly should not like to pitch my tent in Frankfort, even as successor to the great Munch Bellinghausen himself—Heaven grant I may have given him all his consonants!—the President of the Diet. And yet, to the people themselves, few places take such rooted hold on the feelings of the inhabitants as trading cities. Talk of the attachment of a Swiss or a Tyrolese to his native mountains—the dweller in Fleet Street, or the Hoch Gasse, will beat him hollow. The daily occupations of City life, filling up every nook and crevice of the human mind, leave no room for any thought or wish beyond them. Hence arises that insufferable air of self-satisfaction, that contented self-sufficiency, so observable in your genuine cockney. Leadenhall Street is, to his notion, the touchstone of mankind, and a character on "'Change" the greatest test of moral worth. Hamburg or Frankfort, Glasgow or Manchester, New York or Bristol, it is all the same; your men of sugar and sassafras, of hides, tallow, and train-oil, are a class, in which nationality makes little change. No men enjoy life more—few fear death as much—this is truly strange! Any ordinary mind would suppose that the common period of human life, spent in such occupations as Frankfort, for instance, affords, would have little desire for longevity—that, in short, a man, let him be ever such a glutton of "Cocker," would have had enough of decimal fractions and compound interest after fifty years; and that he could lay down the pen without a sigh, and even, for the sake of a little relaxation, be glad to go into the next world. Nothing of the kind: your "Frankforter" hates dying above all things. The hardy peasant who sees the sun rise from his native mountains, and beholds him setting over a glorious landscape of wood and glen, of field and valley, can leave the bright world with fewer regrets than your denizen of some dark alley or some smoke-dried street in a great metropolis. The love of life—it may be axiomized—is in the direct ratio of its artificiality. The more men shut out nature from their hearts and homes, and surround themselves with the hundred little appliances of a factitious existence, the more do they become attached to the world.

The very changes of flood and field suggest the thought of a hereafter to him who dwells among them; the falling leaf, the withered branch, the mouldering decay of vegetation, bear lessons there is no mistaking; and the mind, thus familiarized, learns to look forward to the great event as the inevitable course of that law by which he lives and breathes. While to others, again, the speculations which grow out of the contemplation of Nature's great works, invariably are blended with this thought. Not so your man of cities, who inhabits some brick-surrounded kingdom, where the incessant din of active life as effectually excludes deep reflection as does the smoky atmosphere the bright sky above it.

Immersed in worldly cares, interested, heart and soul, in the pursuit of wealth, the solemn idea of death is not broken to his mind by any analogy whatever. It is the pomp of the funeral that realizes the idea to him; it is as a thing of undertakers and mourning-coaches, of mutes and palls, scarfs, sextons and grave-diggers, that he knows it; the horrid image of human woe and human mockery, of grief walking in carnival! No wonder if it impress him with a greater dread!

"What has all this sad digression to say to Frankfort, Mr. O'Leary?" quoth some very impatient reader, who always will pull me short up, when I'm in for a "four-mile-heat" of moralizing. Come, then, I'll tell you. The train of thought was suggested to me as I strolled along the Boulevard to my hotel, meditating on one of the very strangest institutions it had ever been my lot to visit in any country; and which, stranger still, so far as I know, guide-book people have not mentioned in any way.

In a cemetery of Frankfort—a very tasteful imitation of "Père la Chaise"—there stands a large building, handsomely built, and in very correct Roman architecture, which is called the "Recovery House," being neither more nor less than an institution devoted to the dead, for the purpose of giving them every favourable opportunity of returning to life again, should they feel so disposed. The apartments are furnished with all the luxurious elegance of the best houses; the beds are decorated with carving and inlaying, the carpets are soft and noiseless to the tread; and, in fact, few of those who live and breathe are surrounded by such appliances of enjoyment. Beside each bed there stands a small table, in which certain ivory keys are fixed, exactly resembling those of a pianoforte. On these is the hand of the dead man laid as he lies in the bed; for, instead of being buried, he is conveyed here after his supposed death, and wrapped up in warm blankets; while the temperature of the room itself is regulated by the season of the year. The slightest movement of vitality in his fingers would press down one of the keys which communicate with a bell at the top of the building, where resides a doctor, or rather two doctors, who take it watch and watch about, ready at the summons to afford all the succour of their art. Restoratives of every kind abound—all that human ingenuity can devise —in the way of cordials and stimulants, as well as a large and admirably-equipped staff of servants and nurses, whose cheerful aspect seems especially intended to re-assure the patient, should he open his eyes once more to life.

The institution is a most costly one. The physicians, selected from among the highest practitioners of Frankfort, are most liberally remunerated, and the whole retinue of the establishment maintained on a footing of even extravagant expenditure. Of course, I need scarcely say, its benefits, if such they be, are reserved for the wealthy only. Indeed, I have been told the cost of "this lying in state" exceeds that of the most expensive funeral four-fold. Sometimes there is great difficulty in obtaining a vacant bed. Periods of epidemic disease crowd the institution to such a degree, that the greatest influence is exerted for a place. Now, one naturally asks, what success has this system met with to warrant this expenditure, and continue to enjoy public confidence ? None whatever. In seventeen years which one of the resident doctors passed there, not *one* case occurred of restored animation, nor was there ever reason to believe that in any instance the slightest signs of vitality ever returned. The physicians themselves make little scruple at avowing the incredulity concerning its necessity, and surprised me by the freedom with which they canvassed the excellent, but mistaken, notions of its founders.

To what, then, must we look for the reason of maintaining so strange an institution ? Simply to that love of life so remarkably conspicuous in the people of Frankfort. The failure in a hundred instances is no argument to any man who thinks his own case may present the exception.

It matters little to him that his neighbour was past revival when he arrived there; the question is, what is his
own chance?   Besides that, the fear of being buried alive
—a dread, only chimerical in other countries—must often
present itself here, when an institution is maintained to
prevent the casualty.   In fact, there looks a something of
scant courtesy in consigning a man to the tomb at once,
in a land where a kind of purgatorial sojourn is provided
for him.   But stranger than all is the secret hope this
system nourishes in the sick man's heart, that howeve.·
friends may despond, and doctors pronounce, he has a
chance still—there is a period allowed him of appealing
against the decree of death—enough if he but lift a finger
against it.   What a singular feature does the whole system
expose, and how fond of the world must they be who
practise it?   Who can tell whether this "House of
Recovery" does not creep in among the fading hopes of
the death-bed, and if, among the last farewells of parting
life, some thoughts of that last chance are not present to
the sick man's mind?   As I walked through its silent
chambers, where the pale print of death was marked in
every face that lay there, I shuddered to think how the
rich man's gold will lead him to struggle against the will
of his Creator.   La Morgue, in all its fearful reality, came
up before me, and the cold moist flags on which were
stretched the unknown corpses of the poor, seemed far less
horrible than this gorgeous palace of the wealthy dead.
   Unquestionably, cases of recovery from trance occur in
every land, and the feelings of returning animation, I
have often been told, are those of most intense suffering—
the inch to inch combat with death is a fearful agony; yet
what is it to the horrible sensations of *seeming* death, in
which the consciousness survives all power of exertion,
and the mind burns bright within while the body is about
to be given to the earth.   Can there be such a state as
this?   Some one will say, " Is such a condition possible?"
I believe it firmly.   Many years ago a physician of some
eminence gave me an account of a fearful circumstance
in his own life, which not only bears upon the point in
question, but illustrates in a remarkable degree the powerful agency of volition as a principle of vitality.   I shall

give the detail in his own words, without a syllable of comment, save that I can speak, from my knowledge of the narrator, to the truth of his narrative.

CHAPTER XXVI.

THE "DREAM OF DEATH."

" It was already near four o'clock ere I bethought me of making any preparation for my lecture. The day had been, throughout, one of those heavy and sultry ones autumn so often brings in our climate, and I felt from this cause much oppressed and disinclined to exertion; independently of the fact that I had been greatly over-fatigued during the preceding week—some cases of a most trying and arduous nature having fallen to my lot, one of which, from the importance of the life to a young and dependent family, had engrossed much of my attention, and aroused in me the warmest anxiety for success. In this frame of mind I was entering my carriage to pro-ceed to the lecture-room, when an unsealed note was put into my hands: I opened it hastily, and read that poor H——, for whom I was so deeply interested, had just expired. I was greatly shocked. It was scarcely an hour since I had seen him, and from the apparent improve-ment since my former visit, had ventured to speak most encouragingly; and had even made some jesting allusions to the speedy prospect of his once more resuming his place at ' hearth and board.' Alas! how shortlived were my hopes destined to be ! how awfully was my prophecy to be contradicted.

" No one but he who has himself experienced it, knows anything of the deep and heartfelt interest a medical man takes in many of the cases which professionally come before him ; I speak here of an interest perfectly apart from all personal regard for the patient, or his friends.

Indeed, the feeling I allude to has nothing in common with this, and will often be experienced as thoroughly for a perfect stranger as for one known and respected for years.

"To the extreme of this feeling I was ever a victim. The heavy responsibility, often suddenly and unexpectedly imposed; the struggle for success, when success was all but hopeless; the intense anxiety for the arrival of those critical periods which change the character of a malady, and divest it of some of its dangers, or invest it with new ones; the despondence when that period has come only to confirm all the worst symptoms, and shut out every prospect of recovery; and, last of all, that most trying of all the trying duties of my profession, the breaking to the perhaps unconscious relatives that my art has failed, my resources were exhausted, in a word, that there was no longer a hope.

"These things have preyed on me for weeks, for months long, and many an effort have I made in secret to combat this feeling, but without the least success, till, at last, I absolutely dreaded the very thoughts of being sent for to a dangerous and critical illness. It may then be believed how very heavily the news I had just received came upon me; the blow, too, was not even lessened by the poor consolation of my having anticipated the result, and broken the shock to the family.

"I was still standing with the half-opened note in my hands, when I was aroused by the coachman asking, I believe for the third time, whither should he drive? I bethought me for an instant, and said, ' To the lecture-room '

"When in health, lecturing had ever been to me more of an amusement than a labour; and often, in the busy hours of professional visiting, have I longed for the time when I should come before my class, and divesting my mind of all individual details, launch forth into the more abstract and speculative doctrines of my art. It so chanced, too, that the late hour at which I lectured, as well as the subjects I adopted, usually drew to my class many of the advanced members of the profession, who made this a lounge after the fatigues of the morning.

"Now, however, I approached this duty with fear and trembling: the events of the morning had depressed my mind greatly, and I longed for rest and retirement. The passing glance I threw at the lecture-room through the half-opened door, showed it to be crowded to the very roof, and as I walked along the corridor, I heard the name of some foreign physician of eminence, who was among my auditory. I cannot describe the agitation of mind I felt at this moment. My confusion, too, became greater as I remembered that the few notes I had drawn up were left in the pocket of the carriage, which I had just dismissed, intending to return on foot. It was already considerably past the usual hour, and I was utterly unable to decide how to proceed. I hastily drew out a portfolio that contained many scattered notes, and hints for lectures, and hurriedly throwing my eye across them, discovered some singular memoranda on the subject of insanity On these I resolved at once to dilate a little, and eke out, if possible, the materials for a lecture.

" The events of the remainder of that day are wrapt in much obscurity to my mind, yet I well remember the loud thunder of applause which greeted me on entering the lecture-room, and how, as for some moments I appeared to hesitate, they were renewed again and again, till at last, summoning resolution, I collected myself sufficiently to open my discourse. I well remember, too, the difficulty the first few sentences cost me, the doubts, the fears, the pauses, which beset me at every step as I went on. My anxiety to be clear and accurate in conveying my meaning, making me recapitulate and repeat, till I felt myself, as it were, working in a circle. By degrees, however, I grew warmed as I proceeded, and the evident signs of attention my auditory exhibited, gave me renewed courage, while they impressed me with the necessity to make a more than common exertion. By degrees, too, I felt the mist clearing from my brain, and that even without effort, my ideas came faster, and my words fell from me with ease and rapidity. Simile and illustration came in abundance, and distinctions which had hitherto struck me as the most subtle and difficult of description I now drew with readiness and accuracy. Points of an abstruse and recondite nature, which, under other circumstances, I should not have wished to touch upon, I now approached fearlessly and boldly, and felt, in the very moment of speaking, they became clearer and clearer to myself. Theories and hypotheses, which were of old and acknowledged acceptance, I glanced hurriedly at as I went on, and with a perspicuity and clearness I never before felt, exposed their fallacies and unmasked their errors. I thought I was rather describing events, and things passing actually before my eyes at the instant, than relating the results of a life's experience and reflection. My memory, usually a defective one, now carried me back to the days of my early childhood; and the whole passages of a life long lay displayed before me like a picture. If I quoted, the very words of the author rushed to my mind as palpably as though the page lay open before me. I have still some vague recollection of an endeavour I made to trace the character of the insanity in every case, to some early trait of the individual in childhood, when, overcome by passion, or overbalanced by excitement, the faculties run wild into all those excesses, which, in after years, develop eccentricities of character, and, in some weaker temperaments, aberrations of intellect. Anecdotes illustrating this novel position came thronging to my mind; and events in the early years of some who subsequently died insane, and seemed to support my theory, came rushing to my memory. As I proceeded, I became gradually more and more excited, the very ease and rapidity with which my ideas suggested themselves increased the fervour of my imaginings, till at last I felt my words come without effort, and spontaneously, while there seemed a commingling of my thoughts which left me unable to trace connection between them, while I continued to speak as fluently as before. I felt at this instant a species of indistinct terror of some unknown danger which impended me, yet which it was impossible to avert or to avoid. I was like one who, borne on the rapid current of a fast-flowing river, sees the foam of the cataract before him, yet waits passively for the moment of his destruction, without an effort to save. The power which maintained my mind in its balance had gradually forsaken me, and shapes and fantasies of every odd and fantastic character flitted around and about me. The ideas and descriptions my mind had conjured up assumed a living, breathing vitality, and I felt like a necromancer waving his wand over the living and the dead. I paused; there was a dead silence in the lecture-room · a thought rushed like a meteor-flash across my brain, and bursting forth into a loud laugh of hysteric passion, I cried,— ' AND I, AND I, TOO, AM A MANIAC ! ' My class rose like one man—a cry of horror burst through the room. I know no more.

*   *   *   *   *   *

" I was ill, very ill, and in bed. I looked around me —every object was familiar to me. Through the half-closed window-shutter there streamed one long line of red sunlight—I felt it was evening. There was no one in the room, and, as I endeavoured to recall my scattered thoughts sufficiently to find out why I was thus there came an oppressive weakness over me. I closed my eyes and tried to sleep, and was roused by some one entering the room. it was my friend Doctor G——· he walked stealthily towards my bed, and looked at me fixedly for several minutes, I watched him closely, and saw that his countenance changed as he looked on me; I felt his hand tremble slightly as he placed it on my wrist, and heard him mutter to himself, in a low tone, ' My God ! how altered !' I heard now a voice at the door, saying, in a soft whisper, ' May I come in ?' The doctor made no reply, and my wife glided gently into the apartment. She looked deathly pale, and appeared to have been weeping; she leaned over me, and I felt the warm tears fall one by one upon my forehead. She took my hand within both of hers, and putting her lips to my ear, said, ' Do you know *me*, William ?' There was a long pause I tried to speak, but I could not; I endeavoured to make some sign of recognition, and stared her fully in the face ; but I heard her say, in a broken voice, ' He does not know *me* now ;' and then I felt it was in vain. The doctor came over, and taking my wife's hand, endeavoured to lead her from the room I heard her say, ' Not now, not now,' and I sank back into a heavy unconsciousness.

" I awoke from what appeared to have been a long and
deep sleep. I was, however, unrefreshed and unrested.
My eyes were dimmed and clouded, and I in vain tried
to ascertain if there was any one in the room with me.
The sensation of fever had subsided, and left behind the
most lowering and depressing debility. As by degrees I
came to myself, I found that the doctor was sitting beside
my bed ; he bent over me, and said, ' Are you better,
William ?' Never until now had my inability to reply
given me any pain or uneasiness, now, however, the
abortive struggle to speak was torture. I thought and
felt that my senses were gradually yielding beneath me,
and a cold shuddering at my heart told me that the hand
of death was upon me. The exertion now made to repel
the fatal lethargy must have been great, for a cold, clammy
perspiration broke profusely over my body ; a rushing
sound, as if of water, filled my ears ; a succession of short
convulsive spasms, as if given by an electric machine,
shook my limbs ; I grasped the doctor's hand firmly in
mine, and starting to the sitting posture, I looked wildly
about me. My breathing became shorter and shorter,
my grasp relaxed, my eyes swam, and I fell back heavily
in the bed ; the last recollection of that moment was the
muttered expression of my poor friend G——, saying, ' It
is over at last '

" Many hours must have elapsed ere I returned to any
consciousness. My first sensation was feeling the cold
wind across my face, which seemed to come from an open
window. My eyes were closed, and the lids felt as if
pressed down by a weight. My arms lay along my side,
and though the position in which I lay was constrained
and unpleasant, I could make no effort to alter it ; I tried
to speak, but I could not.

" As I lay thus, the footsteps of many persons traversing
the apartment, broke upon my ear, followed by a heavy,
dull sound, as if some weighty body had been laid upon
the floor ; a harsh voice of one near me now said, as if
reading, ' William H——, aged thirty-eight years ; I
thought him much more ' The words rushed through
my brain, and with the rapidity of a lightning flash, every
circumstance of my illness came before me, and I now

knew that I had died, and that for my interment were intended the awful preparations about me. Was this then death? Could it be that though coldness wrapt the suffering clay, passion and sense should still survive; and that while every external trace of life had fled, consciousness should still cling to the cold corpse destined for the earth? Oh! how horrible, how more than horrible! the terror of the thought! Then I thought it might be what is termed a trance, but that poor hope deserted me as I brought to mind the words of the doctor, who knew too well all the unerring signs of death, to be deceived by its counterfeit, and my heart sank as they lifted me into the coffin, and I felt that my limbs had stiffened, and I knew this never took place in a trance. How shall I tell the heart-cutting anguish of that moment, as my mind looked forward to a futurity too dreadful to think upon; when memory should call up many a sunny hour of existence, the loss of friends, the triumph of exertion, and then fall back upon the dread consciousness of the ever-buried life the grave closed over; and then 1 thought that perhaps sense but lingered round the lifeless clay, as the spirits of the dead are said to hover around the places and homes they have loved in life, ere they leave them for ever; and that soon the lamp should expire upon the shrine when the temple that sheltered it lay mouldering and in ruins. Alas! how fearful to dream of even the happiness of the past, in that cold grave where the worm only is a reveller; to think that though—

Friends, brothers, and sisters, are laid side by side,
Yet none have ere questioned, nor none have replied;

yet that all felt in their cold and mouldering hearts the loves and affections of life, budding and blossoming as though the stem was not rotting to corruption that bore them; I brought to mind the awful punishment of the despot, who chained the living to the dead man, and thought it mercy when compared to this.

"How long I lay thus I know not, but the dreary silence of the chamber was again broken, and I found that some of my dearest friends were come to take a farewell look at me ere the coffin was closed upon me for

ever. Again the horror of my state struck me with all its
forcible reality, and like a meteor there shot through my
heart the bitterness of years of misery condensed into the
space of a minute. And then, I remembered, how gradual
is death, and how by degrees it creeps over every portion
of the frame, like the track of the destroyer, blighting as
it goes, and said to my heart, All may yet be still within
me, and the mind as lifeless as the body it dwelt in ; and
yet these feelings partook of life in all their strength and
vigour. There was the *Will* to move, to speak, to see, to
live, and yet all was torpid and inactive, as though it had
never lived. Was it that the nerves, from some depressing cause, had ceased to transmit the influence of the
brain ? Had these winged messengers of the mind refused their office ? And then I called to mind the almost
miraculous efficacy of the Will, exerted under circumstances of great exigency, and with a concentration of
power that some men only are capable of. I had heard of
the Indian father who suckled his child at his own bosom,
when he had laid its mother in her grave ; yet, was it not
the will had wrought this miracle ? I myself have seen
the paralytic limb awake to life and motion by the powerful application of the mind stimulating the nervous channels of communication, and awakening the dormant powers
of vitality to their exercise. I knew of one whose heart
beat fast or slow as he did will it. Yes ! thought I, in a
transport, the Will to live, is the power to live ; and only
when this faculty has yielded with bodily strength need
death be the conqueror over us. The thought of reani-
mation was ecstatic, but I dare not dwell upon it ; the
moments passed rapidly on, and even now the last preparations were about to be made, ere they committed my body
to the grave. And how was the effort to be made? If
the Will did indeed possess the power I trusted in, how
'was it to be applied ? I had often wished to speak or
move during my illness, yet was unable to do either. I
then remembered that in those cases where the Will had
worked its wonders, the powers of the mind had entirely
centred themselves in the one heart-filling desire to accomplish a certain object, as the athlete in the games strains
every muscle to lift some ponderous weight. And thus, I

knew, that if the heart could be so subjected to the principle
of volition, as that, yielding to its impulse, it would again
transmit the blood along its accustomed channels, and that
then the lungs should be brought to act upon the blood by
the same agency, the other functions of the body would
be more readily restored by the sympathy with these great
ones. Besides, I trusted that so long as the powers of the
mind existed in the vigour I felt them in, that much of
what might be called latent vitality existed in the body.
Then I set myself to think upon those nerves which preside over the action of the heart—their origin, their course,
their distribution, their relation, their sympathies. I traced
them as they arose in the brain, and tracked them till they
were lost in millions of tender threads upon the muscle of
the heart. I thought, too, upon the lungs as they lay
flaccid and collapsed within my chest—the life-blood stagnant in their vessels,—and tried to possess my mind with
the relation of these two parts, to the utter exclusion of
every other. I endeavoured then to transmit along the
nerves the impulse of that faculty my whole hopes rested
on. Alas! it was in vain. I tried to heave my chest and
breathe, but could not,—my heart sank within me, and all
my former terrors came thickening around me, more dreadful by far, as the stir and bustle in the room indicated they
were about to close the coffin. At this moment my dear
friend B——— entered the room. He had come many miles
to see me once more, and they made way for him to approach me as I lay. He placed his warm hand upon my
breast, and oh! the throb it sent through my heart! Again,
but almost unconsciously to myself, the impulse rushed
along my nerves, a bursting sensation seized my chest, a
tingling ran through my frame, a crashing, jarring sensation, as if the tense nervous cords were vibrating to some
sudden and severe shock, took hold on me; and then, after
one violent convulsive throe which brought the blood from
my mouth and eyes, my heart swelled, at first slowly, then
faster, and the nerves reverberated, clank! clank! respon-
sive to the stroke. At the same time the chest expanded,
the muscles strained like the cordage of a ship in a heavy
sea, and I breathed once more. While thus the faint
impulse to returning life was given, the dread thought

flashed on me that it might not be real, and that to my own imagination alone were referable the phenomena I experienced. At the same instant the gloomy doubt crossed my mind it was dispelled, for I heard a cry of horror through the room, and the words, 'He is alive! he still lives!' from a number of voices around me. The noise and confusion increased. I heard them say, 'Carry out B—— before he sees him again—he has fainted!' Directions and exclamations of wonder and dread followed one upon another; and I can but call to mind the lifting me from the coffin, and the feeling of returning warmth I experienced, as I was placed before a fire, and supported by the arms of my friend.

"I will only add that after some weeks of painful debility I was again restored to health, having tasted the full bitterness of death."

CHAPTER XXVII.

THE STRANGE GUEST.

THE "Eil Wagen," into whose bowels I had committed myself on leaving Frankfort, rolled along for twenty-four hours before I could come to any determination as to whither I should go; for so is it that perfect liberty is sometimes rather an inconvenience, and a little despotism is now and then no bad thing; and at this moment I could have given a ten-gulden piece to any one who should have named my road, and settled my destination.

"Where are we?" said I, at length, as we straggled—nine horses and all—into a great vaulted *porte-cochère.*

"At the Koenig von Preussen, Mein Herr," said a yellow-haired waiter, who flourished a napkin about him in very professional style.

"Ah! very true; but in what town, city, or village, and in whose kingdom?"

"Ach du lieber Gott!" exclaimed he, with his eyes opened to their fullest extent. "Where would you be bn in the city of Hesse Cassel, in the Grand Duchy of Seiner Königlichen Hocheit——"

"Enough—more than enough! Let me have supper."

The "Speiss Saal" was crowded with travellers and townspeople as I entered; but the room was of great size, and a goodly table, amply provided, occupied the middle of it; taking my place at which, I went ahead through the sliced shoe-leather, yclept beef, the kalbs-braten and the gurkin salad, and all the other indigestible abominations of that light meal a German takes before he lies down at night. The company were, with the exception of a few military men, of that nondescript class every German town abounds with—a large-headed, long-haired, plodding-looking generation, with huge side-pockets in their trousers, from one of which a cherry-wood pipe-stick is sure to project; civil, obliging, good sort of people they are, but by no means remarkable for intelligence or agreeability. But then, what mind could emerge from beneath twelve solid inches of beetroot and bouilli, and what brain could bear immersion in "Bavarian beer?"

One never can understand fully how atrocious the tyranny of Napoleon must have been in Germany, until he has visited that country and seen something of its inhabitants. Then only can one compute what must the hurricane have been that convulsed the waters of such a land-locked bay. Never was there a people so little disposed to compete with their rulers—never was obedience more thoroughly an instinct. The whole philosophy of the German's mind teaches him to look within, rather than without; his own resources are more his object in life than the enjoyment of state privileges; and to his peaceful temper endurance is a pleasanter remedy than resistance. Almost a Turk in his love of tranquillity, he has no sympathy with revolutions or public disturbances of any kind, and the provocation must indeed be great when he arouses himself to resist it. That, when he is thus called on, he can act with energy and vigour, the campaigns of 1813 and 1814 abundantly testify. Twice the French armies had to experience the heavy retribution on unjust invasion; both Spain and

Germany repaid the injuries they had endured, but with a characteristic difference of spirit. In the one case, it was the desultory attacks of savage guerillas, animated by the love of plunder as much as by patriotism; in the other, the rising of a great people to defend their homes and altars, presented the glorious spectacle of a nation going forth to the fight. The wild notes of the Basque bugle rang not out with such soul-stirring effect as the beautiful songs of Korner, heard beside the watch fire or at the peasant's hearth. The conduct of their own princes might have debased the national spirit of any other people; but the German's attachment to Vaterland is not a thing of courtly rule, nor conventional agreement. He loves the land and the literature of his fathers; he is proud of the good faith and honesty which are the acknowledged traits of Saxon character; he holds to the "sittliche Leben," the orderly domestic habits of his country; and as he wages not a war of aggression on others, he resists the spoliation of an enemy on the fields of his native country

When the French revolution first broke out, the students were amongst its most ardent admirers; the destruction of the Bastile was celebrated among the secret festivals of the Burschenscraft, and although the fever was a brief one, and never extended among the more thinking portion of the nation, to that same enthusiasm for liberty was owing the great burst of national energy that in 1813 convulsed the land from the Baltic to the Tyrol, and made Leipsic the compensation for Jena.

With all his grandeur of intellect, Napoleon never understood the national character—perhaps he may have despised it. One of his most fatal errors, undoubtedly, was the little importance he attached to the traits which distinguish one country from another, and the seeming indifference with which he propounded notions of government diametrically opposed to all the traditions and prejudices of those for whom they were intended. The great desire for centralization, the ambition to make France the heart of Europe, through whose impulse the life-blood should circulate over the entire Continent, to merge all distinctions of race and origin, and make Frenchmen of one quarter of the globe, was a stupendous idea; and, if

nations were enrolled in armies, might not be impossible.
The effort to effect it, however, cost him the greatest
throne of Christendom.

The French rule in Spain, in Italy, and in Holland, so
far from conciliating the goodwill and affection of the
people, has sown the seeds of that hatred to France in each
of these countries, that a century will not eradicate;
while no greater evidence of Napoleon's ignorance of
national character need be adduced, than in the expectations he indulged in the event of his landing an army in
England.

His calculation on support from any part of the British
people,—no matter how opposed to the ministry of the
day, or how extreme in their wishes for extended liberties,
was the most chimerical thought that ever entered the
brain of man. Very little knowledge of our country might
have taught him that the differences of party spirit never
survive the mere threat of foreign invasion; that however
Englishmen may oppose each other, they reserve a very
different spirit of resistance for the stranger who should
attack their common country; and that party, however it
may array men in opposite ranks, is itself but the evidence
of patriotism, seeking different paths for its development.

It was at the close of a little reverie to this purpose,
that I found myself sitting with one other guest at the
long table of the "Speiss Saal;" the rest had dropped off
one by one, leaving him in the calm enjoyment of his
meerschaum and his cup of black coffee.

There was something striking in the air and appearance
of this man, and I could not help regarding him closely;
he was about fifty years of age, but with a carriage as
erect and a step as firm as any man of twenty. A large
white moustache met his whiskers of the same colour, and
hung in heavy curl over his upper lip; his forehead was
high and narrow, and his eyes, deeply set, were of a green-
ish hue, and shaded by large eyebrows that met when he
frowned. His dress was a black frock, braided in Prussian
taste, and decorated by a single cordon, which hung not
over the breast, but on an empty sleeve of his coat, for
I now perceived that he had lost his right arm near the
shoulder. That he was a soldier, and had seen service, the

most careless observer could have detected; his very look and bearing bespoke the militaire. He never spoke to any one during supper, and from that circumstance, as well as his dissimilarity to the others, I judged him to be a traveller. There are times when one is more than usually disposed to let Fancy take the bit in her mouth and run off with them; and so I suffered myself to weave a story, or rather a dozen stories, for my companion, and did not perceive that while I was inventing a history for him, he had most ungratefully decamped, leaving me in a cloud of tobacco-smoke and difficult conjectures.

When I descended to the Saal the next morning I found him there before me; he was seated at breakfast before one of the windows, which commanded a view over the Platz and the distant mountains. And here let me ask,—Have you ever been in Hesse Cassel? The chances are—not. It is the highroad—nowhere. You neither pass it going to Berlin or Dresden. There is no wonder of scenery or art to attract strangers to it, and yet if accident should bring you thither, and plant you in the " König von Preussen," with no pressing necessity urging you onward, there are many less pleasant things you could do than spend a week there. The hotel stands on one side of a great platz, or square, at either side of which, the theatre and a museum form the other two wings; the fourth being left free of building, is occupied by a massive railing of most laboured tracery, which opens to a wide gate in a broad flight of steps, descending about seventy feet into a spacious park. The tall elms and beech trees can be seen waving their tops over the grille above, and seeming, from the Platz, like young timber; beyond, and many miles away, can be seen the bold chain of the " Taunus" mountains stretching to the clouds, forming altogether a view which, for extent and splendour, I know of no city can present the equal. I could scarce restrain my admiration, and as I stood actually rivetted to the spot, I was totally inattentive to the second summons of the waiter, informing me that my breakfast awaited me in another part of the room.

" What, yonder?" said I, in some disappointment at being so far removed from all chance of the prospect.

"Perhaps you would join me here, sir," said the officer, rising, and with a most affable air, saluting me.

"If not an intrusion——"

"By no means," said he; "I am a passionate admirer of that view myself. I have known it many years, and I always feel happy when a stranger participates in my enjoyment of it."

I confess I was no less gratified by the opportunity thus presented of forming an acquaintance with the officer himself than with the scenery, and I took my seat with much pleasure. As we chatted away, about the town and the surrounding country, he half expressed a curiosity at my taking a route so little travelled by my countrymen, and seemed much amused by my confession that the matter was purely accidental, and that frequently I left the destination of my ramble to the halting-place of the diligence.

As English eccentricity can, in a foreigner's estimation, carry any amount of absurdity, he did not set me down for a madman, which, had I been French or Italian, he most certainly would have done, and only smiled slightly at my efforts to defend a procedure, in his eyes so ludicrous.

"You confess," said I, at last, somewhat nettled by the indifference with which he heard my most sapient arguments,—"you confess on what mere casualties every event of life turns : what straws decide the whole destiny of a man, and what mere trivial circumstances influence the fate of whole nations, and how, in our wisest and most matured plans, some unexpected contingency is ever arising to disconcert and disarrange us; why, then, not go a step farther,—leave more to fate, and reserve all our efforts to behave well and sensibly, wherever we may be placed,—in whatever situations thrown,—as we shall then have fewer disappointments, we shall at least enjoy a more equable frame of mind, to combat with the world's chances."

"True, possibly, if a man were to lead a life of idleness, such a wayward course might suffice him as well as any other; but, bethink you, it is not thus men have wrought great deeds, and won high names for themselves. It is not by fickleness and caprice, by indolent yielding to the accident of the hour, that reputations have been acquired——"

"You speak," said I, interrupting him at this place,—
"you speak as if humble men like myself were to occupy
their place in history, and not lie down in the dust of the
churchyard undistinguishable and forgotten."

"When they cease to act otherwise than to deserve
commemoration, rely upon it their course is a false one.
Our conscience may be—indeed often is—a bribed judge;
and it is only by representing to ourselves how our modes
of acting and thinking would tell upon the minds of
others, reading of, but not knowing us, that we arrive at
that certain rule of right, so difficult in many worldly trials."

"And do you think a man becomes happier by this?"

"I did not say happier," said he, with a sorrowful emphasis on the last word. "He may be better"

With that he rose from his seat, and looking at his
watch he apologized for leaving me so suddenly, and
departed.

"Who is the gentleman that has just gone out?" asked
I of the waiter.

"The Baron von Elgenheim," replied he; "but they
mostly call him the Black Colonel. Not for his moustaches," added he, laughing with true German familiarity,
"they are white enough, but he always wears mourning."

"Does he belong to Hesse, then?"

"Not he; he's an 'Ouslander' of some sort—a Swabian,
belike; but he comes here every year, and stays three or
four weeks at a time. And, droll enough too, though he
has been doing so for fifteen or sixteen years, he has not a
single acquaintance in all Cassel, indeed, I never saw
him speak to a stranger till this morning."

These particulars, few as they were, all stimulated my
curiosity to see more of the colonel, but he did not
present himself at the *table d'hôte* on that day or the
following one, and I only met him by chance in the Park,
when a formal salute, given with cold politeness, seemed
to say our acquaintance was at an end.

Now there are certain inns, which, by a strange magnetism, are felt as homes at once; there is a certain air of
quietude and repose about them that strike you when you
enter, and gain on you every hour of your stay. The
landlord, too, has a bearing compounded of cordiality and

respect; and the waiter, divining your tastes and partiali-
ties, falls quickly into your ways, and seems to regard you
as an *habitué* while you are yet a stranger; while the
ringletted young lady at the bar, who passed you the first
day on the stairs with a well-practised indifference, now
accosts you with a smile and a curtsey, and already believes
you an old acquaintance.

To an indolent man like myself, these houses are impossible to leave. If it be summer, you are sure to have
a fresh bouquet in your bed-room every morning when you
awake; in winter, the garçon has discovered how you
like your slippers toasted on the fender, and your robe-de-
chambre airing on the chair, the cook learns your taste
in cutlets, and knows to a nicety how to season your
"omelette aux fines herbes;" the very washerwoman of
the establishment has counted the plaits in your shirt,
and wouldn't put one more or less for any bribery. By
degrees, too, you become a kind of confidant of the whole
household. The host tells you of ma'mselle's fortune, and
the match on the "tapis" for her, and all its difficulties
and advantages, contra and pro, the waiter has revealed
to you a secret of passion for the chambermaid—but for
which, he would be Heaven knows how many thousand
miles off, in some wonderful place, where the wages would
enable him to retire in less than a twelvemonth; and even
"Boots," while depositing your Wellingtons before the
fire, has unburdened his sorrows and his hopes, and asks
your advice, "if he shouldn't become a soldier?"

When this hour arrives, the house is your own. Let
what will happen, *your* fire burns brightly in your bed-
room; let who will come, your dinner is cared for to a
miracle. The newspaper, coveted by a dozen, and eagerly
asked for, is laid by for your reading; you are, then, in
poet's words,—

"Liber, honoratus, pulcher—Rex denique Regum;"

and, let me tell you, there are worse sovereignties.

Apply this to the "König von Preussen," and wonder not
if I found myself its inhabitant for three weeks afterwards.

CHAPTER XXVIII.

"THE PARK."

In somewhat less than a fortnight's time, I had made a bowing acquaintance with some half-dozen good subjects of Hesse, and formed a chatting intimacy with some three or four frequenters of the *table d'hôte*, with whom I occasionally strolled out of an afternoon into the Park, to drink coffee, and listen to the military band that played there every evening. The quiet uniformity of the life pleased and never wearied me; for, happily—or unhappily, as some would deem it—mine is one of those tame and commonplace natures which need not costly amusements, nor expensive tastes to occupy it. I enjoy the society of agreeable people with a gusto few possess; I can also put up with the association with those of a different stamp, feeling sensibly how much more I am on a level with them, and how little pretension I have to find myself among the others. Fortunately, too, I have no sympathy with the pleasures which wealth alone commands. It was a taste denied me; I neither affect to undervalue their importance, nor sneer at their object; I simply confess that the faculty which renders them desirable was by some accident omitted in my nature, and I never yet felt the smallness of my fortune a source of regret. There is no such happiness, to my notion, as that which enables a man to be above the dependence on others for his pleasures and amusements—to have the sources of enjoyment in his own mind, and to feel that his own thoughts, and his own reflections, are his best wealth. There is no selfishness in this—far from it—the stores thus laid by make a man a better member of society—more ready to assist—more able to advise his fellow-men. By standing aloof from the game of life, you can better estimate the chances of success and the skill of the players; and as you have no stake in the issue, the odds are that your opinion is a correct one. But, better than all, how many enjoyments which, to the glitter of wealth, or the grandeur of a high position, would seem insignificant and valueless, are to the humble man sources of hourly delight, and is our happiness anything but an aggregate of these grains of pleasure ? There is as much philosophy in the child's toy as the nobleman's coronet;—all the better for him who can limit his desires to the attainable, and be satisfied with what lies within his reach. I have practised the system for a life long, and feel that if I now enjoy much of the buoyancy and the spirit of more youthful days, it is because I have never taxed my strength beyond its ability, and striven for more than I could justly pretend to. There is something of indolence in all this—I know there is—but I was born under a lazy star, and I cannot say I regret my destiny.

From this little *exposé* of my tastes and habits it may be gathered that Cassel suited me perfectly. The air of repose which rests on these little secluded capitals has something—to me at least—inexpressibly pleasurable : the quaint, old-fashioned equipages, drawn along at a gentle amble—the obsolete dress of the men in livery— the studious ceremony of the passers to each other—the absence of all bustle—the primitive objects of sale exposed in the various shops—all contrasting so powerfully with the wealth-seeking tumult of richer communities—suggest thoughts of tranquillity and contentment. They are the bourgeoisie of the great political world ; debarred from the great game which empires and kingdoms are playing, they retire within the limits of their own narrow but safe enjoyments, with ample means for every appliance of com- fort; they seek not to astonish the world by any display, but content themselves with the homely happiness within their reach.

Every day I lingered here I felt this conviction the stronger. The small interests which occupied the public mind originated no violent passions, no exaggerated party spirit. The journals—those indices of a nation's mind— contained less politics than criticism ; an amicable little contention about the site of a new fountain, or the posi- tion of an elector's statue, was the extent of any discus- sion ; while at every opportunity crept out some little congratulating expression on the goodness of the harvest, the abundance of the vintage, or, what was scarcely less valued, the admirable operatic company which had just arrived. These may seem very petty incidents for men to pass their lives amongst, thought I, but still they all seem very happy: there is much comfort, there is no poverty. Like the court whist-table, where the points are only for silver groschen, the amusement is just as great, and no one is ruined by high play.

I'm not sure but that I should have made an excellent Hessian ! thought I, as I deposited two little silver pieces, about the size of a spangle, on the table, in payment for a very appetizing little supper, and an ink-bottleful of Rhine wine ;—and now for the coffee

I was seated beneath a great chestnut tree, whose spreading branches shaded me from the rays of the setting sun that came slanting to my very feet. At a short distance off sat a little family party—grandfather, grandchildren, and all—there was no mistaking them ; they were eating their supper in the park, possibly in honour of some domestic fête. Yes, there could be no doubt of it; it was the birthday of that pretty, dark-eyed little girl, of some ten years of age, who wore a wreath of roses in her hair, and sat at the top of the table, beside the " Greis." A burst of delighted laughter broke from them all as I looked, and now I could see a little boy of scarce five years old. whose long yellow locks hung midway down his back; he was standing beside his sister's chair, and I could hear his infant voice reciting a little verse he had learned in honour of the day. The little man, whose gravity contrasted so ludicrously with the merry looks about, went through his task as steadily as a court preacher holding forth before royalty ; an occasional breach of memory would make him now and then turn his head to one side, where an elder sister knelt, and then he would go on again as before. I wished much to catch the words, but could only hear the refrain of each verse, which he always repeated louder than the rest,—

" Da, sind die Tage lang genuch
Da, sind die nachte mild "

Scarcely had he finished when his mother caught him

to her arms and kissed him a hundred times, while the others struggled to take him, the little fellow clinging to her neck with all his strength.

It was a picture of such happiness, to look on it were alone a blessing. I have that night's looks and cheerful voices fresh in my memory, and have thought of them many a long mile away from where I then heard them.

A slight noise beside me made me turn round, and I saw the black Colonel, as the waiter called him, and whom I had not met for several days past. He was seated on a bench near, but with his back towards me, and I could perceive he was evidently unaware of my presence. I had, I must confess it, felt somewhat piqued at his avoidance of me, for such the distant recognition with which he saluted me seemed to imply. He had made the first advances himself, and it was scarcely fair that he should have thus abruptly stopped short, after in-viting acquaintance While I was meditating a retreat, he turned suddenly about, and then, taking off his hat, saluted me with a courtly politeness quite different from his ordinary manner.

"I see, sir," said he, with a very sweet smile, as he looked towards the little group, "I see, sir, you are indeed an admirer of pretty prospects."

Few and simple as the words were, they were enough to reconcile me to the speaker; his expression, as he spoke them, had a depth of feeling in it, which showed that his heart was touched.

After some commonplace remark of mine on the sim-plicity of German domestic habits, and the happy im-munity they enjoyed from that rage of fashion which in other countries involved so many in rivalling with others wealthier than themselves, the Colonel assented to the observation, but expressed his sorrow that the period of primitive tastes and pleasures was rapidly passing away. The French Revolution first, and subsequently the wars of the Empire, had done much to destroy the native sim-plicity of German character; while, in latter days, the tide of travel had brought a host of vulgar rich people, whose gold corrupted the once happy peasantry, suggest-ing wants and tastes they never knew, nor need to know.

" As for the great cities of Germany," continued he, "they have scarcely a trace left of their ancient nationality. Vienna and Berlin, Dresden and Munich, are but poor imitations of Paris; it is only in the old and less visited towns, such as Nuremberg or Augsburg, that the 'Alt Deutsch' habits still survive. Some few of the Grand Ducal States—Weimar, for instance—preserve the primitive simplicity of former days even in courtly etiquette, and there, really, the government is paternal, in the fullest sense of the term.

" You would think it strange, would you not, to dine at court at four o'clock, and to see the grand ducal ministers and their ladies—the *élite* of a little world of their own—proceeding, many of them on foot, in court-dress, to dinner with their sovereign? Strange, too, would you deem it—dinner over—to join a promenade with the party in the park, where all the bourgeoisie of the town are strolling about with their families, taking their coffee and their tea, and only interrupting their conversation or their pleasure to salute the Grand Duke or Grand Duchess, and respectfully bid them a 'good e'en.' And then, as it grew later, to return to the palace for a little whist or a game of chess, or, better still, to make one of that delightful circle in the drawing-room where Goethe was sitting. Yes, such is the life of Weimar. The luxury of your great capitals—the gorgeous *salons* of London and Paris—the voluptuous pleasures which unbounded wealth and all its train of passions beget—are utterly unknown there; but there is a world of pure enjoyment and of intercourse with high and gifted minds which more than repay you for their absence.

" A few years more, and all this will be but 'matter for an old man's memory.' Increased facilities of travel, and greater knowledge of language, erase nationality most rapidly. The venerable habits transmitted from father to son for centuries—the traditional customs of a people —cannot survive a caricature nor a satire. The 'Esprit Moqueur' of France and the insolent wealth of England have left us scarce a vestige of our Vaterland. Our literature is at this instant a thing of shreds and patches —bad translations of bad books. The deep wisdom and

the racy humour of Jean Paul are unknown; while the
vapid wit of a modern French novel is extolled. They
prefer the false glitter of Dumas and Balzac to the sterling
gold of Schiller and Herder; and even Leipsic and
Waterloo have not freed us from the slavish adulation of
the conquered to the conqueror."

" What would you have?" said I.

" I would have Germany a nation once more—a nation
whose limits should reach from the Baltic to the Tyrol.
Her language, her people, her institutions, entitle her to
be such, and it is only when parcelled into kingdoms and
petty states, divided by the artful policy of foreign powers,
that our nationality pines and withers."

" I can easily conceive," said I, " that the Confederation
of the Rhine must have destroyed, in a great measure,
the patriotic feeling of Western Germany, the peasantry
were sold as mercenaries; the nobles, little better, took
arms in a cause many of them hated and detested——"

" I must stop you here," said he, with a smile; "not
that you would, or could, say that which should wound
my feelings, but you might hurt your own when you came
to know that he to whom you are speaking served in that
army. Yes, sir, I was a soldier of Napoleon."

Although nothing could be more unaffectedly easy than
his manner as he said this, I feared I might already have
said too much; indeed, I knew not the exact expressions
I had used, and there was a pause of some minutes,
broken at length by the Colonel saying,—

" Let us walk towards the town; for, if I mistake not,
they close the gates of the Park at midnight, and I believe
we are the only persons remaining here now."

Chattering of indifferent matters, we arrived at the
hotel; and after accepting an invitation to accompany the
baron the next day to Wilhelms Höhe, I wished him
good night and retired.

CHAPTER XXIX.

THE BARON'S STORY.

EVERY one knows how rapidly acquaintance ripens into intimacy when mere accident throws people together in situations where they have no other occupation than each other's society, days do the work of years, confidences spring up where mere ceremonies would have been interchanged before, and, in fact, a freedom of thought and speech as great as we enjoy in our oldest friendships. Such, in less than a fortnight, was the relation between the Baron and myself. We breakfasted together every morning, and usually sallied forth afterwards into the country, generally on horseback, and only came back to dinner, a ramble in the Park concluding our day.

I still look back to those days as amongst the pleasantest of my life, for although the temper of my companion's mind was melancholic, it seemed rather the sadness induced by some event of his life than the depression resulting from a desponding temperament—a great difference, by the way; as great as between the shadow we see at noonday and the uniform blackness of midnight. He had evidently seen much of the world, and in the highest class; he spoke of Paris as he knew it in the gorgeous time of the Empire—of the Tuileries, when the *salons* were crowded with kings and sovereign princes—of Napoleon, too, as he saw him, wet and cold, beside the bivouack fire, interchanging a rude jest with some "gronard" of the "Garde," or commanding, in tones of loud superiority, to the marshals who stood awaiting his orders. The Emperor, he said, never liked the Germans, and although many evinced a warm attachment to his person and his cause, they were not Frenchmen, and he could not forgive it. The Alsatians he trusted, and was partial to; but his sympathies stopped short at the Rhine, and he always felt that if fortune turned, the wrongs of Germany must have their recompense.

While speaking freely on these matters, I remarked that he studiously avoided all mention of his own services; a mere passing mention of "I was there," or, "My regiment was engaged in it," being the extent of his observations regarding himself. His age and rank, his wound itself, showed that he must have seen service in its most active times, and my curiosity was piqued to learn something of his own history, but which I did not feel myself entitled to inquire.

We were returning one evening from a ramble in the country, when stopping to ask a drink at a wayside inn, we found a party of soldiers in possession of the only room, where they were regaling themselves with wine; while a miserable-looking object, bound, with his arms behind his back, sat pale and woe-begone in one corner of the apartment, his eyes fixed on the floor, and the tears slowly stealing along his cheeks.

"What is it?" asked I of the landlord, as I peeped in at the half-open door.

"A deserter, sir——"

The word was scarcely spoken when the Colonel let fall the cup he held in his hand, and leaned, almost fainting, against the wall.

"Let us move on," said he. in a voice scarcely articulate, while the sickness of death seemed to work in his features.

"You are ill," said I, "we had better wait——"

"No, not here—not here," repeated he anxiously; "in a moment I shall be well again—lend me your arm."

We walked on, at first slowly, for with each step he tottered like one after weeks of illness; at last he rallied, and we reached Cassel in about an hour's time, during which he spoke but once or twice—"I must bid you a good night here," said he, as we entered the inn; "I feel but poorly, and shall hasten to bed" So saying, and without waiting for a word on my part, he squeezed my hand affectionately, and left me.

It was not in my power to dismiss from my mind a number of gloomy suspicions regarding the Baron, as I slowly wended my way to my room. The uppermost thought I had was, that some act of his past life—some piece of military severity, for which he now grieved deeply—had been brought back to his memory by the sight of the poor deserter. It was evident that the settled melancholy of his character referred to some circumstance or event of his life,—nothing confirmed this more than any chance allusions he would drop concerning his youthful days, which appeared to be marked by high daring and buoyant spirits

While I pondered over these thoughts, a noise in the inn-yard beneath my window attracted my attention, I leaned out and heard the Baron's servant giving orders for post-horses to be ready by daybreak to take his master's carriage to Meissner, while a courier was already preparing to have horses in waiting at the stages along the road.

Again my brain was puzzled to account for this sudden departure, and I could not repress a feeling of pique at his not having communicated his intention of going, which, considering our late intimacy, had been only common courtesy. This little slight—for such I felt it—did not put me in better temper with my friend, nor more disposed to be lenient in judging him, and I was already getting deeper and deeper in my suspicions, when a gentle tap came to my door, and the Baron's servant entered, with a request that I would kindly step over to his master's room—who desired to see me particularly.

I did not delay a moment, but followed the man along the corridor, and entered the *salon*, which I found in total darkness.

"The Baron is in bed, sir," said the servant; "but he wishes to see you in his room."

On a small camp bed, which showed it to have been once a piece of military equipment, the Baron was lying, he had not undressed, but merely thrown on his robe de chambre and removed his cravat from his throat; his one hand was pressed closely on his face, and as he stretched it out to grasp mine, I was horror-struck at the altered expression of his countenance. The eyes, bloodshot and wild, glanced about the room with a hurried and searching look, while his parched lips muttered rapidly some indistinct sounds. I saw that he was very ill, and asked him if it were not as well he should have some advice.

" No, my friend, no," said he, with more composure in his manner ; " the attack is going off now. It rarely lasts so long as this. You have never heard perhaps of that dreadful malady which physicians call ' Angina,' the most agonizing of all diseases, and I believe the least under-stood I have been subject to it for some years, and as there is no remedy, and as any access of it may prove fatal, life is held on but poor conditions——"

He paused for a second or two, then resumed, but with a manner of increased excitement "They will shoot him—yes, I have heard it all; it's the second time he has deserted—there is not a chance left him.——I must leave this by daybreak—I must get me far away before to-morrow evening—there would not come a stir—the slight-est sound, but—I should fancy I heard the ' fusillade.' "

I saw now clearly that the deserter's fate had made the impression which brought on the attack, and although my curiosity to learn the origin of so powerful a sensibility was greater than ever, I would willingly have sacrificed it to calming his mind, and inducing thoughts of less violent excitement.

"I was senior lieutenant of the ' Carabiniers de la Garde ' at eighteen," said he, speaking with a thick and hurried utterance. "We were quartered at Strasbourg; more than half of the regiment were my countrymen, some from the very village where I was born One there was, a lad of sixteen, my schoolfellow and companion when a boy; he was the only child of a widow whose husband had fallen in the wars of the Revolution. When he was drawn in the conscription no less than seven others pre-sented themselves to go in his stead, but old Girardon, who commanded the brigade, simply returned for answer, ' Such brave men are worthy to serve France; let them all be enrolled,' and they were so. A week afterwards Louis my schoolfellow deserted. He swam the Rhine at Kehl, and the same evening reached his mother's cottage He was scarcely an hour at home when a party of his own regiment captured him; he was brought back to Stras-bourg, tried by torchlight, and condemned to death.

" The officer who commanded the party for his execu-tion fainted when the prisoner was led out; the men,

horror-struck at the circumstance, grounded their arms
and refused to fire. Girardon was on the ground in an
instant; he galloped up to the youth who knelt there with
his arms bound behind him, and drawing a pistol from his
holster, placed the muzzle on his forehead, and shot him
dead! The men were sent back to the barracks, and by a
general order of the same day were drafted into different
regiments throughout the army; the officer was degraded
to the ranks—it was myself."

It was with the greatest difficulty he was enabled to
conclude this brief story; the sentences were uttered with
short, almost convulsive efforts, and when it was over, he
turned up his face, and seemed buried in grief.

"You think," said he, turning round and taking my
hand in his,—"you think that the sad scene has left me
such as you see me now; would to Heaven my memory
were charged with but that mournful event. Alas! it is
not so." He wiped a tear from his eye, and with a falter-
ing voice continued. "You shall hear my story; I never
breathed it to one living, nor do I think now that my
time is to be long here."

Having fortified his nerves with a powerful opiate, the
only remedy in his dreadful malady, he began,—

"I was reduced to the ranks in Strasbourg; four years
after, day for day, I was named Chef de Bataillon on the
field of Elchingen. Of twelve hundred men our battalion
came out of action with one hundred and eighty; the
report of the corps that night was made by myself as
senior officer, and I was but a captain.

"'Who led the division of stormers along the covered
way?' said the Emperor, as I handed our list of killed and
wounded to Duroc, who stood beside him.

"'It was I, sire.'

"'You are major of the 7th Regiment,' said he.
'Now there is another of yours I must ask for; how is he
called that surprised the Austrian battery on the Dorran
Kopf?'

"'Himself again, sire,' interrupted Duroc, who saw
that I hesitated how to answer him.

"'Very well, very well indeed, Elgenheim; report him
as "Chef de Bataillon," Duroc, and colonel of his regi-

ment. There, sir, your countrymen call me unjust and ungenerous. Show them your " brevet " to-night, and do *you*, at least, be a witness in my favour.'

" I bowed and uttered a few words of gratitude, and was about to withdraw, when Duroc, who had been whispering something in the Emperor's ear, said aloud, ' I'm certain he's the man to do it. Elgenheim, His Majesty has a most important despatch to forward to Innspruck to Marshal Ney. It will require something more than mere bravery to effect this object; it will demand no small share of address also ; the passes above Saltzbourg are in the possession of the Tyrolese sharpshooters ; two videttes have been cut off within a week, and it will require at least the force of a regiment to push through. Are you willing to take the command of such a party ?'

" 'If His Majesty will honour me with——'

" 'Enough, sir,' interrupted the Emperor ; ' we have no time to lose here—your orders shall be ready by daybreak —you shall have a squadron of Chasseurs, as scouts, and be prepared to march to-morrow.'

" The following day I left the camp with my party of eight hundred men, and moved to the southward. It may seem strange to think of a simple despatch of a few lines requiring such a force ; indeed, I thought so at the time ; but I lived to see two thousand men employed on a similar service in Spain, and, worse still, not always successfully. In less than a week we approached Landberg, and entered the land of mountains. The defiles, which at first were sufficiently open to afford space for manœuvres, gradually contracted, while the mountains at either side became wilder and more lofty; a low brushwood of holly and white oak, scarce hiding the dark granite rocks that seemed actually piled loosely one above another, and ready to crash down at the least impulse. In the valleys themselves the mountain rivulets were collected into a strong current, which rattled along amid masses of huge rock, and swept in broad flakes of foam, sometimes across the narrow road beside it. Here, frequently, not more than four men could march abreast , and as the winding of the glens never permitted a view of much more than a mile in advance, the position, in case of attack, was far from satisfactory. For three entire days we continued our march, adopting, as we went, every precaution against surprise I could think of; a portion of the cavalry were always employed as *éclaireurs* in advance, and the remainder brought up the rear, following the main body at the distance of a mile or two. The stupendous crags that frowned above, leaving us but a narrow streak of blue sky visible—the mournful echoes of the deep valleys—the hoarse roar of the waters —or the wild notes of the black eagle—conspired to throw an impression of sadness over our party, which each struggled against in vain. It was now the third morning since we entered the Tyrol, and yet never had we seen one single inhabitant. The few cottages along the roadside were empty, the herds had disappeared from the hills, and a dreary waste, unrelieved by one living object, stretched far away before us. My men felt the solitude far more deeply than had every step been contested with them. They were long inured to danger, and would willingly have encountered an enemy of mortal mould; but the gloomy images their minds conjured up were foes they had never anticipated nor met before. As for myself, the desolation brought but one thought before me; and as I looked upon the wild wastes of mountain, where the chalet of the hunter or the cot of the shepherd reared its humble head, the fearful injustice of invasive war came fully to my mind. Again and again did I ask myself, what could greatness and power gain by conflict with poverty like this? How could the humble dweller in these lonely regions become an object of kingly vengeance, or his bleak hills a thing for kingly ambition? and, more than all, what could the Tyrol peasant ever have done thus to bring down upon his home the devastating tide of war? To think that but a few days back and the cheerful song of the hunter resounded through those glens, and the laugh of children was heard in those cottages where now all was still as death. We passed a small cluster of houses at the opening of a glen—it could scarce be called a village—and here, so lately had they been deserted, the embers were yet warm on the hearth, and in one hut the table was spread and the little meal laid out, while they who were to have partaken of it were perhaps miles away.

"Plunged in these sad reflections, I sat on a little eminence of rock behind the party, while they reposed themselves during the heat of noon. The point I occupied afforded a view for some miles of the road we had travelled, and I turned to see if our cavalry detachment were not coming up; when as I strained my eyes in the direction, I thought I could perceive an object moving along the road, and stooping from time to time. I seized my glass, and now could distinctly perceive the figure of a man coming slowly onwards. That we had not passed him on the way was quite evident, and he must therefore have been on the mountain or in concealment beside the road.

" Either thought was sufficient to excite my suspicion, and without a second's delay I sprang into the saddle, and putting my horse to his speed galloped back as fast as I could. As I came nearer I half fancied I saw the figure move to one side and then back again, as though irresolute how to act; and fearing lest he should escape me by taking to the mountain, I called to him aloud to halt. He stood still as I spoke, and I now came up beside him. He was an old man, seemingly above eighty years of age; his hair and beard were white as snow, and he was bent almost double with time; his dress was the common costume of a Tyrolese, except that he wore in addition a kind of cloak with a loose hood, such as the pilgrims wear in Austria; and indeed his staff and leathern bottle bespoke him such. To all my questions as to the road and the villages he replied in a kind of *patois* I could make nothing of; and although tolerably well versed in all the dialects of Southern Germany, his was quite unintelligible to me. Still, the question how came he there was one of great moment. If *he* had been concealed while we passed so near, why not others? His age and decrepitude forbade the thought of his having descended the mountain, and so I felt puzzled in no common degree. As these doubts passed through my mind, the poor old man stood trembling at my side as though fearing what fate might be in store for him. Anxious to recompense him for the trouble I had caused him, I drew out my purse, but no sooner did he see it than he motioned it away with his hand, and shook his head in token of refusal.

" ' Come, then,' said I, ' I've met a pilgrim ere this would
not refuse a cup of wine;' and with that I unslung my
canteen and handed it to him. This he seized eagerly and
drained it to the bottom, holding up both hands when he
had finished, and muttering something I conjectured to be
a prayer. He was the only living object belonging to the
country that I had seen,—a sudden whim seized me, and I
gave him back the flask, making a sign that he should
keep it.

' He clutched the gift with the avidity of old age, and
sitting down upon a stone began to admire it with eager
eyes. Despairing of making him understand a word, and
remembering it was time to move forward, I waved my
hand in adieu and galloped back.

" The cavalry detachment came up soon after ; and guess
my astonishment to learn that they had not seen the old
man on the road, nor, although they narrowly watched the
mountain, perceived any living thing near. I confess I
could not dismiss a feeling of uncomfortable suspicion from
my mind, and all the reflections I bestowed upon his age
and decrepitude were very far from reassuring me. More
than once I regretted not having brought him forward with
us ; but again the fact of having such a prisoner would
have exposed me to ridicule at head-quarters, if not a heavy
reprimand.

" Full of these reflections, I gave the word to move forward. Our object was, if possible, to reach the opening of
the Mittenwald before night, where I was informed that
a small dismantled fort would afford a secure position, if
attacked by any mountain party. On comparing the
route of the map, however, with the road, I discovered
that the real distances were in many cases considerably
greater than they were set down, and perceived that with
all our efforts we could not hope to emerge from the
ravine of the Schwartz-thal before the following day.
This fact gave me much uneasiness ; for I remembered
having heard that as the glen approaches the Mittenwald,
the pass is narrowed to a mere path, obstructed at every
step by masses of fallen rock ; while the mountains, more
thickly covered with underwood, afford shelter for any
party lying in ambush. Nothing could be more fatal

than an attack in such a position, where a few determined
men in front could arrest the march of a whole regiment;
while from the close sides of the pass, a well-directed fire
must sweep the ranks of those below.

"This gorge, which, narrowing to a mere portal, has
been called the Mitten-Thor, was the scene of some fearful
struggles between the French troops and the Tyrolese, and
was always believed to be the most dangerous of all the
passes of the Tyrol; every despatch to the head-quarters
of the army, referring to the disasters that befell there,
and suggesting plans for the occupation of the block-
house near it, as a means of defence.

"By the advice of my officers, one of whom was
already acquainted with all the circumstances of the
ground, I determined on halting at a part of the glen
about two miles from the Mitten-Thor, where a slight
widening of the valley afforded more space for movement
if attacked; and here we arrived as evening was beginning to fall. It was a small oval spot between the mountains, through which a little stream ran, dividing it almost
into equal portions, and crossed by a bridge of rude
planks, to which a little path conducted, and led up the
mountains.

"Scarcely were our watchfires lighted when the moon
rose, and although herself not visible to our eyes as we
lay in the deep valley, a rich flood of silver light fell on
one range of the mountains, marking out every cliff and
crag with the distinctness of day. The opposite mountain,
wrapt in deepest shadow was one mass of undistinguishable blackness, and seemed to frown ominously and
gloomily upon us. The men were wearied with a long
march, and soon laid down to rest beside their fires, and
save the low subdued hum of the little encampment, the
valley was in perfect silence. On the bridge, from which
the pass was visible for a good distance in both directions,
I had placed a look-out sentry; and a chain of patrols
were established around the bivouac.

"These arrangements, which occupied me some time,
being completed, I threw myself down beside my fire, and
prepared for sleep; but somehow, though I had passed
a day of fatigue and exertion, I could not slumber; every

time I closed my eyes the vision of the old pilgrim was
before me, and a vague, undefined feeling of apprehension
hung over me. I tried to believe it was a mere fancy,
attributable to the place, of whose terrors I had heard so
much ; but my mind dwelt on all the disasters of the
Schwartz-thal, and banished every desire for repose.

" As I lay there, thinking, my eyes were attracted by a
little, rocky point, about thirty feet above me on the
mountain, on which the full splendour of the moonlight
shone at intervals as the dark clouds drifted from before
her, and a notion took me—why and how I never could
explain to myself—to ascend the crag, and take a view
down the valley. A few minutes after and I was seated
on the rock, from which I could survey the pass and the
encampment stretched out beneath me. It was just such
a scene as Salvator used to paint ; the wild fantastic
mountains, bristling with rude pines and fragments of
granite ; a rushing torrent, splashing and boiling beneath ;
a blazing watch-fire, and the armed group around it,
their weapons glancing in the red light ; while, to add
to the mere picture, there came the monotonous hum
of the soldier's song as he walked to and fro upon his
post

" I sat a long while gazing at this scene ; many a
pleasant thought of that bandit life we Germans feel such
interest in, from Schiller's play, passing through my mind :
when I heard the rustling of the leaves, and a crackling
sound, as of broken branches, issue from the mountain,
almost directly above me. There was not a breath of
wind, not a leaf stirred, save there. I listened eagerly,
and was almost certain I could hear the sound of voices
talking in a low under tone. Cautiously stealing along,
I began to descend the mountain, when, as I turned a
projecting angle of the path, I saw the sentry on the bridge
with his musket at his shoulder, taking a steady and deliberate aim at some object in the direction of the noise.
While I looked he fired, a crashing sound of the branches
followed the report, and something like a cry, and as the
echoes died away in the distance, a heavy mass tumbled
over the cliff, and fell from ledge to ledge, till it rolled
into the deep grass below. I had but time to perceive it

was the corpse of a man fully armed, when the quick roll
of the drum beat to arms. In an instant the men were
formed, the cavalry standing beside their horses, and the
officers crowding around me for orders. It was the discharge of the sentry's musket had given the alarm ; for,
save himself, no one had seen anything Just then a wild
unearthly cry of 'Ha ! ha !' rung out from one mountain
and was answered from the other ; while the sounds,
increasing and multiplied by the echoes, floated hither and
thither, as though ten thousand voices were shouting
there ; they ceased—all was still for a few seconds, and
then a hail-storm of bullets tore through our ranks, and
the valley rang again with the roar of musketry. Every
cliff and crag, every tuft of brushwood, seemed to be occupied , while the incessant roll of the fire showed that our
assailants were in great numbers Resistance was vain—
our enemy was unseen—our men were falling at each
discharge—what was to be done ?—nothing remained but
to push forward to the Mittenwald, where, the valley
opening into a plain, we should be able to defend ourselves against any irregular troops that might be brought
against us. The order was given, and the men advanced
in a run, the cavalry leading the way. Meanwhile the
fire of the Tyrolese increased, and the fatal marksmen
seldom missed a shot ; two of our officers already lay
dead, and three others dangerously wounded could scarce
keep up with our party.

" 'The road is barricaded and entrenched,' cried the
sergeant of the Dragoons, gallopping back to the main
body in dismay.

" A cry broke from the soldiers as they heard the sad
tidings, while some springing from their ranks called out
' Forward, and to the storm !'

" Rushing to the head of these brave fellows, I waved
my cap, and cheered them on ; the others followed, and
we soon came in sight of the barrier, which was formed
of large trees thrown crossways, and forming, by their
massive trunks and interwoven branches, an obstacle far
beyond our power to remove. To climb the stockade was
our only chance, and on we rushed, but scarcely were we
within half-musket-shot, when a volley met us directed

point-blank—the leading files of the column went down like one man, and though others rushed eagerly forward, despair and desperation goading them, the murderous fire of the long rifles dealt death at every discharge ; and we stood among the cumbered corpses of our fellow comrades. By this time we were attacked in rear as well as front, and now, all hope gone, it only remained to sell life as dearly as we could.   One infuriate rush to break through the barricade had forced a kind of passage, through which, followed by a dozen others, I leaped, shouting to my men to follow.   The cry of my triumph was, however, met by a wilder still, for the same instant a party of Tyrolese, armed with the two-handed sword of their country, came down upon us.   The struggle was a brief and bloody one, man for man fell at either side, but overcome by numbers, I saw my companions drop dead or wounded around me. As for myself, I clove the leader through the skull with one stroke,—it was the last my arm ever dealt, the next instant it was severed from my body.   I fell covered with blood, and my assailant jumped upon my body, and drawing a short knife from his belt, was about to plunge it in my bosom, when a shout from a wounded Tyrolese at my side arrested the stroke, and I saw an uplifted arm stretched out, as if to protect me.   I have little memory after this.   I heard—I think I hear still—the wild shouts and the death-cries of my comrades as they fell beneath the arm of their enemies.   The slaughter was a dreadful one—of eight hundred and forty men, I alone survived that terrible night

" Towards daybreak I found myself lying in a cart upon some straw, beside another wounded man dressed in the uniform of the Tyrolese Jagers.   His head was fearfully gashed by a sabre cut, and a musket ball had shattered his forearm.   As I looked at him, a grim smile of savage glee lit up his pale features, and he looked from my wound to his own with a horrid significance.   All my efforts to learn the fate of my comrades were fruitless; he could neither comprehend me nor I him, and it was only by conjecturing from the tones and gestures of those who occasionally came up to the cart to speak to him, that I could learn the fearful reality.

" That day and the following one we journeyed onwards, but I knew nought of time. The fever of my
wound, increased by some styptic they had used to stop
the bleeding, had brought on delirium, and I raved of the
fight, and strove to regain my legs, and get free. To this
paroxysm, which lasted many days, a low lingering fever
succeeded, in which all consciousness was so slight, no
memory has remained to tell of my sensations.

" My first vivid sensation—it is before me as this
minute—was on entering the little mountain village of
the ' Marien Kreutz.' I was borne on a litter by four
men, for the path was inaccessible except to foot passengers. It was evening, and the long procession of the
wounded men wound its way up the mountain defile, and
along the little street of the village, which now was
crowded by the country people, who with sad and tearful
faces stood looking on their sons and brothers, or asking
for those whom they were never to behold again. The
little chapel of the village was converted into an hospital,
and here beds were brought from every cabin, and all the
preparations for tending the sick began with a readiness
that surprised me.

" As they bore me up the isle of the chapel, a voice
called out some words in Tyrolese ; the men halted and
turned round, and then carried me back into a small
chapelry, where a single sick man was lying, whom in an
instant I recognized as my wounded companion of the
road. With a nod of rude but friendly recognition, he
welcomed me, and I was placed near him on a straw mat-
trass stretched beneath the altar.

" Why I had been spared in the fearful carnage, and
for what destiny I was reserved, were thoughts which
rapidly gave way to others of deep despondency at my
fortune—a despair that made me indifferent to life. The
dreadful issue of the expedition would, I well knew, have
ruined more prosperous careers than mine in that service,
where want of success was the greatest of all crimes.
Careless of my fate, I lived on in gloomy apathy, not one
gleam of hope or comfort to shine upon the darkness of
my misery.

" This brooding melancholy took entire possession of

me, and I took no note of the scenes around me. My ear was long since accustomed to the sad sounds of the sick beds—the cries of suffering, and the low moanings of misery, had ceased to move me—even the wild and frantic ravings of the wounded man near broke not in upon my musings, and I lived like one immured within a solitary dungeon.

"I lay thus one night—my sadness and gloom weightier than ever on my broken spirits—listening to the echoed sounds of suffering that rose into the vaulted roof, and wishing for death to call me away from such a scene of misery, when I heard the low chanting of a priest, coming along the aisle, and the moment after the footsteps of several persons came near, and then two acolytes, carrying lighted tapers, appeared, followed by a venerable man robed in white, and bearing in his hands a silver chalice. Two other priests followed him, chanting the last service, and behind all there came a female figure dressed in deep mourning. She was tall and graceful-looking, and her step had the firm tread of youth, but her head was bowed down with sorrow, and she held her veil pressed closely over her face.

' They gathered round the bed of the wounded man, and the priest took hold of his hand, and lifted it slowly from the bed; and letting it go, it fell heavily down again, with a dull sound. The old man bent over the bed, and touched the pale features, and gazed into the eyes, and then, with clasped hands, he sunk down on his knees and prayed aloud; the others knelt beside him— all save one; she threw herself with frantic grief upon the dead body—for he was dead!—and wept passionately. In vain they strove to calm her sorrow, or even withdraw her from the spot. She clung madly to it, and would not be induced to leave it.

"I think I see her still before me—her long hair, black as night, streaming back from her pale forehead, and hanging down her shoulders—her eyes fixed on the dead man's face, and her hands pressed hard upon her heart, as if to lull its agony In all the wild transport of her grief she was beautiful; for, although pale to sickness, and worn with watching, her large and lustrous eyes—

her nose straight and finely chiselled, like the features of an antique cameo, and her mouth—where mingled pride and sorrow trembled—gave her an expression of loveliness I cannot convey.

" Such was she, as she watched beside her brother's death-bed day and night, motionless and still; for as the first burst of grief was over she seemed to nerve her courage to the task, and even when the hour came, and they bore the body away to its last resting-place, not a sigh or sob escaped her.

" The vacant spot—though it had been tenanted by suffering and misery—brought gloom to my heart. I had been accustomed each day to look for him at sunrise, and each evening to see him as the light of day declined; and I sorrowed like one deserted and alone. Not all alone! for, as if by force of habit, when evening came, *she* was at her place near the altar.

" The fever, and my own anxious thoughts, preyed on my mind that night; and as I lay awake, I felt parched and hot, and wished to drink, and I endeavoured with my only arm to reach the cup beside me. She saw the effort, and sprung towards me at once; and as she held it to my lips, I remembered then that often in the dreary nights of my sickness I had seen her at my bed-side, nursing me and tending me. I muttered a word of gratitude in German, when she started suddenly, and stooping down, said in a clear accent,—

" ' Bist du ein Deutscher ?—Are you a German ?'

" ' Yes,' said, I, mournfully, for I saw her meaning.

" ' Shame! shame! cried she, holding up her hands in horror; ' If the wolves ravage the flocks it is but their nature, but that our own kindred, our very flesh and blood, should do this——'

" I turned my head away in very sorrow and self-abasement, and a convulsive sob burst from my heart.

" ' Nay, nay, not so,' said she, ' a poor peasant like me cannot judge what motives may have influenced you and others like you ; and after all,' and she spoke the words in a trembling voice, ' and after all, you succoured *him* when you believed him sick and weary.'

" ' I—how so ? It never was in my power——'

" ' Yes, yes,' cried she, passionately; ' it was you; this " gourde" was yours ; he told me so, he spoke of you a hundred times.' And at the instant, she held up the little flask I had given to the pilgrim in the valley.

" ' And was the pilgrim then——.'

" ' Yes,' said she, as a proud flash lit up her features, ' he was my brother; many a weary mile he wandered over mountain and moor to track you ; faint and hungry, he halted not, following your footsteps from the first hour you entered our land Think you, but for him, that you had been spared that night's slaughter, or that, for any cause but his, a Tyrolese girl had watched beside your sick bed, and prayed for your recovery ?'

" The whole truth now flashed upon me; every circumstance doubtful before became at once clear to my mind, and I eagerly asked the fate of my comrades.

" A gloomy shake of the head was the only reply.

" ' All ? ' said I, trembling at the word.

" ' All ! ' repeated she, in an accent whose pride seemed almost amounting to ferocity.

" ' Would I had perished with them ! ' cried I, in the bitterness of my heart, and I turned my face away and gave myself up to my grief.

" As if sorry for the burst of feeling she had caused me, she sat down beside my bed, took my hand in her's, and placed her cold lips upon it, while she murmured some words of comfort. Like water to the seared, parched lips of some traveller in the desert, the accents fell upon my almost broken heart, suggesting a thought of hope where all was darkness and despair. I listened to each word with a tremulous fear lest she should cease to speak, and dreading that my ecstasy were but a dream. From that hour I wished to live, a changed spirit came over me, and I felt as though with higher and more ennobling thoughts I should once more tread the earth. Yes, from the humble lips of a peasant girl, I learned to feel that the path I once deemed the only road to heroism and high ambition could be but ' the bandit's trade,' who sells his blood for gain. That war, which, animated by high-souled patriotism, can call forth every sentiment of a great and generous nature, becomes, in an unjust cause, the lowest slavery and degradation. Lydchen seldom quitted my bedside, for my malady took many turns, and it was long—many months—after, that I was enabled to leave my bed and move up and down the chapel.

"Meanwhile the successes of our army had gradually reduced the whole country beneath French rule, and, except in the very fastnesses of the mountains, the Tyrolese had nowhere they could call their own. Each day some peasant would arrive from the valleys with information that fresh troops were pouring in from Germany, and the hopes of the patriotic party fell lower and lower. At last, one evening as I sat on the steps of the little altar, listening to Lydchen reading for me some Tyrol legend, a wild shout in the street of the village attracted our notice, which seemed to gain strength as it came nearer. She started up suddenly, and throwing down her book rushed from the chapel. In another moment she was back beside me, her face pale as a corpse, and her limbs trembling with fear.

"'What has happened? Speak, for God's sake, what is it?' said I.

"'The French have shot the prisoners in the Platz at Innspruck; twenty-eight have fallen this morning,' cried she, 'seven from this very village, and now they cry aloud for your blood; hear them, there!'

"And as she spoke a frightful yell burst from the crowd without, and already they stood at the entrance to the chapel, which, even at such a time, they had not forgotten was a sanctuary. The very wounded men sat up in their beds and joined their feeble cries to those without, and the terrible shout of 'blood for blood!' rang through the vaulted roof.

"'I am ready,' said I, springing up from the low step of the altar. 'They must not desecrate this holy spot with such a crime. I am ready to go where you will.'

"'No, no,' cried Lydchen, '*you* are not like our enemies, you wish us nought of evil, your heart is with the struggle of a brave people, who fight but for their homes and Vaterland. Be of us, then, declare that you are with us. Oh! do this, and these will be your brothers, and I your sister; ay, more than sister ever was.'

D D

"'It cannot be; no, never,' said I; 'it is not when life is in the balance that fealty can change.'

"With difficulty I freed myself from the clasp of her arms, for in her grief she had thrown herself at my feet, when, suddenly, we heard the deep accents of the aged priest, as he stood upon the steps of the altar, and commanded silence. His tones were those of severity and sternness, and I could mark that not a murmur was raised as he continued.

"'You are safe,' whispered Lydchen; 'till to-morrow you are safe, before that you must be far away.'

"The respite of the priest was merely to give me time to prepare for death, which it was decreed I should suffer the following morning in the Platz of the village.

"Scarcely had evening begun to fall when Lydchen approached my bed, and deposited a small bundle upon it, whispering gently, 'Lose no time, put on these clothes, and wait for my return'

"The little chapelry where I lay communicated by a small door with the dwelling of the priest, and by her passing through this I saw that the 'Father' was himself conniving at the plan of my escape. By the imperfect glimmer of the fading day I could perceive that they were her brother's clothes she had brought me; the jacket was yet stained with his blood. I was long in equipping myself, with my single arm, and I heard her voice more than once calling to me to hasten, ere I was ready.

"At length I arose, and passing through the door entered the priest's house, where Lydchen, dressed in hat and mantle, stood ready for the road. As I endeavoured to remonstrate she pressed her hand on my mouth, and walking on tiptoe led me forward; we emerged into a little garden, crossing which she opened a wicket that led into the road. There, a peasant was in waiting, who carried a small bundle on his shoulder, and was armed with the long staff used in mountain travelling.

"Again, making a sign for me to be silent, she moved on before me, and soon turning off the road, entered a foot-track in the mountain. The fresh breeze of the night, and the sense of liberty, nerved me to exertion, and I walked on till day was breaking. Our path generally lay in a descending direction, and I felt little fatigue, when at sunrise Lydchen told me that we might rest for some hours, as our guide could now detect the approach of any party for miles round, and provide for our concealment. No pursuit, however, was undertaken in that direction, the peasants in all likelihood deeming that I would turn my steps towards Lahn, where a strong French garrison was stationed ; whereas we were proceeding in the direction of Saltzbourg, the very longest, and and therefore the least likely route through the Tyrol.

" Day succeeded day, and on we went. Not one living thing did we meet in our lonely path. Already our little stock of provisions was falling low, when we came in sight of the hamlet of Altendorf, only a single day's march from the lake of Saltzbourg.

" The village, though high in the mountain, lay exactly beneath us as we went, and from the height we stood on we could see the little streets of the town and its marketplace like a map below us. Scarcely had the guide thrown his eyes downwards, than he stopped short, and pointing to the town, cried out, ' The French ! the French !' and true enough, a large party of infantry were bivouacked in the streets, and several horses were picquetted in the gardens about. While the peasant crept cautiously forward to inspect the place nearer, I stood beside Lydchen, who, with her hands pressed closely on her face, spoke not a word.

" ' We part here !' said she, with a strong, full accent, as though determined to let no weakness appear in her words-

" ' Part, Lydchen !' cried I, in an agony ; for up to that moment I believed that she never intended returning to the Tyrol.

" ' Yes. Thinkest thou that I hold so light my home and country as thou dost ? Didst thou believe that a Tyrol girl would live 'midst those who laid waste her " Vaterland," and left herself an orphan, without one of her kindred remaining ? '

" ' Are there no ties save those of blood, Lydchen ? Is your heart so steeled against the stranger, that the devotion, the worship of a life long, would not move you from your purpose ? '

" ' Thou has refused me once,' said she, proudly ; ' I

offered to be all your own, when thou couldst have made me so with honour. If thou wert the "Kaiser Franz," I would not have thee now.'

" ' Oh ! speak not thus, Lydchen, to him whose life you saved, and made him feel that life is a blessing. Remember, that if *your* heart be cold to me, you have made *mine* your own for ever. I will not leave you. No——'

" ' Is it that thou mayst bring me yonder and show me amongst thy comrades ?—the Tyrol maiden that thou hast captured, thy spoil of war.'

" ' Oh ! Lydchen, dearest, why will you speak thus——'

" ' Never !' cried she, as her eyes flashed proudly, and her cheek flushed red ; ' never. I have the blood of Hofer in my veins ; and bethinkest thou I would stoop to be a jest, a mockery, before thy high-born dames, who would not deem me fit to be their waiting-woman ? Farewell, sir. I hoped to part with thee less in anger than in sorrow.'

" ' Then will I remain,' said I.

" ' Too late, too late,' cried she, waving her hand, mournfully ; ' the hour is past. See, there come your troops ; a moment more, and I shall be taken. You wish not this, at least——'

" As she spoke, a cavalry detachment was seen coming up the valley at a canter. A few minutes more and she would be discovered. I knew too well the ruffian natures of the soldiery to hazard such a risk. I caught her to my arms with one last embrace, and the next moment dashed down the path towards the dragoons. I turned my head once, but she was gone ; the peasant guide had left the breach of the chasm, and they both were lost to my view.

" My story is now soon told. I was tried by a court-martial, honourably acquitted, and restored to my grade, *en retraite*, however, for my wound had disabled me from active service. For three years I lived in retirement near Mayence, the sad memory of one unhappy event embittering every hour of my life.

" In the early part of 1809, a strong division of the French army, commanded by my old friend and companion, Lefebvre, entered Mayence, on their way to Austria ; and as my health was now restored, I yielded to his persuasion

to join his staff as first aide-de-camp. Indeed, a carelessness and indifference to my fortune had made me submit
to anything, and I assented to every arrangement of the
general, as if I were totally unconcerned in it all.

" I need not trace the events of that rapid and brilliant
campaign. I will only remark that Eckmuhl and Ratis-
bon both brought back all the soldier's ardour to my heart;
and once more the crash of battle, and the din of marching
columns, aroused my dormant enthusiasm.

" In the month of April a *corps d'armée* of twenty
thousand men entered the Tyrol, and pushed forward to
the Nieder wald, where Lefebvre had his head-quarters.
I cannot stay to speak of the terrible scenes of that period,
the most fearful in the spirit of resistance that ever our
arms encountered. Detachments were cut off every day
—whole columns disappeared, and never again were heard
of; no bivouac was safe from a nightly attack; and even
the sentinels at the gates of Innspruck were repeatedly found
dead on their posts. But, worse than all, daily instances
of assassination occurred by peasants, who, sometimes
dressed as suttlers, entered the camp, and took the opportunity to stab or shoot our officers, caring nothing, as it
seemed, for the certain death that awaited them.

" These became of such frequent occurrence that scarce
a report did not contain one or two such casualties,
and, consequently, every precaution that could be thought
of was adopted, and every peasant taken with arms—
in a country, too, where none are unarmed—was shot
without trial of any kind whatever.

" That little mercy, or indeed justice, was meted out to
the people, I need only say that Girardon was commandant of the garrison, and daily inspected the executions
on parade. It happened that one morning this savage
old officer was stabbed by an Austrian peasant, who had
long been employed as a camp servant, and trusted in
situations of considerable confidence. The man was immediately led out for execution to the Platz, where was
another prisoner—a poor boy found rambling within the
lines, and unable to give any account of his presence there.

" Girardon, however, was only slightly wounded, and
countermanded the execution of his assassin, not from

motives of forgiveness, but in order to defer it till he was himself able to be present and witness it. And upon me, as next in command, devolved the melancholy duty of being present on the parade. The brief note I received from Girardon reminded me of a former instance of weakness on my part, and contained a sneering hope that I 'had learned some portion of a soldier's duty since I was reduced to the ranks at Strasbourg.'

" When I reached the Platz, I found the officers of the Staff in the middle of the square, where a table was placed, on which the order for the execution was lying, awaiting my signature.

" 'The prisoner begs a word with the officer in command,' said the orderly sergeant.

" 'I cannot accede to his request,' said I, trembling from head to foot, and knowing how totally such an interview would unman me.

" 'He implores it, sir, with the utmost earnestness, and says he has some important secret to reveal before his death.'

" 'The old story—anything for five minutes more of life and sunshine,' said an officer beside me.

" 'I must refuse,' said I, ' and desire that these requests may not be brought before me '

" 'It is the only way, Colonel,' said another; 'and indeed such intervals have little mercy in them; both parties suffer the more from them.'

" This speech seemed to warrant my selfish determination, and I seized the pen, and wrote my name to the order; and then handing it to the officer, covered my face with my hands, and sat with my head leaning on the table.

" A bustle in front, and a wild cry of agony, told me that the preparations were begun, and quick as lightning the roar of a platoon fire followed. A shriek, shrill and piercing, mingled with the crash, and then came a cry from the soldiers, ' It is a woman ! '

" With madness in my brain, and a vague dread—I know not of what—I dashed forward through the crowd, and there, on the pavement, weltering in her blood, lay the body of Lydchen, she was stone dead, her bosom shattered by a dozen bullets.

" I fell upon the corpse, the blood poured from my mouth

in torrents; and when I arose, it was with a broken heart, whose sufferings are bringing me to the grave."

This sad story I have related without any endeavour to convey to my reader either the tone of him who told it or the dreadful conflict of feeling which at many times prevented his continuing. In some few places the very words he made use of were those I have employed, since they have remained fast rooted in my memory, and were associated with the facts themselves. Except in these slight particulars, I have told the tale as it lives in my recollection, coupled with one of the saddest nights I ever remember.

It was near morning when he concluded, tired and exhausted, yet to all appearance calmer and more tranquil from the free current of that sorrow he could no longer control.

"Leave me, now," said he, "for a few hours; my servant shall call you before I go."

It was to no purpose that I offered to accompany him, alleging—as with an easy conscience I could do—that no one was less bound by any ties of place or time. He refused my offer of companionship, by saying that strict solitude alone restored him after one of his attacks, and that the least excitement invariably brought on a relapse. "We shall meet soon again, I hope," was the extent of promise I could obtain from him; and I saw that to press the matter further was both unfair and indelicate.

Though I lay down in bed, I could not sleep; a strange feeling of dread, an anxious fear of something undefined, was over me; and at every noise I arose and looked out of the window, and down the streets, which were all still and silent. The terrible events of the tale were like a nightmare on my mind, and I could not dismiss them. At last I fell into a half slumber, from which I was awakened by the Baron's servant. His master was dangerously ill; another attack had seized him, and he was lying senseless. I hastened to the room, where I found the sick man stretched half dressed upon the bed, his face purple, and his eye-balls strained to bursting; his breathing was heavy, and broken by a low, tremulous quaver, that made each respiration like a half-suppressed sigh. While I opened the window to give him air, and bathed his forehead with cold water, I despatched a servant for a doctor.

The physician was soon beside me; but I quickly saw that the case was almost hopeless. His former disease had developed a new, and, if possible, worse one—aneurism of the heart.

I will not speak of the hourly vacillations of hope and fear in which I passed that day and the following one. He had never regained consciousness; but the most threatening symptoms had considerably abated, and, in the physician's eyes, he was better. On the afternoon of the third day, as I sat beside his bed, sleep overtook me in my watching, and I awoke, feeling a hand within my own : it was Eigenheim's.

Overjoyed at this sign of returning health, I asked him how he felt. A faint sigh, and a motion of his hand towards his side, was all his reply. Not daring to speak more, I drew the curtain and sat still and silent at his side   The window, by the physician's order, was left open, and a gentle breeze stirred the curtains lightly and gave a refreshing air within the apartment. A noise of feet, and a hurried movement in the street, induced me to look out, and I now saw the head of an infantry battalion turning into the Platz. They marched in slow time, and with arms reversed. With a throb of horror, I remembered the deserter! Yes, there he was! He marched between two dismounted gensd'armes, without coat or cap, a broad placard fixed on his breast, inscribed with his name and his crime. I turned instantly towards the bed, dreading lest already the tramp of the marching men had reached the sick man's ear; but he was sleeping calmly, and breathing without effort of any kind.

The thought seized me to speak to the officer in command of the party, and I rushed down, and making my way through the crowd, approached the Staff as they were standing in the middle of the Platz   But my excited manner, my look of wild anxiety, and my little knowledge of the language, combined to make my appeal of little moment.

"If it be true, sir," said a gruff old veteran, with a grisly beard, "that he was an officer of the Empire, the fire of a platoon can scarcely hurt his nerves."

"Yes, but," said I, "there is a circumstance of his life

which makes this ten-fold more dangerous—I cannot explain it—I am not at liberty——"

" I do not desire to learn your secrets, sir," replied the old man, rudely; "stand back and suffer me to do my duty."

I turned to the others, but they could give me neither advice nor assistance, and already the square was lined with soldiers, and the men of the " death party " were ordered to stand out.

" Give me at least time enough to remove my friend to a distant chamber, if you will not do more," said I, driven to madness, but no attention was paid to my words, and the muster roll continued to be read out.

I rushed back to the inn, and up the stairs; but what was my horror to hear the sound of voices, and the tramp of feet, in the sick room I had left in silence. As I entered, I saw the landlord and the servant, assisted by the doctor, endeavouring to hold down the Baron on his bed, who with almost superhuman strength, pushed them from him in his efforts to rise. His features were wild to insanity, and the restless darting of his glistening eye showed that he was under the excitement of delirium.

" The effort may kill him," whispered the doctor in my ear; " this struggle may be his death."

" Leave me free, sir!" shouted the sick man. " Who dares to lay hands on me—stand aside there—the peloton will take ground to the right," continued he, raising his voice as if commanding on parade ; " Ground arms! "

Just at this instant, the heavy clank of the firelocks was heard without, as though in obedience to his word. " Hark! " said he, raising his hand—"Not a word— silence in the ranks." And in the deadly stillness we could now hear the sentence of death, as it was read aloud by the adjutant. A hoarse roll of the drum followed, and then the tramp of the party as they led forward the prisoner, to every step of which the sick man kept time with his hand.

We did not dare to move—we knew not at what instant our resistance might be his death.

" Shoulder arms!" shouted out the officer from the Platz.

" Take the orders from me," cried Elgenheim, wildly. " This duty is mine—no man shall say I shrunk from it."

" Present arms—Fire——"

"Fire!" shouted Elgenheim, with a yell that rose above the roll of musketry; and then with a groan of agony, he cried out, "There—there—it's over now!" and fell back dead into our arms.

*   *   *   *   *   *

Thus died the leader of the stormers at Elchingen,—the man who carried the Hill of Asperne against an Austrian battery. He sleeps now in the little churchyard of the "Marien Hülfe" at Cassel.

CHAPTER XXX.

THE RAPACIOUS OFFICER.

I LEFT Cassel with a heart far heavier than I had brought into it some weeks before. The poor fellow whose remains I followed to the grave was ever in my thoughts, and all our pleasant rambles and our familiar intercourse were now shadowed over by the gloom of his sad destiny. So must it ever be. He who seeks the happiness of his life upon the world's highways, must learn to carry, as best he may, the weary load of trouble that "flesh is heir to." There must be storm for sunshine, and for the bright days and warm airs of summer he must feel the lowering skies and cutting winds of winter.

It was only as I reached Münden to breakfast that I remembered it was Sunday, and so when I had finished my meal I joined my host and his household to church. What a simplicity is there in the whole Protestantism of Germany—how striking is the contrast between the unpretending features of the Reformed, and the gorgeous splendour of the Roman Catholic Church. The benches of oak, on which were seated the congregation, made no distinctions of class and rank. The little village authorities were mingled with the mere peasants—the Pastor's family sat nearest to the reading desk—that was the only place distinguished from the others. The building, like most of its era, was plain and unornamented—some passages from Scripture were written on the walls in different places, but these were its only decoration. As I sat awaiting the commencement of the service I could not avoid being struck by the marked difference of feature, observable in Protestant, from what we see in Roman Catholic communities, not depending upon nationality, for Germany itself is an illustration in point. The gorgeous ceremonial of the Romish Church—its venerable architecture—its prestige of antiquity—its pealing organ, and its incense all contribute to a certain exhaltation of mind, a fervour of sentiment, that may readily be mistaken for true religious feeling. These things, connected and bound up with the most awful and impressive thoughts the mind of man is capable of, cannot fail to impress upon the features of the worshippers an expression of profound, heartfelt adoration, which poetizes the most common place, and elevates the tone of even the most vulgar faces. Retsch had not to go far for those figures of intense devotional character his works abound in—every chapel contained innumerable studies for his pencil. The features of the Protestant worshippers were calm, even to sternness—the eyes, not bent upon some great picture, or some holy relic, with wondering admiration, were downcast in meditation deep, or raised to heaven with thoughts already there. There was a holy and a solemn awe in every face, as though in the presence of *Him*, and in *His* Temple, the passions and warm feelings of man were an unclean offering; that to understand His truths, and to apply His counsels, a pure heart and a clear understanding were necessary—and these they brought. To look on their cold and steadfast faces you would say that Luther's own spirit—his very temperament, had descended to his followers. There was the same energy of character—the indomitable courage—the perseverance no obstacle could thwart—the determination no opposition could shake. The massive head square and strong—the broad, bold forehead—the full eye—the wide nostril, and the thick lip—at once the indication of energy, of passion and of power, are seen throughout Saxony as the types of national feature.

As you approach the town of Eisenach—for I'm not

going to weary you with the whole road—you come upon a little glen in the forest, the "Thuringer Wald," where the road is completely overshadowed, and even at noonday is almost like night A little well, bubbling in a basin of rock stands at the road side, where an iron ladle, chained to the stone, and a rude bench, proclaim that so much of thought has been bestowed on the wayfarer. As you rest from the heat and fatigue of the day upon that humble seat, you may not know that Martin Luther himself sat on that very bench, tired and way-worn, as he came back from Worms, where, braving the power of king and kaiser, he had gone manfully to defend his opinions, and assert the doctrines of the Reformation.

It was there he lay down to sleep—a sleep I would dare to say not the less tranquil because the excommunication of Rome had been fulminated over his head He was alone. He had refused every offer of companionship which zeal for the cause and personal friendship had prompted, when suddenly he was aroused by the tramp of armed men, and the heavy clattering of horses coming up the glen. He knew his life was sought for by his enemies, and what a grateful deed his assassination would be to record within the halls of many a kingly palace. In an instant he was on his legs, and grasping his trusty broad sword, he awaited the attack. Not too soon, however, for scarcely had the horsemen come within sight, than, putting spurs to their steeds, they bore down upon him ; then checking their horses suddenly, the leader called aloud to him to surrender himself his prisoner.

Good Martin's reply was a stroke of his broadsword, that brought the summoner from his saddle to the ground. Parley was at an end now, and they rushed on him at once. Still it was clear that their wish was not to kill him, which, from their numbers and superior equipment, could not have been difficult. But Luther's love of liberty was as great as his love of life, and he laid about him like one who would sell either as dearly as he could. At length, pressed by his enemies on every side his sword broke near the hilt, he threw the useless fragment from his hand, and called out, " Ich kann nicht mehr!"—" I can do no more!"

He was now bound with cords, and his eyes bandaged, conveyed to the castle of the Wartburg about two miles distant, nor did he know for several days after that the whole was a device of his friend and protector, the Elector of Saxony, who wished to give currency to the story that Luther's capture was a real one, and the Wartburg his prison, and not, as it really proved, his asylum. Here he spent nearly a year, occupied in the translation of the Bible, and occasionally preaching in the small chapel of the "Schloss." His strange fancies of combats with the Evil One are among the traditions of the place, and the torn plaster of the wall is pointed out as the spot where he hurled his inkstand at the fiend who tormented him, in the shape of a large blue-bottle fly.

One cannot see, unmoved, that rude chamber, with its simple furniture of massive oak, were the great monk meditated those tremendous truths that were to shake thrones and dynasties, and awake the world from the charmed sleep of superstition, in which, for centuries, it lay buried.

The force of his strong nature, his enthusiasm, and a kind of savage energy he possessed, frequently over-balanced his reason, and he gave way to wild rantings and ravings, which often followed on the longest efforts of his mental labour, and seemed like the outpourings of an overcharged intellect. The zeal with which he prosecuted his great task, was something almost miraculous —often for thirty, or even forty hours did he remain at the desk without food or rest, and then such was his exhaustion, bodily as well as mental, that he would fall senseless on the floor, and it required all the exertions of those about him to rally him from these attacks. His first sensations on recovering, were ever those of a deadly struggle with the Evil One, by whose agency alone he believed his great work was interrupted, and then the scene which succeeded would display all the fearful workings of his diseased imagination. From these paroxysms, nothing seemed to awake him so readily as the presence of his friend Melancthon, whose mild nature and angelic temperament were the exact opposites of his bold impetuous character. The sound of his voice alone would frequently calm him in the wildest moments, and when the torrent of his thought ran onward with mad speed, and shapes and images flitted before his disordered brain, and earthly combats were mingled in his mind with more dreadful conflicts, and that he burst forth into the violent excesses of his passion—then the soft breathings of Melancthon's flute would still the storm, and lay the troubled waters of his soul—that rugged nature would yield even to tears, and like a child, he would weep till slumber closed his eyes.

I lingered the entire day in the Wartburg—sometimes in the Rittersaal, where suits of ancient and most curious armour are preserved ; sometimes in the chapel, where the rude desk is shown at which Luther lectured to the household of the "Schloss." Here, too, is a portrait of him which is alleged to be authentic. The features are such as we see in all his pictures ; the only difference I could perceive was, that he is represented with a moustache, which gives what a Frenchman near me called an " air brigand " to the stern massiveness of his features. This circumstance, slight as it is, rather corroborates the authenticity of the painting, for it is well known that during his residence at the Wartburg, he wore his beard in this fashion, and to many retainers of the castle passed for a Ritter, or a knight confined for some crime against the state.

With a farewell look at the old chamber, where stands his oaken chair and table, I left the Schloss, and as night was falling descended towards Eisenach—for a description of whose watermills and windmills, whose cloth factories and toy shops, I refer you to various and several guide books—only begging to say, on my own account, that the " Reuten Krantz " is a seemly inn, and the host a pleasant German of the old school ; that is, in other words, one whose present life is always about twenty years in advance of his thoughts, and who, while he eats and drinks in the now century, thinks and feels with that which is gone. The latest event of which he had any cognizance, was the retreat from Leipsic, when the French poured through the village for five days without ceasing. All the great features of that memorable retreat, however, were absorbed in his mind, by an incident which occurred to himself, and at which, by the gravity of his manner in relating it, I could not help laughing heartily.

When the Commissariat arrived at Eisenach, to make arrangement for the troops on their march, they allowed the inhabitants the option—a pleasant one—of converting the billets imposed upon them for a certain sum of money, in virtue of which they obtained an exemption from all intrusion on the part of men and officers, save those of the rank of colonel and upwards; and in evidence, a great placard was affixed to their door, setting forth the same, as a "general order." Now as it was agreed that only one officer should be accommodated at a time, the privilege was worth paying for, particularly by our host of the "Rue Garland," whose larder was always stored with delicacies and whose cellar was famed for thirty miles round. He accordingly counted down his reichs-thalers, gulden, and groschen—with a heavy heart it is true, but to avert a heavier evil, and with his grand patent of immunity hung out upon his sign-post, he gave himself no farther trouble about the war or its chances. On the third evening of the retreat, however, a regiment of the Chasseurs de la Garde, conspicuous by their green coats and white facings, the invariable costume of the Emperor himself, entered the town, and bivouacked in the little square. The colonel, a handsome fellow of about five-and-thirty, or forty, looked about him sharply for a moment or two, irresolute where he should fix his resting-place; when a savoury odour of sausages frying in the "Reuten Krantz," quickly decided his choice. He entered at once, and making his bow to mine host, with that admirable mixture of deference and command a Frenchman can always assume, ordered his dinner to be got ready, and a bed prepared for him.

It was well worth the host's while to stand on good terms with the officers of rank, who could repress or wink at the liberties of the men, as occasion served, and so the "Rue Garland" did its utmost that day to surpass itself.

"Je dois vous prévenir," said the colonel, laughing, as he strolled from the door, after giving his directions, "Je dois vous prévenir, que je mange bien, et beaucoup."

"Monsieur shall be content," said the host, with a tap

on his own stomach, as though to say,—"The nourishment that has sufficed for this, may well content such a carcass as thine——"

"And as for wine——" continued the colonel.

"Zum kissen!" cried the host, with a smack of his lips that could be heard over the whole Platz, and which made a poor captain's mouth water, who guessed the allusion

I shall not detail for my reader, though 1 most certainly heard myself, the long bill of fare, by which the "Rue Branch" intended to astonish the weak nerves of the Frenchman, little suspecting, at the time, how mutual the surprise was destined to be. I remember there was "fleisch" and "braten" without end, and baked pike, and sausages, and boar's-head, and eels, and potted mackerel, and brawn, and partridges; not to speak of all the roots that ever gave indigestion since the flood, besides sweet-meats and puddings, for whose genera and species it would take Buffon and Cuvier to invent a classification. As I heard the formidable enumeration, I could not help expressing my surprise at the extent of preparations, so manifestly disproportionate to the amount of the company; but the host soon satisfied me on this head, by saying, "that they were obliged to have an immense supply of cold viands always ready to sell to the other officers throughout the town, whom," he added, in a sly whisper, "they soon contrived to make pay for the heavy ransom imposed on themselves." The display, therefore, which did such credit to his hospitality, was made with little prospect of injuring his pocket—a pleasant secret, if it only were practicable.

The hour of dinner arrived at last, and the colonel, punctual to the moment, entered the *salon*, which looked out by a window on the Platz—a strange contrast, to be sure, for his eyes, the great sideboard loaded with luscious fare, and covered by an atmosphere of savoury smoke, and the meagre bivouac without, where groups of officers sat, eating their simple rations, and passing their goblets of washy beer from hand to hand.

Rochefoucauld says "There is always something pleasant in the misfortunes of our best friends;" and as I suppose he knew his countrymen, I conclude that the colonel arranged his napkin on his knee with a high sense

of enjoyment for the little panorama which met his eyes
on the Platz.

It must certainly have been a goodly sight, and somewhat of a surprise besides, for an old campaigner to see
the table groaning under its display of good things; amid
which, like Lombardy poplars in a Flemish landscape,
the tall and taper necks of various flasks shot up—some
frosted with an icy crest, some cobwebbed with the touch
of time

Ladling the potage from a great silver tureen of antique
mould, the host stood beside the colonel's chair, enjoying
—as only a host can enjoy—the mingled delight and
admiration of his guest, and now the work began in
right earnest. What an admirable soup, and what a glass
of "Nieder thaler!"—no hock was ever like it; and
those *patés*—they were *en bechamelle.* "He was sorry
they were not oysters, but the Chablis he could vouch
for." And well he might; such a glass of wine might
console the Emperor for Leipsic.

" How did you say the trout was fried, my friend?"

" In mushroom gravy, dashed with anchovy."

" Another slice, if you'll permit me." Pop! "That
flask has burst its bonds in time; I was wishing to taste
your 'Œil de Perdrix'"

The outposts were driven in by this time, and the heavy
guns of the engagement were brought down; in other
words, the braten, a goodly dish of veal, garnished with
every incongruity the mind of man could muster, entered;
which, while the host carved at the sideboard, the colonel
devoured in his imagination, comforting himself the while
by a *salmi* of partridges with truffles

Some invaluable condiment had, however, been forgotten with the veal, and the host bustled out of the
room in search of it The door had not well closed,
when the colonel dashed out a goblet of champagne, and
drank it at a draught; then springing from the window
into the Platz, where already the shadow of evening was
falling, was immediately replaced by the major, whose
dress and general appearance were sufficiently like his own
to deceive any stranger

Helping himself without loss of time to the *salmi*, he

E E

ate away like one whose appetite had suffered a sore trial from suspense.

The *salmi* gave place to the veal, and the veal to the baked pike; for so it is, the stomach in Germany is a kind of human ark, wherein, though there is little order in the procession, the animals enter whole and entire. The host watched his guest's performance, and was in ecstacies—good things never did meet with more perfect appreciation; and as for the wine, he drank it like a Swabian, whole goblets full at a draught. At length, holding up an empty flask, he cried out, "Champagne!" And away trotted the fat man to his cellar, rather surprised, it is true, how rapidly three flasks of his "Ai Mousseux" had disappeared.

This was now the critical moment, and, with a half-sigh of regret, the major leaped into the street, and the first captain relieved the guard.

Poor fellow! he was fearfully hungry, and helped himself to the first dish before him, and drank from the bottle at his side, like one whose stomach had long ceased to be pampered by delicacies.

"Du Heiliger!" cried the host to himself, as he stood behind his chair, and surveyed the performance. "Du Heiliger! how he does eat, one wouldn't suppose he had been at it these fifty minutes. Art ready for the capon now?" continued he, as he removed the keel and floor-timbers of a saddle of mutton.

"The capon," sighed the other; "yes, the capon now." Alas! he knew that delicious dish was reserved for his successor. And so it was; before the host re-entered, the second captain had filled his glass twice, and was anxiously sitting in expectation of the capon.

Such a bird as it was!—a very sarcophagus of truffles —a mine of delicious dainties of every clime and cuisine!

"Good—eh?"

"Delicious!" said the second captain, filling a bumper, and handing it to the host, while he clinked his own against it in friendly guise.

"A pleasant fellow, truly," said the host, "and a social —but, Lord, how he eats! There go the wings and the back! Himmel und Erde! if he isn't at the pasty now!"

"Wine!" cried the Frenchman, striking the table with the empty bottle, "Wine!"

The host crossed himself, and went out in search of more liquor, muttering, as he shuffled along, "What would have become of me if I hadn't paid the indemnity!"

The third captain was at his post before the host got back, and whatever the performance of his predecessors, it was nothing to his. The pasty disappeared like magic, the fricandeau seemed to have melted away like snow before the sun; while he drank indiscriminately Hock, Hermitage, and Bordeaux, as though he were a camel victualling himself for a three weeks' tramp in the desert.

The poor host now walked round the board, and surveyed the débris of the feast with a sad heart. Of all the joints which he hoped to have seen cold on the shelves of his larder, some ruined fragments alone remained. Here was the gable end of a turkey—there the side-wall of a sirloin; on one side, the broken roof of a pasty; on the other, the bare joists of a rib of beef. It was the Palmyra of things eatable, and a sad and melancholy sight to gaze on.

"What comes next, good host?" cried the third captain, as he wiped his lips with his napkin.

"Next!" cried the host, in horror, "Hagel und regen! thou canst not eat more, surely?"

"I don't know that," replied the other, "the air of these mountains freshens the appetite—I might pick a little of something sweet."

With a groan of misery, the poor host placed a plum pie before the all-devouring stranger, and then, as if to see that no legerdemain was practised, stationed himself directly in front, and watched every morsel, as he put it into his mouth. No, the thing was all fair, he ate like any one else, grinding his food and smacking his lips like an ordinary mortal. The host looked down on the floor, and beneath the cloth of the table—what was that for? Did he suspect the stranger had a tail?

"A glass of mulled claret with cloves!" said the Frenchman, "and then you may bring the dessert."

"The Heavens be praised!" cried the host, as he swept the last fragments of the table into a wide tray, and left the room.

E E 2

" Egad! I thought you had forgotten me altogether,
captain," said a stout, fat fellow, as he squeezed himself
with difficulty through the window, and took his seat at
the table. This was the quartermaster of the regiment, and
celebrated for his appetite throughout the whole brigade.

" Ach Gott, how he is swelled out!" was the first
exclamation of the host, as he re-entered the room ; "and
no wonder either, when one thinks of what he has eaten."

" How now, what's this? " shouted the quartermaster,
as he saw the dessert arranging on the table, " Sacré
tonnere! what's all this? "

" The dessert—if you can eat it," said the host, with a
deep sigh.

" Eat it!—no—how the devil should I? "

" I thought not," responded the other, submissively,
" I thought not, even a shark will get gorged at last! "

" Eh, what's that you say? " replied the quartermaster,
roughly ; " you don't expect a man to dine on figs and
walnuts, or dried prunes and olives, do you? "

" Dine! " shouted the host, " and have you not dined? "

"No, mille bombes, that I haven't, as you shall soon see?"

" Alle Gute Geisten loben den Hernn! " said the host,
blessing himself; " an thou be'st the Satanus, I charge
thee, keep away! "

A shout of laughter from without prevented the quartermaster's reply to this exorcism being heard ; while the
trumpet sounded suddenly for " boot and saddle."

With a bottle of wine stuffed in each pocket, the
quartermaster rose from table, and hurried away to join
his companions, who had received sudden orders to push
forward towards Cassel ; and as the bewildered host stood
at his window, while the regiment filed past, each officer
saluted him politely as they cried out in turn, " Adieu,
Monsieur! my compliments to the braten "—" the turkey
was delicious"—"the salmi perfect"—"the capon glorious"
—" the venison a chef-d'œuvre!" down to the fat quartermaster, who, as he raised a flask to his lips, and shook his
head reproachfully, said, " Ah! you old screw, nothing
better than nuts and raisins to give a hungry man for his
dinner!" And so they disappeared from the Platz, leaving
mine host in a maze of doubt and bewilderment, which it

took many a day and night's meditation to solve to his own conviction.

Though I cannot promise myself that my reader will enjoy this story as much as I did, I could almost vouch for his doing so if he heard it from the host of the " Reuten Krantz" himself, told with the staid gravity of German manner, and all the impressive seriousness of one who saw in the whole adventure nothing ludicrous whatever, but only a most unfair trick, that deserved the stocks or the pillory.

He was indeed a character in his way; his whole life had only room for three or four incidents, about and around which his thoughts revolved, as on an axis, and whose impression was too vivid to admit of any occurrence usurping their place. When a boy, he had been in the habit of acting as guide to the " Wartburg" to his father's guests —for they were a generation of innkeepers time out of mind—and even yet he spoke of those days with transport.

It was amusing, too, to hear him talk of Luther as familiarly as though he had known him personally, mentioning little anecdotes of his career, and repeating his opinions as if they were things of yesterday; but indeed his mind had no more perspective than a Chinese tea-tray —everything stood besides its neighbour, without shadow or relief of any kind; and to hear him talk, you would say that Melancthon and Marshal Macdonald might have been personal friends, and Martin Luther and Ney passed an evening in the blue *salon* of the "Reuten Krantz." As for Eisenach, and all about it, he knew as little as though it were a city of Egypt He *hoped* there was a public library now—he *knew* there was in his father's time, but the French used to make cartridges with the books in many towns they passed through—perhaps they had done the same here. These confounded French—they seemed some way to fill every avenue of his brain; there was no inlet of his senses without a French sentinel on guard over it.

Now—for my sins, I suppose—it so chanced that I was laid up here for several weeks with a return of an old rheumatism I had contracted in one of my wanderings. Books they brought me; but, alas! the only volumes a German circulating library ever contains are translations

of the very worst French and English works. The weather was, for the most part, rainy and broken; and even
when my strength permitted me to venture into the
garden, I generally got soundly drenched before I reached
the house again. What insupportable ennui is that which
inhabits the inn of a little remote town, where come few
travellers and no news! What a fearful blank in existence is such a place! Just think of sitting in the little
silent and sanded parlour, with its six hard chairs, and
one straight old sofa, upholstered with flock and fleas;
counting over the four prints in black wood frames upon
the walls. Scripture subjects, where Judith, with a
quilted petticoat and sabots, cuts the head off a Holo-
fernes in buckskins and top-boots, and catches the blood
in a soup-tureen; an Abraham, with a horse-pistol, is
threatening a little Isaac in jacket and trousers, with a
most villanous expression about the corners of his eyes;
and the old looking-glass, cracked in the middle, and
representing your face in two hemispheres, with a nose and
one eye to each—the whole tinged with a verd antique
colouring which makes you look like a man in bronze.

Outside the door, but near enough for every purpose of
annoyance, stands a great hulking old clock, that ticks
away incessantly—true type of time that passes on its
road whether you be sick or sorry, merry or mournful.
With what a burr the old fellow announces that he is
going to strike—it is like the asthmatic wheezing of some
invalid making an exertion beyond his strength; and
then, the heavy plod of sabots back and forward through
the little hall, into the kitchen, and out again to the
stable-yard; with the shrill yell of some drabbled wench
screaming for "Johann," or "Iacob;" and all the little
platitudes of the *ménage* that reach you, seasoned from
time to time by the coarse laughter of the boors, or the
squabbling sounds that issue streetwards, where some
vendor of "schnaps" or "kirch-wasser" holds his tap.

What a dreary sensation comes over one, to think of
the people who pass their lives in such a place, with its
poor, little, miserable interests and occupations, and how
one shudders at the bare idea of sinking down to the level
of such a stagnant pool—knowing the small notorieties,

and talking like them; and yet, with all this holy horror, how rapidly and insensibly is such a change induced. Every day rubs off some former prejudice, and induces some new habit, and, as the eye of the prisoner in his darksome dungeon learns to distinguish each object, clear, as if in noon-day, so will the mind accommodate itself to the moral gloom of such a cell as this, ay, and take a vivid interest in each slight event that goes on there, as though he were to the " manner born."

In a fortnight, or even less, I lay awake, conjecturing why the urchin who brought the mail from Gotha had not arrived ;—before three weeks I participated in the shock of the town, at the conduct of the Frow von Butterwick, who raised the price of Schenkin or Schweinfleisch, I forget which, by some decimal of a farthing; and fully entered into the distressed feelings of the inhabitants, who foretold a European war from the fact that a Prussian corporal, with a pack on his shoulders, was seen passing through the town that morning before daybreak.

When I came to think over these things, I got into a grievous state of alarm. " Another week, Arthur," said I, " and thou art done for; Eisenach may claim thee as its own; and the Grand Duke of ——, Heaven forgive me! but I forget the potentate of the realm ; he may summon thee to his counsels as the Hoch Wohlgeborner und Gelehrter, Herr von O'Leary; and thou mayest be found here some half century hence, with a pipe in thy mouth, and thy hands in thy side pockets, discoursing fat consonants, like any Saxon of them all. Run for it, man, run for it; away, with half a leg, if need be, out of the kingdom with all haste ; and if it be not larger than its neighbours, a hop, step, and jump, ought to suffice for it."

Will any one tell me—I'll wager they cannot—why it is, that if you pass a week or a month in any out-of-the-way place, and either from sulk or sickness lead a solitary kind of humdrum life, that when you are about to take your leave, you find half the family in tears. Every man, woman, and child think it incumbent on them to sport a mourning face. The host wipes his eye with the corner of the bill; the waiter blows his nose in the napkin; the chambermaid holds up her apron; and

Boots, with a side wipe of his blacking hand, leaves his countenance in a very fit state for the application of the polishing brush. As for yourself, the position is awkward beyond endurance.

That instant you feel sick of the whole household, from the cellar to the garret. You had perilled your soul in damning them all in turn; and now it comes out that you are the " enfant cheri " of the establishment. What a base, black-hearted fellow you must be all the time; in short, you feel it; otherwise, why is your finger exploring so low in the recesses of your purse. Confound it, you have been very harsh and hasty with the good people, and they did their best after all.

Take up your abode at Mivart's or the " Clarendon;" occupy for the six months of winter the suite of apartments at Crillon's or Meurice's , engage the whole of the "Schwann," at Vienna; ay, or even the " Grand Monarque," at Aix; and I'll wager my head you go forth at the end of it without causing a sigh in the whole household. Don't flatter yourself that Mivart will stand blubbering over the bill, or Meurice be half choked with his sobs. The " Schwann " doesn't care a feather of his wing, and as for the " Grand Monarque," you might as well expect his prototype would rise from the grave to embrace you. A civil grin, that half implies, " You've been well plucked here," is the extent of parting emotion, and a tear couldn't be had for the price of Tokay.

Well, I bid adieu to the " Reuten Krantz," in a different sort of mood from what I expected. I shook the old " Rue-branch " himself heartily by the hand, and having distributed a circle of gratuities—for the sum total of which I should have probably been maltreated by a London waiter—I took my staff and sallied forth towards Weimar, accompanied by a shower of prayers and kind wishes, that, whether sincere or not, made me feel happier the whole day after.

CHAPTER XXXI.

THE FORTRESS.

I NARROWLY escaped being sent to the guard-house for the night, as I approached Erfurt; for, seeing that it was near nine o'clock, when the gates of the fortress are closed, I quickened my pace to a trot, not aware of the "reglement" which forbids any one to pass rapidly over the drawbridges of a fortification. Now, though the rule be an admirable one when applied to those heavy diligences, which, with three tons of passengers, and six of luggage, come lumbering along the road, and might well be supposed to shake the foundations of any breastwork or barbican; yet, that any man of mortal mould, any mere creature of the biped class—even with two shirts and a night-cap in his pack—could do this, is more than I can conceive; and so it was, I ran, and if I did, a soldier ran after me, three more followed him, and a corporal brought up the rear, and, in fact, so imposing was the whole scene, that any unprejudiced spectator, not over versed in military tactics, might have imagined that I was about to storm Erfurt, and had stolen a march upon the garrison. After all, the whole thing was pretty much like what Murat did at Vienna, and perhaps it was that which alarmed them.

I saw I had committed a fault, but what it was I couldn't even guess; and as they all spoke together, and such precious bad German, too, (did you ever know a foreigner not complain of the abominable faults people commit in speaking their own language!) that though I cried "peccavi," I remembered myself, and did not volunteer any confessions of iniquity before I heard the special indictment, and it seemed I had very little chance of doing that, such was the confusion and uproar.

Now, there are two benevolent institutions in all law, and, according, to these, a man may plead either "in formâ pauperis" or "in formâ stultus." I took the latter plea, and came off triumphant, my sentence was recorded as a "Dummer Englander," and I went my way rejoicing.

Well, "I wish them luck of it!" as we say in Ireland,

who have a fancy for taking fortified towns. Here was I inside of one—the gates closed, locked, and barred behind me, a wall of thirty feet high, and a ditch of fifty feet deep, to keep me in—and hang me if I could penetrate into the interior. I suppose I was in what is called a parallel, and I walked along, turning into a hundred little crooked corners and zig-zag contrivances, where an embrasure, and a cannon in it, were sure to be found. But as nothing are so like each other as stone walls, and as I never, for the life of me, could know one seventy-four pounder from another, I wandered about, very sadly puzzled to ascertain if I had not been perambulating the same little space of ground for an hour and a half. Egad! thought I, if there were no better engineers in the world than me, they might leave the gates wide open, and let the guard go to bed. Hollo! here's some one coming along—that's fortunate, at last—and just then, a man wrapped in a loose cloak, German fashion, passed close beside me.

"May I ask, mein Herr, which is the direction of the town, and where I can find an inn?" said I, taking off my hat most punctiliously—for although it was almost pitch-dark, that courtesy cannot ever be omitted, and I have heard of a German who never talked to himself without uncovering.

"Straightforward, and then to your left by the angle of the citadel; you can take a short cut through the covered way——"

"Heaven forbid!" interrupted I, "where all is fair and open my chance is bad enough—there is no need of a concealed passage to confuse me."

"Come with me, then," said he, laughing; "I perceive you are a foreigner—this is somewhat longer, but I'll see you safe to the 'Kaiser,' where you'll find yourself very comfortable."

My guide was an officer of the garrison, and seemed considerably flattered by the testimony I bore to the impregnability of the fortress; describing as we went along, for my better instruction, the various remarkable features of the place. Lord, how weary I was of casemates and embrasures, of bomb-proofs and culverins, half-moons and platforms; and as I continued, from politeness, to express my surprise and wonderment, he took the more pains to expound those hidden treasures; and I verily believe he took me a mile out of my way to point out the place, in the dark, where a large gun lay, that took a charge of one hundred and seventy livres weight. I was now fairly done up, and having sworn solemnly that the French army dare not show their noses this side of the Rhine so long as a corporal's guard remained at Erfurt, I begged hard to have a peep at the "Kaiser."

"Won't you see the Rothen Stein?" said he.

"To-morrow,—if I survive," said I, dropping my voice for the last words.

"Nor the Wunder Brucke?——"

"With God's blessing, to-morrow, I'll visit them all; I came for the purpose." Heaven pardon the lie, I was almost fainting.

"Be it so, then," said he, "we must go back again now. We have come a good distance out of our road."

With a heavy groan, I turned back; and if I did not curse Vauban and Carnot, it was because I am a good Christian, and of a most forgiving temper.

"Here we are now—this is the 'Kaiser,'" said he, as after half an hour's sharp walking we stood within a huge archway, dimly lighted by a great old-fashioned lantern.

"You stop here some days, I think you said?"

"Yes, for a fortnight; or a week, at least."

"Well, if you'll permit me, I shall have great pleasure in conducting you through the fortress to-morrow and next day. You can't see it all under two days, and even with that, you'll have to omit the arsenals and the shot-batteries."

I expressed my most grateful acknowledgments, with an inward vow that if I took refuge in the big mortar, I'd not be caught by my friend the next morning.

"Good night, then," said he, with a polite bow. "Bis Morgen."—"Bis Morgen," repeated I, and entered the "Kaiser."

The "Römischer Kaiser" was a great place once; but now, alas! its "Diana is fallen!" Time was when two emperors slept beneath its roof, and the ambassadors of kings assembled within its walls. It was here Napoleon exercised that wonderful spell of enchantment he possessed above all other men, and so captivated the mind of the Emperor Alexander, that not even all the subsequent invasion of his empire, nor the disasters of Moscow, could eradicate the impression. The Czar alone, of his enemies, would have made terms with him in 1814; and when no other voice was raised in his favour, Alexander's was heard, commemorating their ancient friendship, and recalling the time when they had been like brothers. Erfurt was the scene of their first friendship. Many now living have seen Napoleon with his arm linked within Alexander's, as they walked along, and marked the spell-bound attention of the Czar, as he listened to the burning words and rapid eloquence of Buonaparte, who, with a policy all his own, devoted himself completely to the young emperor, and resolved on winning him over. They dined, and went to the theatre together each evening; and the flattery of this preference, so ostentatiously paraded by Napoleon, had its full effect on the ardent imagination and chivalrous heart of the youthful Czar.

Fêtes, reviews, gala parties, and concerts, followed each other in quick succession. The corps of the "Français" was brought expressly from Paris; the ballet of the Opera also came, and nothing was omitted which could amuse the hours of Alexander, and testify the desire of his host —for such Napoleon was—to entertain him with honour. Little, then, did Napoleon dream that the frank-hearted youth, who hung on every word he spoke, would one day prove the most obstinate of all his enemies; nor was it for many a day after that he uttered in the bitter venom of disappointment, when the rugged energy of the Muscovite showed an indomitable front to the strength of his armies, and was deaf to his attempted negotiations, "Scrape the Russian, and you'll come down on the Tartar."

Alexander was indeed the worthy grandson of Catherine, and, however a feeling of personal regard for Napoleon existed through the vicissitudes of after-life, it is no less true that the dissimulation of the Russian had imposed on the Corsican; and that while Napoleon believed him all his own, the duplicity of the Muscovite had over-reached him. It was in reference to that interview and its pledged good faith, Napoleon, in one of his cutting sarcasms, pronounced him "Faux comme un Grec du Bas Empire."

Nothing troubled the happiness of the meeting at Erfurt. It was a joyous and a splendid fête, where, amid all the blandishments of luxury and pleasure, two great kings divided the world at their will It was Constantino and Charlemagne, who partitioned the East and West between each other. The sad and sorrow-struck King of Prussia came not there as at Tilsit, nor the fair Queen of that unhappy kingdom, whose beauty and misfortunes might well have claimed the compassion of the conqueror.

Never was Napoleon's character exhibited in a point of view less amiable than in his relations with the Queen of Prussia. If her position and her personal attractions had no influence over him, the devoted attachment of her whole nation towards her should have had that effect. There was something unmanly in the cruelty that replied to her supplication in favour of her country, by trifling allusions to the last fashions of Paris, and the costumes of the boulevard; and when she accepted the moss-rose from his hand, and tremblingly uttered the words—" Sire, avec Magdebourg?"—a more suitable rejection of her suit might have been found than the abrupt " Non!" of Napoleon, as he turned his back and left her. There was something prophetic in her speech, when relating the anecdote herself to Hardenberg, she added—" That man is too pitiless to misfortune ever to support it himself, should it be his lot!"

But what mean all these reflections, Arthur? These be matters of history which the world knows as well or better than thyself. " Que diable allez-vous faire dans cette galère?" Alas! this comes of supping in the Speiss Saal of the " Kaiser" and chatting with the great round-faced Prussian in uniform at the head of the table; he was a lieutenant of the guard at Tilsit, and also at Erfurt with dispatches in 1808; he had a hundred pleasant stories of the fêtes, and the droll mistakes the body-guard of the Czar used to fall into by ignorance of the habits and customs of civilized life. They were Bashkirs, and always bivouacked in the open street before the Emperor's quarters, and spent the whole night through chanting a wild and savage song, which some took up as others slept, and when day broke the whole concluded with a dance, which, from the description I had of it, must have been something of the most uncouth and fearful that could be conceived

Napoleon admired those fellows greatly, and more than one among them left Erfurt with the cross of the Legion at his breast.

Tired and weary as I was, I sat up long past midnight, listening to the Prussian who rolled out his reminiscences between huge volumes of smoke in the most amusing fashion. And when I did retire to rest, it was to fall into a fearful dream about Bashkirs and bastions, half-moons, hot shot, and bomb-proofs, that never left me till morning broke.

"The Rittmeister von Otterstadt presents his compliments," said the waiter, awakening me from a heavy sleep —" presents his compliments —— "

" Who ? " cried I, with a shudder.

" The Rittmeister von Otterstadt, who promised to show you the fortress."

" I'm ill—seriously ill," said I, " I should not be surprised if it were a fever.

" Probably so," echoed the immovable German, and went on with his message. " The Herr Rittmeister regrets much that he is ordered away on Court Martial duty to Entenburg, and cannot have the honour of accompanying you before Saturday, when——"

" With Heaven's assistance, I shall be out of the visible horizon of Erfurt," said I, finishing the sentence for him.

Never was there a mind so relieved as mine was by this intelligence ; the horrors of that two days' perambulations through arched passages, up and down flights of stone steps, and into caves and cells, of whose uses and objects I had not the most remote conception, had given me a night of fearful dreams, and now I was free once more.

Long live the King of Prussia! say I, who keeps up smart discipline in his army, and I fervently trust that Court Martial may be thoroughly digested and maturely considered ; and the odds are in my favour that I'm off before it's over.

What is it, I wonder, that makes the inhabitants of fortified towns always so stupid ? Is such the fact ? first of all, asks some one of my readers. Not a doubt of it; if you ever visited them and passed a week or two within their walls, you would scarcely ask the question. Can curtains and bastions, fosses and half-moons, exclude intelligence as effectually as they do an enemy? are batteries as fatal to pleasure as they are to platoons? I cannot say; but what I can and will say is, that the most melancholy days and nights I ever passed have been in great fortresses. Where the works are old and tumbling, some little light of the world without will creep in through the chinks and crevices, as at Antwerp and Mentz; but let them be well looked to—the fosses full, no weeds on the ramparts, the palisades painted smart green, and the sentry-boxes to match, and God help you!

There must be something in the humdrum routine of military duty that has its effect upon the inhabitants. They get up at morning by a signal gun, and they go to bed by another, they dine by beat of drum, and the garrison gives the word of command for every hour in the twenty-four. There is no stir, no movement; a patrol or a fatigue party are the only things you meet, and when you prick up your ears at the roll of wheels, it turns out to be only a tumbril with a corporal's guard!

Theatres can scarcely exist in such places; a library would die in a week; there are no soirées; no society. Billiards and beer form the staple of officers' pleasures in a foreign army, and certainly they have one recommendation, they are cheap.

Now as there was little to see in Erfurt, and still less to do, I made up my mind to start early the next day, and push forward to Weimar—a good resolution as far as it went, but then, how was the day to be passed? People dine at "one" in Germany, or if they wish to push matters to a fashionable extreme, they say "two." How is the interval till dark to be filled up, taking it for granted you have provided some occupation for that? Coffee and smoking will do something, but except to a German they can't fill up six mortal hours. Reading is out of the question after such a dinner; riding would give you apoplexy; sleep alone is the resource. Sleep "that wraps a man as in a blanket," as honest Sancho says, and sooth to say one is fit for little else; and so, having ordered a pen and ink to my room, as if I were about to write various letters, I closed the door and my eyes within five minutes after, and never awoke till the bang of a "short eighteen" struck six.

CHAPTER XXXII.

A PLAY BY COMMAND

" WHICH is the way to the theatre ? " said I to an urchin who stood at the inn door, in that professional attitude of waiting your street runners in all cities can so well assume ; for holding a horse and ringing a bell are accomplishments, however little some people may deem them.

" The theatre ? " echoed he, measuring me leisurely from head to foot, and not stirring from his place.

" Yes," said I, " they told me there was one here, and that they played to-night."

" Possibly," with a shrug of the shoulders, was the reply, and he smoked his short pipe, as carelessly as before.

" Come, then, show me the way," said I pulling out some kreutzers, "put up that pipe for ten minutes, and lead on "

The jingle of the copper coin awakened his intelligence, and though he could not fathom my antipathy to the fumes of bad tobacco, he deposited the weapon in his capacious side pocket, and with a short nod bade me follow him.

Nowhere does nationality exhibit itself so strikingly as in the conduct and bearing of the people who show you the way in different cities. Your German is sententious and solemn as an elephant. He goes plodding along with his head down and his hands in his pockets, answering your questions with a sulky monosyllable, and seeming annoyed when not left to his own meditations. The Frenchman thinks, on the contrary, that he is bound to be agreeable and entertaining ; he is doing the honours of La Grande Nation, and it stands him upon that you are not to go away discontented with the politeness of " the only civilized people of Europe." Paddy has some of this spirit, too, but less on national than individual grounds; he likes conversation, and leads the way to it; beside, no one, while affecting to give information himself, can pump a stranger like an Irishman. The Yankee plan is cross-examination outright, and no disguise about it; if he shows the way to one place, it is because you must tell him where you came from last; while John Bull, with a brief "Don't know, I'm sure," is equally indifferent to your road and your fortune, and has no room for any thoughts about you.

My "avant courier" was worthy of his country; if every word had cost him a molar tooth he couldn't have been more sparing of them, and when by chance I either did not hear or rightly understand what he did say, nothing could induce him to repeat it; and so on we went from the more frequented part of the town till we arrived at a quarter of narrow streets, and poor-looking houses, over the roofs of which I could from time to time catch glimpses of the fortifications; for we were at the extreme limits of the place.

"Are you quite certain this is the way, my lad?" said I, for I began to fear lest he might have mistaken the object of my inquiry.

"Yes, yes—there it was—there was the theatre," and so he pointed to a large building of dark stone, which closed the end of the street, and on the walls of which various playcards and announcements were posted, which, on coming nearer, I found were bills for their night's performance, setting forth how the servants of His Majesty would perform "Den Junker in den Residentz," and the afterpiece of "Krahwinkel." There was a very flourishing catalogue of actors and actresses, with names as hard as the dishes in a bill of fare, and something about a "ballet" and a "musical interrmezzo."

Come—said I to myself—this is a piece of good fortune. And so dismissing my little foot page, I turned to the door, which stood within a deep porch.

What was my amazement, however, to find it closed. I looked on every side, but there was no other entrance; beside, the printed list of places and their prices left no doubt that this was the regular place of admission. There's no knowing, after all, thought I; these Germans

F F

are strange folks; perhaps they don't open the door with-..
out knocking, and so here goes.

"In Himmel's namen was ist das?" screamed an angry
voice, as a very undignified-looking vrau peeped from a window of a foot square above the door—"What do you want
with that uproar there?" roared she, louder than before.

"I want to get in—a place in the boxes or a ' stalle' in
the ' balcony'—anywhere will do."

"What for?" cried she again.

"What for!—for the play, to be sure—for the ' Junker
in den Residentz.'"

"He is not here at all—go your ways—or I'll call the
Polizey," yelled she, while, banging the window, there
was an end of the dialogue.

"Can I be of any service to you, mein Herr?" said a
portly little fellow, without a coat, who was smoking at
his door—"What is it you want?"

"I came to see a play," said I in amazement at the
whole proceedings, "and here I find nothing but an old
beldam that threatens me with the police."

"Ah! as for the play I don't know," replied he, scratching his head; "but come with me over here to the 'Fox,' and
we're sure to see the Herr Director."

"But I've nothing to do with the Herr Director," said I;
"if there's no performance I must only go back again—
that's all."

"Ah! but there may, though," rejoined my friend;
"come along and see the Herr himself, I know him well,
and he'll tell you all about it."

The proposition was at least novel, and as the world goes,
that same is not without its advantages, and so I acceded,
and followed my new guide, who in the careless "negli-
gée" of a waistcoat and breeches, waddled along before me.

The "Fox" was an old-fashioned house, of framed
wood, with queer diamond-shaped panes to the windows,
and a great armorial coat over the door, where a fox, in
black oak, stood out conspicuously.

Scarcely had we entered the low arched door, when the
fumes of schnaps and tobacco nearly suffocated me; while
the merry chorus of a drinking song proclaimed that a
jolly party was assembled.

I already repented of my folly in yielding to the strange man's proposal, and had he been near, would at once have declined any further step in the matter; but he had disappeared in the clouds,—the disc of his drab shorts was all I could perceive through the nebulæ. It was confoundedly awkward, so it was. What right had I to hunt down the Herr Director, and disturb him in his lair. It was enough that there was no play; any other man would have quietly returned home again,when he saw such was the case.

While I revolved these thoughts with myself, my fat friend issued from the mist, followed by a tall, thin man, dressed in deep black, with tights and hessians of admirable fit; a pair of large bushy whiskers bisected his face, meeting at the corners of his nose; while a sharp and pointed chin tuft seemed to prolong the lower part of his countenance to an immense extent.

Before the short man had well uttered his announcement of the "Herr Director," I had launched forth into the most profuse apologies for my unwarrantable intrusion, expressing in all the German I could muster, the extent of my sorrow, and ringing the changes of my grief and my modesty, my modesty and my grief; at last I gave in, fairly floored for want of the confounded verb one must always clinch the end of a sentence with in German.

"It was to see the play, then, Monsieur came?" said the Director, inquiringly, for alas! my explanation had been none of the clearest.

"Yes," said I, "for the play—but——" Before I could finish the sentence, he flung himself into my arms, and cried out with enthusiasm, "Du bist mein Vater's Sohn!"

This piece of family information was unquestionably new to me, but I disengaged myself from my brother's arms, curious to know the meaning of such enthusiasm.

"And so you came to see the play?" cried he, in a transport, while he threw himself into a stage attitude of great effect.

"Yes," said I, "to see the 'Junker,' and 'Krähwinkel.'"

"Ach Gott! that was fine, that was noble!"

Now, how any man's enterprising a five franc piece or two gulden-muntze could deserve such epithets, would have puzzled me at another moment; but as the dramatist

said, I wasn't going to "mind squibs after sitting over a
barrel of gunpowder," and I didn't pay the least attention
to it.

"Give me your hand!" cried he, in a rapture, "and let
me call you friend."

The Director's mad as a March hare! thought I, and I
wished myself well out of the whole adventure.

"But as there's no play," said I, "another night will
do as well; I shall remain here for a week to come, perhaps longer——" But while I went on expressing the
great probability of my passing a winter at Erfurt, he
never paid the least attention to my observations, but
seemed sunk in meditation, occasionally dropping in a
stray phrase, as thus—"Die Wurtzel is sick, that is, she is
at the music garden with the officers; then, Blum is drunk
by this; der Ettenbaum couldn't sing a note after his supper
of schenkin. But then there's Grundenwald, and Catinka,
to be sure, and Alte Kreps—we'll do it, we'll do it! Come
along, mein aller Liebster, and choose the best 'loge du
premier,' take two, three, if you like it—you shall see a
play."

"What do you mean? you are surely not going to open
the house for me!"

"An't I though! you shall soon see—it's the only
audience I ever had in Erfurt, and I'm not going to lose
it. Know, most worthy friend," continued he with a
most melodramatic tone and gesture, "that to-night is
the twelfth time I have given out an announcement of a
play, and yet never was able to attract—I will not say an
audience—but not a row—not a 'loge'—not even a 'stalle'
in the balcon. I opened, why do I say I opened? I
advertised, the first night, Schiller's 'Maria Stuart,' you
know the Maria—well, such a Mädchen as we have for
the part! such tenderness—such music in her voice—such
grace and majesty in every movement; you shall see for
yourself, Catinka is here. Then I gave out 'Nathan
der Weise,' then the 'Goetz,' then 'Lust und Liebe,'—why
do I go on? in a word, I went through all our dramatic
authors from Schiller, Göthe, Lessing, Werner, Grill-
parzer, down to Kötzebue, whose two pieces I advertized
for this evening.

"But—pardon my interruption—did you always keep the doors closed as I found them?"

"Not at first," responded he, solemnly; "the doors were open, and a system of telegraphs established between the bureau for payment and the orchestra, by which the footlights were to be illuminated on the arrival of the first visitor; but the bassoon and the drum, the clarinette and the oboe, stood like cannoneers, match in hand, from half-past six till eight, and never came the word 'Fire!' but here we are."

With these words he produced from his pocket a massive key, with which he unlocked the door and led me forward by the arm into a dark passage, followed by our coatless friend, whom he addressed as "Herr Stauf," desiring him to come in also. While the Herr Director was waiting for a light, which the vrau seemed in no hurry to bring, he continued his recital. "When I perceived matters were thus, I vowed two vows, solemnly and before the whole corps—ballet, chorus, and all; first, that I would give twelve representations—I mean announcements of representations—from twelve separate dramatists before I left Erfurt; and, secondly, that for a single spectator, I would open the house and have a play acted. One part of my oath is already accomplished; your appearance calls on me for the other. This over, I shall leave Erfurt for ever; and if," continued he, "the Fates ever discover me again within the walls of a fortified town—unless I be sent there in handcuffs and with a peloton of dragoons—may I never cork my eyebrows while I live!"

This resolve, so perfectly in accordance with the meditations I had lately indulged in myself, gave me a higher opinion of the Herr Director's judgment, and I followed him with a more tranquil conscience than at first.

"There are four steps there—take care," cried he, "and feel along by the wall here; for though this place should be, and indeed is by right, one blaze of lamps, I must now conduct you by this miserable candle."

And so, through many a narrow passage, and narrower door, up-stairs and down, over benches, and under partitions we went, until at length we arrived upon the stage itself. The curtain was up, and before it in yawning blackness, lay the audience part of the house—a gloomy and dreary cavern; the dark cells of the boxes, and the long, untenanted benches of the "balcon," had an effect of melancholy desolation impossible to convey. Up above, the various skies and moon scenes hung, flapping to and fro with the cold wind, that came, heaven knows whence, but with a piercing sharpness I never felt the equal of within doors, while the back of the stage was lost in a dim distance, where fragments of huts, and woods, mills, mountains, and rustic bridges, lay discordantly intermixed —the chaos of a stage world.

The Herr Director waved his dip candle to and fro above his head, like a stage musician, invoking spirits and goblins damned, while he repeated, from one of Werner's pieces, some lines of an incantation.

"Gelobt sey Marie!" said the Herr Stauf, blessing himself devoutly, for he had looked upon the whole as an act of devotion.

"And now, friend," continued the Director, "wait here at this fountain, and I will return in a few minutes;" and so saying he quitted the place, leaving Stauf and me in perfect darkness, a circumstance which I soon discovered was not a whit more gratifying to my friend than myself.

"This is a fearful place to be in the dark," quoth Stauf, edging close up to me; "you don't know, but I do, that this was the Augustine Convent formerly, and the monks were all murdered by the Elector Frederick, in—What was that?—Didn't you see something like a blue flame yonder?"

"Well, and what then? You know these people have a hundred contrivances for stage purposes——"

"Ach Gott! that's true; but I wish I was out again, in the Mohren Gasse; I'm only a poor sausage maker, and one needn't be brave for my trade."

"Come, come, take courage; here comes the Herr Director," and with that he entered with two candles in large gilt candlesticks

"Now, friend," said he, "where will you sit? My advice is, the orchestra; take a place near the middle, behind the leader's bench, and you'll be out of the draught of wind. Stauf, do you hold the candles, and sit in the 'pupitre.' You'll excuse my lighting the foot-lights, won't you?—well, what do you say to a great coat?—you feel it cold—I see you do."

"If not too much trouble——"

"Not at all—don't speak of it;" and with that he slipped behind the flats, and returned in an instant with a huge fur mantle of mock sable. "I wear that in 'Otto von Bohmen,'" said he, proudly; "and it always produces an immense effect. It is in that same 'peltzer' I stab the king, in the fourth act; do you remember where he says (it is at the chess table),—'Check to the Queen;' then I reply, 'Zum Koenig, selbst,' and run him through."

"Gott bewahr!" piously ejaculated Stauf, who seemed quite beyond all chance of distinguishing fiction from reality.

"You'll have to wait ten or twenty minutes, I fear,' said the Director. "Der Catinka can't be found, and Der Ungedroht has just washed his doublet, and can't appear till it's dry; but we'll give you the Krahwinkel in good style. You shall be content, and now I must go dress too."

"He is a strange carl," said Stauf, as he sat up on a tall bench, like an office stool; "but I wish from my soul it was over!"

I can't say I did not participate in the wish, notwithstanding a certain curiosity to have a peep at the rest of the company. I had seen, in my day, some droll exhibitions in the dramatic way, but this, certainly if not the most amusing, was the very strangest of them all.

I remember at Corfu, where an Italian company came one winter, and gave a series of operas, amongst others, "Il Turco in Italia." The strength of the corps did not, however, permit of their being equal to those armies of Turks and Italians who occasionally figure "en scene," and they were driven to ask assistance from the Commandant of the garrison, who very readily lent them a company of, I believe, the 88th regiment.

The worthy Director had sad work to drill his troops, for unhappily he couldn't speak a word of English, and as they knew little or no Italian, he was reduced to signs and pantomime. When the piece, however, was going forward, and the two rival armies should alternately attack and repulse each other, the luckless Director, unable to make them fight and rally to the quick movement of the orchestra, was heard shouting out behind the scenes, in wild excitement, "Avanti Turki!—Avanti Christiani!—Ah, bravo Turki!—Maledetti Christiani!" which threw the whole audience into a perfect paroxysm of laughter.

Come, then, thought I, who knows but this may be as good as Corfu. But lo! here he comes; and now the Director, dressed in the character of the "Herr Berg-Bau und Weg-Inspector," came to the front of the stage, and, beginning thus, spoke, "Meine Herren und Damen—there are *no* ladies," said he, stopping short; "but whose fault is that? Meine Herren, it grieves me much to be obliged on this occasion——Make a row there, why don't you?" said he, addressing me—"ran-tan-tan!—an apology is always interrupted by the audience; if it were not, one could never get through it."

I followed his directions by hammering on the bench with my cane; and he continued to explain that various ladies and gentlemen of the corps were seriously indisposed, and that, though the piece should go on, it must be with only three out of the seven characters. I renewed my marks of disapprobation here, which seemed to afford him great delight, and he withdrew, bowing respectfully to every quarter of the house.

Kotzebue's Krähwinkel, as many of my readers know, needs not the additional absurdity of the circumstances under which I saw it performed to make it ludicrous and laughable. The Herr Director played to the life; and Catinka, a pretty, plump, fair-haired "fraulein"—not, however, exactly the idea of Maria Stuart—was admirable in her part. Even Stauf himself was so carried away by his enthusiasm, that he laid down his candles to applaud; and, for the extent of the audience, I venture to say there never was a more enthusiastic one. Indeed, to this fact the Director himself bore testimony, as he more than once interrupted the scene to thank us for our marks of approval. On both sides the complaisance was complete. Never did actors and audience work better together · for while *we* admired, *they* relished the praise with all the gusto of individual approbation, frequently stopping to assure us that we were right in our applause, that their best hits were exactly those we selected, and that a more

judging public never existed. Stauf was carried away in his ecstasies; and, between laughing and applauding, I was regularly worn out with my exertions.

Want of light—Stauf's candles swilled frightfully from neglect—compelled them to close the piece somewhat abruptly; and in the middle of the second act, such was the obscurity, that the Herr Berg-Bau und Weg-Inspector's wife fell over the prompter's bulk, and nearly capsized Stauf into the bowels of the big fiddle. This was the *finale ;* and I had barely time to invite the corps to a supper at the " Fox," which they kindly accepted, when Stauf announced that we must beat a retreat by "inch of candle." This we did in safety, and I reached the " Fox " in time to order the repast, before the guests had washed off their paint and changed their dresses.

If it has been my fortune to assist at more elegant " réunions," I can aver with safety I never presided over a more merry or joyous party than was our own at the " Fox." Die Catinka sat on my left, Die Vrau von " Mohren-Kopf," the " Mère noble " of the corps, on my right; the Herr Director took the foot of the table, supported by a " bassoon" and a "first lover ;" while various " trombones," " marquis," waiting-maids, walking gentlemen, and a " ghost " occupied the space on either side, not forgetting our excellent friend Stauf, who seemed the very happiest man of the party. We were fourteen souls in all, though where two-thirds of them came from, and how they got wind of a supper, some more astute diviner than myself must ascertain.

Theatrical folks, in all countries. are as much people in themselves as the Gipsies. They have a language of their own, a peculiarity of costume and habit of life They eat, drink, and intermarry with each other, and, in fact, I shouldn't wonder, from their organization, if they have a king in some sly corner of Europe, who, one day, will be restored with great pomp and ceremony. One undeniable trait distinguishes them all—at least, wherever I have met them in the Old world and in the New—and that is, a most unbounded candour in their estimation of each other. Frankness is unquestionably the badge of all their tribe; and they are, without exception, the most free of hypocrisy, in this respect, of all the classes with whom it has ever been my fortune to forgather. Nothing is too sharp, nothing too smart to be said, no thrust too home, no stab too fatal; it's a mêlée tournament, where all tilt, and hard knocks are fair. This privilege of their social world gives them a great air of freedom in all their intercourse with strangers, and sometimes leads even to an excess of ease, somewhat remarkable, in their manners. With them, intimacy is like those tropical trees that spring up twenty feet high in a single night. They meet you at rehearsal, and before the curtain rises in the evening there is a sworn friendship between you. Stage manners, and green-room talk, carry off the eccentricities which other men dare not practise, and though you don't fancy " Mr. Tuft " asking you for a loan of five pounds, hang it! you can't be angry with Jeremy Diddler! This double identity, this Janus attribute, cuts in two ways, and you find it almost impossible to place any weight on the opinions and sentiments of people, who are always professing opinions and sentiments learned by heart. This may be—I'm sure it is— very illiberal—but I can't help it. I wouldn't let myself be moved by the arguments of Brutus on the Corn Laws, or Cato on the Catholic question, any more than I should fall in love with some sweet sentiment of a daylight Ophelia or Desdemona. I reserve all my faith in stage people, for the hours between seven and twelve at night; then, with footlights and scenery, pasteboard banquets, and wooden waves, I'm their slave, they may do with me as they will, but let day come, and " I'm a man again! "

Now as all this sounds very cross-grained, the sapient reader already suspects there may be more in it than it appears to imply, and that Arthur O'Leary has some grudge against the Thespians, which he wishes to pay off in generalities. I'm not bound to answer the insinuation; neither will I tell you more of our supper at the '' Fox," nor why the Herr Director Klug invited me to take a place in his waggon next day for Weimar, nor what Catinka whispered, as I filled her glass with champagne, nor how the " serpent" frowned from the end of the table ; nor, in short, one word of the whole matter, save that I settled my bill that same night at the "Kaiser," and the next morning left for Weimar, with a very large, and an excessively merry party

CHAPTER XXXIII.

CONCLUSION.

THE Platz of Weimar was all astir as we drove up to the "Elephant," dingiest and filthiest of all "hostels." Troops of horses were picquitted before the house, and crowds of peasants poured in from every side with all manner of quadrupeds, gaily decorated with ribbons, and caparisoned with flaring saddlecloths and bright head-stalls.

"What does all this mean?" asked I. "Is it a fair, or a great holiday?"

"No, Mein Herr," replied the landlord; "but there is an officer of rank in the French service just arrived to purchase 'remounts' for the Chasseurs d'Afrique, and the whole country for miles around is eagerly hurrying it to the market."

Promising myself some amusement from the scene, I ordered my breakfast at once, telling the host I should remain for a day or two.

"Ach Gott!" sighed he, "I can give you nothing. The Frenchman and his staff have ordered all in the house. They have bespoken the rooms, engaged the stable, and retained every scullion in the kitchen."

"But surely," said I, "they would not suffer a traveller to starve amidst this more than plenty that I see here, nor would they ask him to lie in the streets while there is shelter to be had in some nameless corner? Go, mine host, and say that a middle-aged gentleman, of engaging manners and social disposition, is here, standing on the threshold, houseless and hungry, that for his entertainment he would willingly pay in cash or conviviality, but that as to leaving an inn without a hearty meal and a good bed, if he wishes it, he'd see all the Frenchmen that over sacréd—particularly well——"

"What! say it out, *mon brave;* don't balk your good

intentions," broke in a deep bass voice; while a broad-chested fellow, all glittering with crosses and orders, presented his bearded face very close to my own,—"Say it out, I say," cried he.

"So I mean to do, *mon Général*," said I, saluting him. "I was going to observe, that of all people in Europe for a refined sense of hospitality, for a just idea of what constitutes real politeness, for a truly elevated sense of human intercourse, there is nothing like a Frenchman."

"Diantre, sir, I am not a Frenchman," was the stern reply.

"A German, it is true," I remarked, "is almost his equal; in some respects a trifle his superior."

"Taper tole; I am no German."

"Nor a Swede? a Russian? a Spaniard? an Italian? a Greek?—You can't be English!" said I, at last, fairly beaten in my attempts to fix his nationality.

"Devil a bit, my darling!" said he, "I'm your own countryman, and what's more, an old friend into the bargain."

There is no need of mystification—it was Con O'Kelly himself, now "Fourrier en chef" in the French service, whose honest hand I grasped. We dined jovially together that evening, and the next morning set out for Marseilles and Africa.

Ah, my dear reader, what a temptation is it that I resist here. To stop, just when a new and singular existence opens before me; to throw down my pen at the very moment I could become most engaging and agreeable. By this time you have learned to see the invariable accuracy of my views, the liberality of my sentiments and the unprejudiced breadth of all my speculations in life, while I, on my side, am as deeply penetrated with the general kindliness which for so long a period has marked your companionship with Arthur O'Leary.

May we meet again; but if not, may your memory be as indulgent as my sense is deep, of all I owe to your forbearance, all I hope from your forgiveness.

Woodfall & Kinder, Printers, Milford Lane, Strand, London, W.C.

Printed in Great Britain
by Amazon

23888782R00256